Scotland's
LOST
VILLAGES

Other books by Dane Love:

Scottish Kirkyards	Robert Hale
The History of Auchinleck – Village and Parish	Carn Publishing
Pictorial History of Cumnock	Alloway Publishing
Pictorial History of Ayr	Alloway Publishing
Scottish Ghosts	Robert Hale
Scottish Ghosts	Barnes & Noble
The Auld Inns of Scotland	Robert Hale
Guide to Scottish Castles	Lomond Books
Tales of the Clan Chiefs	Robert Hale
Scottish Covenanter Stories	Neil Wilson
Ayr Stories	Fort Publishing
Ayrshire Coast	Fort Publishing
Scottish Spectres	Robert Hale
Scottish Spectres	Ulverston Large Print
Ayrshire: Discovering a County	Fort Publishing
Ayr Past and Present	Sutton Publishing
Lost Ayrshire	Birlinn
The River Ayr Way	Carn Publishing
Ayr – the Way We Were	Fort Publishing
The Man Who Sold Nelson's Column	Birlinn
Jacobite Stories	Neil Wilson
The History of Sorn – Village and Parish	Carn Publishing
Legendary Ayrshire	Carn Publishing
The Covenanter Encyclopaedia	Fort Publishing
Scottish Ghosts	Amberley Publishing
Scottish Kirkyards	Amberley Publishing
A Look Back at Cumnock	Carn Publishing
A Look Back at Girvan	Carn Publishing
A Look Back at Ayrshire Farming	Carn Publishing
Ayr Then and Now	The History Press
Ayrshire Then and Now	The History Press
The History of Mauchline – Village and Parish	Carn Publishing
The Galloway Highlands	Carn Publishing
Ayrshire's Lost Villages	Carn Publishing
A Look Back at Dalmellington	Carn Publishing

www.dane-love.co.uk

Scotland's LOST VILLAGES

Dane Love

CARN PUBLISHING

© Dane Love, 2018.
First Published in Great Britain, 2018.

ISBN - 978 1 911043 05 8

Published by Carn Publishing Ltd.,
Lochnoran House,
Auchinleck, Ayrshire, KA18 3JW.

Printed by Bell & Bain Ltd,
Glasgow, G46 7UQ.

The right of the author to be identified as the author of this work has been asserted by him in accordance with the Copyright, Designs and Patents Act 1988.

All rights reserved. No part of this publication may be reproduced, stored, or transmitted in any form, or by any means, electronic, mechanical or photocopying, recording or otherwise, without the express written permission of the publisher.

Contents

List of Illustrations 7

Introduction 11

  1   Adamsrow 15

  2   Arden 22

  3   Avonhead 27

  4   Balclevie 33

  5   Benquhat 37

  6   Binnend 45

  7   Bothwellhaugh 55

  8   Burn Row 67

  9   Cullen 74

10   Darnconner 84

11   Darngavil 95

12   East Benhar 103

13   Eastfield 112

14   Fairfield 119

15   Fochabers 124

16   Forvie 132

17   Gavieside 137

18   Glenbuck 144

19   Haywood 158

20   Hermand 169

21   Inveraray 174

22   Kincardine 182

23   Kingscavil 190

24   Lassodie 197

25	Lethanhill	210
26	Longrigg	224
27	Midbreich	233
28	Mossend	238
29	Oakbank	245
30	Oldtown of Roseisle	252
31	Rattray	258
32	Riccarton Junction	266
33	Roughrigg	274
34	South Cobbinshaw	281
35	Southfield	288
36	Westerton	293
37	Whiterigg	298
38	Woodend	308
39	Woodhead	314
40	Woodlands	324

Appendix	330
Bibliography	332
Index	334

List of Illustrations

1.1	Adamsrow from the south-west	16
1.2	Adamsrow from 1895 Ordnance Survey map	20
2.1	Arden from 1898 Ordnance Survey map	24
3.1	Avonhead from 1898 Ordnance Survey map	31
4.1	Lady's Tower, Elie (Kevan Aitken)	35
5.1	Benquhat Store (left) and old School (right)	40
5.2	Benquhat from 1909 Ordnance Survey map	43
6.1	Binnend from the west in 1907 (Burntisland Heritage Trust)	48
6.2	Binnend (Burntisland Heritage Trust)	49
6.3	Low Binnend (Burntisland Heritage Trust)	51
6.4	Binnend from 1894 Ordnance Survey map	52
6.5	Low Binned from 1894 Ordnance Survey map	54
7.1	Bothwellhaugh – Hill Place (George McPhee)	56
7.2	Bothwellhaugh – Raith Place (George McPhee)	58
7.3	Bothwellhaugh Co-operative shop (George McPhee)	59
7.4	Bothwellhaugh – Brandon Place (George McPhee)	61
7.5	Bothwellhaugh – Haugh Place (George McPhee)	63
7.6	Bothwellhaugh Memorial Cairn	64
7.7	Bothwellhaugh from 1912 Ordnance Survey map	66
8.1	Burn Row from 1898 Ordnance Survey map	71
9.1	Cullen Market Cross	76
9.2	Cullen Parish Church	78
9.3	Plan of Cullen drawn in 1762	81
10.1	Darnconner – the last resident	85
10.2	Darnconner – the Parish Church and manse	87
10.3	Detail of Darnconner village centre from 1908 Ordnance Survey map	90
10.4	Darnconner from 1908 Ordnance Survey map	93
11.1	Darngavil from 1898 Ordnance Survey composite map	97
12.1	East Benhar – ruins of old school	106
12.2	East Benhar from 1897 Ordnance Survey map	109
13.1	Eastfield School, c. 1915 (North Lanarkshire Council)	114
13.2	Eastfield from 1898 Ordnance Survey composite map	117
14.1	Fairfield from 1896 Ordnance Survey map	121
15.1	Fochabers – old Market Cross	125
15.2	Fochabers – details of chain that one held the jougs	130
16.1	Forvie – ruins of old church	133
16.2	Forvie – old font from kirk (right)	135
17.1	Gavieside School in the 1950s (Almond Valley Heritage Trust)	138
17.2	Gavieside from 1917 Ordnance Survey map	140
18.1	Glenbuck from south-east showing school to left of centre	146
18.2	Glenbuck Parish Church	147
18.3	Glenbuck from west, with post office to right	149

18.4	Glenbuck from 1896 Ordnance Survey map	151
19.1	Haywood from the north (South Lanarkshire Council)	159
19.2	Haywood Store (South Lanarkshire Council)	161
19.3	Haywood War Memorial	163
19.4	Haywood – ruins of Greenbank	164
19.5	Haywood – inscribed window sill at Greenbank	165
19.6	Haywood Parish Church (South Lanarkshire Council)	166
19.7	Haywood Wanderers Football Club (South Lanarkshire Council)	167
19.8	Haywood from 1897 Ordnance Survey composite map	168
20.1	Hermand from 1894 Ordnance Survey map	171
21.1	Inveraray Market Cross	175
21.2	Inveraray from painting by Paul Sandby (SCRAN)	178
22.1	Kincardine – solitary gravestone in kirkyard	184
22.2	Kincardine – view of old kirkyard from main street	185
22.3	Kincardine's old Market Cross, now in Fettercairn	187
23.1	Kingscavil (West Lothian Council)	192
23.2	Kingscavil from 1897 Ordnance Survey map	194
24.1	Lassodie – St Ninian's Church (Mary Searles)	198
24.2	Lassodie Post Office (Mary Searles)	201
24.3	Lassodie School (Mary Searles)	202
24.4	Lassodie Tavern (Mary Searles)	204
24.5	Lassodie – the New Rows (Mary Searles)	206
24.6	Lassodie from 1896 Ordnance Survey composite map	207
24.7	Lassodie War Memorial	208
25.1	Lethanhill from south-west	211
25.2	Lethanhill School (left) and Parish Church	215
25.3	Lethanhill War Memorial	218
25.4	Lethanhill from 1909 Ordnance Survey map	221
26.1	Longrigg – David Masterton and family (Graeme Johannessen)	228
26.2	Longrigg from 1898 Ordnance Survey map	231
26.3	East Longrigg from 1898 Ordnance Survey map	232
27.1	Midbreich from 1917 Ordnance Survey map	234
28.1	Mossend – Front Street (West Lothian Council)	239
28.2	Mossend from south-east (Almond Valley Heritage Trust)	241
28.3	Mossend from 1917 Ordnance Survey map	243
29.1	Oakbank from north-east (West Lothian Council)	246
29.2	Oakbank from 1895 Ordnance Survey map	249
30.1	Oldtown of Roseisle (Gordon Castle Muniments)	253
31.1	Rattray Kirk	258
31.2	Rattray Castle	264
32.1	Riccarton Junction from south-east	267
32.2	Riccarton Junction from south-west	269
32.3	Riccarton Junction from 1898 Ordnance Survey map	271
33.1	Roughrigg from 1898 Ordnance Survey map	278

ILLUSTRATIONS

33.2	Low Roughrigg from 1898 Ordnance Survey map	276???
34.1	Cobbinshaw Parish Church (Almond Valley Heritage Trust)	284
34.2	South Cobbinshaw from 1895 Ordnance Survey map	285
35.1	Southfield from 1897 Ordnance Survey map	290
36.1	Westerton – No. 4 Westerton Cottages in the 1930s (Almond Valley Heritage Trust)	294
36.2	Westerton from 1915 Ordnance Survey map	296
37.1	Whiterigg – Meadowhead Cottage (North Lanarkshire Council)	299
37.2	Whiterigg – Airdriehill Square (North Lanarkshire Council)	300
37.3	Whiterigg from 1898 Ordnance Survey map	305
38.1	Woodend from the west	309
38.2	Woodend from 1916 Ordnance Survey map	311
39.1	Woodhead from east	317
39.2	Woodhead from east	317
39.3	Woodhead from 1895 Ordnance Survey map	321
40.1	Woodlands from 1912 Ordnance Survey map	327

Introduction

This book is a history of forty villages in Scotland that are 'lost', or no-longer exist. In some cases, they have been replaced with newer communities, built on a different site, but most of the villages herein were simply abandoned when their need had expired, and in many cases the location where they stood has returned to nature, perhaps overgrown with scrub or planted in trees. In some cases, the site of the villages has returned to open fields, with little to hint at what existed there at one time.

The definition of both 'lost' and 'village' is one that the author had to wrestle with when he compiled his earlier book, *Ayrshire's Lost Villages*. That volume contains fifty villages in one single county that have all gone, or at least disappeared by 99% or so! In some cases, if a single house or two survives of a village which had a considerable population at one time, then it was felt it merited being included. In this volume, all of the villages were probably large enough to be classed as such, whereas in Ayrshire a few smaller hamlets which comprised little more than a row of homes, were included. Similarly, there may be an odd house or two surviving of the communities in this book, but in general most of the village has gone.

The disappearance of villages can occur for a variety of reasons. The biggest percentage of villages in this collection had their origin as workmen's houses, often for miners and associated trades, and when the mines closed they moved on to new jobs, finding accommodation elsewhere. The contracts and leases drawn up by many of the mining companies were such that once their lease to the minerals had expired, then they had to remove the buildings and return the site of them back to grass, or at least what had existed beforehand. Advertisements selling the materials used to construct the houses were not uncommon, and no doubt many houses were dismantled and the windows, slates, roof trusses, etc., recycled in the construction of new homes elsewhere.

In style, miners' houses changed gradually over the years. The oldest designed communities were often formed around an open courtyard and were described as being 'colliery squares'. One of these existed at Adamsrow, where the houses were known as Square Town. Rows followed, and most mineworkers' homes were formed in this way. In many cases the coal companies spent as little as possible in building the homes, resulting in back-to-back dwellings, and long rows, requiring as few proper walls as possible. The longest miners' row was probably Commonloch Row at Darnconner in Ayrshire, where 96 houses were built in a single terrace without a break.

By the middle of the twentieth century, after the wars, many old mining villages were cleared away, it being realised that conditions in the rows did not meet what was deemed satisfactory for the times. Although outsiders often regarded the conditions as being below standard, many residents loved their communities, if not exactly their house itself, and in many cases were unwilling to leave. Even the promise of a new house with running water, electricity and sewerage was not enough to persuade them. In some cases, the council required to use a Slum Clearance Act in order to clear communities away, such as at East Benhar and elsewhere. Almost every community has its tale of the last resident being almost forcibly removed from the house that they may even have been born in, to be given the keys to a new property, where folk were regarded as being generally much less friendly than those in the village from where they came.

The rehousing of the occupants of many villages and their clearance often came about as a result of campaigning by the likes of the National Union of Mineworkers. In 1910 many county medical officers conducted surveys of the rows, quickly followed by the Royal Commission of Housing (Scotland) surveys, which took place between 1913-18. Reports were compiled by the inspectors sent to various communities across the coalfields, and their findings make unpleasant reading. The filth and dampness in many villages was almost unbearable, and facilities that included basics such as running water were often missing. In many villages water could be obtained from pumps in the street, but there was no drainage, other than open drains which smelled terrible in the summer.

Some of the villages in this book were very old in their origin, such as Kincardine and Rattray, even being designated royal burghs or burghs of barony, but they simply declined over a period of years, their field of influence having evaporated. In the case of Rattray, the blocking of its harbour by sand was one of the main reasons for its decline, whereas at Kincardine – a community that was the 'county town' at one time – it declined when other communities located in more accessible locations, began to take over some of it jurisdictions.

Other villages were moved purposefully, such as Fochabers and Inveraray. Though the new houses were far superior to those that they replaced, the rebuilding of a new community was not carried out by the landowner as a means of public-spirited goodwill, it was more as a mark of superiority, clearing the lower classes and their hovels away from their own new country houses. In places such as Cullen, the village, which had descended into considerable poverty from a lack of trade, had become an embarrassment to the Earl of Findlater. He laid out a new community nearer the Moray Firth, where the new harbour allowed the residents to take up fishing, which, for many, must have been a new trade altogether.

There are a fair number of other lost villages that were removed in order to 'improve' the policies around a country house or castle. In addition to those mentioned in this volume, we could add those of Scone, Tyninghame, Grantown and Duffus. Writing in *The Picture of Scotland* in 1827, Robert Chambers makes a short reference to Scone: 'At a little distance farther [from the remnants of Scone Abbey], stands the old market-cross of Scone, surrounded by a wilderness of pleasure-grounds, which has come in place of the ancient village. There are many instances of towns losing their market crosses; but we believe this is the only cross which has lost its town.' Chambers was wrong, of course, for the market cross at Fochabers still stands in the ground of Gordon Castle.

A few townships or 'ferm-touns' were cleared away at the time of the Highland Clearances, but this book has not included any, mainly because they were not large enough to be classed as villages, and in the main were more disparate settlements. Perhaps a second volume will rectify this omission.

There are scores, perhaps hundreds, of other lost villages across Scotland, and this book is only a selection of the larger ones. Four of the villages are in Ayrshire, which more or less replicates chapters from the *Ayrshire's Lost Villages* book, but to ignore Ayrshire in this volume seemed senseless. That the Ayrshire volume includes fifty villages indicates just how many lost villages there probably are across the rest of the country.

Dane Love
Auchinleck, 2018

Acknowledgements

In compiling this book, I must acknowledge a number of people who have supplied either information or illustrations. In no particular order, they are: Kevan Aitken, Almond Valley Heritage Trust; Burns Monument Centre, Kilmarnock; Burntisland Heritage Trust; Stephen Fisk (www.abandonedcommunities.co.uk); Gordon Castle Muniments; Historic Environment Scotland; National Records of Scotland; Lanark Library; George McPhee; Moray Council Libraries and Archives; Alistair Adams; Graeme Johannessen; Mary Searle; National Library of Scotland; North Lanarkshire Libraries; West Lothian Libraries; and, of course, the many people who have passed on their memories and assisted me over the years, their contributions perhaps supplied over a period of time, not necessarily with this book in mind. The Ordnance Survey maps were supplied by the National Library of Scotland.

1
Adamsrow

★

The village of Adamsrow is thought to have been erected around 1792, mainly to house miners who were employed in the local pits. It was located to the south-east of Edinburgh, in the rural parish of Newton. Musselburgh lay a couple of miles to the north-east, Dalkeith a similar distance to the south, and Craigmillar to the north-west. Prior to the houses being built, a small settlement known as Cuffabout is said to have occupied the site. The village comprised of a long row of houses, arranged along the north side of the road, with a shorter row on the south side, plus a square group of houses, also on the south side of the road. This last group had the name of Square Town.

The long row on the north side of the road had around 35 houses in it initially, prior to the arrival of the railway. One means of accessing the village was from the north-east end, where the road entered the village on crossing a little un-named burn, which forms the boundary of Newton parish with neighbouring Inveresk. The houses were built right on the edge of the roadway, the front doors opening directly onto the road. The houses were in the main built of stone and had slate roofs. Each house had its own single fireplace, and on the ridge of the roofs were line upon line of chimney stacks, each having two chimney pots, one for each house. Each house had its own strip of garden ground to the rear, the tenants cultivating it to grow vegetables for the kitchen.

On the south side of the road was a single row of around five houses, again with gardens to the rear. At the south-west end of this row, at the back of the gardens, was a well from where the villagers could draw water. By 1893, when the Ordnance Survey returned to update their maps (as shown in the map), most of this row had been demolished, leaving just two houses.

Square Town was located at the south-west end of the village. As its name suggests, the cottages here were erected to form a large square of buildings. The houses enclosed the square on three sides, with no gaps. On the north-west side, adjoining the road, was a fourth row of cottages, numbering five homes, but at the end of the row were pends leading through to the central square. This had a well, positioned in the centre. Cottages in Square Town had their gardens to either side of the square, on its external sides. The style of Square Town's layout indicates its age, for prior to miners' rows, many mineworkers homes were in what was known as 'colliery squares'.

1.1 Adamsrow from the south-west

Although Square Town was probably newer than Adamsrow, it did exist as early as 1798, when John Baxter, collier at Square Town, is listed in the names associated with the Mid Lothian Militia. Square Town was the first part of Adamsrow to disappear. It was mostly in ruins by 1875, and was cleared away by the 1890s, apart from the single row alongside the main road through Adamsrow. Five houses here were still standing in 1893.

Adamsrow owed its existence to the presence of coal beneath the green swards of Midlothian countryside. Coal had apparently been worked there since at least the early 1600s. The community may have been named after the Adam family, who certainly lived in the parish as early as 1710. Andrew Adam was born around 1690 and died in 1743 and is buried in the Newton churchyard. His family lived in the area for a number of generations, most of them being colliers.

In the early eighteenth century, many of the miners from Newton parish were barred from attending worship in Newton Parish Church. The colliers fought for fifteen years to be allowed to return, their wish finally being granted in 1747. To commemorate this, a Collier's Loft was constructed in the church, its frontage adorned with a pseudo-heraldic badge containing the miners' tools – hammers, picks and shovel. Eight of the miners had their names inscribed on the façade – Robert Archibald, Hugh Adam Sr., Thomas Archibald, Hugh Adam Yr., Hendry Adam, James Kinghorn and John Adam. By 1839, the collier overseer at Edmonstone Colliery was David Adam.

There were many small mines around Adamsrow. In Inveresk parish most of the pits were referred to as Craighall mines. The closest pit to the village was located at the west end, behind the northern row. This had a tramway leading to it from the railway line. A shaft sunk into the ground was used for raising coal, and a weighing machine was located on the surface. Here too, was a chimney, indicating that a steam engine existed, perhaps to pump water or raise coal.

Mining was in decline in the area when the *New Statistical Account* was being compiled in the 1830s. The minister of Newton parish, Rev John Adamson, noted that the population was in decline, mainly due to the state of the collieries, 'which are not wrought to the same extent as formerly.' He continued, 'The Sheriffhall Colliery, belonging to the Duke of Buccleuch, is nearly wrought out; and in that of Edmonstone, belonging to John Wauchope, Esq., a few years will suffice to exhaust all that can be wrought by levels from the present engines. The field, however, is far from being exhausted, and by a powerful engine farther to the dip than the present, a large winning of very valuable coal may be obtained.' By 1845 this was undertaken, Sir John Hope having taken a lease of Edmonstone Colliery, and a large steam engine, brought from Cornwall, was used for pumping water from a depth of 100 fathoms.

The miners in Adamsrow, and neighbouring rows, such as Redrow, Millerhill and Cocklerow, suffered from a disease which was known as black-spit, or melanosis. This was caused by them inhaling coal dust whilst working in the bowels of the earth. The *New Statistical Account* noted that, 'Many strong men are cut off by it before they reach the age of forty, especially if they have, for any length of time, been engaged in what in opposition to coal-hewing is called stone-work, (sinking of pits, driving of mines, etc.). Almost all the men are affected by it sooner or later, so as to be rendered unfit for any active exertion for years before they drop prematurely into the grave, between the ages of forty and sixty or sixty-five. The vicissitudes of temperature to which they are daily exposed on issuing from the pits throughout a great part of the year, coupled with irregular habits in the case of too many, no doubt contribute to this mortality.'

Although working conditions in the pits hereabouts were poor, it was noted that miners enjoyed a better income than agricultural labours. However, the minister noted that the miners were wont to spend their cash in excess eating and drinking. They also acquired all of their goods on credit, to be paid off at the next payment of wages.

There was a school at nearby Redrow which educated the children of the area. Prior to attendance being compulsory by law, the children of the miners were expected to assist in working. The *New Statistical Account* noted that, 'The young, even, where not previously neglected as to their education, are taken from school often as early as eight years of age, to be set to work in the pits.'

In Edmonstone Colliery in October 1859, Alexander Flockhart and James Wilson were being lowered in a bucket down the mineshaft. The rope snapped as they descended, plunging them to the bottom of the pit shaft, fifteen fathoms, or ninety feet below. The injuries sustained by Flockhart were so severe that he died three hours later. Wilson survived, but his injuries were of a serious nature.

By 1846 the *Topographical Dictionary of Scotland* noted that Adamsrow itself (excluding Square Town) had 249 inhabitants. This was based on the 1841 Census, from which we find that many of the houses had large families in residence.

Taking Adamsrow in isolation, the 1841 Census indicates that there were 55 houses there at the time. Two of these were unoccupied. Taking the occupation of the head of each household, of those which were specified, 38 were coal miners. In many cases, other occupants of the house were also employed as coal miners. In four cases, the head of the household was a female whose occupation was described as 'coal labourer'. One of these, Marion Wilson, shared the house with John Wilson, a tailor. Two heads of households were employed as agricultural labourers. One house was occupied by Jane Drylie, grocer, her husband Robert Drylie, saddler, Christian Drylie, milliner and Margaret Drylie, dressmaker. Most of the residents had been born in Midlothian, though there were one or two who had come from farther afield. The average occupancy per house was 4.5, but two households had as many as ten living under one roof – the families of Andrew Archibald and Donaldson Watson. Four households had nine residents – Abraham Loch, Thomas Ross, Thomas Dunlop and Hugh MacGill.

At Square Town there were 25 houses, with a population of 77 in 1841. Ten of the houses were unoccupied at the time of the Census, the houses gradually being cleared of residents. Of the heads of households, eight were listed as being coal miners, one as an agricultural labourer, one as a coal labourer (again female) and Widow Robertson was a grocer. Again, two of the houses had ten occupants – that of Alexander Brown and John MacGill, both coal miners.

In 1849 the North British Railway was constructed through part of the village, linking Edinburgh with Hawick. The line made its way from Edinburgh to Eskbank, for Dalkeith, and south to the Border town. When the line was laid it actually split the village in two, and it is reckoned that eight miners' cottages had to be demolished to allow the track to be laid. The railway was raised on an embankment at the village, allowing it to pass over the village street on a flat iron-plate bridge deck. Despite the proximity of the railway, there was to be no station in the village, for Millerhill Station was constructed a few hundred yards to the south, a footpath across the fields from Adamsrow allowing access.

A report into the condition of miners' housing in 1875 makes mention of Adamsrow:

> At Adam's Row, about a quarter of a mile from Millerhill, the houses are tenanted by miners in the employment of the Niddrie Coal Company. There are two rows of old houses, some of them uninhabited, and the remnant of an ancient square, which in its prolonged tussle with time has had greatly the worst of it, some of the houses being roofless, and others reduced to the foundations. No regular ashpit is erected and the village is in a very dirty state, the roadway in front and the garden ground behind being alike untidy. There is not a closet in the place, but a deposit of bricks near the end of the long row is the forerunner, I am told, of such outhouses. For small room and kitchen houses the rent is 5s a month, and for single apartments 3s 4d a month. They are poor houses, but not positively unhealthy. Two wells give a never-failing supply of good spring water.

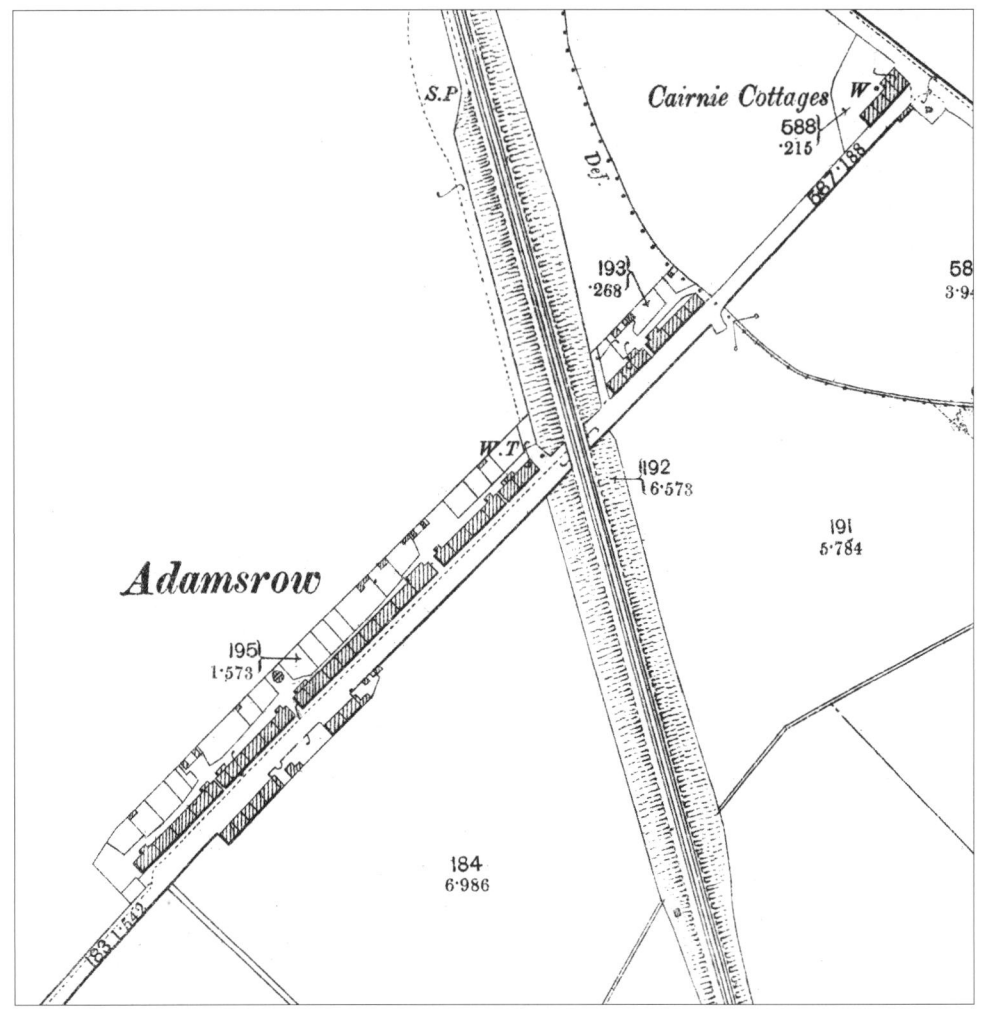

1.2 Adamsrow from 1895 Ordnance Survey map

The old wells used by the residents of the village were eventually replaced by a water supply to a pump, located at the side of the railway bridge. This was in operation by 1893.

When Adamsrow was demolished is not known, but it was certainly gone by the end of the Second World War. An aerial photograph of the time shows the site of the village returned to nature, with fields occupying where the community once existed.

In 1953 the land around Adamsrow was developed for deep mining, when the new Monktonhall Colliery was sunk by the National Coal Board, one of a trio of modern 'super-mines'. Where the community of Adamsrow once existed was cleared, the site being largely covered over by an extensive series of railway sidings, known as Millerhill marshalling yards, constructed in 1957. The two shafts associated with Monktonhall were sunk 3,000 feet into the earth, reaching the deep limestone coal seams. The pit suffered from water ingress, but survived until 1987, when it was mothballed. It was taken over by a miners' co-operative in 1992 but closed for good in 1997, the tower being demolished soon after.

2
Arden

*

On most maps, the village of Arden is named as Arden Rows, and yet it was more than just a row, for it formed a sizeable community of 51 houses. Located on the hill above Plains in Lanarkshire, the community was formed in an 'L' shape, following the line of the minor road which served a number of farms hereabouts. On the Ordnance Survey map of 1859, it was named simply as Arden.

From near Plains and Caldercruix, a minor road made its way straight up the hillside. This roadway was known locally as 'The Fancy'. On climbing the hill from another small lost village – Barblues, which lay by the side of the railway, near to Stepends Junction – one came to the T-junction near to West Arbuckle. This road was known locally as the Red Road, so-called as it was surfaced with red blaes. Turning right, the South Row of Arden was soon reached, a terrace of twenty houses, looking over their small gardens to the glen of the North Calder Water below. Amongst the gardens were two small buildings, used as wash-houses.

A sharp left turn at the end of the row is made, and facing the roadway here was the East Row, a longer terrace of houses, in this case numbering 27 homes. They were not all of the same size, the houses at the southern end of the row being larger than those to the north. These houses had their gardens and allotments across the road from the row, the front doors facing directly onto the road. Both rows at Arden were built of stone and were probably erected early in the nineteenth century.

At the north end of the East Row was a building which was originally erected as a school sometime around 1838 for the village by the coalmasters, but it was eventually closed and the building converted into four homes. It was located alongside a track striking west from the public road. This track continued as a footpath, joining the public road that led to the lost village of Stanrigg. It also led to a coal pit, just one of many which dotted the moorland heights on which Arden was built. Further west, near to the old pit, was another row of houses, shown on the Ordnance Survey map of 1859, but even then it was indicated as being partially in ruins.

Most of the menfolk at Arden worked in the local coal or ironstone mines. The estate of Arden, which extended to 700 acres, had been offered for sale in 1809, in which the minerals below the ground were noted. In 1836 the owner offered the lease allowing the right to mine the minerals, and in 1838 this was bought by John Wilson of the Dundyvan Ironworks for £18,000. By the 1870s much of the estate was leased by the Shotts Iron Company.

John Wilson, who died in 1851, established Arden as a community where the workers in his pits and mines could live. Wilson's obituary, which appeared in the *Falkirk Herald* of 13 November 1851, noted that, 'at Arden Mr Wilson has erected a beautiful country village for the workmen on the estate, with an endowed school, in which the children are educated at no small expense'.

The trustees of John Wilson (under the control of his son, William Wilson) appear to have established a small oil-refinery at Arden around 1866, which produced oil from the shale-coal mined in the vicinity. This doesn't appear to have lasted very long, perhaps as short a period as seven years. Ownership of the works and the mineral rights passed to John Kirk in 1869. Certainly, by February 1874, the full plant and works were offered for sale by auctioneers, J. Shirlaw & Son of Wishaw. The auction advertisement gives an indication of the size of the plant – one eighteen-inch cylinder horizontal steam engine and connections with boiler, 27 feet by 5 feet; 31 retorts of various kinds with connections; about twelve tons of pit rails and crossings; about six tons of platform rails and pit pump pipes in various sizes; six boilers, cranes, hutches, hutch sleepers, smiddy tools, etc. It is assumed that the goods were sold and taken away, there being no more references to a shale oil refinery at Arden thereafter.

The ironstone mines were worked out firstly, but coal-mining continued for some years thereafter. There were quite a number of these in the immediate surroundings of the village, and the miners had to move from one to another as they opened and closed. Just to the north-east of Arden was Midtown Colliery – Pit Number 1, one of the last mines to operate here. Just west of West Arbuckle was Barblues Colliery – Number 9 Pit. To the south-east was the large Barblues Colliery – Arden Pit.

On 27 July 1899 Peter Sherry, a miner who lived at Longriggend, was working in the Gorehill Colliery Number 4 Pit at Arden when there was a gas explosion. He suffered serious burns to his body and was thrown against the wall. He had been engaged in clearing an air course but, as was common at the time, naked lights were being used, resulting in the explosion. Suffering the loss of a foot was a young lad of nine years, James Mallon, who had been playing on a moving railway waggon on a siding at Arden. He jumped off and landed on the rails in front of the waggon, the wheels running over his foot, severing it from his leg. He was attended by Dr Alston from Airdrie who sent him to Glasgow Royal Infirmary for further treatment.

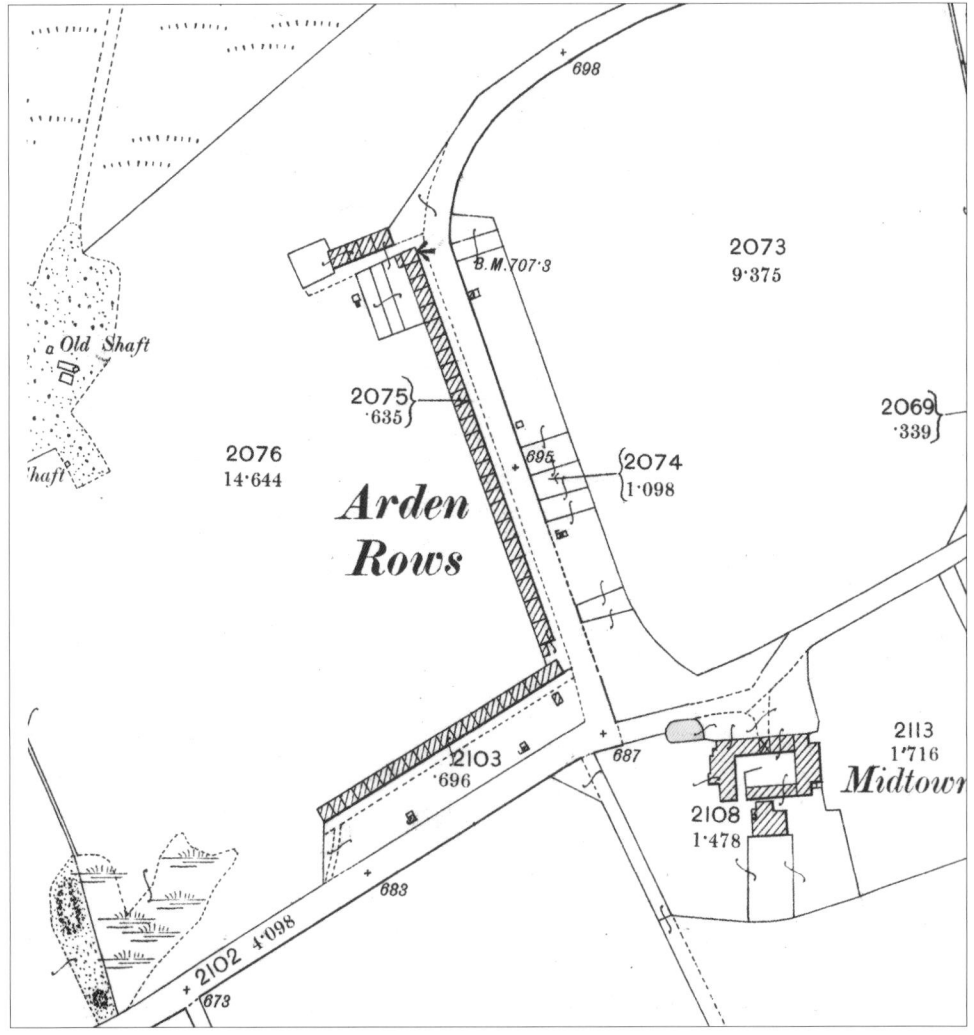

2.1 Arden from 1898 Ordnance Survey map

Studying the birth-places of the residents of Arden in the Census of 1881 indicates that the village had a high percentage of Irish-born families. These had come to Scotland to find work when the Irish potato famine kicked in.

At the right-angled corner in Arden's street was a minor road that led into Midtown of Arden farm, and thence on to Arden House (sometimes referred to as Arden Cottage), and the various buildings usually associated with a country estate, such as the kennels, and stables. Arden House was, for a time, occupied by William and Beatrice Johnstone.

Services at Arden were sparse, and there were only two water pumps to serve the whole community. One of these was located near to the top end of the long row, the other at the road junction at the village corner, next to Midtown road-end.

Staying at Number 18 South Row in 1881 was David and Mary Clarkson. He had moved here from Douglas, also in Lanarkshire, and with his wife brought up at least four children. He seems to have died before 1891, for by this time Mary Clarkson had converted the houses at 19 and 20 South Row into a grocery, selling provisions to the other residents.

In 1910 a report in *The Housing Condition of Miners* by the Medical Officer of Health, Dr John T. Wilson, summarised how the residents of Arden lived when he inspected the houses. He noted that one of the rows had sixteen single-apartment houses in it, the rent payable for which varied from £3 5s to £5 4s. These houses were all built of local stone, one storey in height. The walls did not have a damp-proof course and internally they had been plastered directly onto the solid stone. The floors were of concrete, and as could be surmised, the internal surface of the walls and ceilings were described as 'rough'. With the apartments being fairly large, it was reckoned that there was no overcrowding. An area of garden was supplied to each occupier, but these did not appear to be used. There were two privy middens in front of the houses to serve the row, but there were no wash-houses or coal cellars allocated to each property. Homes did not have sinks, and the drainage was simply by open surface drains. The rubbish was scavenged each week at the expense of the mine-owners.

The other row had thirty houses in it, comprising seven two-apartment homes and 23 single-apartment houses. The single apartment houses were let at £3 13s 8d, whereas the larger houses had a rental of £6 2s. As with the first row mentioned, these houses were erected of stone, without damp-proof courses, and were finished in the same way. The rough walls and ceilings were damp, and facilities matched the first row.

The population of Arden reached 646 in 1841, dropped to 204 in 1861, and rose again to 397 by the time the 1891 Census was compiled.

After the First World War the emptying of Arden had begun, and the village was totally cleared of residents by 1930. The old stone rows were demolished, leaving only the foundations, which can still be seen poking through the grass.

3
Avonhead

*

In 1868 the colliery manager at Avonhead described the little community as 'this outlandish place', from its remote position on a bleak and windy moor, far from other civilisation. Access to the village was either by means of a narrow and meandering road, or else on foot across the moors to the nearest public road which could be around two miles distant.

The community at Avonhead was located high on moors that separated Lanarkshire and West Lothian. The village gained its name from being positioned near to the Head of Avon Water, the source of the watercourse that becomes the River Avon and flows generally north-east to the Firth of Forth between Bo'ness and Grangemouth. The village sat over 700 feet above sea level on a high moss, the aspect generally north-west.

Mining is noted at Avonhead in 1851-54 when William Jack is recorded as being a coalmaster at Avonhead and Greengairs. In 1857 the mineral rights to Avonhead farm were offered for lease by the landowner, John Thomson of Upperton. A few firms appear to have tried to make a success of the coal and shale-coal seams below the moors, including Douglas & Boag in the 1860s and M. & J. Kelt, the latter business being sequestrated in July 1867. Shale oil machinery, including fifteen retorts, five furnaces and other machinery, were subsequently offered at auction. Around this time the Avonhead Coal Company was formed, which was more successful, perhaps due to the fact that one of the shareholders owned the Clifton Ironworks at Coatbridge, providing a ready market for the coal. Avonhead Coal Company was sold in 1875, along with around thirty to forty houses, a manager's house and stores. The Avonhead Coal Company owned the mines by the turn of the twentieth century, having their headquarters in Coatbridge Main Street. In 1911 the company was reformed as the Avonhead Coal Company Ltd., with its offices at 166 Buchanan Street, Glasgow. In 1924 it was working the Lady Grange and Kiltongue seams of coal, used for household burning and manufacturing. At the time the directors were R. T. Walker and R. H. Walker. Avonhead Mine was managed by James Shanks, employing 58 men underground and a further dozen on the surface.

Avonhead was spread along the moss-side in a generally east-west direction. At the western end were three rows of houses, separated perpendicularly by one of the minor access tracks that made its way into the village. On passing Avondale Cottage, which survives, the track turned south. On the right-hand side was a row of fourteen houses, all built together at right angles to the road. These houses all comprised of a single apartment. Parallel with this terrace was a second row of houses, different in size to the first row, but this terrace only had thirteen houses in it. These houses were slightly larger, having two apartments.

Across the track was a third row, built with cottages back-to-back, totalling twenty homes, each containing a single apartment. These rows appear to have been the oldest ones erected in the village, for they were referred to as Auld Avonhead. In 1868 there is reference to a store in one of the buildings at Old Avonhead, but this probably closed when a new larger shop was established in the central rows. All of the three western rows were abandoned by 1910, the walls standing roofless on the moor.

A footpath struck east to the central part of the village. Here were two more rows of back-to-back houses. The western row had a total of sixteen houses in it, the second, larger row, having 24 houses.

Adjoining the middle rows were a number of other buildings, which served a variety of purposes. These were arranged facing each other across the eastern access road to Avonhead. One of the buildings was the village store, another the public house. These were erected in 1874 by the Glasgow Steam Coal Company. A few names of managers in the store at Avonhead are known. It was operated by Messrs Carrick and Yuill in 1889. In 1887 James Aitken ran a licensed grocery in the village.

To the east of the central part of the village was a further set of back-to-back houses, referred to as the Shale Row. There were sixteen houses in this row. This row had been abandoned by 1910, being depicted as roofless on the Ordnance Survey map of the period. One of the rows at Avonhead was known as the Steamboat Rows, though why is not known.

The houses at Avonhead were at first the property of a Mr Muir, who erected them around 1874 to house miners employed in his coal-mines. A correspondent of the *Glasgow Herald* visited in 1875 and noted that the houses had been built of bricks. He wrote that they had a large room and kitchen, the floors being made from wood. The ceilings were regarded as being quite high, making the houses appear airier. Occupants of the houses paid Muir twelve shillings a month in rent.

Water was piped into the village and water pumps were positioned around the central rows. There were two pumps provided, one adjacent to the two central rows. These replaced the original means of gathering water, which was collected from pools on the moss. It was noted that water was difficult to obtain in the summer months.

At the village centre was a public house, known as the Heather Bell. In addition to this, a number of householders sold beer and spirits, often illicitly. One of these was John Hendry, a miner, who lived in one of the houses. He was taken to Airdrie Justice of the Peace Court in April 1887, charged with selling beer and porter without having a licence. The *Lanarkshire Examiner* reported that 'Constable Simpson of Meadowfield states that he had suspected Hendry of shebeening for the last four months, having observed numbers of men visiting his house on Sunday mornings and leaving it very much the worse of drink. It was also noted that a beer cart called at the accused's house twice a week, and several parties spoke of Hendry carrying on the illicit traffic, and being supplied with liquor which they drank and paid for in his house.' Hendry was found guilty and was fined £7, the maximum penalty possible.

Another amusing tale includes the time in July 1887 when Greengairs Brass Band visited the community and was playing tunes outside Mr Aitken's Grocery. Two miners, John Gillan and James Miller, both of whom were described as being the 'worse of drink', began dancing to the tunes. It wasn't known whether it was in fun or in earnest, but Miller knocked Gillan to the ground and struck him. Gillan's brother jumped in, only to be struck by a Michael Neilus. Eventually a large crowd gathered to watch the fracas, Miller and Neilus eventually being fined fifteen shillings.

Clarkston School Board erected a public school at Avonhead, located about one quarter of a mile to the north of the village, at the road bridge over the Avon Water. The site of the school is now Avalon, a cottage south of Upperton. The roll at the school in 1886 was 64 pupils, with an average attendance of 55; in 1891 the roll was 74, however, it had a capacity for 191 children. The Scottish Education Department awarded it a grant of £63 13s 6d that year. In the 1880s the head mistress was a Mrs Grace P. Herriot (up to 1887) after which Miss Maggie Main was appointed. In 1884 Her Majesty's Inspectors visited the school and noted that, 'this school is taught with great earnestness and success. The pupils performed their work most expeditiously and correctly, and the results reflect much credit on the teacher. Sewing is a special feature of this school, and is worthy of the highest praise'. On Christmas Day, 1885, the pupils of the school were presented with an orange on leaving the classroom, gifted by John Wylie, of Avonhead Colliery. He had noted that, 'it afforded him the greatest pleasure to give them this small treat, as it was the custom when he was a scholar himself, and he just wished to continue the good old custom'. The school was reroofed with new slates in 1891, and at the same time it was noted that water barrels should be fitted up at the school, so as to supply the children with drinking water, 'otherwise so scarce in the district'. In April 1917 New Monkland School Board announced that Avonhead School would close at the end of the month. Most of the families whose children attended the school had moved elsewhere, resulting in the school roll falling to nine children.

Although there was no church at Avonhead, in 1880 a branch of Meadowfield Church Sabbath School was formed in the village. This proved to be a great success initially, and in August 1880 seventy sabbath scholars enjoyed taking part in a Sunday school trip to Drumbow farm.

Many of the miners who lived at Avonhead worked in the Avonhead Pits. Pits numbered 1 and 8 were located across the moor to the south. Pit Number 9 was located to the west. In 1875 the coal mines worked the Virtuewell seam, which was around 2 feet 6 inches thick, and the Lady Grange seam of around two feet.

The mines at Avonhead appear to have been safer than some of the others in the county, or else seem to have been more fortunate in that there were fewer deaths recorded in them. Two deaths noted occurred on the evening of Friday 25 June 1869 when two pit sinkers were killed. They were part of a group of three who were in the process of sinking a pit and had set some dynamite. They returned to the surface until the shot had went off. Once the dust had settled, the three had stepped into a kettle, or bucket, to descend into the pit when it went out of control and plummeted to the bottom. The engine which was used to haul the kettle up and down had not been put into gear (it was also used for pumping water from the pit bottom), resulting in the shaft being in neutral. Two of the miners, who had only started their first shift at the pit, were killed instantaneously. They were James Murdoch of Arden Rows and Michael Queen, of Meadowfield Rows, Longriggend. A third man, John Henderson of Arden, who also fell with the kettle, received serious injuries. John Anderson, the

AVONHEAD

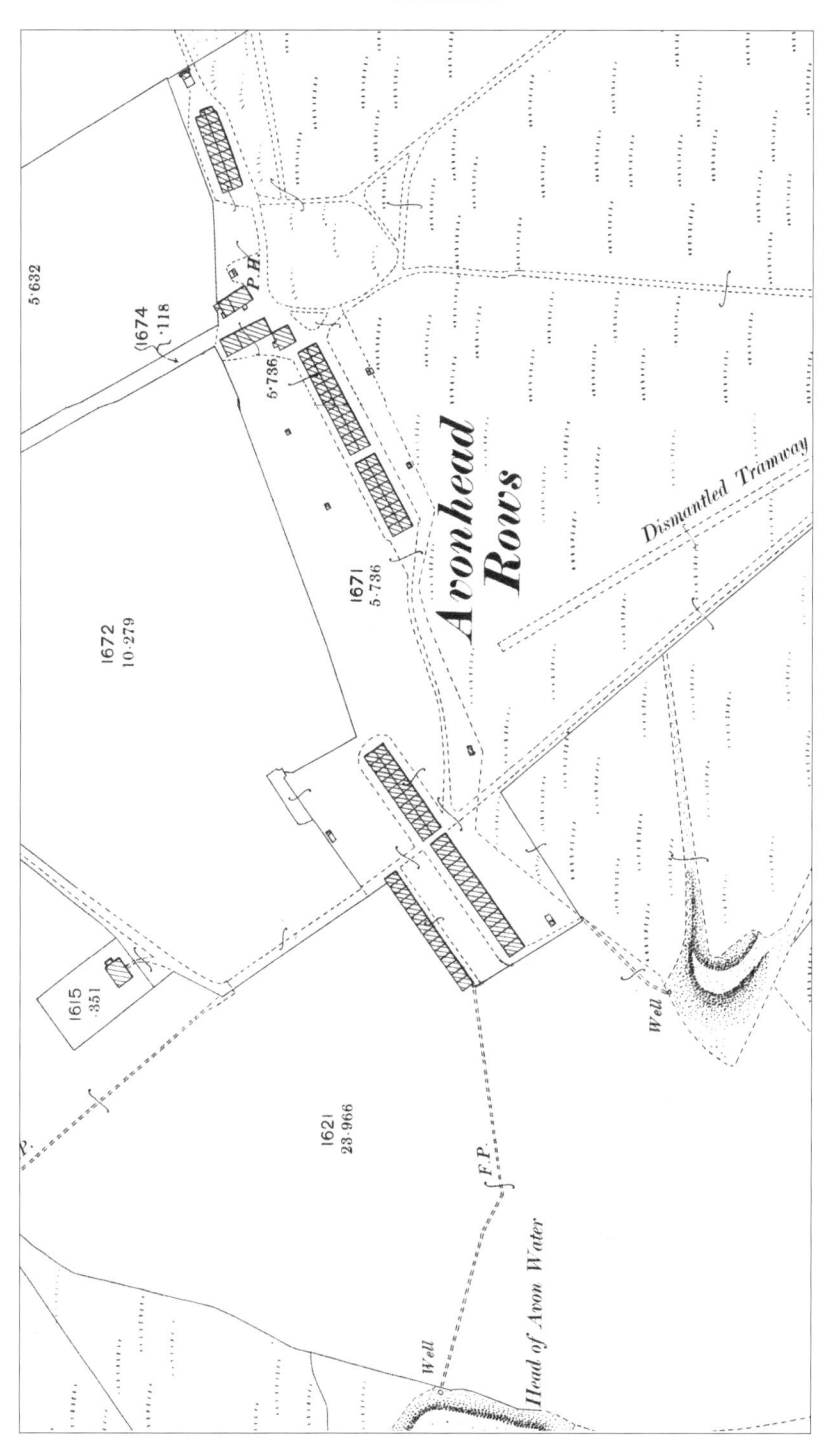

3.1 Avonhead from 1898 Ordnance Survey map

engineman who was supposed to have been in charge of the winding engine, was arrested and charged with culpable neglect of duty. Sheriff Logie bailed him on a charge of £15. When his case came up at court he did not attend, and it was later discovered that he had absconded to America.

In April 1871 the engine house at Avonhead Pit Number 3 was burned to the ground. It was thought that flames from the boiler house had reached the timber building, setting it ablaze.

On the evening of Tuesday, 23 April 1901, James Little, aged 24, who lived at Low Avonhead Rows, was injured when a block of stone, weighing around ten hundredweight, fell from the roof of Avonhead Number 4 pit. He was engaged in brushing on the roadhead around four feet from the splint coal face. The rock fell on Little, pushing him to the ground and crushing part of his body. He received injuries to his left leg and right side of his body, including internal damage.

The population of Avonhead was 194 in 1871, 435 in 1881, 472 in 1891 and 399 in 1901. In 1885, when the Longriggend Registrar made a return on the number of people living at Avonhead, he noted that there were 468 people living in 92 houses. Most of the village was cleared away in the 1900s, the last house standing being the public house manager's home, which was demolished around 1943. The school was the only building still standing in 1960. It was noted at the time that former residents who returned often pointed to a field where at one time the village pub stood.

An advertisement in the *Hamilton Herald and Lanarkshire Weekly News* of 4 December 1909 indicated the outcome of some of the buildings at Avonhead, which were being cleared away at the time. Messrs. Shirlaw, Allan & Co., auctioneers in Hamilton, advertised, 'On an early day, at Avonhead, near Longriggend Station, N.B.R., Building Material of Workmen's Houses.'

4
Balclevie

★

Sir Walter Scott's novel, *Guy Mannering, or the Astrologer,* which he wrote in 1815, has a scene in it in which the Laird of Ellangowan evicted a community of gypsies from the clachan of Derncleugh. This community had built up over the years, becoming a semi-permanent village, but something of a blot in the refined landscape around Ellangowan New House. Scott describes Derncleugh in his novel:

> They had there erected a few huts, which they denominated their 'city of refuge,' and when not absent on excursions, they harboured unmolested, as the crows that roosted in the old ash-trees around them. They had been such long occupants, that they were considered in some degree as proprietors of the wretched shealings which they inhabited.

The presence of the gypsy community had become an embarrassment to the Laird of Ellangowan, and he was determined to remove it. To start the process, he hoped to devise some form of quarrel with them, but this came about quicker than he planned. Finding some gypsy boys on his property, they were whipped by the grieve, or farm oversser. The gypsies retaliated, steeling Ellangowan's hens and destroying other property. 'Every door in the hamlet was chalked by the ground-officer, in token of a formal warning to remove at next term…. At length the term-day, the fatal Martinmas, arrived, and violent measures of ejection were resorted to. A string posse of peace-officers, sufficient to render all resistance vain, charged the inhabitants to depart by noon; and, as they did not obey, the officers, in terms of their warrant, proceeded to unroof the cottages, and pull down the wretched doors and windows.'

One of the gypsies, Meg Merrilies, cursed the laird, claiming that only six generations of his family would ever live in the mansion.

Scott is thought to have based this part of his novel on the story of the village of Balclevie, sometimes spelled Bucklyvie or Bucklevie, which used to exist in the parish of Elie in Fife. This community was located on Elie House estate, between the mansion itself and Kilconquhar Loch to the north. Elie House comprises of an ancient castle, rebuilt as a tower house in 1697 by Sir William Anstruther, who had bought the estate at that time.

By the middle part of the eighteenth century, Balclevie was owned by Sir John Anstruther (d. 1811), who was an eminent judge of the period. In 1750 he was to marry Janet Fall (d. 1802), whose ancestors were the gypsy Fall, or Faa, family, which claimed to be the royal gypsy line. She, however, was the second daughter of Charles Fall, Provost of Dunbar. Janet Fall was something of a catch for Sir John, for she was regarded as one of the society beauties. Thomas Carlyle referred to her as 'a coquette and a beauty'. Elie House was extended by the addition of a large north wing around 1760, perhaps influenced by Lady Anstruther's taste in style.

It was Lady Anstruther who was also responsible for having the bathing tower erected at Sauchar Point, on Elie Ness, known as the Lady's Tower. This is a simple structure, comprising of four arches, the seaward one affording spectacular views of the Firth of Forth. When Lady Anstruther wished to take a dip in the waters of the firth, she would go to the tower, to change, and from the building drop down into the sea. To keep prying eyes away from her, she would instruct an estate worker to ring a bell at the approach to the headland and around the lanes of Elie, to warn people away, so that she could bathe in private.

When Lady Anstruther moved into Elie, she was annoyed at the proximity of Balclevie village, and is said to have claimed that it 'interfered with the privacy of the mansion'. The residents were said to hold regular outdoor religious services, the sound of which also annoyed her. Some claimed that the humble inhabitants of the village, often regarded as little more than tinkers, reminded her of her lowly background too much. In any case, she persuaded Sir John that it should be cleared away, so that the view from the house would be more attractive.

Sir John acquiesced, despite having lived at Elie for years and not having regarded the village's proximity a problem until she brought it to his attention. Sir John bought all of the feus in 1771 and the residents were given notice to quit their properties. Once they had moved out, the houses, which were probably little more than thatched cottages with rubble walls held together with clay, were flattened.

4.1 Lady's Tower, Elie (Kevan Aitken)

Sir Walter Scott may also have taken the tale of the curse of six generations from the Bucklyvie story, for it is said that one of the villagers placed a curse on Sir John and his family, foretelling that only six generations of Anstruthers would occupy the house. This prediction was to become true.

Writing in 1836, Dr Milligan wrote: 'The prophecy is still devoutly believed by a number of people; and the fact has added strength to their faith, - the sixth proprietor, within the memory of middle-aged men, being now in possession, and some disaster having occurred in the history of them all.'

Evidence of the existence of Balclevie village is difficult to come by. John Adair's map entitled, 'The East Part of Fife', sketched by him around 1684, names the community. His map shows Elie House as Ardross, replacing the ancient Ardross Castle which still stands in ruins by the shore. Around the mansion is a large enclosure, with trees and gardens. To the north of this, on the shore of Kilconquhar Loch, is Balclevie, indicated by a solitary building, but this is perhaps just a symbol which may represent a larger community.

The Ordnance Survey 25 Inch map of 1894 uses the 'site of' cross symbol on its map to show where the village once existed. The map spells the name as 'Buchlyvie' and positions it where a line of trees indicated an old fence line that ran east to west, almost due north of Elie home farm. By the time of the 1914 edition of the same map, the tree line had gone, but the map still indicated the village site with its cross of antiquity. Looking at aerial surveys of the area, no indication of any crop marks appear, perhaps an indication that the village was little more than a collection of turf-built homes, ones that melded back into the landscape once they had been emptied of families and residents.

In the kirkyard at Kilconquhar can be found an old stone effigy, purportedly of a knight in armour. To locals, this is referred to as 'Jock o' Bucklevie'. If this name has any significance in history, then it implies that Balclevie may have been an estate of its own at one time, and that the lairds thereof were buried here. It is thought that the effigy may have been located within the church building itself in the past.

A minister of Kilconquhar Parish Church, Rev R. S. Armstrong, penned a poem in which he told the tale of Balclevie. He wrote:

>Balclevie was a village fair,
>Balclevie is no longer there,
>They took and cast its houses down,
>Balclevie was a bonnie town.
>
>---
>
>She cursed the tongue that gave command
>That not one stone be left to stand,
>She cursed the Lady Jenny Fa'
>That their wee toon had ta'en awa'.

5
Benquhat

★

There's something about Benquhat that seems to attract descendants of villagers back to the remote moor where the rows of houses once stood. It is perhaps the lonely war memorial that does this, a solitary obelisk perched on the slopes of Benquhat Hill itself, overlooking a wide and bleak expanse of countryside, covered with gorse and heather, high above the Doon valley in southern Ayrshire. Thus it was in November 2014 that Diana May, her husband and son, came on a pilgrimage to the memorial, to pay her respects to her great uncles, whose names are chiselled into the stone. Her great-grandmother, Agnes Wilson, had unveiled the monument in 1921. She wasn't the first person to return to the home of her ancestors, for annually the lonely roadway from Dalmellington is walked by others, keen to see the wild place that moulded their characters.

There must have been an old shepherd's cottage or croft around this area known as Benquhat that existed in the seventeenth century. It was here that Roger Dun (1659-1689) lived, the son of the farmer, James Dun. Roger and his brothers, Allan and Andrew, were to become supporters of the National Covenant. On one occasion, they attended a conventicle at Craignew in Carsphairn parish but, on their return home, the soldiers apprehended the two brothers. They were never to be seen again. Roger managed to escape and had to spend much of his time in hiding, often in secluded Dunaskin Glen. One day he met the soldiers searching for him, but as they didn't know what he looked like, he was able to act as though he was someone else, and assisted them in their search! Dun made a number of other escapes, the most notable being at Caldons in Glen Trool. When a prayer meeting was attacked by the dragoons, Dun managed to make his way to Loch Trool, where he submerged himself in the water. Although Dun survived the 'killing times' of the Covenanting period, he was actually shot dead by someone who was intent on killing another. This was at the time of Carsphairn Fair, and his body lies in the kirkyard at Carsphairn, where a small headstone marks his grave.

In 1847 a new village was created on the southern slopes of Benquhat Hill by the Dalmellington Iron Company. The village was located on remote moorland, bare of trees, and stood over 1,000 feet above sea level. The name given to the village, Benquhat, came from the hill below which it was located, but the locals preferred the simpler spelling of 'Benwhat'. Though this variant appeared on the Ordnance Survey Six Inch map of 1860, in general the spelling Benquhat was insisted upon by the authorities.

At first only one row was built, with 34 single-apartment houses, constructed from the handmade Dunaskin brick. This row was named the Laight Row, after the castle ruins which existed lower down the glen. To the east of the row a school and store were built, also by the Dalmellington Iron Company, but stone from the Dunaskin Quarry was used in their construction.

Sometime between 1870 and 1874 a further four rows of 98 houses were erected, located behind the Laight Row and contouring along the hillside. Behind Laight Row was the Stone Row, of twenty houses. East of this was the Store Row (of twenty houses), so-called because it stood behind the co-operative store. Next again was the Post Office Row with thirty houses, one of which contained the small post office. The last row of 28 houses was called the Heath Row, so-called because it overlooked the remote moor. The Stone Row was built of Dunaskin stone, the other three rows of Dunaskin bricks. The Store Row was sometimes known as the Middle or Brick Row, perhaps implying that the four rows were not erected simultaneously, with the Stone Row erected first, the Heath Row last. On the south side of the rows were the gardens.

The houses at Benquhat were let for 2s 3d per week for a room and kitchen in 1875. At that time there were no closets or ash pits in the community, but the water supply appears to have been fairly good.

Benquhat, like many other mining communities of the time, attracted folk from all over Scotland and beyond, all in search of work, and a better lifestyle than they hitherto enjoyed. Thus, Benquhat was to become home to exiles from Ireland, the Highlands, Cornwall, Wanlockhead, Cumbria, Lincolnshire, Wigtownshire, Argyll, Renfrewshire, and many other locations. In most cases, the local industry or agriculture had taken a turn for the worse, resulting in hundreds being laid off. Such was the case in the Highlands, where folk were still being removed from the land, Cumbria, where the lead mines were in decline, Cornwall, where a similar tale existed in the tin mines, and Ireland, where the potato famine and agricultural decline were still having a severe effect on the residents.

The population of Benquhat in 1881 had risen to 772 people, housed in 131 dwellings. This was probably the largest it ever reached, for by 1891 it had dropped to 523. Gradually, as the mines closed on the high moors, families were keen to move out of the community, there being twenty empty houses in 1914. By 1951 the population had dropped to 460.

As the years passed, basic facilities were provided at Benquhat. A water pipe was laid across the back of the houses, and residents were allowed to ask blacksmiths to connect cast iron pipes to the water main and run the water into their homes. Prior to this, water had to be obtained from pumps, of which two existed per row. Alternatively, water from springs and wells could be used, and Campbell's Spoot and Squibbie's Well were such sources.

Electricity didn't arrive to Benquhat until 1933. A power station had been constructed at Waterside in 1917-18 by the iron company for use in the local pits, brickworks and workshops. As surplus power was generated, cables were strung across the moor to the village, and residents had the opportunity of connecting to them.

At Benquhat the Dalmellington Iron Company erected a school sometime in the early 1870s, located south of the Post Office Row, at the top of the Store Brae. Built of Dunaskin stone, the school had three classrooms. At the time its roll was around 200, but only about 140 pupils attended. In 1879 the roll was 140, taught by two assistants and one pupil teacher. One classroom was divided by a glass screen which was removable. This was often done to allow various functions to take place, from weddings to tea dances. Pupils of primary age were taught here - they had to travel to Dalmellington for secondary education.

The school proved to be too small for the population, especially with the raising of the school-leaving age, and in 1926 a new school was erected at the west end of the village, between the rows and the bing of Corbie Craigs Number 4 ironstone pit. In addition to the usual classrooms, the new seminary had a new domestic science room, where sewing and cooking was taught, a gymnasium and a woodwork room. A unique feature was the introduction of water closets, the only ones that ever existed in the village. In 1930 the roll was around 120 pupils, dropping to 80 by 1950. Headmasters at Benquhat included Alex MacArthur (appointed in 1909), Arthur Halcrow Gear (died 1921) and Francis Ferguson (1932-1944). As the village was cleared, the school roll plummeted. When it was finally closed in 1951 there were only three pupils still attending – Doreen Atkinson, Jean MacHattie and Maureen Wilson. The last teacher, Mrs Paterson, only worked there for a few months.

5.1 Benquhat Store (left) and old School (right)

The store at Benquhat was operated by the Dalmellington Iron Company. A railway siding was laid to its side, which allowed pugs to arrive with provisions. The store had two halves, one which sold groceries and general supplies. The other sold beer, but not spirits, which was the iron company's decision. Among the storemasters who ran the shop was John Talman.

A number of women, often widows, ran small shops from their homes. Among those which existed at times were Maggie Fisher's – she sold 'cough cakes' and other sweets; Mrs Dick had a post office which also sold confectionery and mineral waters; Mrs Moffat sold cigarettes and Granny Hainey sold a variety of sweets, mostly homemade. George Park, who spoke at Benquhat Re-union in 1967, recalled that he would 'watch her make her famous stalks and candy – a pennyworth lasted Saturday and Sunday. She also made Boston cream and Burdock Stout which went down well in the hot summer days we had then.'

There was no church established at Benquhat, but the minister from Dalmellington, Rev George Hendrie, travelled up the hill every fortnight to hold Sunday evening services, in the former school building. In 1917 a joint communion service was initiated, run by the parish church and the United Free Church. In addition to formal services, there were fortnightly 'kitchen meetings'.

The workmen banded together to form societies which were instrumental in improving conditions for their members. Among those formed in the nineteenth century were the Benquhat and Lethanhill Aboveground Workmen's Society, Benquhat and Lethanhill Underground Workmen's Society, Dunaskin and Doon Aboveground Society, and the Jellieston and Drumgrange Friendly Society. For the men, two cottages at the end of the Laight Row were converted into a Miners' Institute, or reading room, where many of the meetings were held. Boys aged fourteen or over, if they were in work, could join. Among the games and pastimes on offer were cards, dominoes, billiards, skittles, snooker, summer ice and carpet bowls. There was a small library with books supplied from Dalmellington, in addition to daily newspapers. To be a member, the men had four pence per month deducted from their wages.

The Hope of Benwhat Tent of the International Order of Rechabites was founded on 7 July 1906 and the juvenile branch, the Ark of Safety Juvenile Tent, was established in 1907. In 1913 there were 86 state members of the Hope Tent, plus 80 order members and 43 juvenile members.

The Benquhat Silver Band was founded either in 1869 or 1871 depending on which source is used. It may even have existed in 1867. Certainly, it was up and running by the latter date, entertaining the villagers and performing at every main social function in the community, from Sunday School trips to weddings. The band survived the demise of the village, latterly merging with an Ayr band to form the Ayr-Benwhat Silver Band. In 1971 the band celebrated its centenary, at which long-standing conductor, James Armour, was honoured for his fifty years as bandmaster, most of which was with Benquhat.

Little changed at Benquhat from the Victorian era until the rows were eventually cleared after the Second World War. The post office was operated by Mrs Jane Dick for over thirty years until she retired. It was then taken over by Mrs MacHattie, who was born at Burnhead farm nearby and who married Andrew MacHattie, son of Adam MacHattie who lived at 1/2 Corbie Craigs, two houses converted into one. Mrs MacHattie closed the post office in 1951. In the late 1930s work had commenced on rehousing the residents of the rows at Bellsbank and Dalmellington, but this scheme was temporarily abandoned following the outbreak of war.

The Benquhat war memorial was unveiled on 31 July 1921. The memorial was sculpted by James Vallance of Prestwick from Kemnay granite and it stands 13 feet 6 inches tall. It was erected on the slopes of Benquhat itself, so that the memorial was visible on the horizon from the village. On it are the names of 22 residents who set off to serve in the First World War but never returned.

As with most miners' rows, the sport of football was followed with considerable passion. A football pitch was created on the old hearth of Corbie Craigs Number 5 pit, and here Benwhat Heatherbell played in their light blue tops. They were to win the Ayrshire Junior Challenge Cup in season 1899-1900. The club temporarily folded during the Great War. When the Ayr and District League folded in 1926 the club joined the South Ayrshire League. In 1928 they achieved one of their greatest goal records, beating Lugar Boswell Thistle 9-2 at home. They did not survive much longer, closing down in the middle of the 1930-31 season. In that season they only played five games, winning two and drawing one. One of their defeats was 8-0 at Cumnock Juniors. At the January 1931 meeting of the club it was announced that it was to fold.

Another keen association was the Doon Harriers, established in 1927 as a cross-country running and athletics club. The members took part in many events across the county, their strength in cross-country running being developed with running across the moors and hillsides.

About half a mile to the south of Benquhat was a row of ten single-apartment houses known as Corbie Craigs. This was officially classed as a separate village, but its proximity to Benquhat and the fact that the residents shared all the facilities of the larger village, meant that most residents regarded themselves as being part of the same community. Corbie Craigs dates from the 1850s. The houses were built for the workers who were employed in the operation of the railway incline from Waterside up to the Corbie Craigs pits. This line was erected at the same time as the houses. Each house had one main room, of twenty feet by twelve feet, plus a small scullery of nine feet by eight feet, which projected to the rear, or north. On the south side of the row were the tenants' gardens.

When the incline was closed in 1866 it became a pathway commonly used by Corbie Craigs and Benquhat residents. The community at Corbie Craigs was probably intended to be larger, but the Dalmellington Iron Company decided to erect the village of Benquhat instead. It had few facilities, the water obtained from nearby burns, sanitation limited to dry closets located in wooden huts. The rent was 1s 9d per week. Though there were only ten houses, the 'village' had a population of around 50 people. Latterly houses numbered one and two were joined to create one unit.

When the coal mines were nationalised in 1947, Benquhat became the property of the National Coal Board. They were keen to off-load many older

BENQUHAT

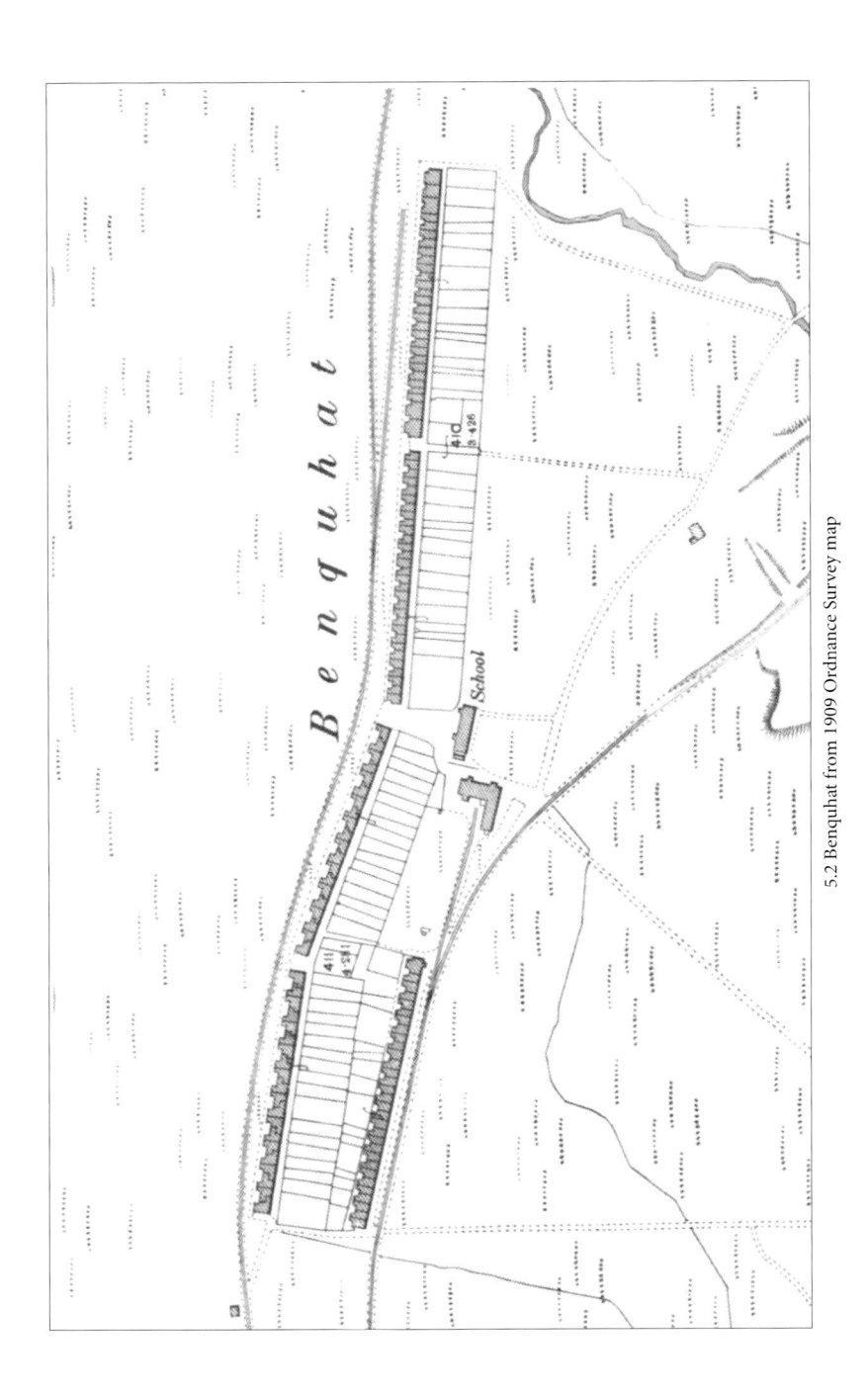

5.2 Benquhat from 1909 Ordnance Survey map

properties, and the fact that the houses did not meet modern standards meant that they were subject to the slum clearance acts. Ayr County Council built new houses in Dalmellington, and also established a new community on the outskirts of the village, named Bellsbank. Most of the Benquhat residents were evacuated in 1951, when 460 residents were to make the journey down from the hill and into the valley below. The last family to move out of Corbie Craigs was Mr and Mrs Joseph Thomson, he being a miner. At Benquhat the last resident was John Reilly. He was such a noted resident that he was nicknamed the 'Provost of Benquhat'. The village was demolished, but the foundations of many of the buildings can still be made out on the ground.

The Benquhat name survived, however, for Benquhat Burns Club continued to hold Burns' Suppers long after the village had gone. The club was founded in 1941 and joined the Burns Federation three years later. It had its roots as part of the Discussion Club, which originally met in the school. When the village was abandoned, the club moved to Dalmellington's church hall, which meant that the suppers were dry, something of a novelty among traditional Burns' Suppers. The club usually had 160 attending the suppers, but by 1970, twenty or so years after the village was demolished, there were still fifty folk attending. Another group with Benquhat connections was the annual Benquhat Re-union, which was instituted in 1965, inviting speakers such as John P. Kennedy, manager of Minnivey Colliery.

In 2015 a memorial stone was erected at the site of the village by three men, William McCluskie, William Rowan and Scott Filson. The granite boulder was sculpted by Kevin Roberts and bears the legend *Benwhat Village 1860-1952 Erected by S. Filson, W. McCluskie, W. Rowan*.

6
Binnend

★

Above the Fife coastal port of Burntisland rises the hill known as The Binn, its wooded slopes prominent to the north of the community. At its eastern end was a farm known as Binnend, reached by climbing a steep track through the woods from the road linking Burntisland with Kinghorn. The farm had been positioned on a flat area of ground, its elevated position affording wide panoramas of the Firth of Forth. It was here that the Burntisland Oil Company decided to erect a village to house its workers.

The Burntisland Oil Works had a rather amazingly-short history, especially when we consider that at one time it employed in excess of 1,000 workers. In total, it only lasted for thirteen years, in which time a large factory was erected, operated, closed and demolished! The company was founded in 1878 by George Simpson, an Edinburgh coalmaster, and it soon established the Binnend Oil Works, as it was originally called. This was operated on a small scale, for three years later there were still just 36 employees. Shale coal was mined in the locality and taken to the works by a number of mineral railways. The shale coal was crushed and then placed in retorts, where it was heated to 500°C, releasing the oil. This was used in a variety of industries for manufacturing other products. The company survived a winding-up order in October 1879, but did not last much longer.

In 1880 the company proposed laying a large pipe from the works down to Burntisland and thence to the shore, from where the waste liquid from the plant would be discharged. This was considered by the court, which refused to allow it, for fear that the noxious substance would affect the bathing facilities nearby. Instead, it was proposed that the works should build settling tanks, and allow the liquid to evaporate instead. At the time the company employed from 100-150 people, who were at threat of being paid off.

In 1881 the oil works were sold to a new company, the head of which was John Waddell of Edinburgh. He had considerable finance behind him, and the works were greatly expanded. He sunk new mines to work the coal up to 365 feet below sea level. The new buildings, retorts and ancillary works were capable of processing 500 tons of shale oil daily, producing 15,000 gallons of crude oil. This was then refined and usable products were produced, including oils for burning and lubricating. Paraffin was produced, and from this paraffin wax and paraffin candles. In addition, sulphate of ammonia was created, used as a fertiliser on the land.

In 1887 the works were to undergo a considerable rebuilding and extension. One of the pits at the time was working shale coal 100 feet below sea level, reached by a shaft 450 feet deep. Two major difficulties existed for the business – the lack of coal at the site and the expense of transporting produce and resources to and from the works. Coal for the furnaces had to be purchased from the Fife coalfields and conveyed to the works in carts.

In an attempt to alleviate the problems, a branch line was laid from Kinghorn Station into the works, allowing the produce to be transported more readily, opening on 2 May 1887. The arrival of the railway was not to be the boon that the company had anticipated, for by then the works were in decline. Things trundled on slowly for a number of years, but the inevitable occurred in September 1892 – the company went into liquidation. In January 1893, the factory was placed on the market, but with no interest coming, all the workers were laid off. The buildings and machinery were kept on a care-and-maintenance basis for a further year, but in 1894 the factory was closed completely. All of the machinery was dismantled and sold.

As well as the works being extended, a new candle works was erected in 1887 near to Kinghorn, owned by the same company. The five buildings, measuring around 100 feet by 50 feet, contained refining departments (two of them), a candle-manufactory, and two used for storage purposes.

The extensive oil works at Binnend had a number of large cylindrical tanks to hold the oil produced, and a number of large buildings in which the various processes were carried out. In addition, the skyline was punctuated with a series of very tall chimneys, from which dirty smoke belched into the sky. William Erskine described the light pollution which was also a by-product of the factory: 'The blaze of light that emanated from the works at night illumined not only the surrounding district but formed a beacon to indicate to mariners their whereabouts in the Forth.'

As with all large works, deaths occurred at various times due to industrial accidents. On 4 November 1878, Richard Green, aged 28, was killed when a wagon that he was sitting on was making its way through a small tunnel. It was filled with spent shale, being taken to the dump, but Green hit his head on the roof of the tunnel, killing him instantaneously.

Binnend village was established in 1883 following a large extension to Burntisland Oil Company's works. It was built around Binnend farm itself, and comprised of twelve terraces of houses, positioned at right angles to each other. By August 1883 it was home to 100 families, with a population around 300-400. The steep access road to Binnend passed by the farm steading and beyond to Common and Longloch. The ascent of the brae from the public road through the woods was particularly steep, but a second road to the community came by way of Whinnyhall. Although less steep, this added quite a distance to the walk to Burntisland. To the east of the road were seven terraces, arranged approximately north/south. Reached firstly was the first row of eight houses, positioned adjoining the road. Behind it were three other rows, each of them also containing eight houses.

Beyond were a second set of three terraces, located parallel with each other, each terrace having eight houses in it.

On the west side of the original farm road were five rows, four of which were in a west/east alignment, with the fifth row perpendicularly placed to the west end. In each of the five rows there were six houses.

According to the *Fifeshire Advertiser* of August 1883, 'the houses at Binnend are of a superior class for miners' houses. They are one-storeyed, built of substantial stone and lime…. Some difficulty has been experienced in providing the people with a supply of water for domestic use, and a reservoir to catch the surface and other water has just been constructed in the valley above Rodenbraes by throwing up 1,200 yards of earthwork. The water is conveyed a distance of about a mile through 8-inch iron pipes, to a new filter-house, and hence to the village.'

The reporter continued to note that 'the village has begun to develop within itself some of the "resources of civilisation".' This included a village store and a newsagent, and Sunday services were held in the open-air and in private houses by a missionary from the Free Church.

In addition to the workers' rows, and the old farm, there were a number of other buildings at Binnend. Next to the farm, on the north side of the steading, was a Free Church Mission Hall. This had been erected in 1889 as a mission from the Free Church in Burntisland, which had intended making it a regular mission under the charge of a probationer. Ministers came to the village on

Sundays and held services in the hall. Apparently, it wasn't just Free Church ministers who preached in the building, for ministers of other denominations are known to have held services there. The hall was also in demand for other community activities, including being used as a school from 1889. The hall, which was a corrugated-iron structure, lined in timber, was later dismantled and rebuilt in Burntisland's Union Street, where it served as a mission church for workers employed in building the new docks. It was then a church hall for the Couper, renamed St Andrew's, Church until 1934, when a permanent building replaced it. When the mission church at Binnend closed, Mr Farley continued to hold services in the school.

Not using the Free Church hall for church services were the Roman Catholic residents. The village had around one third of its population being associated with that church, and its adherents had to walk to the Burgh Chambers in Burntisland where services were held. In 1886 a new school was erected in Lochies Road, after which the Catholics held their services there.

On the opposite side of the road from the mission hall was Binnend School, erected in 1890-1. The Scottish Education Department had approved the construction of the school in 1888, but the financial position of the business meant that it took a few years to materialise. The school was opened on 2 February 1891 by Mr Rettie, advocate, Edinburgh, chairman of Burntisland

6.1 Binnend from the west in 1907 (Burntisland Heritage Trust)

Landward School Board. For the size of the village, the school was a comparatively large seminary, and when it opened it had a roll of around 170 children. It was of a simple design, built of brick, with accommodation for 240 pupils. The cost of building and furnishing it was reckoned to be £1,600. The first headmaster appointed was a Mr Smith, who previously had taught in Burntisland's Burgh School, assisted by Miss Isles, head teacher in the infant department. The school had been closed by 1913, but the building survived for a number of years.

The oil company had provided a building that was used by the residents as a reading room. This soon proved to be too small for the number of folk that used it, so in 1887 it was extended. This was formally opened by the works manager, John Spencer, on 9 December 1887.

East of the rows at Binnend was a football ground, home to the local football team, Binnend Rangers. This is known to have existed in the period 1889-1902. Binnend United played in 1922 and Binnend Albion were another team. For a number of years in the 1880s and 1890s there was also an annual gymnastic games event, held in July. Competitions undertaken included quoiting, road-races, dancing, tug-of-war, high jump, putting the ball, old men's race and 'go-as-you-please' races. By the 1920s the Binnend Children's Gala took place in September, with football now popular, along with various races.

6.2 Binnend (Burntisland Heritage Trust)

The population of Binned varies over the years, as the works waxed and waned. In 1881, according to the Census, there were 564 residents. At the time, there were 95 houses, almost all of which had only two rooms in them. By 1891, the Census noted that the population had increased to 756. The *Ordnance Gazetteer* of the 1890s noted that Binned was 'a prosperous village'.

The village of Binnend was often referred to as High Binn, for there was another small community located by the side of the Kinghorn road, known as Low Binn. There were five rows of houses here, arranged parallel with the main road, but only two of which were located at the roadside. Each of these terraces had six homes in them. Locals regarded Low Binn as being inferior to High Binn, perhaps because the occupants of the houses passed through quicker, and thus there was less of a sense of community. It also lacked the facilities that had been established at High Binn.

Parallel with the front row were two terraces immediately behind, again with six houses in each. The fifth terrace was located further west, and was located slightly further back from the road than the back row, but again had six houses. All of the rows were single-storey, with chimneys on the roof ridge.

Low Binn, according to the 1881 Census, had a population of 192, occupying the 33 houses that existed at that time. There was a small hall here, used for many years by the Binnend branch of the Women's Rural Institute.

On the hill overlooking Low Binn was Whinnyhall, where the works manager lived. Before the arrival of the works, this house was a favourite summer residence of Dr (later Bishop) Daniel Sandford (1766-1830), and Professor James Lorimer (1818-1890).

In 1893 the Burntisland Oil Works had closed, and most of the industrial buildings were demolished in the following years. Binnend village remained, the houses still occupied by families whose working-aged folks had to travel to find work. The population began to dwindle somewhat, and some of the houses were demolished, or remained empty. A good number were offered to let as holiday homes, in particular in the Edinburgh papers, hoping to attract city dwellers across the Firth of Forth to Fife. Examples include that in the *Edinburgh Evening News* of 14 August 1905 – 'House, furnished, room and kitchen, three beds, own key.'

In November 1910 a number of improvements were being made to the houses in an attempt at increasing the demand for holiday lets. Sanitary improvements were being made and the streets were being repaired. At the time it was noted that the community was 'practically a summer resort for city people'.

During the First World War the houses at Binnend were in demand to house workers in Burntisland dockyard, which was booming due to war work, and also by troops who were serving locally. In 1917 the new aluminium works opened at Burntisland, attracting employees from other areas. The lack of housing in Burntisland itself meant that many of the workers moved into those at Binnend.

Although Binnend had neither 'a system of drainage nor up-to-date sanitary equipment', in February 1922 it was 'considered the healthiest little community in Scotland'. This was calculated by the fact that there were only five deaths in the district, equal to 6 people per 1,000.

6.3 Low Binnend (Burntisland Heritage Trust)

In 1938 the Whinnyhall Estate, which included the site of the works and the village, was purchased by the British Aluminium Company. At the time of the Second World War the houses at Low Binn had been demolished and the site cleared away. Scrubby trees and gorse took over, and soon much of the area was covered in vegetation.

6.4 Binnend from 1894 Ordnance Survey map

At High Binn the western rows had been abandoned by 1943, and the two rows nearest the top of the hillside had been demolished. The other three rows were left in ruins, the walls standing but the roofs gone. By 1950 there were sixteen residents, six of which were children. Most of them were to be rehoused in Burntisland.

Only the seven rows east of Binnend farm were still roofed. Letting of these rows continued into the 1950s, the *Fifeshire Advertiser* noting on 5 March 1955, 'There has been a run on cottages to let as summer quarters in Binnend village, Burntisland. During the past ten days between 50 and 60 families have engaged houses for Whitsunday term. As they have the privilege of sub-letting it is estimated that during the summer months between 200 and 300 visitors will be resident in the village.' It was common for holidaymakers from Edinburgh and Leith to rent a house for a month in the summer, the man of the house joining the wife and children at the weekends. At the time it only cost 7½ old pence for the ferry.

In May 1952 an article in the *Fifeshire Advertiser* noted that Binnend only had a permanent population of four - Mr and Mrs George Hood and Mr and Mrs T. MacLaren. Both couples were grand-parents and desirous of moving out of the community into more populous villages. The MacLarens had been resident in the village since 1932, having moved from Kirkcaldy to take over a small shop. They closed their business at the outbreak of the Second World War and applied for a house from Fife County Council in 1940, but still hadn't been offered one, despite the fact that their home was condemned. As a consequence, they occupied their home rent and rates free. They had neither gas nor electricity, and water had to be carried from an outside pump. In January 1954, the *Advertiser* noted that George Hood, 'the 74-year-old last inhabitant of Binnend, is now living in Newcastle and the village is, using the word loosely, dead!'

6.5 Low Binned from 1894 Ordnance Survey map

7
Bothwellhaugh

*

In Scottish history, the name Bothwellhaugh is linked to the assassination of James Stewart, 1st Earl of Moray. He was making his way through the main street of Linlithgow on 23 January 1570 when James Hamilton of Bothwellhaugh and Woodhouselee shot him from the steps of his uncle's home. Hamilton was a supporter of Mary, Queen of Scots, whereas Moray was the regent after the queen was imprisoned in England, on behalf of the young James VI.

The estate of Bothwellhaugh was located on the banks of the Clyde, due north of Hamilton and east of Bothwell itself. Latterly, the lands were subordinate to Hamilton estate, and the house became little more than a farmhouse. This farm survived for many years, working the low-lying grounds on the banks of the Clyde.

In 1884 a large coal mine, known as Hamilton Palace Colliery (Pits Number 1 and 2), was sunk immediately north of the farm steading, in what was part of the large Bothwellhaugh Plantation. The mine was known locally as 'The Pailis', a rather grand-sounding name for what was a dark and black place of work. In 1913 the pit produced 2,000 tons of coal each day, there being 1,120 miners working underground and a further 280 on the surface. It was established by the Bent Coal Company.

The coal won from the ground here had a reputation for being some of the finest. It was in great demand for firing industrial boilers, and many steam engines on the railway used it. It is claimed that when the 'Flying Scotsman' train set the record for speed from Scotland to London it was fired on Palace coal.

The earliest miners' houses erected at Bothwellhaugh dated from 1884. The first phase was built immediately south of the pithead buildings, parallel with the workshops. Calder Place was a double-storey terrace of houses, 48 in number. The south front faced onto Bothwellhaugh Road. The rear had external stairways leading to the upper floor, which was occupied by houses, too. The terrace was built of red bricks, with lighter coloured bricks marking the door and window surrounds.

It was noted that the houses at Bothwellhaugh were of a superior standard to those erected by mine-owners in other parts of the county. These houses were of the tenement type, and had damp-proof courses and floor ventilation, ensuring that dampness was less of a problem.

A further group of three terraces was located west of the workshops and smithy, and collectively was known as The Square. The name was properly used to refer to the rear row of houses, a line double-storey in height, with external stairways to the front and rear making their way up to the houses on the first floor. The houses were built back-to-back, so that they only had windows on one façade. In total there were 28 houses in this row.

Parallel with The Square, and forming the southern side of the open courtyard, was a row of houses known as Haugh Place. This had 28 houses in it, again built over two levels with stairways on the courtyard side leading to the upper floor. Each house had two rooms, one of which was a kitchen. In house number 1, William and Elizabeth Mair ran a small shop, known simply as 'Mair's', supplying sandwiches to working miners, often on tick.

At the west end of the courtyard stood Store Place, positioned perpendicular with the road. Again, the houses were over two levels, and stairs front and rear led to the upper apartments. There were thirteen houses in this

7.1 Bothwellhaugh – Hill Place (George McPhee)

terrace. These last three rows were the poorest standard houses at Bothwellhaugh. They were single-apartment homes, and originally most of the residents had to get their water from an outside pump. They shared a dry midden, but in the 1920s these were replaced with water closets.

As the name implies, at the southern end of Store Place, at the gable end, was the village store. At the corner was a post box.

The village had other places where you could buy goods. George McPhee ran a small newsagent in his house in Haugh Place before moving into new premises – a converted railway wagon.

Alongside Bothwellhaugh Road, west of Store Place, was a long terrace of houses, known as Clyde Place. This, like Calder Place, had 48 houses in it, built over two levels with staircases to the north.

Beyond Clyde Place, between the road and the railway siding, there was a narrow stretch of open land, beyond which were more houses, known as Roman Place. This piece of open ground was where the new co-operative shop was erected. The Hamilton Palace Colliery Co-operative Society was founded in August 1886 by the miners and was greatly supported by them for many years. In its first year there were only 39 members, but this increased considerably as the residents appreciated its worth, as well as the annual dividend payable on sales. By 1919 there were over 500 members, 25 employees, and the dividend of three shillings in the pound was one of the highest in the country. Membership remained constant until the 1950s, after which it declined. The co-op building itself was quite distinctive in style. Two ornate Dutch-style gable ends faced the street at either end of a seven-bay frontage, a pedimented doorway between three sets of windows. The whole building was of one storey.

Built onto the east end of the co-operative was the village police station. This had a bay window on the single-storey building. Police were stationed in the village from around 1900 until August 1950, when the station was closed.

Roman Place was built over two levels, with external staircases, and had 44 houses in it. On the opposite side of the road was an open area of grassland which was the village playpark. At an angle to Roman Place was Park Place, comprising 20 houses on two levels.

At a later date, around 1904-5, a further five terraces of houses were built at Bothwellhaugh. These were located to the west of Park Place, four of the rows being erected parallel with Park Place, the fifth, Avon Place, being built alongside the road. Avon Place had 28 houses in it, built over two levels.

Facing Park Place, and forming a narrow street with it, was a row of houses named Douglas Place. This row had 28 houses in it. Each couple of houses had to share a single toilet.

The final three rows at Bothwellhaugh had houses that were larger than most of the others. They were also far superior in that they had an inside toilet and front and back doors. Hill Place (with 18 houses), Brandon Place (24 houses on two levels) and Raith Place (28 houses), were erected parallel to each other, Hill and Brandon places facing each other to form a street. Between the rows were back courts, with drying areas and places where children played. Anyone living in Bothwellhaugh saw these three rows of houses as the best in the community, and many aspired to become tenants there. Hill Place was built of brick, the roofs slated and chimney stacks on the ridge. The north-west side had a straight façade, whereas the south-east had stairs to the upper floor, passing through a projecting wing with additional chimneys. Brandon Place was built of brick, with a rendered finish. The houses had Georgian-paned sliding sash windows. The slate roofs had large chimney stacks on them, the four pots indicating each house. The east side of the row had a straight façade, occupied only by windows, whereas the west side had projecting wings, with

7.2 Bothwellhaugh – Raith Place (George McPhee)

external stairs leading to the upper flat. Raith Place was also built over two levels, the main frontage facing north-west. On the south-east side of the terrace were external stairs, with iron balustrades, leading to the upper flat. Raith Place had two house styles in it, four blocks of them of one type, the other ten of another. These ten blocks had rather distinctive arched openings on their rear façade, paired chimneys over them.

7.3 Bothwellhaugh Co-operative shop (George McPhee)

Probably the last four houses to be erected at Bothwellhaugh were the highest quality – four semi-detached homes built on the south side of the road, facing Calder Place, next to the farm. These were simply referred to as The Cottages, numbered one to four. Here lived the mine managers. Perhaps as these were the best houses in the community, they were the last to be emptied, the last residents being Robert and Janet Frew, who lived at cottage number 1. Robert had been Deputy Pit Manager but was injured in a car accident and died in 1971, after which his wife moved out.

In 1910 there were reckoned to be 485 houses in the village, with 965 residents employed in the Palace Colliery. There was a large population in addition to this number, comprising wives and children.

The residents of Bothwellhaugh had to share outside lavatories and ashpits, which were located outside the rows, often to the rear. Four wash-houses served the 48 houses at Calder Place. Residents had a rota to arrange when they were able to use the wash-houses, and should someone decide to have a bath then they covered the window with a cloth to provide some privacy.

To provide lighting in the houses, residents originally relied on candles or oil lamps. Around the 1930s gas was installed, for which one penny was paid into the meter. Electricity was to arrive even later.

One of the major problems of living at Bothwellhaugh was the proximity to the River Clyde. On a number of occasions, it flooded the lower stretches of the village, and on many other times the river level meant that the sewerage pipes backfilled.

A mission hall was erected at the east end of The Square in the centre of the community in the late 1800s. Bothwell Parish Church held services here, as well as establishing a Sunday school and bible class. The Free Church in Bothwell also held services in the community. The mission hall was later to become a village hall, once a new church had been erected. Here many dances, whists and tea bingos were held, as well as village weddings. This hall was erected, like most of the colliery buildings, with red facing bricks. The windows and door surrounds had white brick borders, and the external corners of the walls were similarly treated. The roof was slate, with a central fleche, affording ventilation. On the gables were white-brick decorative arches with circular window. At the southern gable was a single-storey semi-octagonal apse.

In the 1920s a church was built at Bothwellhaugh, at the west end of the village, on the opposite side of the road from Raith Place. This was a fairly simple building, its Tudoresque timber framed walls being infilled with brick. Facing the street was a small porch. On the roof was a small fleche for ventilation. Known as Bothwellhaugh Memorial Church, it was ministered to by Rev Crawford (around 1924), Rev Arthur G. Taylor (in the 1930s and 1940s - he died in 1952), Rev J. Simpson Smith (around 1947) and Rev J. B. Smith (in the 1950s).

A second place of worship was located at the west end of the village – the Gospel Hall. The assembly was formed in 1920 following a period of planting by other groups. A place of worship was erected in April 1921, created from an adapted army hut acquired from Glencorse Barracks. Bothwellhaugh Assembly survived until 1978.

A miners' institute, or welfare club, was established between the church and the gospel hall. It was opened in August 1924 and comprised of a large hall, where most of the bigger organisations of the village moved to, and a reading room, smoking room and kitchen. This had the new facility of a bath, the use of which was charged at a shilling. In the 1950s new pithead baths were erected at the mine. The institute was extended when a new hall containing a billiard room, carpet bowling area and a games room was added. This facility was opened in April 1936 at a cost of around £3,000. The institute was closed in 1965.

7.4 Bothwellhaugh – Brandon Place (George McPhee)

In the 1880s an infant school building was erected at the eastern end of the village by the Bent Colliery Company. It soon proved to be too small to cater for all of the children in the village and had to be extended. It passed into the hands of Bothwell School Board, which set about making further additions. The new extended school was opened in 1902, at which time there were 379 pupils on the roll. By the time of the First World War there were over 500 pupils in attendance, after which it began to decline, in line with the demise of the village itself. By 1948 there were 175 pupils, 64 in 1964, and only ten the following year.

The school incorporated an infant department, the two classrooms there having 168 pupils in 1906. Head teachers over the years included a Mr MacCallum (1920s) and Mr Brown (1930s). The school was closed in 1965. The building was erected of red bricks, with white brick surrounds to the window and door openings. The roof was of slate and there was a decorative red-tile ridge.

A second school was erected sometime in the 1900s opposite Calder Place. This was St Bride's Roman Catholic School.

Bothwellhaugh residents loved their sport, and a bowling green was laid out on ground adjoining Bothwellhaugh farm, sometime between 1900 and 1914. A small clubhouse overlooked the manicured grass, where numerous competitions took place. At the eastern extremity of the village, beyond the public school, was a small building which was home to Bothwellhaugh Billiard Club.

At one time there was a full-sized football ground, located across the mineral siding from Roman Place, at the end of Bothwellhaugh Plantation. Here played Palace Rangers. This area was later to be requisitioned during the war, and a new football field was created to the west of the village, reached through a bridge under the railway. This was the home ground of Palace United and later Bothwellhaugh Athletic (which existed in the 1930s and 1940s). The field was owned by the colliery company, but in December 1938 they gifted it to the football club, allowing it to charge for admission, rather than just take a collection. The club closed in August 1940, due to the war, but reformed afterwards.

The old football field and the former recreation ground, or 'public park' were taken over as allotments at the outbreak of the First World War. Many residents were keen on their plots, and various competitions were held to promote the growing of the best vegetables and for the tidiest plot. Each autumn, Bothwellhaugh Horticultural Society held an annual show, with prizes for flowers and vegetable produce.

Bothwellhaugh's population grew over the decades, and by 1911 it was reckoned that 2,500 people lived there in the 450 houses.

A number of well-known people either lived or were born in Bothwellhaugh. Robin Cook MP, who was the Foreign Secretary for a time, was the son of Peter Cook, who was born in the village. John McPhee came from Bothwellhaugh and was to play for Motherwell Football Club in the 1950s and 60s, being noted as redoubtable midfielder. Another footballing connection was

7.5 Bothwellhaugh – Haugh Place (George McPhee)

the fact that the wife of the football manager, Sir Matt Busby, Jean, worked at the Palace colliery.

As with most mining communities, the residents were keen supporters of a variety of organisations and clubs. The Bothwellhaugh Silver Band was active for many years, as was the Bothwellhaugh Thistle Flute Band. The Rechabites had a local branch, meeting in the colliery hall. There was a Scout group for boys, under the leadership of Robert Lang, who was also manager at the pit, and a Girl Guide unit. The Boys' Brigade had a company in the village. The Ancient Order of Shepherds and the Salvation Army held meetings in the colliery hall.

One of the organisations based in the community was the Bothwellhaugh Players, which entertained at various events in the district. In the 1930s the leader was Dick Anderson, who was to compose a song entitled 'Bothwellhaugh', the chorus of which reads:

> Bothwellhaugh, good old Bothwellhaugh,
> That's where we reside,
> Happy we shall be, there tae live and dee,
> In that wee place near the Clyde.
> All the folks are friendly, each wi' yin and a',
> So altogether sing, let your voices ring,
> Guid auld Bothwellhaugh.

Just before the outbreak of the Second World War, the houses at Bothwellhaugh were beginning to be emptied, the residents rehoused in new housing schemes at Bellshill. The war halted the process for a number of years, and it wasn't until 1948 that decanting of the homes continued, this time on a larger scale. The sanitary conditions endured in the community was the main reason for the closure. Many of the residents were rehoused at Orbiston.

Hamilton Palace Colliery was closed in May 1959, and the miners redeployed elsewhere, or else made redundant. The last houses still occupied at Bothwellhaugh were gradually emptied, and the final buildings were demolished in 1965-66. Clyde Place was demolished in February 1966. Most of the occupants moved to new council houses in nearby communities, such as Motherwell, Bellshill or Hamilton, but many took the opportunity to emigrate to Australia or Canada, starting a new life. The colliery bing was dug away to

7.6 Bothwellhaugh Memorial Cairn

provide bottoming for the new M74 which was being built at that time.

With the site cleared, in the early 1970s it was decided to incorporate it in a new country park, created in the valley of the Clyde between Hamilton and Motherwell. Named Strathclyde Park, it extends to around 1,000 acres, incorporating the former sites of Clydeside Haugh, part of Hamilton Low Parks and Bothwell Haugh. In the valley a large man-made loch was created, running parallel to the River Clyde, named Strathclyde Loch. This was to cover over part of the area formerly occupied by Bothwellhaugh, but most of the site of the village wasn't submerged. Instead, it became the site of M. & D.'s theme park.

In 1977 the Bothwellhaugh Ex-Residents Committee was formed, to keep the memory of the old village alive. They agreed to meet for a reunion on the first Saturday in June – the traditional day of the village miners' gala day, and this has continued for forty years. The first gathering had about two hundred people in attendance, but as the years have passed, the numbers have dwindled, until only a few dozen show up.

The only real marker of the old village of Bothwellhaugh is a stone-built cairn, standing about seven feet in height, located near to the Alona Hotel. The cairn was erected in 1980 to commemorate the villagers who either suffered in the wars, or were killed in the mine. Within the structure is a time capsule, containing a number of mementoes of the village. On it is a small plaque, noting that:

> This cairn was erected on the site of the former mining village of Bothwellhaugh. In its heyday in the 1920s it was a thriving community of approximately 2000 people. At its centre the Hamilton Palace Colliery, virtually the sole employer and the way of life for the entire village. When the colliery finally closed in 1959 the village slowly died and by the 1960s nothing was left but memories. To all the people who ever lived there it was always affectionately known as 'The Pailis'.

On the opposite side of the cairn a second plaque commemorates the villagers who died in the Great War (no names are given), plus those who died in the Second World War: R. Alexander, J. Bradley, W. Crawford, J. Crawford, A. Dougan, E. Friel, S. Little, J. McGarrity, F. McMahon, William Mitchell, William Nelson, A. Semple and J. Watson.

SCOTLAND'S LOST VILLAGES

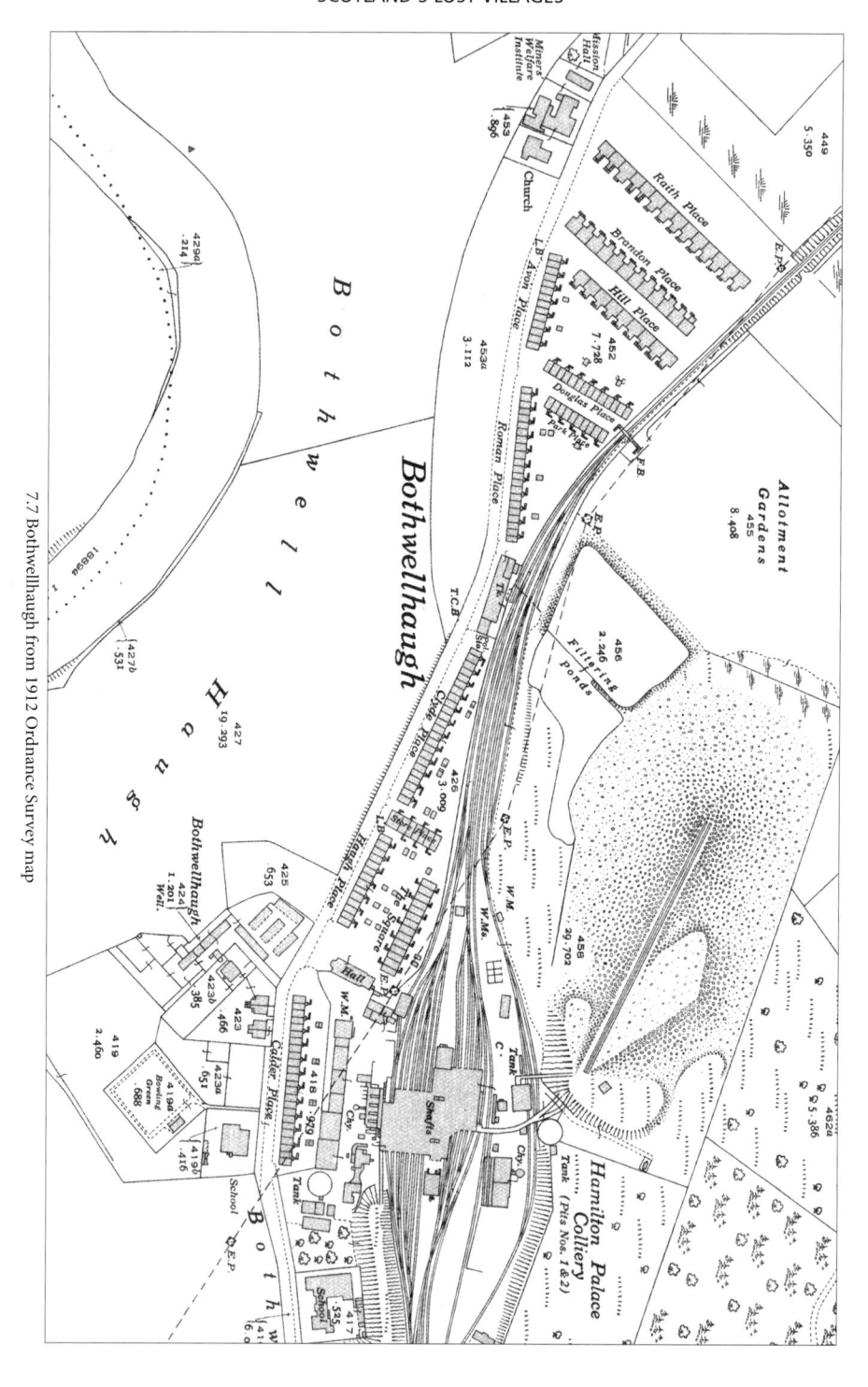

7.7 Bothwellhaugh from 1912 Ordnance Survey map

66

8
Burn Row

★

Slamannan Station, Station Row, Burn Row, Low Limerigg, Limerigg and High Limerigg were, or are, a series of small villages that were strung out alongside the road heading south from Slammannan village centre in Stirlingshire. The three Limeriggs survive, as does nearby Binniehill, but the houses at Burn Row have gone, other than a couple of buildings. One of these is a modern cottage named Tigh an Uillt, Gaelic for Burnhouse, an old name hereabouts which referred to a cottage on the other side of the stream.

Burn Row was located at a shallow bend on the road, where it lies closest to the Culloch Burn. The rows were positioned on both sides of the road, forming a short street. Arriving at the community from Slamannan, on the right were two short rows of houses. The first had three houses of different sizes, their gardens to the rear, their front doors opening directly onto the street.

Immediately following the row of three houses was a short terrace of four houses, the first larger than the other three. Again, the front doors faced the main road, the gardens to the rear dropping to the burn. After this row was a gap in the street line, where three other houses were located. These sat back from the road, a semi-detached pair and a single house, with gardens around them. These three houses were known as Rosebank. In 1860 the semi-detached houses probably formed one cottage, known simply as Rosebank, with an extensive garden around it.

Beyond Rosebank, remaining on the west side of the street, was a terrace of six small houses. These had no gardens, but to the rear, between the burn and the houses themselves, were two outhouses, used as washhouses. These houses appear on the 1860 Ordnance Survey map, indicating their age, but the map hints that at that time the six houses were only three, being subdivided at a later date.

The road swung gently to the left, and beyond the dog-leg was a long terrace of 22 houses with no gaps. The first fourteen houses were small single-apartments, accessed from the main road. To the rear was a roadway alongside the terrace, and beyond this was an area occupied by gardens. The last eight houses were larger in size, no doubt double-apartment, but again facing the street.

On the opposite side of the road from this long terrace was another terrace of sixteen houses. Again, these were of two sizes, the twelve houses to the south being single-apartment, with projecting wings to the rear. The four houses at the north end were double-apartment. This terrace sat back from the road, and to the rear of the houses, beyond an access lane, were gardens. When these houses were erected the little burn which ran to their rear, had to be redirected, formerly running closer to the road.

The final two terraces at Burn Row were located north of this terrace, facing the rows to either side of Rosebank, their front doors opening directly onto the public road. The southernmost row had seven single-apartment houses. A narrow lane between the gables separated this row with that to the north, which had ten houses in it. These varied in size and were probably rebuilt over the years. This row appeared on the 1860 Ordnance Survey map, though at that time the map-maker only indicated five different-sized houses. At the northern end of this last row was a building, erected in the gusset between the public road and a small burn that ran down the east side of the community.

As with many local mining villages, a representative from the *Glasgow Herald* visited in 1875 to report on the conditions endured by the miners' families. He wrote:

> It is a village of some pretensions as to size, consisting as it does of two old rows and three new brick rows. Giving our attention first to an old row of nine stone houses, we find that they are single apartments with wooden floors, and that the beds are placed against the back wall, in which there is no window. They are poor houses, rented at 1s 3d a week. On the opposite side of the road, which, by the way, is in a disgraceful state, is what appears to be a still older row of single apartments, the interiors being quite as dark and uninviting as those we have just quitted. The houses in the new rows, which are of brick, have high ceilings and a small window at the back. They are much healthier places to live in than the others, and the rent is 1s 6d a week. There are also in the village a few room-and-kitchen houses with scullery, for which a

rent of 1s 9d a week is charged. The old rows are not provided with ashpits or closets, and the cleanliness of the village is looked after by a man who was recently appointed for this purpose. Water is taken from a going pit, and after being filtered is led into a large barrel at the end of the village. In rainy weather it is said to be dirty, but at the time of my visit it looked well enough.

The villagers in Burn Row sourced their water from a well located at the southern end of the south-western terrace.

Many of the residents of Burn Row worked in the local coalmines. Most of these were named after the estate on which they stood – Balquhatstone. The mansion lay to the south of Slamannan, a much-extended eighteenth-century building. To the south-west of Burn Row, in the field adjoining the village, was Balquhatstone Colliery, Pit Number 8. North of the village, at Burnbrae Cottages, was Balquhatstone Colliery, Pit Number 7, and to the east was another pit, with a row of six miners' houses known as Salterhill Houses near to it. Across the Culloch Burn were more pits, including a pair of terraces of six houses each, known as Thorn Row. As these small coal mines opened and closed, the miners moved from one to the other.

The miners at Burn Row appear to have been more militant and unruly than many of those living elsewhere. In local newspapers from the time that the village existed, there are numerous accounts of breaches of the peace occurring within the community. A short list here only hints at the number of incidents that took place over the years, events that no doubt would have been discussed at length behind closed doors in such a small community.

In March 1894 James Wardrope of New Monkland entered the home at Burn Row of Helen Whyte, widow, and smashed ten panes of glass and the window frame, then pulled Thomas Wardrope, miner, from his bed, kicked and punched him. James Wardrope was fined fifteen shillings. In 1899 William Whiteman, Samuel MacCracken, Richard Brown, John Blair and William MacMillan were charged with breach of the peace committed within the house at Burn Row occupied by Peter MacNaughton. The first two pleaded guilty and were fined ten shillings each. The other three's plea of not guilty was accepted. In July 1899 Agnes Morrow of Burn Row was found guilty of assaulting Jessie Hynds by striking her on the head with a poker. Apparently, Jessie had asked for a loan of money, her son not being in work. When Agnes only gave her sixpence for a dram, the son, Mrs Hynds and another attacked her, resulting in the act of defence. Despite this claim, she was fined fifteen shillings.

In March-April 1878 the miners of the Slamannan area had been on strike for six weeks. As the weeks passed, the coalmasters decided to evict the families from their homes, as these were supplied with their jobs. A number of the miners began to riot on 18 April 1878, resulting in considerable damage to various properties. The reporter from the *Evening Telegraph* visited Slamannan and reported:

> From a visit to Slamannan to-day, the destruction of property appears greater than formerly reported. The mansion of Mr McKillop, coalmaster, is fearfully wrecked. His wife and children had, when the rioters appeared, to hide in a press, and the servants to shelter themselves where they could. Stones as large as turnips crashed through the windows. Mr McKillop had to run a long distance for his life. Several times he has received threatening letters, with cross bones upon them, and one represented his house, with the word 'Dynamite' written below. Four other houses of coalmasters and managers were also wrecked last night. Only three policemen were in town to cope with the rioters, and they hid themselves. Eleven more arrived to-day with the Sheriff, but they also kept out of sight because large crowds of excited miners were going about. A strong body of Glasgow police arrived tonight. A disturbance is apprehended. The Magistrates are prepared to read the Riot Act. The riot arose from the strike, which commenced six weeks ago, against a reduction of sixpence per day. The men and their families are in great destitution, and are enraged at their employers.

In August some of the miners were placed on trial and a number were sentenced to sixty days imprisonment. Others were to be imprisoned for thirty days or else fined thirty shillings.

In 1898 Esau Edwards, who resided in Burn Row, was killed in Balquhatstone Colliery Number 7 Pit. The pit, which was managed by Arthur MacGregor at the time, worked two seams of coal – the Lady Grange seam, which was nine fathoms below ground, and the splint coal seam, which was a further 24 fathoms below the Lady Grange seam. Linking the two seams was a

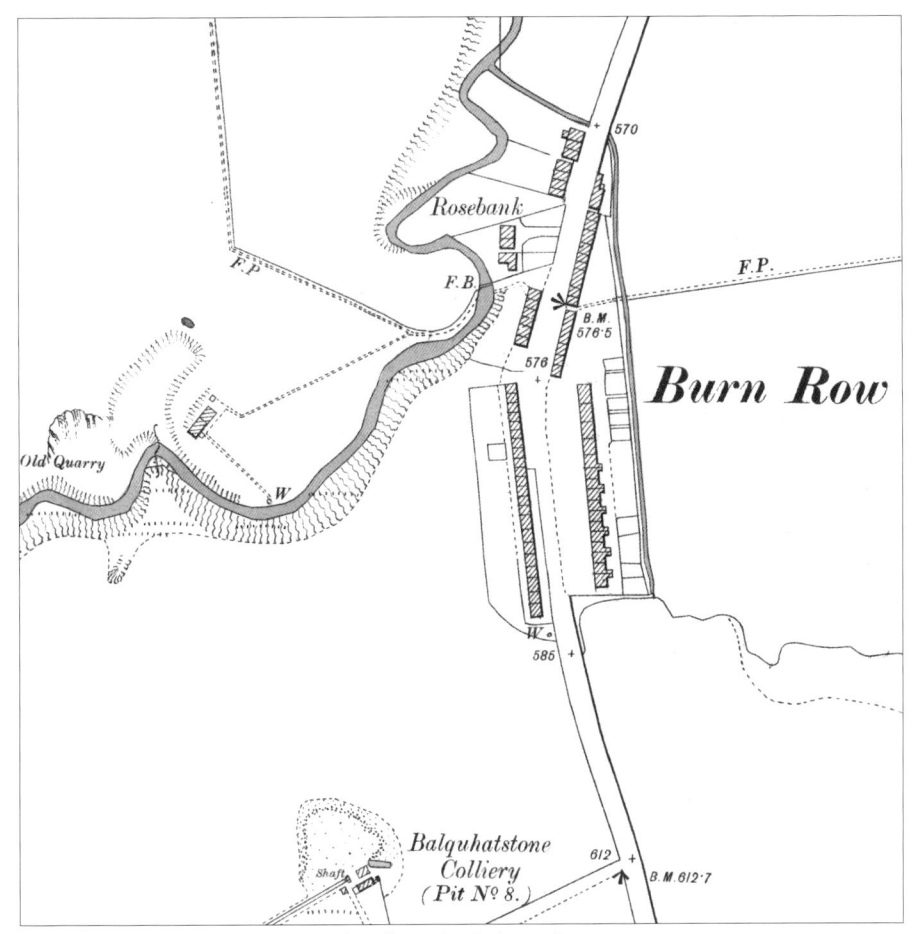

8.1 Burn Row from 1898 Ordnance Survey map

shaft, which had a pair of doors at the upper level to close it off. It was Esau Edwards' job to ensure that the doors were closed, and that two sleepers were laid over the doors to ensure that they weren't easily opened. On the day of his death, the pit foreman, James Waugh, went down the shaft to the lower level to start the engine. It was Waugh's theory that Edwards had forgotten to close one of the doors, and as he laid the sleepers in place, had fallen down the pit.

Balquhatstone, or Balquhatston as it was spelled historically, had been in the Waddell family for generations, the lands having been presented to James Waddell by King James IV in the early sixteenth century. In the early nineteenth century James Waddell did a fair amount of prospecting across his estate, looking for coal and ironstone, but he was unsuccessful, so much so that he had to sell the estate in 1818. It was purchased by a collateral branch, and George Waddell of Ballochney successfully worked the coal seams which lay below the rolling hills of the parish. The family name became Peddie-Waddell. One of the Peddie-Waddells was killed in the Boer War. Within Slamannan is a memorial clock in his honour, bearing the inscription:

> Erected by the tenantry and the inhabitants of Slamannan and neighbourhood in memory of the patriotic devotion of George Ralston Peddie Waddell, only son of Mr & Mrs Peddie Waddell of Balquhatstone, who volunteered for active service in South Africa with the Lothians & Berwickshire Imperial Yeomanry and after the hardships of a year's campaign died at Germiston Transvaal on 8th February 1901 aged 26 years. Amiable, generous, esteemed by all, he freely gave his services and life in the cause of the country that he loved.

He is also commemorated on a marble plaque on the wall of the Waddell burial ground at Slamannan Parish Church.

There was a grocer's shop in Burn Row at the end of the nineteenth century. In 1896 it was the property of John MacIntyre and his wife, Christina Cowan. The shop was later occupied by John Hugh Fulton, who also had a grocer's shop at Glasgow Road, Camelon, Falkirk. His business interests were sequestrated in November 1901.

A number of residents of Burn Row formed the Blue Bell Cricket Club to play against other teams. How successful they were on the field is unknown, but they weren't very good financially. In June 1885, James M. Watson, who ran a tailor's business in Slamannan, had to take the club, which consisted of the following members – Malcolm Baxter, James Hamilton, Robert MacLuckie, John MacLuckie, James Thomson, James MacCracken, Robert Baxter, Alexander Baxter, James Gibb and Alexander MacLuckie – to the small claims court in Falkirk. The club had purchased ten cricket suits, ten caps and ten belts for their strip, but had failed to make the full payment. A sum of £11 6s was still outstanding. Unfortunately for Watson, of the four men cited to appear in court, two had gone to America, the whereabouts of the third wasn't known, but Alexander Baxter was issued with a decree.

At the turn of the twentieth century the village started to decline. The mines were closing, the coal being unprofitable. By 1910 almost all of the community had gone – the three terraces on the east side of the road being removed, leaving only weeds and scrub to reclaim the land. The rows south of Rosebank were also removed, but Rosebank itself survived. The little row of four houses north of Rosebank was still standing, as was the terrace of three next to it. On the east side of the road the only surviving building was that at the northernmost end. The village remained this size for the next thirty years, though on the 1940 survey the northernmost house of the terrace of three had gone.

In November 1927 the remnants of the village were offered for sale in the *Falkirk Herald*: 'For Sale by private bargain, the property at Burn Row, Slamannan, consisting of (1) cottage containing three rooms and kitchen, occupied by Mr David Johnston; (2) cottage containing 2 rooms and kitchen, occupied by Mrs Hoggan; (3) 6 houses each containing room and kitchen, occupied by Mr McColm and others. There is a large piece of ground attached to the property. Rental £41. Apply to James Wilson & Sons, Solicitors, Falkirk.' By November 1946, J. Black of Burn Row was trying to sell his property there – 'highest offer secures'.

9
Cullen

★

The old village of Cullen was located half-a-mile inland from the present village of the same name, which is located on the Moray Firth, west of Banff. The present village appears to be of some antiquity, its old stone cottages and harbour belying the fact that it was created in a single plan, the work of the local laird.

The old village of Cullen was a community that was based on the linen industry. This boomed in the second half of the eighteenth century. When Thomas Pennant made his tour of Scotland in 1769, he found Cullen to be 'mean; yet [it] has about a hundred looms in it, there being a flourishing manufacture of linnen and thread, of which near fifty thousand pounds worth is annually made there and in the neighbourhood'. Things were not always so, for the compiler of the *Statistical Account* of the parish in 1794, Rev Robert Grant, wrote:

> Before the year 1748, the inhabitants of Cullen were as poor and idle as any set of people in the north. There was no industry, trade, nor manufacturing among them; their only employment was to labour a few acres of land, and to keep tippling houses; and often to drink with one another, to consume the beer for want of customers. The late Earl of Findlater, that true patriot, pitying the situation of the people, resolved to introduce the linen manufacture among them. And here, perhaps it may not be improper to mention the method he adopted to promote this purpose. He brought two or three gentlemen's sons from Edinburgh, who had been regularly bred there to the business, and who had some patrimony of their own; but for their encouragement to settle so far north, he gave to each £600 free of interest for seven years, after which, the money was to be paid by £50 yearly, the remainder in their hands to be always free of interest. Besides this, he built excellent weaving shops, and furnished every accommodation at very reasonable rates: and as his lordship presided at the Board of trustees at Edinburgh,

he obtained for his young manufacturers, premiums of looms, heckles, reels, and spinning wheels, with a small salary to a spinning mistress. So good a plan, and so great encouragement, could not fail of success. In a few years, the manufacture was established to the extent desired. All the young people were engaged in the business; and even the old found employment in various ways by the manufacturers: and thus a spirit of industry was diffused over the place and neighbourhood in a very short time, which soon appeared in their comfortable mode of living, and their dress. This manufacture here, as well as in other places, has had its vicissitudes, owing to good or bad markets and demands; but still it continues on the whole in a comfortable state. There are in this small place 65 looms, constantly employed in weaving linen, some few of them in weaving damask. The manufacturers also give out a great number of webs to be woven by country weavers in their own shops. There are also 7 stocking looms constantly employed.

However, by the early nineteenth century this trade was in considerable decline, and the village was struggling as a result.

The Earl of Seafield decided that the old village of Cullen at the gates of his fine policies should be cleared away, to enhance his property. There was already a community nearby, known as Seatown of Cullen, which comprised of a sweep of cottages, gables facing the bay, where fishermen lived. This community had existed in the sixteenth century, but by 1762 there were still only twenty-seven houses there. With the growth in fishing, the village grew, so that by the time the *New Statistical Account* had been written around 1840, it had around two hundred houses. The Earl decided to create a new community adjoining this village, on the ground above the slopes to the south-east. On what had been fields, he laid out a grid pattern of streets, centred on a large square. A new harbour was developed from 1817 onward, with the north pier the work of Thomas Telford.

Although the earliest known reference to a new town is drawn on a sheet of paper with an 1811 watermark, consideration for improving Cullen had been made earlier. In the late eighteenth century, Robert Adam provided a drawing of a new town house and in 1788 James Playfair drew plans and elevations of a simpler building. Both were unbuilt.

9.1 Cullen Market Cross

Work on the new village eventually commenced in 1821, after the earl commissioned the Elgin architect, William Robertson, to create a plan. He also designed most of the principal buildings, notably the new Town Hall and Seafield Arms Hotel (originally the Cullen Hotel), occupying the south-east corner of the square. This fine classical edifice was erected in 1822-23 at the Earl of Seafield's expense, reputedly around £3,000. A multi-purpose building, it included the assembly room for the council, council chamber, court room, post office, inn and stables. The building showed the earl's determination to establish a new community, and the residents of the old village were persuaded to move there in the following years.

In *Reminiscences of the Old Town of Cullen*, published in 1882, William Cramond wrote, 'To demolish and remove, within the space of ten years, a town that had existed for, probably, ten centuries, and had risen to the rank of a Royal Burgh, is an undertaking that at the present day would be deemed incredible in Scotland; yet such was done to the old town of Cullen, and done, too, so adroitly, that except a few ill-conceived murmerings, the echoes of which have not yet quite died away, after the laps of sixty years, no voice was raised to oppose.'

As the new houses in Cullen were completed, the tenants in the old cottages were moved into them. As the streets and lanes were emptied of people, the houses were pulled down. Most of them had thatched roofs, which were quickly burned, and the walls were little more than stones held together with clay.

The original village of Cullen consisted of one long street, stretching roughly on an east-west axis, north of the Burn of Cullen gorge, and north of the castle. The layout of the village is clearly indicated on an estate plan of 1764, surveyed by Peter May. From the west, the road enters the village, where houses are located on both sides of the street. From the plan, it is most likely that many of the houses were built with their gables facing the street, an old Scottish style common in ancient communities. Each house had its own area of garden or stackyard to the rear of it, and beyond these, separated by a narrow lane, were larger plots. According to the plan, these were 'Common land divided in lotts among the people of Cullen according to a separate plan.' From this western street a couple of side lanes struck off, one to the south leading to farms on the other side of the Cullen glen, that heading north giving access to the common allotments.

The street reached the place where the church was located – it being positioned on the southern side of the highway, in a walled kirkyard. This church still survives, and serves the village of Cullen to this day. The church is an ancient one, originally a side chapel of Fordyce, but in 1236 a petition was accepted, raising it to a parish church. Prior to the Reformation, around 1536, a chaplainry of St Anne was established, at which time the south transept was erected. In 1543 the church was elevated to the status of a collegiate church, when Alexander Ogilvy of Findlater and others established it. It was to be the second-last collegiate church founded in Scotland, and the church was probably rebuilt at this time, the chancel being extended. A 'college' comprising of a provost, six prebendaries and two singing boys were based here, ensuring that masses were sung daily. The north aisle was added around 1798.

From near the church a couple of roadways struck off to the south, one accessing what appears to have been larger buildings around what could have been a small village square. These may have been an inn, where many travellers are known to have halted to change horses and rest, a tolbooth and the estate offices. From one corner of the kirkyard a tree-lined drive made its way the short distance to Cullen Castle. To either side of it were gardens and orchards, associated with the castle.

9.2 Cullen Parish Church

There is some information on the old tolbooth which stood in Cullen. It is known to have existed in 1614, for burgh courts were held in it at that time. A new building was started in 1618, but it appears to have taken some time to complete, for the Convention of Royal Burghs was demanding that work on it was carried out six years later. Even in 1642 there is reference that 'upputing and edifeing the tolbuith' was taking place, perhaps the finishing touches being made. The ground floor had two vaulted chambers, one of which was used as a prison, the other for storing meal. On the upper floor there were two apartments, one used as a guard room, the other as a slightly less oppressive cell, used as a debtors' prison. In 1719 the building needed some major repair work, and at this time the roof was re-slated. At the time a new bell was acquired from the Aberdeen founders, Albert Gely. This weighed 150 pounds. In 1767 the Cullen Burgh Council minutes make reference to the unsuitability of the tolbooth for a gaol, the walls of the building being too thin, and the woodwork was by this time starting to rot.

Another known set of buildings in the village was Lawtie's Mortifications, a bedehouse, which was endowed by William Lawtie of Myrehouse. This was located at the south-eastern end of the village. Lawtie mortified a croft of land, with some houses and money, from which was purchased some additional acres of land. This ground was let, the rent being used to buy 10½ bolls of barley which, with fifteen shillings was distributed amongst the poor. An older bedehouse was under the gift of the Earl of Findlater, who allowed them peat for the fire and 6½ bolls of meal per year. This bedehouse had been taken down before 1794, having been ruinous, after which the earl allowed the free use of a house, but this was rarely taken up.

From the church, the road continued in an easterly direction, again built up on both sides, with domestic buildings facing onto the highway. Another lane struck north to the allotments and the back lane. The post office was located at the top of the Wynd, as the road from Enzie was called. A smithy, operated by Alexander Leishman, existed on he south side of the kirkyard, on the roadway to Cullen House.

A little to the east, the south side of the street was unbuilt, for here was a high stone wall which enclosed the castle's formal garden and kitchen garden. Only on the north side of the street were there any domestic buildings. Beyond the gardens, the street was built up on both sides once more, and it continued thus for a few hundred yards. On the right, a lane struck from the main road southwards, dropping down to the mill, powered by water from a lade diverted from the Cullen Burn.

Within the village were one or two larger dwellings. These included the Laird of Findochty's town house. Another building was the property of the owners of Findlater Castle. The house was dated 1603, supposedly the date when the old castle was abandoned. Some of the cottages were double-storeyed, and yet still sported thatched roofs. In 1718 Elspet Strachan was granted a warrant by the council to erect a house at Townhead. This measured 12 ells by 5 ells (around 45 feet by 18 feet) and had 4¼ roods of ground.

The description of the village given by Cramond is a useful indicator of what it appeared like: 'The houses … are … mostly low one-storey buildings, many of them built of stones half way up the walls, the rest of the walls being turf or clay, generally thatched, and with their gable ends, like the houses of Flanders, to the street, and situated with the most complete disregard to uniformity … the street is high in the middle; and many of the houses, being below the general level of the street, are continually subject to flooding, the water sometimes lying in pools below the beds.'

Cullen had its own school, in 1794 described by the parish minister as 'good … where from 40 to 50 boys are taught Latin, English, writing, arithmetic, and book-keeping'. Known as the Grammar School, this was located on the main street, next to the kirkyard. The town council had a room over the school, and over it was the schoolmaster's room. Around 1745 the schoolmaster had to teach in the Sunday School in addition to the day school, but he also ran a public house! The presbytery stepped in and stopped this as it was 'inconsistent with office of school-master.' The old school had been built in 1713, but by the late eighteenth century was ruinous, and was moved into the old weaver's shop on the west side of the street, next to the Grand Entry to Cullen House. There was a 'pretty good school-house', with a convenient room for the schoolmaster, but his salary was noted as being very small – only receiving about £6 10s a year. There was also a schoolmistress in the village, who taught the girls to read and sew, for which she was paid a salary of £5. The school at Old Cullen remained open until 1821 when Mr Hoyes and around eighty pupils marched to the new school. The headmaster gave every child threepence and the rest of the day off.

In 1773 Johnson and Boswell passed through the village. The latter wrote, 'Cullen has a comfortable appearance, though it is but a very small town, and the houses mostly poor buildings.' They breakfasted at the village inn, but the fare was not to Johnson's taste.

CULLEN

9.3 Plan of Cullen drawn in 1762

Writing in the *Statistical Account*, Rev Grant lists the advantages and disadvantages of the old village:

> The town of Cullen, by its situation, has many advantages. It lies on the post road, which is kept in good repair. It has, in general, good schools. It has the advantage and accommodation of a post-office, a pretty good butcher market, plenty of all the necessaries of life supplied from a rich country, on the one hand, and, an ample supply all of kinds of fish from the sea, on the other, with command of plenty of moss for fuel. The disadvantages are, a scanty supply of water. There is not a good spring in the parish of Cullen but one, and that lies without the town. To the burn of Cullen, there is access only at two places, and there the roads are so steep, that it is difficult to carry up water. The only supply, is a cistern in the centre of the town, where water is brought in leaden pipes from the annexed part of the parish of Rathven. To accommodate the town properly, they would need at least other two cisterns. The houses, in general, though cheap rented, are mean and bad; and most of them being with their ends to the street, it offends the eye of the traveller.

Eventually, Cullen was totally removed, leaving little to indicate its former existence. Of the village itself, the old church remained, beyond the control of the Earl, standing in its little kirkyard. Old Cullen House stands near to the church, now the seat of the Earl of Seafield - Cullen House itself having been sold and subdivided into large apartments. It is claimed that Old Cullen House is the sole survivor of the old village, apart from the church. However, it is known to have been considerably extended, notably in 1827 when William Robertson produced a U-plan front façade with a pedimented porch. Around 1899 the single-storey house was raised to two floors. According to Cramond, it was 'only ten years ago [i.e c.1870] did the Town Council legally renounce its claims to the old place'. It was also noted in *The Annals of Cullen* that 'The Town Council minute books contain not the slightest references to the removal of the town, no more than if such an event had never occurred. The earliest allusion after the event is in 1851.'

In addition to the church, other fragments of the old village can be seen on Castle Hill, the remains of a Norman motte which was later occupied by a tower.

Here, in a rustic enclosure, are carved stones that originated in the old village. They include one which depicts the Royal Arms of Scotland, another having the quartered arms of Ogilvy and Sinclair, and a third with the boar passant representing the Baird family. A fourth stone contains the date 1688 and the initials M. P. O., indicating *Magister* Patrick Ogilvy, son of the Earl of Findlater. A stone with the initials and date *WO KH 1671* was taken from a house in the old village and rebuilt into the walls of the Commercial Hotel in the new town. The initials are thought to represent William Ord and Katherine Henry.

For a time the market cross of Cullen stood on Castle Hill. It was removed from the old village of Cullen to this spot around 1826 and set up on the hilltop. The cross was first sculpted in 1675, when the master mason, Daniell Ross, was commissioned to make it. He was told to base it on the cross in Banff – an octagonal shaft with a representation of the royal arms. In 1695-6 the Cullen mason, Lachlan MacPeter, was charged with 'building, finishing and perfytting' it. Cullen's market cross was later re-sited in the centre of the new town, but it was incorporated in a much larger structure, erected in 1872 to plans by John Millar.

10
Darnconner

*

There has been a farm on the low hill at Darnconner, in the parish of Auchinleck, Ayrshire, for centuries. A rounded knoll protrudes above the wet surroundings of Airds Moss, its soil dry enough to grow grass and other crops. In the seventeenth century it was home to the Gibson family who were supporters of the National Covenant. A Covenanting minister, Rev David Houston, held a conventicle, or field-meeting, on the farm of Polbaith, near Kilmarnock, on 16 January 1687. Hugh Gibson in Darnconner attended. He probably took all of his family with him and it is thought that his young child was baptised at the event.

The government dragoons were sent out in pursuit of those who had attended and a number of Covenanters from the Auchinleck, Sorn and Ochiltree areas were captured and imprisoned. Among them was Hugh Gibson who was seized at his home. Apparently, he had a number of illegal arms, including a gun and gunpowder. He also had in his possession a collection of books which were regarded as being seditious, and he was caught trying to dispose of them when the soldiers arrived. He was taken to Ayr for trial, which took place before Captain Douglas on 21 January 1687. The charge read:

> Heuge Gibson in Dargoner, Watersyde's tenant in the parish of Auchenfleck, baptised tuo children with the indulged minister of the Sorn; refuises to tell where his youngest child was baptised. There was a gune and halfe a pund of pouder found in his house; he sayes the gune was his goodfathers; his wyfe gott pairt of the pouder from the dragounes for rubbing his cattell; these rebelliouse books were found betuixt his house and his cottars throune out of ane window.

The case appears to have been un-proven and we next find him appearing before the Earl of Linlithgow and Foulis of Colinton in Edinburgh courthouse. There the charge laid before him was that:

Hewgh Gibsone in the paroch of Auchinleck, in Watersyde's land, depones he wes not at any of these conventicles, and never wes in any armes against the King; lives regularlie, and swears he will never be in armes against him; owns his authoritie and prayes heartily for him, his long life and prosperous government; and depones he cannot write.

Gibson appears to have been set free thereafter.

The lands of Darnconner were acquired by the Alexander of Ballochmyle family in the late eighteenth century. They were expanding their estates, having made profits from the new cotton mills at Catrine and foreign plantations. Darnconner appeared to be a rather strange purchase, being but a small farm steading on a rounded knoll surrounded by peat bogs, but the potential of minerals below the ground had been recognised.

The first coal workings on Darnconner lands appear to have been sunk in the early 1800s, for by 1843 the *New Statistical Account of Scotland* noted that shallow seams of around 3-4 feet in thickness, approximately 50 fathoms (300 feet) below ground level, were dug. Approximately twenty to two dozen men worked in each pit, producing coal that earned around five shillings per ton.

10.1 Darnconner – the last resident

An old map belonging to Ballochmyle estate, dating from the mid-1850s, shows Roundshaw, Darnconner and Common farms. There are five small mines depicted on the south-eastern part of Darnconner farm, west of the Mill Dam, and at the foot of the dam is Common Row, an early line of miners' homes. No village existed at Darnconner itself, but the potential for mining coal was pencilled in – a proposed railway siding from the Auchinleck to Muirkirk line is shown, called the 'Shiells and Hilliar Branch'. This was never constructed, but a different mineral siding was laid across the moss at a later date, positioned a bit further to the east.

It was alongside this second railway line that the first part of Darnconner village was created. Two separate blocks of housing were constructed, formed into the High and Low Squares, totalling 34 houses.

William Baird, the coal- and iron-masters, extended the community by erecting new rows to either side of the two existing squares. North-west of the High Square two rows (the Railway Rows) of 24 single-apartment houses were built parallel to each other. Next to the Low Square, in which the Co-op operated by Baird was located, were the new Store Row of six houses and a School Row also of six houses.

The school was located north east of Darnconner farm and had five rooms. The building was erected in 1853 by the Eglinton Iron Company who deducted a monthly fee from its employees in order to pay the school-master an annual salary of £50. It had been erected at the instigation of Rev Dr Chrystal, minister of Auchinleck. Over the years it was added to a few times. On 5 January 1875 William Tweedie was appointed headmaster, previously being assistant teacher at Lugar. He was paid a salary of £150, and had the assistance of five teachers, some of them pupil teachers.

On 1 November 1887 Darnconner, Lugar and Cronberry schools were transferred to the School Board who took over their running. At Darnconner William Tweedie continued until after the Great War. In 1899 he moved into the new schoolmaster's house which the board erected next to the school.

The school at Darnconner was leased from Bairds, but by the turn of the century it was deemed unsuitable for educational purposes, and if it was not brought up to standard then Scotch Education Department grants would be withheld. Accordingly, in 1904 it was resolved to have a replacement erected, capable of holding 300 pupils. James Hay, architect, of Kilmarnock, drew up plans for a new building, erected at the southern end of Common Row, a more central location to cover Darnconner, Common and Commondyke villages. The first sod was cut in the spring of 1905. The mason and plumbing work was carried out by Messrs Melville & MacPherson of Newmilns; the joinery work by Cook of Catrine; H. & T. Morrison of Cumnock did the slating, and M. Taylor of Cumnock the plasterwork. Opened on Monday 15 March 1906 by Robert Angus, the new school had cost £3,934 16s 1d to build. A gold key was gifted to Mrs Angus by Mr Hay and a banquet was held in one of the classrooms. The new school building was erected with terracotta bricks, with dressed stone at the doors, windows and gable tops. The roof comprised green slate. The main entrance was located at the west end of the building, reaching a lobby that ran through the centre of the building. There were seven classrooms, each with 'Boyle's patent air pump ventilators'.

10.2 Darnconner – the Parish Church and manse

The school board instructed the headmaster at Darnconner that no pupils residing in Sorn parish should be admitted to the new school when it opened. Prior to the school's erection the board had been in contact with the Sorn parish board to discuss the possibilities of a joint school, but the Sorn board turned this down and refused to offer the Auchinleck board any money in respect of its residents educated at Darnconner. When no Sorn pupils were allowed into the new school the board at Sorn quickly contacted the Auchinleck board and agreed to grant some funds to assist in the running of Darnconner School. Most of the Sorn parish pupils resided at Burnside Row, just 1,500 yards from the school. The roll at Darnconner in 1917 was 195.

William Tweedie retired as headmaster in July 1919 after over fifty years of service. Tweedie himself lived until 4 November 1926 when he died aged 74. He was buried in Auchinleck. At Darnconner he was followed by Mr W. Rattray (1919-1926), after which the school was closed.

A mission station of the parish church had been established at Darnconner in 1874, but the 'more airy than comfortable' corrugated-iron shed in which the villagers worshipped was blown over in a storm. On 14 March 1897 a new Gothic church with adjoining manse was erected with funds provided by Robert Angus of Craigston. Built of red Ballochmyle sandstone externally, internally it was finished in white Kilwinning freestone. It comprised a nave, small transepts and chancel, the latter floored with small tiles. The architect of the kirk was Robert S. Ingram and it was built to accommodate 300 worshippers at a cost of £3,000. The opening service was conducted jointly by the Revs Chrystal and Hill.

The church at Darnconner had a number of ministers over a short time, amongst these being Rev Benjamin Brown (nephew of Rev Dr Chrystal), Rev A. D. Scott MA, and Rev James Higgins. The latter's first charge was at Darnconner, where he married the infant mistress at Darnconner School, Grace Johnston Girvan, on 21 April 1910. They had four children. Higgins was to serve as the minister at Rendall, Orkney, from 1910. In 1919 he was translated to Orphir, also Orkney, and in 1926 moved on again to Amulree in Perthshire.

Another minister for a time was Rev William Eadie, and Rev William Petrie performed baptisms in 1913. Latterly the parish minister visited to perform baptisms, the weekly services being conducted by 'missionaries'. These were James Eaglesham, W. Ross and George Laird. Traditionally, only one wedding was ever to take place in the church. The last baptism performed at Darnconner was of Hendryna Dickson (born 16 September 1937) which took place on 5 June 1938. She lived with her parents at 116 Peesweep Row, Lugar. As the rows in Darnconner were being abandoned and the villagers rehoused in Auchinleck, the church was closed in 1939 but stood for many years thereafter.

In addition to the local Church of Scotland congregation, there was an assembly of brethren which met in a former house at Ballochmyle Row. The brethren were formed in 1891 and continued to meet until 1929. At Darnconner there were many busy groups, including the Rechabites, Free Gardeners, and the Darnconner Branch of the Independent Labour Party which held an annual social and dance from 1910. The Rechabite movement was established at Darnconner in 1896, the juvenile branch the year following. The membership in 1913 was 76 state members, 107 order members and 69 juveniles.

Other groups which were represented at Darnconner included the Boy Scouts and a branch of the British Order of Ancient Free Gardeners, known as the Heatherbell Lodge. In 1901 Darnconner Airds Moss Burns Club was established, becoming federated on the roll of Burns clubs in the Burns Federation as number 122.

Darnconner Store was the principal shop in the immediate district, the store at Commondyke being smaller. In 1861 the storekeeper was John Provan. Adjoining it was a bakery. There was no butcher's – meat being brought by horse-drawn van from the main Baird store at Lugar. Baird's employees were expected to buy all their requisites in the company store, indeed they often bought items on tick, to be paid for from their next wage. At Darnconner an office next to the store opened for a couple of hours each Wednesday to allow employees to draw out a little of their wages if required. In April 1913 fire ripped through the store at Darnconner, destroying the building and stock, and causing some damage to neighbouring properties. John Dempsey managed to photograph the fire-ravaged ruins and sold postcards of the scene soon after. The manager at the Ironworks Co-op branch at the time was Robert Thomson. At the end of the Great War John MacDonald was the manager of Darnconner Co-op branch and he remained until the shop closed in 1931.

The post office at Darnconner was run by Mrs Annie Rae, postmistress, until 1911 when she retired. David Brown was postmaster until he died in November 1927. Postmen were Andrew Mitchell, who lived at Common Row, and Hugh Mullen.

The village had a police station in one of the rows, to which constables seem to have been appointed for a short period. These include George Smith (1878), John Innes (1881), James Mowat (1885) and G. R. Mair (1887). The village constable at the turn of the century was James Wilson. By 1928 the Darnconner Nursing Association existed.

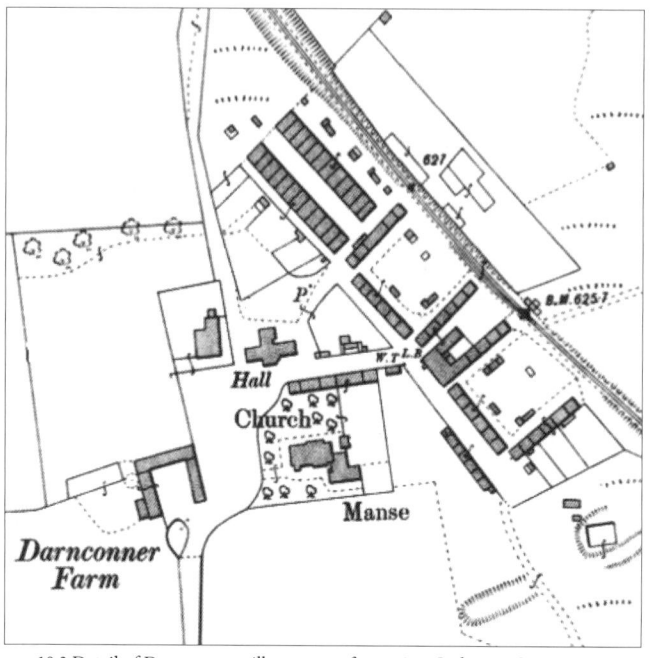

10.3 Detail of Darnconner village centre from 1908 Ordnance Survey map

By 1900 the new Common Row (or Commonloch Row) was built at Darnconner, the original Common Row of six houses becoming known then as the Stable Row. The Common Row was built alongside the old tracks which were laid to the Common Coalworks of the early nineteenth century, facing across the road to the Common Loch. To reduce the cost of erecting houses, the row was built continuous, with a total of 96 houses forming a dog-leg. Built of stone, some of the materials were brought from old houses which Bairds owned at Dalry. This was probably Swinlees Row, which was demolished around the same time.

Behind the Common Row was the much shorter Walker's Row of twelve houses, located perpendicular to the roadway into Darnconner farm. This row was owned by the William Walker Coal Company, hence its name. Also owned by Walker's were the Ballochmyle Rows, two rows of 24 houses each, on both sides of the road between Common and Glenshamrock farms. These probably date to around 1876 when the Ballochmyle Pit was sunk. Outwith the parish was the Burnside Row, of twelve houses, better known as 'The Poverty' from the fact that the residents were some of the poorer in the district, which was also owned by Walker.

Over the lifetime of the village, Darnconner's population rose and fell. At the 1871 census there were 928 residents. By 1881 this had fallen to 550, but it was to increase again by 1891, when 1,198 people lived in the community.

Darnconner continued to be an active community in the new century even although most of the local mines were beginning to be closed. The population in 1901 was 457. In 1914 there were 80 houses in the various squares and rows.

Thomas MacKerrell visited the village as part of the survey into miners' housing in 1914. He noted that there were 94 houses, 17 each in Low and High Squares, 48 houses in the two Railway Rows, built back to back, and six each in the School and Store rows. The total population was around 400. In the Low (or Laigh) Square there were no washing-houses, but a few boilers stood in the open air. Two doorless closets served the seventeen families who lived there, the open ash pits overflowing with stinking refuse. The condition of some of the coal-houses was such that a few tenants kept their fuel beneath their beds. The High Square had similar conditions, and the 'glaur' was inches deep at the house doorways. The Railway Rows, let at five shillings per month, were very damp, the floors made of broken brick tiles. The closets had no doors, some surrounded by a sea of human excrement. The School and Store rows likewise had poor amenities, the Store Row having no closets and needing to share those in the School Row. The village also had a church and store, the whole owned by William Baird and Company.

Although the population of Common Row stood at 506, there was not a single wash-house and only seventeen doorless closets for the whole row. The smell from the closets was described as abominable, the floor being covered in human excrement. The pathway in front of the row was unpaved, and the inspectors could not walk along it without going up to the ankles in dirt. The sewage passed down an open syvor before being discharged into the Auchinleck Burn.

Ballochmyle Rows stood to either side of the road which separates Darnconner and Barglachan farms and, like the Common Row, were owned by Bairds. There were 24 houses in each row, let at two shillings per week, the total population 227. When the Ballochmyle Colliery was closed one of the buildings was converted into a branch of the Auchinleck Co-op to serve this community.

The Stable Row, owned by Sir Claud Alexander of Ballochmyle's trustees, had only six two-apartment houses and one single apartment. There were 37 people living here, the rent £5 per annum. There was a single wooden closet for the six houses, and no ash pits or wash-houses. The sewage ran into a ditch which took it to the nearby burn. This row stood at the southern end of the Common Loch.

On 11 November 1914 William Baird gave up the mineral lease of Darnconner and ownership of the houses passed back to Ballochmyle estate.

The estate did not really want much to do with the houses, and it was noted that no repairs were carried out on them thereafter. By 1925 Darnconner and Commonloch rows were owned by James Clark of Carskeoch, near Patna.

By the end of the First World War the community at Darnconner was in decline. Messrs Baird's tenancy of some of the houses expired at Martinmas 1920 and the tenants were told to leave by December that year. In 1920 many of the houses in the Squares, Front and Back rows were empty. Only squatters occupied some of the houses, or at least those who failed to leave by the due date were termed squatters. Ownership of the houses returned to Ballochmyle estate, who became liable for the rates. The estate claimed that the houses were uninhabitable, and therefore should not be subject to rates, and that anyone still living there had not been asked for rent and had paid none. At the Lands Valuation Appeal Court in Edinburgh in February 1922, Ballochmyle estate was deemed responsible for the houses.

In 1926 a group of labourers built rough homes for themselves in the side of the former Common Pit Number 10 bing, half a mile from Darnconner itself. These were partially dug into the side of the bing, and rough stone walls were constructed to support the sides as well as the roof of timber and turves. The semi-subterranean community stayed here for a number of years, in 1929 there being nine occupants occupying the dwellings. One of the residents, Michael Mulryan, was murdered by three other men. Mulryan, who was 57 years of age, was known locally as 'Mad Harry'. Charged for the murder were Hugh MacNaughtan, James Kelly and Joseph Donnelly.

By 1930 the Ballochmyle, Walker's and Stable rows were uninhabitable. Ownership of them had passed to Mrs Christina Gordon of Carskeoch, near Patna, who bought Darnconner and Common farms from Ballochmyle estate. She also owned the Common Row which was abandoned in 1928. In the 1930s a start was made by the county council on rehousing the remaining occupants in new houses at Auchinleck. By 1932 only 27 families remained at Darnconner.

In 1933 many of the tenants from Darnconner and Commondyke went on a rent strike in their new Auchinleck homes, claiming that Ayr County Council were charging them rents in excess of what the Slum Clearance Act allowed. Twenty-one court summonses were issued by the council in December 1933 and at court the tenants were found in the wrong, having agreed to the new rents prior to their moving.

DARNCONNER

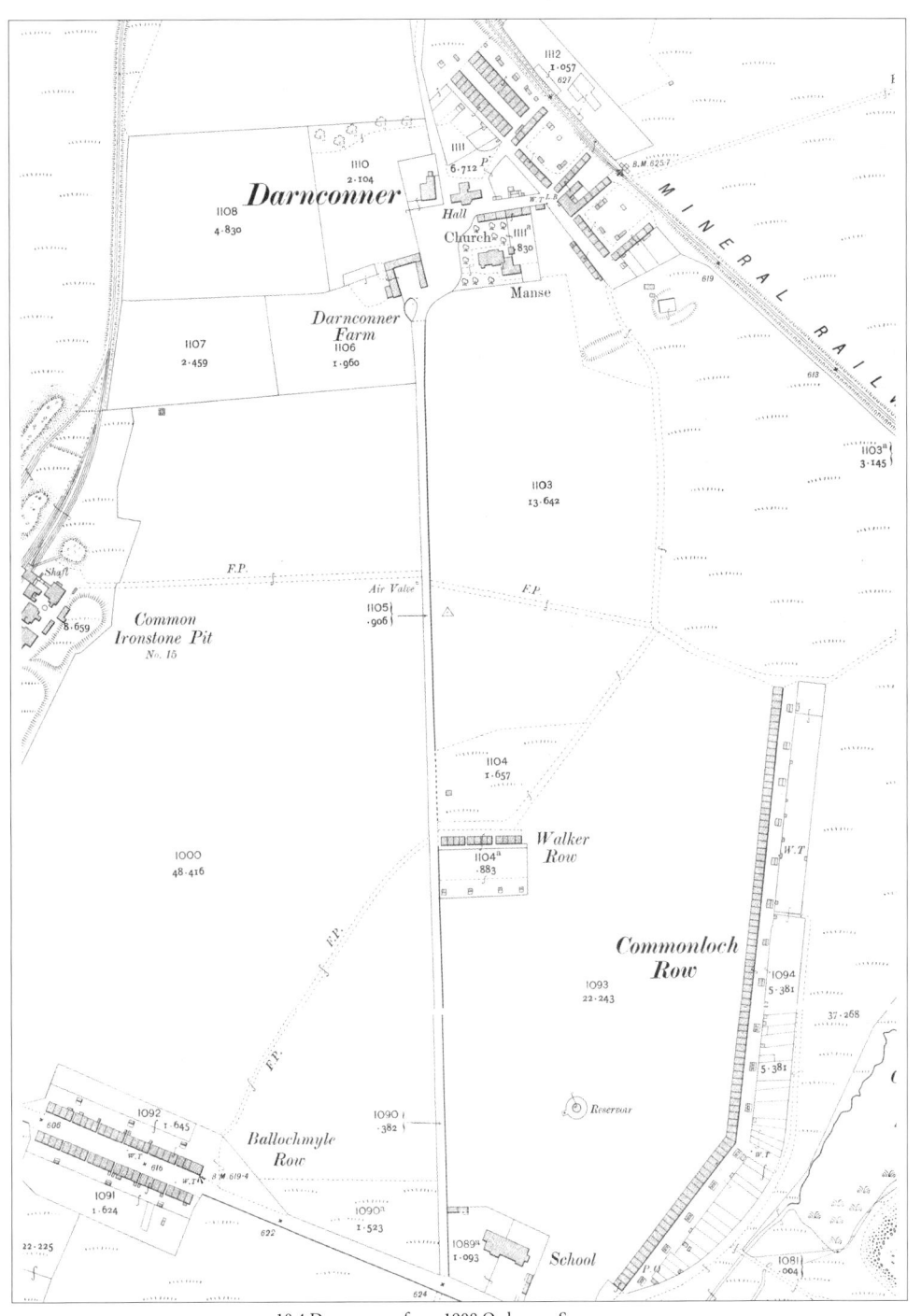

10.4 Darnconner from 1908 Ordnance Survey map

93

In the year the Second World War broke out, both the school and the church were closed, each building becoming stores, the former for the council, the latter for the farmer. In 1940 the Common Row was demolished, the final row at Darnconner to be removed. The school was demolished in 1955, the church in 1979, leaving the manse standing. In 1958 the belfry had been removed and the bell gifted to Catrine Congregational Church. The font was gifted to the Peden Kirk in Auchinleck. J. L. MacArthur came to Darnconner after the Second World War with the job of demolishing the church, but found it so attractive that he bought it and the manse and resided there for many years.

Playing football at Junior level was Darnconner Britannia Football Club, existing from around 1888 to 1900. Their field was known as Pablin Ground, their colours red, white and blue.

In the late twentieth century open cast coal mines were developed at Darnconner and Common farms (the former from 1985, the latter from 1990). The open cast mine at Darnconner produced over 600,000 tons of coal before 1991. Darnconner was also used for the extraction of clay for brick-making. Brick-making collapsed, and so the site became abandoned. It was sold to a waste management company for landfill purposes, planning permission for it being granted in 1996. However, the site was never used and permission for dumping expired. The hole had also filled with water, creating a lochan of around 30 acres in extent. The site was subsequently subject to a variety of semi-restoration schemes, whereby the loch would be retained and the surrounding mounds landscaped to reduce their impact on the countryside.

Today, the site of Darnconner village has mostly been obliterated by surface coal mining, and much of the land has been infilled and planted with trees. Only the former schoolhouse and manse survive, alongside Darnconner farmhouse itself.

11
Darngavil

★

Coal has been worked in the Darngavil area of Lanarkshire for centuries. In 1793, when the *Statistical Account* was compiled, it was noted that there was an 'ingaun e'e' pit there, where five miners worked a seam of coal three feet eleven inches deep. This coal was transferred to local communities and sold at 2s 9d per ton. In 1840 the landowner, Patrick Rankin, began mining on a larger scale, and in the 1850s coal mines were sunk on the moor north east of Airdrie, in the parish of New Monkland. Located distant from any centre of population, the mine owners erected simple houses for the miners, more or less at the pit head.

The first houses at Darngavil were located on both sides of the Dykehead Branch Railway which was laid by the Monkland Railway Company to serve the Darngavil, Drumgray and Greengairs pits. To locals, it was affectionately known as 'Gavil. On the south side, located by the minor road which became known as Darngavil Road, was a row of six homes. To the south west of this row were a couple of other buildings, facing each other across the road. The oldest rows at Darngavil were erected of stone and dated from the early nineteenth century. The second row at Darngavil was located on the north side of the railway, again numbering six homes. This was all that existed at the time the Ordnance Surveyors made their maps in 1859.

To the east of the southern part of Darngavil were two rows of houses, built parallel to each other, though slightly offset. The rows were separated by a narrow 'street'. At the west end of the southern row was an old coal pit, abandoned by 1859. These two rows had seven houses in each, each comprising of a single apartment. These rows were known as Mossbank and were erected prior to 1859 by the Coltness Iron Company to house workers employed in the mines. When the Coltness company's lease expired, the houses were acquired by Mrs Thomas Scotland, of Motherwell Street, Rawyards (Airdrie). She didn't do much with the houses, which were deemed to be in a poor condition. Indeed, action was taken against Mrs Scotland around 1908 regarding the dilapidated state of the conveniences and the lack of a water supply. Some improvements were made after this, and the houses were then regarded as being in a fair order.

They were demolished soon after, however.

In 1847 the houses at Darngavil were owned by the Langloan Iron Company (Messrs. Addie, Miller and Rankin). A rare survivor of an agreement from the company with their tenants survives:

> 1. Every workman who is in possession of a house or garden, or both, shall, on notice being given by either party, be held bound to remove from such possession and to have authorised instant ejection therefrom and on the expiry of such notice.
> 2. Every workman who is in possession of a house or garden, or both, shall be held liable to pay all damages done to his house during his occupancy thereof; and the amount of such damage shall be chargeable and form a deduction from the amount of his wages in like manner as the charge for rent.
> 3. Every workman who is in possession of a house shall use it only for the accommodation of his own family and shall on no account take in thereto any lodger or lodgers without special consent in writing being previously procured from his employer and, in the case of contravention, he shall be subject to a payment of 1s 6d a week for each lodger kept during the period of contravention; and all occupants of such houses are hereby prohibited from keeping dogs, swine or poultry on the premises under a penalty of 5s for each offence.
> 4. Every workman having a house or garden, or both, from his employer, shall be held to have specially agreed that the wages remaining unpaid to him at the time of quitting his service shall not be claimed by him or be payable to him until he shall actually cede possession of the said house, garden, or both to his employer.
> 5. Every workman in possession of a house or garden, or both, from his employer is hereby prohibited from selling or disposing of any dung or ashes made on the premises, which dung or ashes are hereby declared to be the property of his employer and to be placed where he may direct under a penalty of 5s; but he will be allowed therefrom what may be required for manure to the garden attached to his house; and, if his garden is not planted before the tenth day of April, the employer is empowered to plant the same and deduct the expense from the workman's wages at the first pay day thereafter and, in the event of his

DARNGAVIL

removing from his house or garden before receiving the benefit of such crop, the employer to pay the value of the crop at the sight of men.

By 1896, when the second edition of the Ordnance Survey map was surveyed, the village had grown considerably, new rows having been erected between the surveys. Adjoining the southern row was a second terrace of six houses, built immediately parallel to the first, with a narrow lane between them. To the east of the paired rows was a third row, of six houses. At the west end of the paired rows was a large building. The rows here were let to their tenants at the cost of £4 4s 2d per annum. The houses were one storey in height and were built of

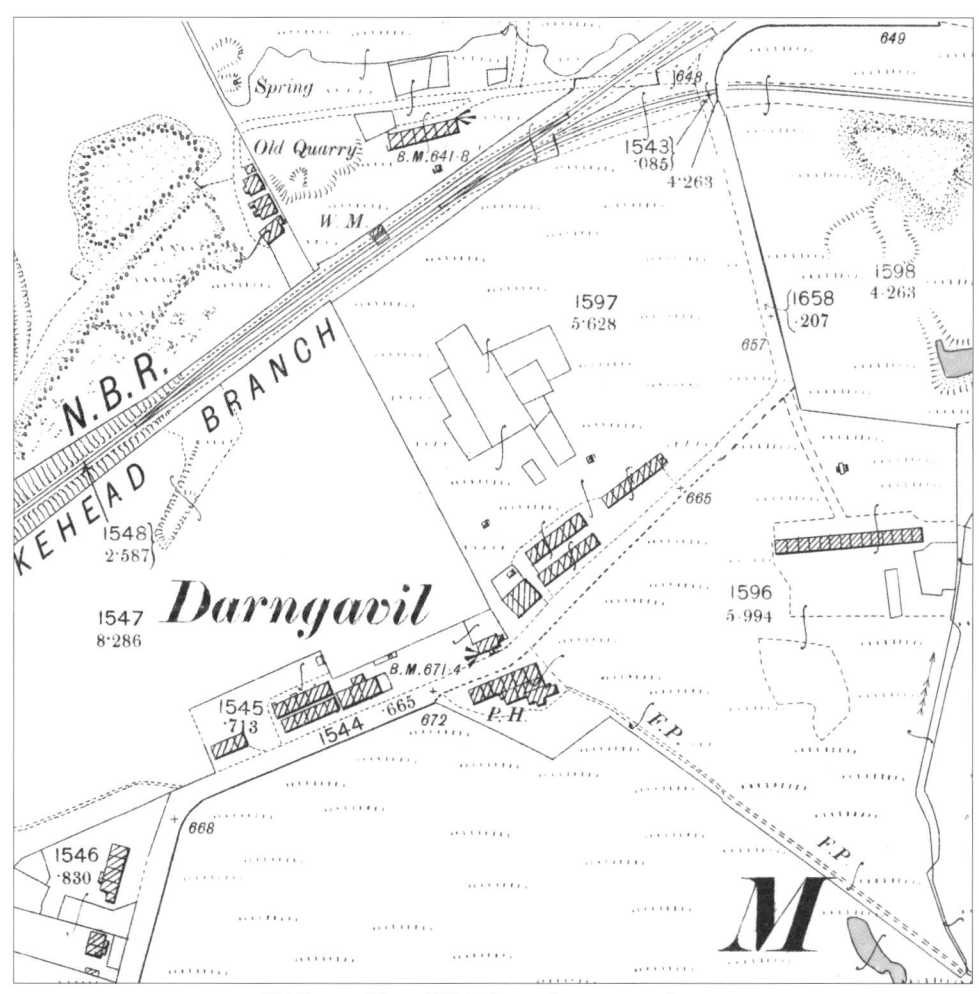

11.1 Darngavil from 1898 Ordnance Survey composite map

bricks. They had been erected around 1873, but even then there had been no desire to install damp courses. The walls were consequently sodden, and there was no ventilation in the houses. Building standards hadn't improved from the older stone cottages, for the walls were simply plastered directly onto the brick and the floors were wooden. There were garden areas allocated to each house, but these were not being cultivated. There were two open privy middens, located about forty feet to the rear of the houses. Water was obtained from standpipes located at the gable of one of the rows, and there were four outside sinks for the use of the residents.

On the south side of the road through Darngavil six houses were built, and immediately to their south, and part of the same complex of buildings, was a public house.

West of this was the Stone Row and the Long Row. The Stone Row was located behind the Long Row and comprised three single-apartment houses and a two-apartment house. Between it and the street was the Long Row, of seven single-apartment houses and a double-apartment house. The rental payable for the single-apartment houses in 1910 was £2 18s 6d and the double-apartment houses was £5 12s 6d per annum. The houses were built of stone but did not have damp-proof courses. The walls were plastered internally directly onto the stone, and the floors were composed of wooden slabs. Inside, the houses were in a poor condition – the walls were damp, many of the ceilings and floors were broken. The ceilings were low, making the rooms appear small, but it was noted that there was no overcrowding. The residents of the two rows had their own gardens, but appeared to be unwilling to cultivate them. There were no wash-houses or coal cellars and only one open privy midden, located thirty feet in front of the houses. Water was obtainable from a standpipe located in front of the rows, but there were no sinks in the houses, and drainage from them was by means of open gutters. The rubbish from the rows was scavenged daily by the owners.

By 1896, when the Ordnance Survey map-makers returned to Darngavil, the community had grown considerably. The original row in the village itself was now joined by a second row, built parallel to it, and close together, leaving a narrow lane between the houses. Again, this row had six homes, the second row built between the old row and the road. To the east of the old row was a new row of another six homes.

The two old buildings that faced each other across the road had been extended. On the south side of the road the old building had been rebuilt, to form a line of six houses. Incorporated in this row was the old public house. It was referred to as Johnnie Miller's Pub.

Further rows of houses had been built to the west of the old rows. These rows contained a number of houses which were rather irregular in size, the eastern row having three houses, the western comprising five houses. Immediately behind the latter, with a narrow lane between, was another row of four houses.

The main road strikes to the south around here, and on the western side were a row of four houses and a pair of semi-detached houses.

On the north side of the railway, the old row of houses was still occupied in 1896, but to the west of it were now a further four houses, each one different in shape and size.

The rows at Darngavil all had names. Among these were Brick Row, Cheyne's Land (known locally as Brandy Row), Laigh Row, Young's Row, MacGrady's Land, MacMillan's Land, Stone Row, Store Row and Shank's Land. Mossbank Row was known locally as the Billy- or Bully-Ruffian Row. Store Row was named after the co-operative shop that existed there, managed at one time by James Gilchrist, followed by James Kerr. There was also a small sweet shop in the village, run by Jessie Miller.

In 1910, housing inspectors visited Darngavil and made some comments regarding Mossbank Rows. They described the houses as being one storey in height, having been built of stone. The walls were plastered internally, directly onto the stone, resulting in the walls being cold and often damp. The houses had a wooden floor, but there was no ventilation. It was noted that the houses, which were of a single apartment, were in a fair condition, and that there was no overcrowding. Adjoining the rows there were areas of garden ground allocated to each house, but the inspectors noted that these were not being cultivated. There were also no wash-houses or coal cellars in the rows. There was one privy midden, located about 200 feet in front of the houses.

Mossbank houses had no sinks in them, and any water drainage was by means of surface water channels. To obtain water, the residents had to use a standpipe located immediately in front of the houses, the single water source being shared by the fourteen houses. There was no scavenging carried out at the rows, resulting in piles of rubbish being located around the houses. The residents occupying Mossbank had to pay a rental of £3 5s.

A mission church was established at Darngavil by the Church of Scotland in the late nineteenth century. Among the missionary ministers was Rev John Davidson, who was later to become a Congregational minister at Lancaster in 1902. When he left he was presented with a gold albert by the workers at Darngavil Mission. A sabbath school was held weekly and had an annual soiree, held in the schoolroom.

The Darngavil Coal Company had numerous pits in the area, numbered in succession. In June 1911 the engine-house and pit-head frame of Number 14 Pit went on fire, destroying most of the surface buildings, which had been made from wood. The Darngavil Coal Company Ltd. was taken over by Wilsons & Clyde Coal Company Ltd. in 1933.

Just before the outbreak of the Second World War, a new coal mine had been sunk at Darngavil. The Braeside Coal Mine was located right in the midst of the village, accessed from the dog-leg in the street. Adjacent to it was the Drumshangie Coal Mine, pit number four.

On 18 August 1920 an inrush of water into Darngavil Colliery Number 4 threatened the lives of seven miners at work below. In addition to the water from the incessant rain, water from a disused working also plunged into the shaft. The engineman engaged at the surface was unsure what to do, so rushed to awaken John Shields, who lived nearby. Shields persuaded the engineman to lower him through the waterfall into the shaft, which was filling up at the pit bottom. He then made his way to the coalface, where the men were still at work, oblivious to the danger they were in. All eight managed to make their way back to the pit bottom and were lifted back to safety by the engineman. In 1922 Shields was awarded the Edward Medal for bravery.

As with all mines, there were many fatal accidents. John Queen was killed in the Stanrigg or Arbuckle Colliery disaster of 1918, when nineteen men were entombed below ground. Other strange deaths included that of Neil Reid (aged 63), who was a colliery storekeeper at Darngavil. He was found dead in a snowdrift in March 1916, having been overcome in a storm.

The miners at Darngavil were keen on football, and the village sported a junior football team for some time. They played on a field located between the main village and the Dykehead branch of the railway. A Darngavil team played in the Lanarkshire leagues in the late nineteenth century. This may have developed into Darngavil Star Football Club, which was active in 1905-6. In the latter year the team merged with three other local teams, Airdriehill Shamrock,

Plains Bluebell and Greengairs, to form Darngavil United. The team survived for a few years longer, but the outbreak of the First World War probably put an end to it. In 1931 a team known as Darngavil Hibs won the Cinema Cup.

Another sport that was commonly played by the miners was 'hainchin'. This required the miner to throw a rough spherical stone, about three inches in diameter, along a public road of a prearranged distance. The person who managed it in the least number of throws was deemed the winner. Although the sport appears to be harmless, it was regarded as illegal, and on 1 June 1861 the *Airdrie and Coatbridge Advertiser* reported that Nicholas Easton, a brusher in the pit, and Robert Sharp, a spirit dealer in Airdrie, were fined for playing the game along the road from Whiterigg to Darngavil. This was in contravention of the Highways Act, and to the annoyance of the other road users.

In addition, locals played at quoits on the green behind the Big Barn. They were also keen on greyhound and whippet racing, walking their dogs for miles, and pigeon racing.

Darngavil was beginning to decline as the twentieth century arrived. By 1910 the four houses north of the railway had been abandoned and their roofs removed. The old row here was still occupied. South of the railway, in the main community, the houses were still roofed and most were occupied. The Darngavil pits closed in 1926, resulting in a drift of population from the community. A brickwork was established, operating in the 1950s and 1960s, employing a few locals and using blaes from some of the local bings.

Most of Darngavil was cleared away by the Second World War, but a good number of residents were reluctant to leave. They continued to live in their homes for some time, but mining operations took place under them, and eventually the buildings began to crack and were deemed unsafe. When this was discovered, they were evacuated and given new accommodation in prefabricated houses in Main Street, Plains, around Christmas 1945. As late as 1960, when the *Third Statistical Account*, detailing the parish of New Monkland, was written, it was noted that the village was being cleared of its last residents, who were to be rehoused in either Plains or Caldercruix.

Today, Darngavil has gone. The village was gradually abandoned as the residents moved to better quality housing in the nearby communities. As they moved out, the houses were razed to the ground, leaving only foundations poking through the moorland grasses. In more recent years, the whole site of the village has virtually been obliterated. Surface coal mines were established on the moors and these removed the top-soil and peat to reveal the coal measures below. The countryside around the lost village has been changed forever, and a new landscape created, unrecognisable to any former resident who should return.

12
East Benhar

★

The village of East Benhar was located on the moors to the north of Fauldhouse, on the road to Harthill, in West Lothian. It was established in 1870 by Benhar Coal Company, which was headquartered in Edinburgh, but it leased the land from the Duke of Hamilton. When the Census enumerators arrived in 1871 to count the population living there, they discovered that there were 72 houses in the community, occupied by 418 people. This worked out at just short of six people per house. Most of the dwellings only had two rooms, so it was obvious that the houses were overcrowded almost from the day they were built. Of this population, 229 were males. Of the total populace, 121 of them were natives of Linlithgowshire, or West Lothian as it was also known. A larger percentage (45%) had been born in Lanarkshire. The population in 1881 was 658; in 1891 it was 707, dropping to 673 by 1901. In 1897 there were 170 houses. In 1932 it was reckoned the population was still as high as 588.

The main centre of East Benhar was the long main street which existed on the Fauldhouse to Harthill Road. The east side of this street had the most houses. The first row on the right when approaching from Fauldhouse had a terrace of ten houses and was known locally as the Reekie Row. It was followed by the school building. Beyond the school was a second terrace of eight houses, known as the School Row. Next again was a row of small dwellings, six in number, known as the Red Row, followed by a fourth row of eighteen houses. This last row was built in a sharp dog-leg, four of the houses built at an angle to the main road, looking north-west. This row was probably the most modern row in the village, with better quality housing. The houses here had sculleries added to them, after which it became known as the Scullery Row – the Scots' tradition of attributing names after the basic things has been long-practised!

On the west side of the main street was a row of twelve houses at the southern end. Known as the Garret Row, it had a first floor, hence its name, and it was occupied by the better-off mining staff. It was sometimes referred to as the Dandie Row, from the better-dressed occupants, or Paton's Row. This was followed by a row of six smaller houses, which were to be demolished by 1914. At the end of this second row a road striking to the west existed.

Next again was a row of six small houses, again cleared away by 1914. This spot was later occupied by the Welfare Hall, erected by East Benhar Miners' Welfare Society around 1924.

The roadway heading south-west from the main street had three terraces of houses alongside it. The first terrace had ten small houses. The second row had twelve houses in it, and the third terrace comprised of eight houses. The second two terraces had gardens facing the houses, across the road. Together, these three terraces were known as the Long Row.

Behind the western road was a further series of houses, following a road which for no apparent reason took two doglegs. Two rows of six small houses were followed by a single row of four houses at right angles to the first pair of rows. Beyond this was another two rows, again of six small houses. These 28 houses were demolished before 1914.

A gap in the line of the street was followed by a short row of six houses. Two of these were at one time occupied by the co-operative store, hence the row being known as the Store Row. It was around the turn of the twentieth century that the Crofthead Co-op opened its store in the village.

To the south-west of this, across the railway siding, was a row of four houses. Attached to the north end was a building occupied for years by Jean Wilson's dairy. Other shops existed in the community, often run by women who had been widowed due to either the war or losing their husbands in mining accidents. Mrs Thomson ran a small grocery from her house at 123 East Benhar.

To the south of this part of the village, separated from it by a stretch of open moor, was the older part of East Benhar. The rows here were built parallel to each other, almost running on an east-west axis. One of them was known as the Castle Row. The north side of the community here had a row of six small houses on the west side of the railway siding, and two rows of eight houses on the east.

Facing the row was a fourth row of six houses to the west of the mineral siding, and two other rows of six houses each, separated by a very narrow pend. When the village went into decline, these three southern rows were demolished, certainly sometime between 1895 and 1914. Most of the houses at East Benhar were built of red brick, making them look slightly more comfortable than they actually were. In 1917 it was reckoned that there were 105 houses in East Benhar.

Originally, there was no proper water supply to the community. Latterly, however, the residents enjoyed a fairly good supply of water, originally obtained from a spring located near the village. In the early years of the twentieth century the water supply was piped to the community, and a number of water pumps were positioned around the rows. One of these was located in the street in front of the school. A second pump was positioned at the western end of the central rows. A third pump was located at the southern rows.

In 1878 a mission station of the Church of Scotland existed in the village, run by the church at Harthill. The two churches formed a quoad sacra parish, having been disjoined from Shotts parish. Rev Alexander Watt served as minister from 1877 until 1919. He was followed by Rev Kennedy Adams.

In the late nineteenth century, there was a church group known as the East Benhar Evangelistic Association. This did much good work in the village and held numerous services in the community. In July 1885, they held a large conventicle at Peden's Stone, which still survives around one mile to the west of the village, near to what had been Benhar farm. The stone commemorates Rev Alexander Peden, one of the most noted Covenanter ministers of the seventeenth century, who held secret field meetings here. At the Evangelistic Association's conventicle, 2,000 worshippers turned up to hear Mr Ronaldson of Longridge and Mr Crawford of Fauldhouse preach.

There was also a group of worshippers who were members of the East Benhar branch of the Lanarkshire Christian Union, formed in 1886 and meeting weekly in the school.

A school building was located by the side of the main road through East Benhar, located between two of the eastern rows. In 1896 it was referred to as East Benhar Colliery School. It had three rooms, used for infants, junior and senior pupils. The playground was divided into two, separated by railings, for boys and girls. In 1897 there were eighty pupils on the roll, rising to 100 the following year. In 1900 it had increased to 156 and by 1902 had reached 170. In 1896 a new evening school was started and in the following year the infant room was furnished with a harmonium. In 1908 a new bookcase furnished with books was presented to the school by James Coats of Paisley. Headmasters included John Purdie and Robert MacDonald. The schoolmaster's house was quite unique in the village for many years – it had a private privy located in the garden. Water closets for the pupils were supplied at some point, but in December 1902 the roof blew off them. In the same winter, snow blew through gaps in the structure into the classrooms. In 1906 new water closets were added to the school, but the headmaster only turned on the water with a special key when 'washing time' took place. The school continued to educate the children of the village until 1933, when it was closed. The log books from 1896 until 1933 are held in the local history library at Linlithgow. The school building was later converted into a private house but has subsequently been abandoned.

12.1 East Benhar – ruins of old school

East Benhar, being a sizeable community, had a number of societies in existence which provided education and leisure for the villagers. There was a library with a reading and recreation room. East Benhar Penny Savings Bank assisted many households to save money. For those of an artistic bent, the Crofthead and East Benhar Amateur Dramatic Association put on a number of shows and plays after it was formed in 1886. There was a Brass Band, Burns Club, Quoiting Club and Angling Club. The community held its first gala day in 1920, held on the golf course at Fallahill. East Benhar Friendly Society existed in 1886 when Hugh Kerr was president. Its income that year was £82, the expenditure £43. In 1886 a grand concert was held in aid of East Benhar Instrumental Brass Band. A Works Library was instituted in 1886 in an empty house. Subscribers had to pay two pence per month to be able to access the 150 books.

Although most of the original residents of East Benhar had been born in either West Lothian or Lanarkshire, by 1891 it was reckoned that 20% of the population had moved here from Ireland, or at least were of Irish birth. The religious tension in the community did not appear to be much of a problem, the colliery here being referred to as an 'Orange pit'.

East Benhar owed its existence to the presence of coal below the surface of the moor. The seams were not far below the ground, the alluvial overburden being just seven fathoms and three feet in thickness. Beneath this was a seam of coal eighteen inches thick, plus a second seam of splint coal three feet eight inches thick. The Benhar Coal Company was taken over by the Niddrie and Benhar Coal Company, but it gave up the lease to the minerals in 1897. The village went into decline as a consequence, the miners often moving elsewhere in order to find work. At the time, fifty of the houses lay empty.

The Fallahill Colliery had a number of shafts in the vicinity of East Benhar, and most of the male residents worked in them. Pit Number 1 was located between the two halves of the community. The pit was operational in 1897, but by the start of the First World War it had been abandoned, and the pithead buildings removed. Similarly, Pit Number 4 was located to the west of the southern rows, and it, too, was abandoned by 1914.

In 1906 Barr and Thornton took over the lease, the business owned by Thomas Thornton of Hermand House and George Barr of Bonnington House, East Calder. In 1947, when the private coal mines were taken over by the National Coal Board, East Benhar pit had 64 miners working below ground and a further 21 above.

Miners in the local communities struggled with low wages and poor conditions for many years, but in 1886 the miners met at Peden's Stone to demand a wage rise. This proved to be unsuccessful, but the mine owners did agree to reduce the rents of the houses and also the cost of coal supplied to the households.

As in all mining communities, there were to be a fair number of men killed in the pits from roof falls, collapses and other accidents. Among those from East Benhar who died was George Martin, who was a brusher in the pits. He fell down the shaft at Starryshaw Coal Pit early one morning in December 1874. His body plunged almost 200 feet to the bottom, where it was later found in a mangled condition. The community had the services of a general practitioner - in 1886, for example, threepence per week was deducted from miners' wages to pay for his services, at the time being Dr Clarke.

In the evidence of conditions in the mining houses of Scotland, compiled in 1918, James Doonan, a miners' agent from West Lothian, visited the village and reported back on what he saw. He noted that the houses had been erected forty years earlier. They were built of brick, but when they had been erected there was no damp-proof course included, resulting in moisture seeping up from the wet mossy ground on which the village had been built. So bad was the dampness that in some houses the moisture came to the surface and exuded on internal walls. Some of the residents had tried to cover the damp walls with wallpaper, but it was noted that this was only a temporary measure, for the dampness soon discoloured it, and in many instances the surface was so damp that the paper fell from the wall.

In the village, the sanitary conditions were poor, too. Adjacent to the rows were a number of buildings, which doubled as ash-pits and which had open privies erected alongside. James Doonan noted that the smell from these was abysmal, particularly when the summer sun came and the odour permeated about the village. There was no proper sewerage system, but an open drain ran in front of each row, taking some of the sewage away, but when there was no rain it often lay stagnant. Doonan reported that there were no wash-houses – in fact he claimed that the nearest bath to the village would either be in Edinburgh or Glasgow!

At the time of Doonan's visit, he counted 29 single-room houses, for which the occupant paid a rent of 1s 7d to 1s 8d per week. There were also 62 double-roomed houses, for which the rent was 2s 4d per week. There were eleven houses that had three rooms, one of which was a kitchen, the rent for these being 3s 1d per week.

James Doonan reported that, 'It is only fair to say that since the present colliery owners acquired these houses, they have spent a considerable sum in repairs, but as these houses were built for the workers employed at another colliery which has been wrought out, they have now practically reached the period when the cost of repairs will almost surpass the amount secured in rent after taxes and feu-duty have been paid.' The old coal company was the Benhar Coal Company Limited, which went into liquidation in 1882. The company owned the local mines, as well as others nearer Edinburgh. A public roup took place on 7 June 1882 in Edinburgh at which the 'workmen's houses, workshops, pit buildings, machinery and plant' were auctioned. This included the rows at East Benhar, as well as at other communities such as Muirhead and Dykehead.

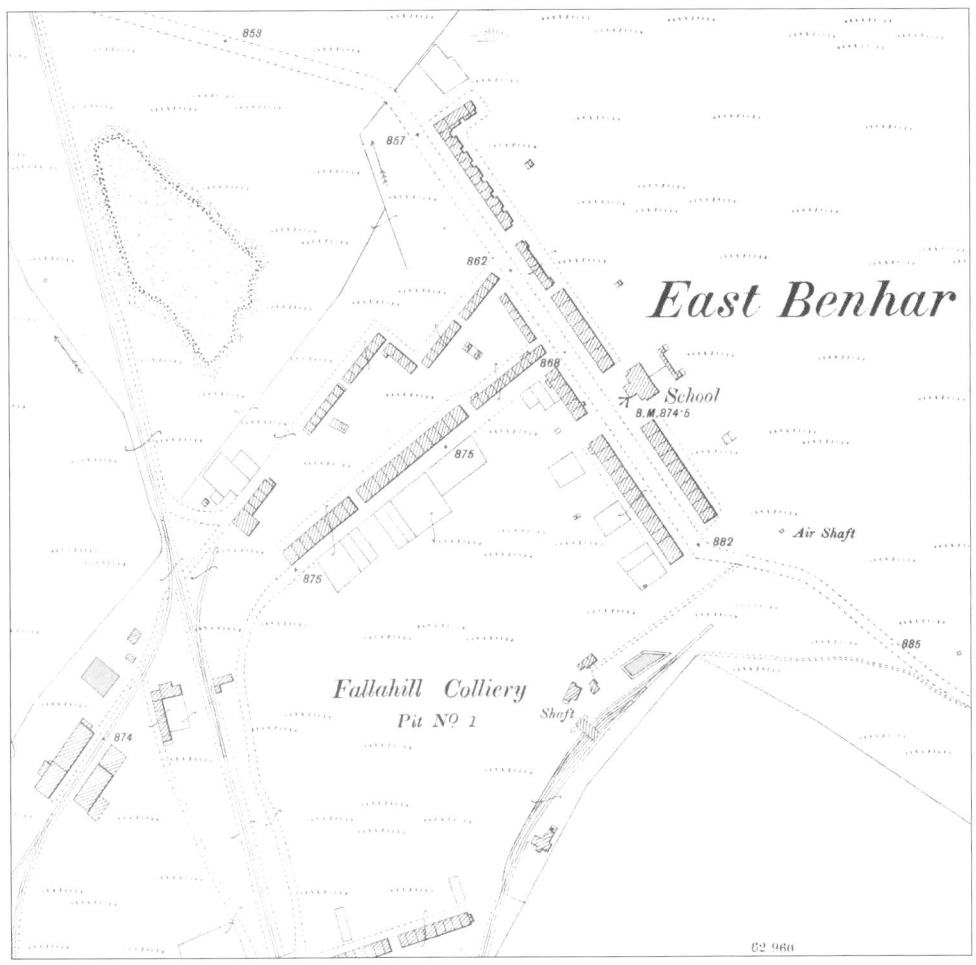

12.2 East Benhar from 1897 Ordnance Survey map

A new coal company came to sink a pit in the early twentieth century and it required housing quickly for their workers. In addition to the houses at East Benhar, the company erected around one hundred new houses at Fauldhouse, and gradually most of the workers moved there – indeed, as soon as a new house at Fauldhouse had been completed it was filled immediately. These had the bonus of an inside lavatory and running water, plastered internal walls, but no baths.

East Benhar had its own Miners' Welfare Society. The Fauldhouse and East Benhar Burns Club was founded in 1907 and joined the Burns Federation in 1914.

East Benhar had its own junior football team, known as East Benhar Heatherbell. The club was founded in 1886 and played in a blue and white strip. In 1888 they won the MacLagan Junior Cup, beating Cardross Rovers of Broxburn. When they returned to the village, East Benhar Brass Band welcomed them by playing 'Hail the Conquering Heroes'. Cardross appealed the result, complaining that the referee at the game was inefficient. This was upheld by the Linlithgowshire Junior Association, from which Heatherbell resigned. The association foundered soon after. West Lothian and District Junior Football Association was established soon after, and Heatherbell won the trophy in 1890, 1891, and the Moffat Cup in 1905. The Heatherbell club was at its peak at the start of the twentieth century, winning the Lanarkshire Junior Football Club League Cup in season 1906-07. The team was also Second Division champions in 1904-05, 1908-09 and 1914-15. The club, like many others, folded in 1916 during the First World War and was not restarted at the resumption of peace.

Four players from Heatherbell went on to play for senior teams, including Arsenal, Hearts, Liverpool, Manchester United, and Portsmouth. Robert MacLaren and David Wilson were both signed by Liverpool in 1899. Other notable players included John 'Sailor' Hunter.

One of the more noted players with East Benhar Heatherbell was Tommy Robertson (1876-1941). He was born at East Benhar and played with the Heatherbell whilst still a youngster. He moved on to play for Motherwell and Fauldhouse, before signing for Hearts in 1896. With that club he won a Scottish League winners' medal. After two years he moved on to Liverpool for four years, scoring nineteen goals in his first two seasons, even although he played outside left. He moved back to Hearts, followed by Dundee and Manchester United. He left the professional ranks thereafter, finishing his career at Bathgate. Robertson only played for Scotland on one occasion, on 26 March 1898, at Belfast against Ireland. He was one of the scorers in Scotland's three-nil victory.

In addition to the junior football club, a senior club played at East Benhar for a couple of seasons, from 1900-02. This was East Benhar Rangers, playing in a light blue strip. Patrick Slavin (1877-1916), a former outside-right player with Celtic and Motherwell played for the club for a time. He served with the Royal Scots but was killed at the Somme on 13 November 1916 and is buried there.

EAST BENHAR

In December 1932 West Lothian County Council decided to rehouse the residents of East Benhar, the reasoning being that the houses were sub-standard and that the community had little chance of a future. A Slum Clearance Order was obtained to force this through. A site adjoining Fauldhouse was selected to build new council houses, and thus the population of some 600 residents were gradually moved out. At Fauldhouse, 106 new houses were built, forming the streets of Scott Place, Barton Terrace and a few in Langrigg Road. Fauldhouse School was expanded to cope with the influx of new pupils, the cost being £2,500. The last of the houses at East Benhar were cleared away in 1933. At that time there were only two rows left. T. Thomson, a resident in the community, was to pen 'Benhar, a Poem on Life in East Benhar':

We had the Castle and the Dandy, that made twa,
Then we had the Garret and the Reekie Raw,
The Schill Raw, the Red Raw, doon the Scullery,
Right up the Long Row and the Store Row tae,
But in case there's someone who wants to be contrary,
We had the brickwork, the Jubilee, the School, the Welfare and the Dairy.

Ye can aye tell a chap frae Benhar,
No' by the claes that he wears,
No' by the muffler that's tied roon his neck,
But the heather that grows out his ears.

13
Eastfield

★

Eastfield was a fairly large village which was located on the hill to the north east of Caldercruix, in Lanarkshire. The village was established by the local mining company, James Nimmo & Company, which already had created a mining community at Longrigg. The village at Eastfield was built to house workers in the various pits associated with Longriggend Colliery, of which Eastfield Pit Number 1 was located just south-east of the village. The firm had acquired the mineral rights to Eastfield and Drumbreck, two farms which surrounded the village. Other old mine shafts existed in the near vicinity, one abandoned shaft being located in the field just south of the public house. The village was established sometime after 1871, for it does not appear in the Census carried out that year, although Eastfield farm does. There were no coalmines or ironstone pits depicted on the map at that time either. By 1881, when the next Census was undertaken, the village had a population of 780, dropping to 701 in 1892 and rising again to 990 in 1901.

In some early accounts, the village is referred to as Drumbreck, the name of the farm to the west of the community. The name Drumbreck was adopted when the school board erected a school to serve the children of the district.

Eastfield was basically two main streets, at right angles to each other, the roads of which still survive and which form Caldercruix Road, running south-west to north-east in direction, and Telegraph Road, which more-or-less heads in a north-south direction. A third street existed behind the right angle to the east, the long terrace located in a triangle of land between the main roads and the mineral railway which served Eastfield Pit. In total there were ten rows of houses making up Eastfield.

Driving from Caldercruix to Eastfield today, a distance of just half a mile from the last houses in Caldercruix's Eastfield Road, one comes to a small group of buildings on the left-hand side of the road, the vestiges of a much larger village. Originally there were a couple of semi-detached cottages here, facing onto Caldercruix Road. Immediately following these cottages was Drumbreck School, built in 1887 by Clarkston School Board to serve the considerable population that existed here. The building was designed in two halves, the infants and senior end, as was common in many village schools, and in the small playground to the rear were toilet blocks. The schoolmaster's house was located behind the school. It was erected in 1890.

The *Lanarkshire Examiner* of 10 December 1887 tells the story behind the school:

> As our readers are aware, the enterprise of Messrs James Nimmo & Company in opening up new mineral fields on the lands of Eastfield and Drumbreck has necessitated the erection of a large number of workmen's houses in the neighbourhood within the last year or two, and as these are nearly all occupied, and a considerable number of children of school age have to be looked after, the Clarkston School Board, with characteristic foresight and consideration of the convenience of the parents and comfort of the children, at one proceeded with the erection of a new school to meet the necessities of the case; otherwise, the children would have had to attend Caldercruix or Longriggend Schools, which are a long way off, and which would have had to be enlarged before the extra children could be accommodated. The Board have therefore taken a wise and judicious step in building a new school for what is practically a new population.
>
> The school is situated on the north side of the road from Caldercruix to Slamannan near its junction with the road to Longriggend. It consists of an infants' room for 87 and a senior room for 100 children. Each of these rooms has separate outdoor porches. The school is built of dull red pressed brick having a very smooth surface. The door and window openings are semi-circular headed, and the gables are pierced with two-light and triplet windows. These openings are finished with hood-mouldings, and these, with bands of white brick carefully but most sparsely introduced, giving a pleasant and artistic relief. In designing in brick, failure is frequently attained by a too elaborate introduction of white ornament. The buildings are well grouped and have a decidedly picturesque appearance. Each room has a Grahtryx ventilator for the extraction of foul air, and fresh air is admitted by circular openings over the two-light windows at the level of the ceilings, so that complete ventilation is got without any draughts.

In an ornamental circular panel over the boys' entrance is the following inscription cut out in stone – 'Drumbreck Public School, Jubilee of the Reign of Queen Victoria, 1887'. Baillie Arthur of Airdrie is the architect, and the following are the contractors, whose work is of a very satisfactory kind:- Builders, D. & A. McPhee, Chryston; carpenter and joiner work, Robert Eadie, Airdrie; plumber work, Dugald Rankine, Airdrie; slater and plaster work, Matthew Thom & Co., Airdrie; draining, levelling and fencing work, David Waddell, Plains. The lamps and pendants were supplied by Robert Ferguson, and the grates and fittings by Henry Crombie, both of Airdrie.

The school was formally opened on Monday 5 December 1887 by William Black, chairman of the school board, after which 130 children enrolled. James Miller and Miss Young were the first teachers, both having transferred from Airdriehill school at Whiterigg. By 1891 the school had a roll of 243 with an average attendance of 180 children.

Following the school was a double row of cottages, twelve in number, six facing the main road and a further half dozen facing away from it. A pathway made its way around this row, and to the north were allotments.

13.1 Eastfield School, c. 1915 (North Lanarkshire Council)

At the corner of Telegraph Road was a public house, serving the thirsty residents of the village. In 1890 William MacAllister, hotel-keeper in Slamannan, was successful in getting a licence for a property he had acquired at Eastfield, at least two previous applicants failing to get a licence. One of these was James Hunter, who in 1887 managed to get a grocery licence. In 1900 this was transferred to James Gilmour. One of the barmen employed in the pub here related that he experienced more fights between the miners on pay day at Eastfield than he had at any other pub he had served in.

Continuing along Caldercruix Road, on the way towards Limerigg, was a terrace of ten houses. Following the first terrace was a second, this one also comprising of ten houses.

On the same side (west) of Telegraph Road as the public house were three terraces of houses. The first, nearest the inn, had ten houses, and the second, which had houses of a similar size, had a further ten. The third terrace, which had smaller homes, also had ten homes in it.

On the east side of Telegraph Road were three more terraces. The first had ten houses, and were larger like the two terraces across the road. The second and third terraces were of smaller houses, each also having ten houses in it.

The last street at Eastfield faced onto the railway line, though there was a stretch of grass and a roadway in between. There were two terraces of ten houses in each here, the terraces separated by a narrow lane between the two gables, from where a footpath led across the back yards to Telegraph Road.

Eastfield was located on an elevated hillside, around 670-690 feet above sea level. When originally built, there were forty double-apartment houses and sixty single-apartment homes. However, as the years passed, some of the house floor-plans were reconfigured, smaller houses being knocked into one.

The general manager in the mines at one time was John Murray. Eastfield Pit Number 1 was located a few hundred yards along a track from Slamannan Road. A mineral siding from Longriggend made its way past Eastfield, across the road and terminated at the pithead. Among the more serious accidents that took place in the pit was the time Richard Tobbin, aged 55, was killed. He was at work in the lower Drumgray anthracite seam with his son. The son left him for a time, during which the roof collapsed, tons of rubble landing on Tobbin, crushing his spine and killing him instantly. His body was discovered by his son when he returned. Tobbin lived in a house in what was known as Murray's Land, Eastfield.

In the late nineteenth century, the village supported three football teams. Eastfield Worthies was a senior team which is known to have played in the 1876-7 season. There were two junior teams in the village, Eastfield Thistle existing in 1881. In 1886-7 Eastfield Athletic played some games, after which no junior teams existed.

A number of other organisations existed in the village over the decades. In 1886 reference is made to the Eastfield branch of the Glasgow Foundry Boys' Religious Society, under the chairmanship of Mr A. F. Brown.

On 24 June 1913 housing inspectors visited Eastfield to look at the conditions endured by the occupants of the houses. The evidence gathered was presented to the Royal Commission on 25 March 1914. The inspectors were…

> … of opinion that it ought not to be available for inspection. There are 3 one-roomed houses, 3 two-roomed houses, and 3 back-to-back with the one-roomed houses. There are no sculleries, no coal-cellars, no closets, no ash-pits, and the water supply is from one stand in the street. The houses are old-looking, and should be pulled down. Rent here is 1s. 8d. for a house of one apartment, and 2s. 8d. for one of two apartments; is paid weekly, and does not include rates.

They also made notes on their sheets that the 'Whole place and houses disgraceful, and should be pulled down. This place cannot be described at all; it must be seen.'

Another report that was almost contemporary noted that Eastfield had twenty single-apartment houses, the rental of which was £5 12s 6d per annum. There were forty double-apartment houses, the rent payable being £7 7s 4d. The houses were all of one storey, built of brick, but having no damp-proof courses were subsequently sodden. The houses were erected around 24 years before the report, showing just how quickly they had deteriorated. The walls had no cavities, and internally they were plastered straight onto the brickwork, resulting in them being very cold. Most houses had wooden floors, and there was some ventilation, but the internal surface of the walls and ceilings were noted as being rough and broken.

The inspectors noted that there was no overcrowding at Eastfield, and that in general the kitchens were of a fair size. However, the back rooms were comparatively small. The community had no wash-houses and no coal cellars,

EASTFIELD

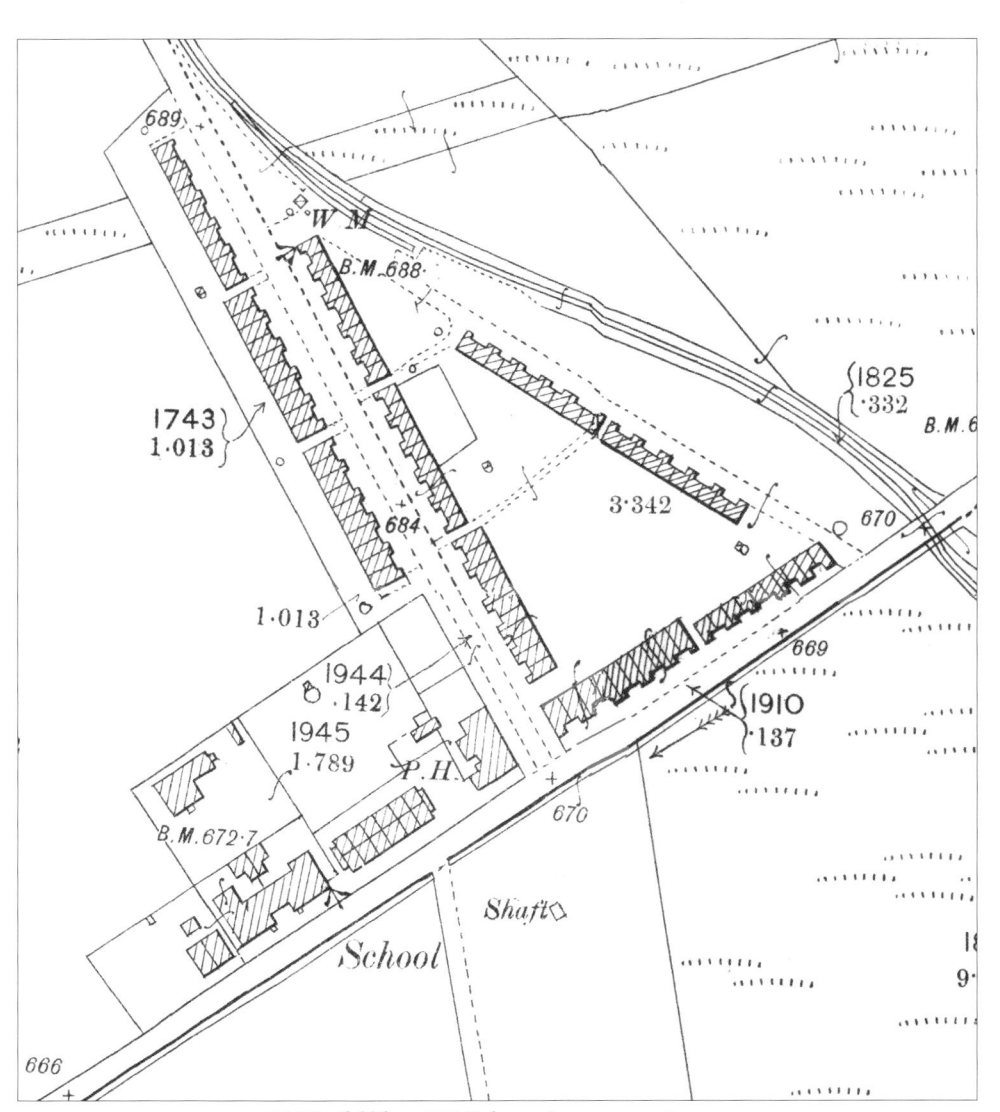

13.2 Eastfield from 1898 Ordnance Survey composite map

but garden ground was available to each tenant if required, but this was often not taken advantage of. The rows had two open privy middens, and three separate ashpits, located about twenty feet to the rear of the houses. Water was available from two standpipes in the street, fed from a gravitation water supply. The rubbish and detritus thrown onto the roads and streets was scavenged by the owners. At the time, some action had been taken regarding the damp conditions of the houses, with some improvements attempted. Twenty of the houses with two apartments had been rebuilt internally, and new coal cellars, wash-houses, sculleries and sinks had been provided. The houses also had new water closets built into the porches that were added. Forty of the houses which were deemed beyond renovation had been demolished.

In 1929 the last pits operated by Nimmo's in the district were closed and the village was given up by the firm. Ownership passed into private hands, but with no employment many of the residents moved away to find work elsewhere.

In 1942 there was a mission arranged by the Christian Brethren to Eastfield, as a result of which a Gospel Hall and brethren group was established. This appears to have continued to meet until around 1960.

By 1960, when the *Third Statistical Account* of Lanarkshire was compiled, the only houses still surviving in Eastfield was the school house plus three or four other cottages. The residents of the community were rehoused at Caldercruix, but there is a tale that the first old couple to get a new house only stayed there for a short period, moving back to their original home. The reason for returning is not confirmed, some think it was because they couldn't afford the dearer rent, but the most common tale relates that they missed the friendliness of the neighbours of their old community.

14
Fairfield

✶

The village of Fairfield was located at the east end of Loch Fitty in Fife, just over three miles north-east of Dunfermline. Some say that the village actually formed part of the larger community of Lassodie, mentioned later in this book, but the Ordnance Survey treated it as a separate community, and certainly, it was separated from Lassodie itself by a few hundred yards of open countryside.

Fairfield was built as a new community to replace older houses that had existed at the Old Rows of Lassodie. It was less remote than the latter village, being positioned just a few hundred yards off the main road from Dunfermline to Kelty, and thus it didn't suffer from the remote feeling that the older rows had.

From the south, the only access road into Fairfield and Lassodie crossed the Loch Fitty Burn by a stone bridge and then on ascending the embankment, turned into Fairfield's main street. The proximity of the burn could be something of a problem over the years. In September 1928 a three-year-old boy, named James Rankine Scott, was drowned in the water. His father, Robert Scott, a miner who lived in a house close-by, had the misfortune of finding his son dead in the stream. Although the burn was a popular spot for lads to play and folks to gather, no-one saw the young lad fall into the water. The boy had been at home and had left the house to play. His mother went outside to shout for him, but when no reply was forthcoming, her husband went to look for him. The burn was in spate at the time, and it is thought that he had slipped on the bank and tumbled in.

On making one's way across the bridge over the burn, the road swung to the right up a small slope, then took a sharp left into the main street of the community. This ran uphill at an angle, generally heading north-west. Almost all of the buildings were located along this street, apart from three rows of houses which were positioned on the east side of the street, at right angles to it. In layout, the village resembled the traditional Scottish planned village style, with its regular grid pattern, with a long main street and shorter transverse streets perpendicular to it.

At the bottom of the main street the first side street led eastwards. In it were two short terraces of four houses each, overlooking the roadway to the valley of the burn below. Behind this row was a second row, again with two terraces of four houses. In the open land behind the houses were wash-houses, shared by the residents.

The main street had a series of terraces built along it, each house's front door stepping right onto the roadway. Unlike much of the older part of Lassodie, there were pavements here. On the left side of the street, heading towards the village centre, were three terraces of four houses, their washhouses to the rear. On the east side of the street, stretching to the village centre, were four terraces, each containing four houses.

At the centre of the village were a number of other buildings, situated on the west side of the road. Here was a small branch of the co-operative society, and at a later date a post box was affixed to the wall. The shop was operated by the Kelty Co-operative Society and remained open until the village was abandoned in 1931.

On the main street, north of the village centre were more terraces of houses. On the east side of the street were four rows of four houses, again with gardens and washhouses to the rear. On the west side of the roadway were five terraces, stretching farther up the road. These were not regular in length, or in the number of houses in each. That nearest the centre of the community had six houses. The next one had seven. The third terrace had five homes. The fourth row of houses had six dwellings in it. The last row also had six houses in it. At some time, these houses were rebuilt, so that each terrace contained six homes.

Within the streets were a number of water pumps. One of these was positioned at the foot of the main street. A second one was located at the end of the second side street, but on the main street. A third pump was located right in the centre of the village, and it appears to have served all of the upper end of the community. As with Lassodie nearby, the water supply was installed by the coal company and was officially inaugurated by Mrs Brownlie, wife of the company chairman, on 12 September 1887.

Events in the life of the community of Fairfield are random and typical of any little community. Among the more notable is the account of the death of Jane Dryburgh, a young girl of two years and four months. She was described in the newspapers of the time as the 'illegitimate child of Margaret Brown, residing with John Brown, miner, Fairfield.' On the afternoon of Saturday 21

FAIRFIELD

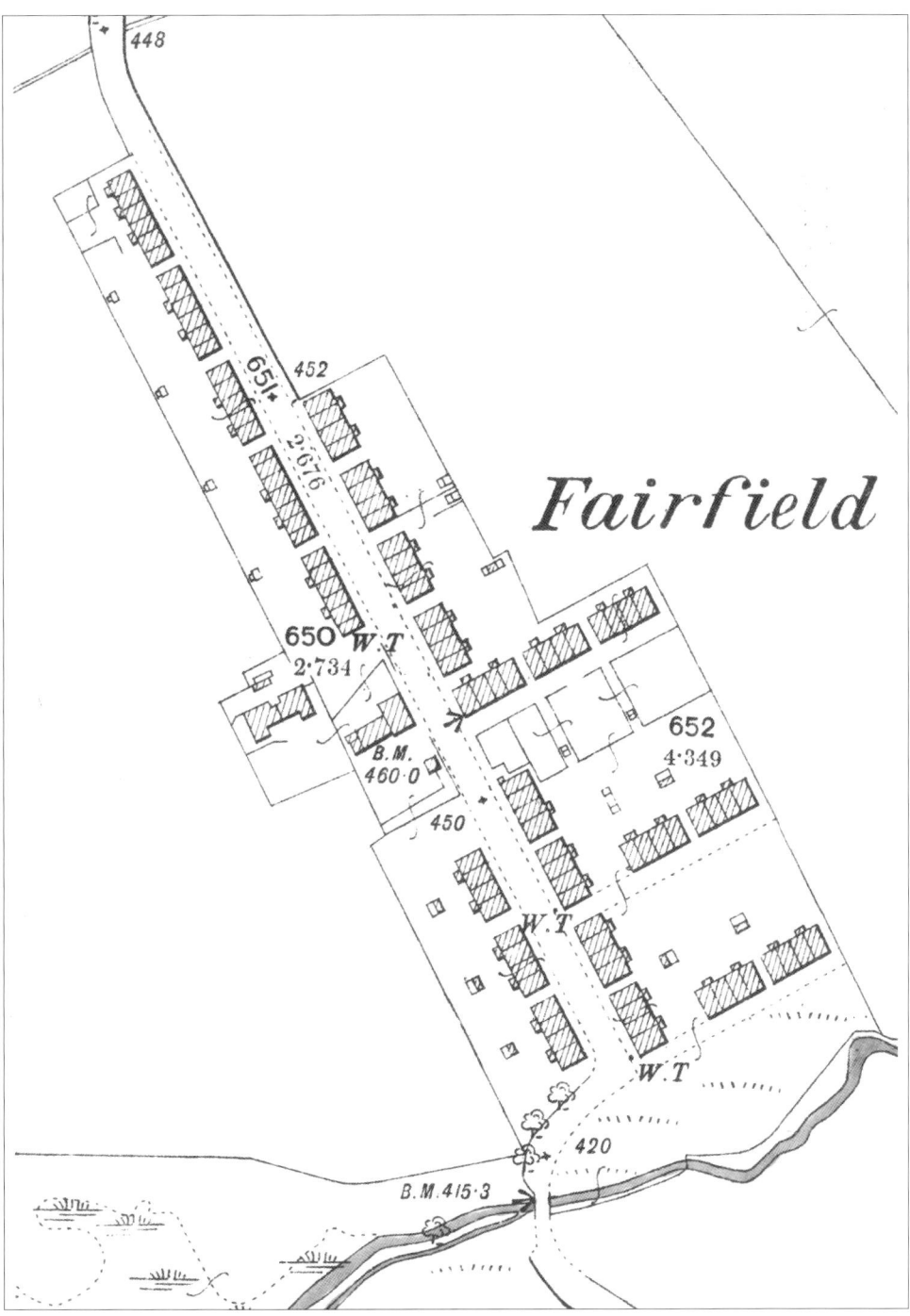

14.1 Fairfield from 1896 Ordnance Survey map

November 1863, the girl ran through the house and fell into a pot of boiling water. Before she was able to be removed from the pot, the girl suffered burns that were so severe that she died on the Monday.

Peter Harrower, a drawer at Number 9 pit at Lassodie, lived in Fairfield in 1880. He became involved in a brawl in the underground workings at the pit with Andrew Downie and had assaulted him by striking him with several severe blows to the face. Harrower was taken to court, charged with assault, and was fined ten shillings by Sheriff Lamond.

John Robson was fined £3 in October 1887 for selling three pints of ale and one gill of whisky without having a liquor licence. The illegal supply of alcohol was something that occurred often in many of the mining villages across the country. In July 1892 the story of a Fairfield shebeen was cited as a classic example to 'those temperance reformers who pin their faith upon the restriction of licences, or even the total prohibition of the liquor trade, as a panacea for the evils of intemperance', according to *The Scotsman*. Apparently, there had been a house in Fairfield that was well-known for operating as a shebeen for a period of two years, but which the police could not find enough evidence to allow them to press charges. Eventually, they managed to get evidence, but only following a disturbance when two topers began to quarrel and the police became involved. The Chief Constable said, during the trial, that if the premises had been granted a proper licence, then they would have been able to police it properly. He said, 'here is a village without licensed premises. The want of legal facilities for obtaining drink, instead of making the people sober, as the advocates for restriction say it should, resulted in a system of shebeening so elaborate that the Chief Constable sees no way of combating it'.

A number of Fairfield men were killed in the Great War, and their names appear with those of Lassodie on the war memorial that survives, now located by the side of the Dunfermline road. Private J. Wilson of the Black Watch was killed when a German aerial torpedo exploded in September 1915. Private William Taylor was a miner at Lassodie prior to signing with the Royal Army Medical Corps with his brother in 1915. Taylor was wounded in 1916 and died of his wounds at the age of 25 years. On 22 April 1916 Private William Gillespie, Black Watch, was killed in action at the age of 22 years. He, too, had been a miner prior to enlisting.

As with Lassodie, Messrs Thomas Spowart & Co. Ltd., the mining company, closed the pit in May 1931 and ordered the residents to move out of their homes, giving them two weeks' notice. Many workers refused to accept this, and remained in their houses for many years, the title to the houses returning to Lassodie estate. When a reporter from the *Dunfermline Press* visited Fairfield in May 1931, he found quite a number of houses that were unoccupied and appeared to have been tenantless for some time. He was also told that, 'it was found necessary to close several of the houses, because of ominous cracks which were beginning to make their appearance on the walls and ceilings, the result of underground workings. In some instances, indeed, the collapse of the houses was only prevented by a process of shoring up between the gables of adjoining groups of buildings'.

In August 1933, there were still thirty people living at Fairfield. Again, they were given orders to leave, a few days' notice given, but some refused to budge. Many claimed that the rent for the new homes they had been offered in Kelty or Cowdenbeath was too expensive to pay when they had no income. The water supply was later turned off, but still, in 1937, a few residents remained, their homes sub-standard, with no running water or sanitary facilities. Eventually, by 1940, the houses were more or less totally vacated and the remaining buildings were pulled down.

Today, Fairfield cannot be identified on the ground, for the site of it was to be subject to the massive St Ninian's Open Cast Coal Mine.

15

Fochabers

*

Drivers, on the main road from Aberdeen to Inverness, should they decide to leave the main road that by-passes the village of Fochabers, will find it is a striking community - a long main street, attractively lined with old Georgian houses, here and there embellished with pillars and porticos. The Parish Church of Bellie is a fine Georgian edifice, designed by John Baxter and erected in 1795-8. The Gordon Arms Hotel has a nucleus of 1777-9, and the former town hall and school were also designed by Baxter and erected in 1792.

The Fochabers we see today dates from 1776 onwards, being a planned town laid out by Alexander Gordon, 4th Duke of Gordon. He had proposed to remove the old village that was located slightly to the north of the present community as early as the 1760s, when he commenced work on remodelling Gordon Castle and the policies. The duke inherited the estate as a minor in 1752. He went on the Grand Tour of Europe and came home with many innovative ideas which he hoped to create in Scotland. He engaged John Baxter to extend the castle from 1768-74. As this was taking place, the extensive gardens to the south of the house were considerably redeveloped and changed into parkland, which extended far into the surrounding farmland. He wished the old village to be relocated, as he was 'desirous to remove the present town or village of Fochabers upon account of inconvenient nearness to Gordon Castle.'

In 1772 the road from Elgin to Cullen was realigned, taking a new route south of the castle and policies. In 1775, over a series of old fields, a grid pattern was laid out on the fairly level ground, and feus were marked out on the former fields, ready for tenants to take possession. In January 1776, the solicitor acting for the duke starting selling off feus in the new town and bought up old feus. The bulk of the tenants came from the old village of Fochabers. However, he does not appear to have offered anything by way of an incentive to the residents to move. He also did not encourage them to move to new homes nearer places of employment, for there were no new industries attracted to the village.

FOCHABERS

The old Fochabers was a fair-sized community, having a population of around 600 in 1720. It seems to have grown in the preceding years, for in the 1660s its population was much smaller, for there were only half a dozen cottages or so there. In 1720, the village also 'possessed a Grammar School and several good lodgings and inns'. There was also a weekly market. By 1764 it was reckoned that there were 150 households in the village.

15.1 Fochabers – old Market Cross

In 1735-6 a new courthouse was erected in the village, for by this time the community had become the centre of a local jurisdiction. The building, which stood next to the market cross, was rectangular in plan, and measured around fifty feet by twenty-two feet. On the façade, facing the market square, was a double forestair, climbing to the first floor, where the court room would have been. No doubt the ground floor was where the vaulted cells were located, and where malefactors were locked up. In 1766 plans for a new tolbooth were produced by Abraham Roumieu. This would have been a fairly prominent building in the old burgh, for it was to have a seven-bay façade, the wall topped with a pediment and the roof containing a tall spire. On the first floor was to be the large courtroom, the ground floor having a girnal, weigh-house, and prison. This building was never erected, for by this time there may have been inklings of a new burgh to be erected elsewhere.

In 1753 some of the houses at the east end of the village were demolished to allow the creation of a new eastern avenue leading into Gordon Castle. The estate carried out a survey of the properties that were to be removed, around twenty in number, and noted that they were built of 'mud and stone work'.

From the old kirk session minutes, one can add a bit of colour to the little that is known about the village. A character in the village was Katherine Ross, 'a woman of infamous character and practice.' She had co-habited with a Peter MacKay, but after he had died she became pregnant. Who the father was, wasn't known, and she wouldn't divulge it. Three men in the village were named, including a John Grant, merchant in the village, but he appears to have taken umbrage at this and had his name publicly read out in the church as being innocent. Katherine was banished beyond the bounds of the Presbytery of Strathbogie.

When Dr Johnson and James Boswell passed through Fochabers on 26 August 1773 they saw little indication of any development. Indeed, Boswell wrote, 'Fochabers, the neighbouring village [to Gordon Castle], is a poor place, many of the houses being ruinous; but it is remarkable, they have in general orchards well stored with apple-trees'.

In August 1776 the Duke instructed J. Ross to send letters to the various tenants in the village, informing them of his proposal to relocate the village:

> You are to be paid ___ pounds Stg. in consideration of your disponing to the Duke of Gordon your present tenement ground in Fochabers

and agreeing to remove to the New Town besides having right to the materials of your present houses and dykes.

The residents were offered from £5 to £52 for their properties, depending on the size and quality.

Many of the occupants were unwilling to move, and a petition against their relocation was signed by a number of them. This was presented to the Duke, but he doesn't appear to have taken any notice of it. A letter of 20 November 1776, written to Charles Gordon at Edinburgh, shows how the residents of the old village were unwilling (or perhaps couldn't afford) to move:

> Sir,
> The Duke is anxious to have the present town of Fochabers removed – And, with that in View, has marked out a situation for a new Town – I have bargained with a few of the present Tenementers – and some houses are going on in the New Town – the fact however is, that many of the present possessors are unwilling to part with their old Habitations, but as the Duke is determined and intent upon it, Every method must be taken to force their removal ….

In *A Survey of the Province of Moray*, written in 1798, Rev Leslie of Darkland, notes that:

> The turbulent state of society in ancient times generally raised a village in the vicinity of every castle, for the mutual security which both the fortress and the people afforded to each other; but which in the peaceful security which the wisdom and energy of the present constitution has so long maintained, it is more pleasant to have the palace environed by the ornamental grounds of an extensive park; in this regard, the Duke of Gordon, several years ago, purchased the property of the town, then situated not far from his gate, and feued off the present village, at a handsome yet commodious distance. This new town is a clean neat burgh of barony; all its streets are straight, crossing each other at right angles; and the great road to London conducted through the centre of its grand square, three sides of which, pretty uniformly built, are the mansions of the inhabitants; the fourth is

occupied by the public buildings, the church, detached in the middle between two large handsome houses of uniform exterior, one occupied as the manse, the other containing the parochial school and town-hall.

The old Fochabers was a community that appears to have grown fairly quickly. In the 1660s it only had a few houses, occupied by workers on the estate. Soon after, the village began to grow. By 1720 the community had 'above 600 inhabitants --- a grammar school, several good lodgins & inns'. There was also a weekly market which attracted folk from the surrounding countryside. In the mid eighteenth century, the village did not have much of a positive reputation, for it was described as being a 'place of miserable huts'. Even worse, many of these were occupied by 'strumpets who are notorious Thieves'.

From the Spey ferry the roadway arrived at the west end of the village, where a street made its way up a gradual slope to the square. The street was built up on both sides, houses and commercial premises facing onto the roadway, with gardens behind. Those houses on the north side of the street had gardens that ended against the estate policy wall. Over this wall was the main western driveway into Gordon Castle, tree-lined and far grander than the main road into the village.

Just short of the square was a road striking off to the south, which made its way up the east side of the Spey towards Boharm and Mulben. Again, this road was built up on both sides.

Parallel with the southern road was a second street of houses, but this one started on the south side of the square. Both of the south-heading roads ended in a large open area, perhaps a market or fair ground.

The square in the centre of the burgh was quite a large one, with a church located in the centre. On all four sides of the open area were buildings facing onto the market place.

From the square, a roadway headed eastwards, again with housing on both sides. At the end of this street the road latterly took a sharp turn to the right, but no doubt originally would have travelled on through the ducal grounds.

To the south of the eastern street, and running back to the southern fairground, was a back lane, along which a number of buildings had been erected.

A survey of many of the cottages in the village was made by Gordon estate in 1735. One of these, the home of squarewright, John Gray, was noted as being built of stone held together with clay mortar, harled with lime. It only had three windows but its hearth and chimney were built of brick.

The old village of Fochabers was enlarged considerably around 1754 when the dowager Duchess of Gordon sold off around fifty new feus. It is likely that these were located on the road that made its way from the east end of the older community in a southerly direction, before a right-angle bend took one on the Banff and Aberdeen road.

In 1758 Fochabers was visited by Sir William Burrell who was partaking in a grand tour of northern Scotland. He noted that the community was 'a poor, miserable collection, or rather cluster, of huts remarkable for the Duke of Gordon's seat adjoyning to it, one part consisting of an old castle, the other of a modern building tacked to it'. When Thomas Pennant passed this way in 1769, he was fairly blunt in his comments about the community – 'a wretched town, close to the castle.'

The first residents of the new town were often those who were employed more closely with the duke, and thus quite readily influenced by him. He offered some 'removal expenses' to those willing to move, but the figure was insufficient to cover little more than that. In fact, those who did accept the new feus would find themselves considerably out of pocket, for the new dwellings that they were to move to had to be built according to Baxter's plan and specifications.

The cost of moving was no doubt the principal factor in the time it took to remove the old village completely. It was not until 1802 that the last building in the old village was emptied and the whole site came back into ducal control. This tenement was soon demolished, and the rubble from the walls was used for other purposes. The site of the market place, roads, walls, gardens and buildings were all cleared away, and the area returned to pasture. Through part of the site a new avenue was created, the principle drive from the main road into the estate. A new kitchen garden was laid out over much of the remainder of the village, and a pond, known as the Fish Pond, over other parts.

In a field to the north of Garden Cottage, which adjoins the kitchen garden, stands the only remnant of the old village – the Old Fochabers Cross. Known locally as 'The Jougs', this is a well-preserved cylindrical pillar, or Tuscan column, about twelve feet tall with a shallow square capital. The cross was left by the Duke as a marker, standing alone, wondering where the buildings and folk who used to crowd round it went. For many years the old jougs were still attached to the cross, but these have gone, leaving only a length of chain. It is said that the footings of the old tolbooth cell can be seen on the ground nine feet away from the pillar, measuring around thirty by fifteen feet, but this is not obvious today.

It is said that the former estate fruit store was also part of the village and was the last cottage in it. Why this was kept is unknown, but it was for many years thatched.

A native of old Fochabers was William Marshall, born on 27 December 1748. His parents being poor, he received little education and at the age of twelve he found work in the Gordon Castle estate. He was

15.2 Fochabers – details of chain that once held the jougs

to become the 4th Duke's butler and then factor. He was married in 1773 to Jane Giles. In 1790 Marshall took on the lease of a farm at Keithmore, in the Banffshire parish of Mortlach. In his spare time, he was a keen player of the fiddle, and he composed over two hundred tunes, some of which it is said were adopted by the other famous Scots fiddler, Neil Gow. Some of his tunes are still popular, such as 'O' a' the airts the wind can blaw' and 'Farewell to Keithmore'. In addition to being a skilled fiddler and composer, Marshall was a self-taught engineer. He built a magnificent large clock, which depicted the time in minutes, hours, days, months and years. It also shows the moon's revolutions around the Earth and its various phases, when high and low tides take place, and how long each day is in darkness, amongst other things. The clock is regarded as being one of the finest in Britain and survives in a private collection. However, a long-case clock that he made can be seen in Fochabers Folk Museum. Marshall died on 29 May 1833 and was buried in the old kirkyard at Bellie.

If one goes into the present village of Fochabers, a house located on the south side of the eastern half of High Street has a lintel with the date 1776 carved on it, as well as the initials J. A. This represents James Allan, one of the first residents of the old village to accept a new feu in the planned village.

16
Forvie

*

There is an ancient ballad that tells of the loss of the Buchan village of Forvie. 'The Sands of Forvie' recounts how at one time in far-flung history, referred to as around four hundred years ago in Rev John B. Pratt's *Buchan*, itself written in 1858, the owner of the parish died, leaving his estate to his three daughters. However, the country was in a lawless state at the time, and within a short period the girls were defrauded of their inheritance by foul means. They had to move elsewhere, but they would often pray that their defrauders should be suitably punished, and that the lands they had gained would become worthless.

What seemed like an interminable period was to pass before the prayers were answered by providence. A great storm blew up, and the North Sea waves crashed upon the shores at Forvie for days on end. The wind blew sands from the beaches over the lush green meadows of Forvie estate, and as the days passed the depth of sand grew thick and deeper. Once the storm had abated the farms and crofts had been covered, the fields buried below massive dunes, and the whole estate had become impossible to farm. The sisters' revenge had come to pass, and the lands of Forvie were not worth the parchment that the titles had been written upon.

The ancient rhyme recounts some of the story:

> Yf evyr maydenis malysone
> Did licht upon drye lande,
> Let nocht bee funde in Furvye's glebys
> Bot thistle, bente, and sande.

The actual date that the Sands of Forvie obliterated the ancient village has not been determined. However, there are some accounts which claim that it took place in 1688, when a storm of nine days' duration covered the lands. As late as 1830 there was an old rent book held at Slains Castle which listed all of the farms and tenants in the parish, including the lost ones around Forvie. Rev Pratt had not seen this, and wrote, 'The recovery of this volume is much to be desired, as it would throw considerable light on this interesting subject.'

There are others who claim that the date of the great sandstorm that obliterated the estate of Forvie took place on 10 August 1413. It is said that the sands were washed ashore from the bowels of the North Sea, and when dried in the wind were blown northwards from the mouth of the Don, spreading across the coastline of Aberdeenshire. The largest dunes were left at Forvie. Whether history can confirm this or not is unknown, but the same account also claims that the same storms blocked the port of Rattray, mentioned later on in this volume. Whether or not it was significant or a coincidence of history, it was also claimed that Mount Hekla erupted on Iceland, creating a terrific hurricane, and that Vesuvius erupted in Italy.

It has also been discovered that, although the sands traditionally obliterated the lands of Forvie in a single, though major, storm, the occupants of the lands had struggled against wind-blown sand for centuries. A local farmer who did some excavation work discovered that the old rigs and furrows that were created by farmers in the past, were in a number of places partially covered with sand,

16.1 Forvie – ruins of old church

then soil was laid on top of the sand, only to be smothered by the sand again. It indicated that there had been various storms over the years where the sand had covered the fields, but which had not been deep enough to totally destroy the farms.

Thomas Pennant, on his tour of Scotland in 1769, passed by Forvie and related that he went, 'through the parish of Forvie now entirely overwhelmed with sand, (except two farms) and about 500 L. per ann. lost to the Errol family, as appears by the oath of the factor made before the court of sessions in 1600 to ascertain the minister's salary.' Writing in 1680, the Countess of Erroll noted that, 'The parish of Forvey, which is wholly overblown with sand, and, it is said, the sand and sea is encroaching in many places.' The date of this indicates that the supposed date of the storm as 1688 being unlikely.

A track from Waterside, at the Ythan Bridge, leads through the heath-covered dunes to the site of the village. The only vestige to remain visible above the level of the sand are the remnants of the ancient parish church. It is said that this was built at the highest part of the original village, hence it remaining visible today. However, at the end of the nineteenth century it was actually dug out from the sand dunes by a local doctor. During this excavation he discovered the piscina. The walls of the church are up to six feet in height, but within them it is still possible to make out the ancient piscina. The ruined walls, which are two feet thick, measure 50 feet by 20 feet. Constructed of a dark stone, red sandstone was used at the door and window jambs. There are two entrances, located at the north and south sides. The walls were restored to roof level in 1981.

Forvie kirk was dedicated to St Adamnan. He was an Irishman who was descended from St Columba. Born in 625, he was elected abbot of Iona in 679. He established churches at Aboyne and Forvie in Aberdeenshire, plus others in Banffshire. He died on 23 September 705. The earliest reference to the kirk at Forvie dates from the thirteenth century, when it was mentioned in the records of the Chartulary of Arbroath. There are also claims that the kirk was associated with the early Knights Templar. Forvie kirk was the centre of a parish of the same name, but in 1573 it was united with the adjoining parish of Slains. In 1574 King James VI granted the rights of Forvie kirk to King's College, Aberdeen. The church was perhaps totally abandoned by this period, for burials that post-date this time were found within the confines of the building. In the *New Statistical Account* of the parish, it is written that, 'graves have been discovered around it, but nothing found in them except a few bones.'

In 1858 Rev John Pratt wrote in *Buchan* that he was unsure that the ruins were, in fact, those of a church. His reasons were sound – the walls were rather plain and did not look ecclesiastical to him. The other difficulty that he spotted was, 'the complete departure from the rule observed by our forefathers in the *orientation* of their churches is of itself sufficient to throw suspicion on the ecclesiastical origin of this ruin.' Nevertheless, he was unwilling to rock local tradition which was adamant that the ruins were, indeed, those of the ancient parish kirk. Pratt's doubts may have inspired the 'local doctor' to have carried out the removal of the surrounding sand.

16.2 Forvie – old font from kirk (right)

Archaeologists made a number of excavations at Forvie in 1957-58, under Professor W. Kirk of the University of Aberdeen. They cleared away the site of the church, and in further trenches they were able to identify a number of square-shaped houses, constructed of stone and clay. South of the kirk, further house-bases were found, one of which had a paved floor. Here sherds of pottery were discovered, dated to the thirteenth to fourteenth century. Also found were coins and some pieces of metalwork.

An ancient octagonal font, carved from a solid block of Peterhead granite, is thought to have been from Forvie kirk and is now on display at the Stevenson

Forvie Centre, located at the northern end of the Forvie nature reserve, near Collieston. Although partially broken, the tapered stone block had a rounded hollow where baptismal water was held. Belonging to Slains Parish Church, it is on loan to the centre. Another relic from the church is the piscina which was gifted to the National Museum of Antiquities in Edinburgh in 1876. When the church was dug out, an ancient aumbry, or mural cupboard was discovered in the wall, a place where the sacred vessels would have been kept for safekeeping. Some small fragments of coloured glass and lead that were discovered on site are also on display in the centre.

The site of Forvie is now within the Forvie National Nature Reserve, established to protect the dunes and the wildlife which makes them their homes. When signs were being erected to indicate items of interest, one was proposed near to the old church. When holes were being dug for the posts, remains of human bones were found, indicating that the burial ground associated with the church was larger than at first thought. The sign was relocated to avoid disturbing the bodies.

17
Gavieside

★

The village of Gavieside consisted of what was virtually one long row of houses. This stretched eastwards from the road linking West Calder with the small village of Livingston, at that time little more than a church, post office and a few cottages, not the large New Town it was to become.

Gavieside was named after a farm that lay to the north of the village, beyond Briestonhill Moss. The village occupied some elevated ground between the valleys of the Breich Water to the west, and the Calder Burn to the east. The village was established around 1862, at the time the Gavieside Paraffin Oil Works were erected by the West Calder Oil Company. This oil company failed in 1878 and the whole business was placed on the market. It was acquired by the expanding Young's Paraffin Light and Mineral Oil Company. In the advertisement offering the business for sale is a description of the works:

> The pits at Gavieside are in good working order with a command of Shale at the very best quality, and which can be raised at low cost…. The Machinery and Buildings at Gavieside are to a large extent of recent construction, and the appliances are of the most modern and approved description. They include Retorts for the Manufacture of Crude Oil; Stills, Washers, etc., for the Manufacture and Refining of Burning and Lubricating Oils; Plant for the Freezing and Pressing of Crude Paraffin and for the Manufacture of Sulphate of Ammonia. There are Counting-Houses, Stores, Stables, Workshops, etc., provided with all necessary Fittings; also a School-House, Manager's House, and Workmen's Dwellings – all in good condition. The Refinery is at present capable of working over Two Million Gallons of Crude Oil per Annum, and with a small outlay could be made to accomplish about a half more. Upset Price, £40,000.

On the main road passing by Gavieside was a short row of six houses, known as Raeburn Row. One edition of the Ordnance Survey map spelled this as

Reaburn, probably in error. This terrace of single-storey houses was built of brick with a pantiled roof. The four houses at the southern end of the row were smaller than the northern two, but not by much. Each house had two fireplaces, resulting in twelve chimney cans on the chimneys. The roof was used to collect water, directed through downpipes into barrels at the front of the house. In addition to the barrels as a source of water, there was a water pump, located in the street in front of the houses. The houses had narrow gardens to the rear.

Striking east from near Raeburn Row was a minor road, heading across a small bridge over the Calder Burn, and joining the main Edinburgh road at Polbeth, east of West Calder. The houses were all located on the north side of the road, forming a long terrace almost half a mile in length. The first row comprised of ten houses.

The next group of houses was probably built simultaneously. There were five blocks, four of four houses, followed by one of two. Two of the blocks of four may in fact have been blocks of eight, the houses comprising two flats.

Following this were rows of smaller houses, each terrace apparently of different sizes and lengths, with a variety of house sizes in them. The first had four houses, the second had five. There followed five rows of four houses each.

The final rows at Gavieside had blocks of four houses, their gables tight together, leaving only a narrow pend between them. There were two blocks of four houses, then a row of six houses and one of three. These numbers were not

17.1 Gavieside School in the 1950s (Almond Valley Heritage Trust)

always precise, for over the years a number of smaller dwellings were knocked together to form one larger house, usually for larger families.

Lighting in most houses was obtained from paraffin lamps, and outside toilets, usually referred to as 'shunkies', were located at random places to serve the houses. Most houses had shutters on the windows, so that at night they could be closed, helping, in a little way, to keep in some heat.

To the east of the row was the West Calder Oil Works, also known as the Gavieside Oil Works. When this went bankrupt, it was dismantled and the machinery re-deployed elsewhere, leaving just bings and railway lines, ruins and reservoirs. At the start of the twentieth century, the bing formed a safety backdrop to a rifle range. The target was located on the north side of the bing, the shooters taking aim from the north-east. To warn the villagers that live ammunition was being used, a flagstaff was positioned on top of the bing. The former cooling reservoir, which survives as a fishing pool, was known to the locals as the Work Pond, often resorted to by young lads for a swim.

Between Raeburn Row and the railway bridge was the school. This was erected sometime in the nineteenth century and served both Gavieside and another lost village – Mossend. The school building was rebuilt, or at least extended, in 1906. A single-storey building, erected of stone, it was distinguished by its gables and tall chimneys, with tall window openings. The school remained in use for two decades after Gavieside village had been demolished. Local primary children were brought to it up until 1948, after which it remained as a nursery school until 1961. It was demolished soon thereafter. Headmasters in the school included Joseph Taylor. In 2003 a group of former pupils decided to organise a reunion, forty years after having left the school. When they were pupils only 48 attended the school

Gavieside did not have a church, being close enough to West Calder for worshippers to walk there on a Sunday morning. However, there was a mission hall in the village, where Sunday services were often held by devout miners, with singing to accompaniment on the organ. In addition, a travelling group of missionaries brought what was the Gospel Tent, erecting it on the grass in front of the rows. A regular Sunday School was held in the school building.

Playing quoits was a popular past-time, and a quoiting green existed on a stretch of Briestonhill Moss, near the east end of the row. Another leisure facility was the reading room, located in two old cottages which had been knocked into one. A few national papers were available there, and various indoor games could

SCOTLAND'S LOST VILLAGES

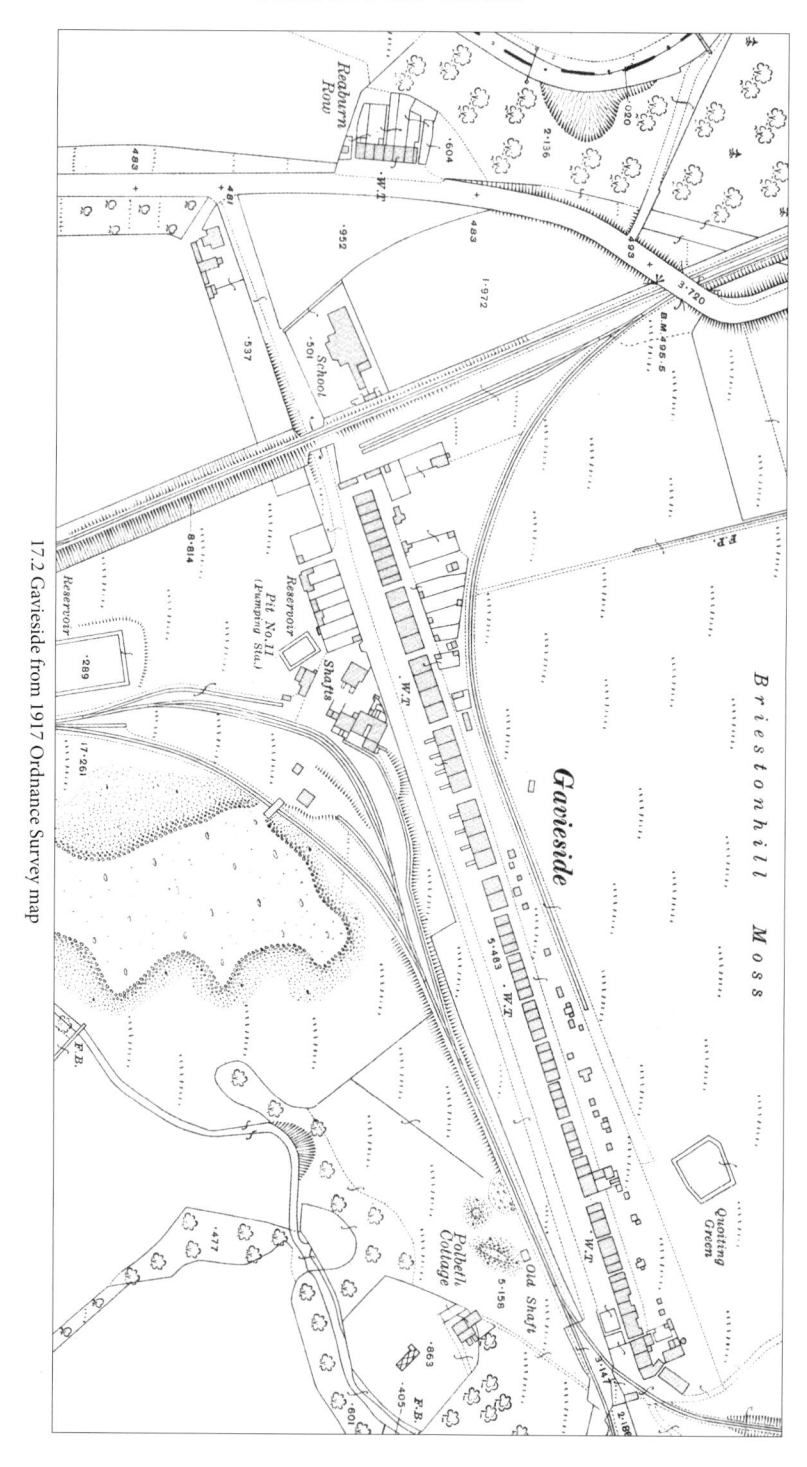

17.2 Gavieside from 1917 Ordnance Survey map

be played. The reading room was also used for various meetings and one or two weddings.

Football was played with some keenness around 1880 when Gavieside Football Club existed, playing in the junior leagues.

The menfolk of Gavieside worked in a variety of local mines. What was known as Pit Number 11 was located on the opposite side of the road from the main Gavieside row, a series of mineral lines leading into it, and a large pit bing rising up to the south-east of it. This pit appears to have been closed early in the twentieth century, but its pithead buildings were retained and acted as a pumping station.

In early references to Gavieside, it is sometimes referred to as 'Fell's Row'. This was after A. M. Fell, who was the first manager at the oil works and a partner in the West Calder Oil Company. There was also a seam of shale coal named after him. In 1914 Theodore K. Irvine carried out an inspection on the housing conditions at Gavieside and reported that:

> There are 8 single and 84 double houses, 44 of which are back to back. Many of the houses are below the level of the road, and rents range from 1/- to 2/3 per week. There are no coal cellars, wash-houses or sculleries. A few stand-pipes supply the water. The refuse is removed weekly. Dry privies of a kind exist. These houses are of a very poor type, and ought to be condemned.

There was a small co-operative society in the village. It was run by a committee of four – Robert Kinsman, David Brown, Alexander Fairley and Robert Fowler. In the shop Mary Brown and Helen Peden served the customers, though the choice of goods was limited. Nevertheless, Gavieside Co-op paid a dividend of four shillings in the pound. Three old ladies ran sweet shops from their houses, selling candy to the children.

On 16 March 1885 four men were killed at Gavieside Number 11 Pit and two others were injured, though the latter were not serious. The accident occurred at around six o'clock in the morning, when men were being lowered in the cage to the bottom of the shaft. Each cage-load held six men, and six or seven loads had already been lowered to the pit bottom when the cage became stuck around twenty fathoms down. The winding-man at the pit-head was not aware that the cage had stuck and continued unwinding the rope. This began to coil on the top of the cage, leaving the cage with no means of supporting itself, other than the fact that it had jammed.

Somehow, perhaps the movement of the men on board helped, the cage became unstuck, but with no rope to support it, plunged headlong down the shaft. When the rope eventually became taught, perhaps after the cage had fallen thirty fathoms or so, the cage came to a sudden halt. This had two effects – the jerk of the rope of the winding engine caused it to seize, and the sudden fall and stop threw four of the men from the cage. They fell down the remaining section of the pit shaft, landing at the bottom. The men killed were all fairly young – Alexander Bulloch (aged thirteen), who lived at 31 Clyde Street, West Calder; Thomas Dugan (aged nineteen), of 21 East Street, Mossend; Samuel MacCurley (aged twenty), of 20 East Street, Mossend; and Andrew Sanderson (aged fifteen), who lived in Gavieside Row. *The West Lothian Courier* gives a graphic account of their injuries:

> They were all frightfully bruised and mutilated. Dugan, it is said, being almost unrecognisable. MacCurley's skull had been fractured and his head otherwise injured; Sanderson's head had been fractured on the left side, while both arms were broken. Bulloch had been cut on the face and head, besides having his left thigh and right ankle broken.

The bodies were removed by way of Pit Number 21, which lay to the east and which was connected to Number 11 underground. The two men who survived had been badly shaken, their lights blown out by the fall, leaving them in darkness. Once the bodies and injured had been rescued, the pit was closed for the day.

At the time the incident took place, Number 11 Pit was regarded as one of the most profitable pits in the area, being just one of thirty pits owned by Young's Paraffin Light and Mineral Oil Company. The pit employed over 200 men and boys. The shaft was over seventy fathoms, or 420 feet, deep.

Other fatalities in the village occurred as a result of random accidents. These include the death of Michael Mackee, aged 45, who fell into the Mossend Burn on a Saturday in January 1901 as he was making his way home. His body was found the following morning by a young boy.

As with many mining communities, the number of men killed in the Great War was fewer than the size of the village would otherwise suggest. Mining was a reserved occupation, so only sons and others not employed there were called up. Gavieside lost six men in the First World War – Alexander Brown, Alexander Chapman, James Calder, Alexander Holmes, Thomas Martin and James Stones.

One son of Gavieside made a bit of a name for himself. Lawrence Ennis was born in Raeburn Row on 31 August 1871. He worked in the local pits from the age of twelve but in 1886 emigrated to the United States with his family. He worked in engineering, at first with the American Bridge Company and then with Dorman Long. From 1924-32 he lived in Australia where he was the manager during the construction of Sydney Harbour Bridge. When this was completed he returned to Britain and died on 5 May 1938.

With the closure of the local shale-coal mines, and the realisation that the condition of the housing was unsatisfactory, the village of Gavieside was identified for demolition in 1939. In March that year the residents were given notice to quit, and within a short period of time the first tenants moved to new houses built in the Polbeth scheme, adjoining West Calder. The outbreak of war meant that the clearance took longer than planned, and the last residents moved out later in the 1940s, after which the community was cleared away. Today, much of the site is covered in trees, although there are some newer buildings on site. Amongst these is the Five Sisters Zoo, established in 2005 to encourage the conservation of endangered species, with over 180 different species of mammals, birds and reptiles.

18
Glenbuck

✶

The furthest east one can be on a public road in Ayrshire is on the A70, Edinburgh to Ayr road, where it leaves the county at the old toll cottage at Glenbuck Loch. Local lore claims that the cottage is actually located in two counties, having been built exactly on the boundary when tolls were exacted on passing carts and other vehicles. Glenbuck Loch is an attractive sheet of water, nestling across the boundary line between two steep hills – Hareshaw Hill to the north and Bell Knowe to the south. At the dam a minor road strikes north, signposted Glenbuck. This leads to the site of the former village of that name – access to which is blocked by a locked gate – and to the former estate policies of Glenbuck House.

The village of Glenbuck will probably be remembered much longer than it might be, due to one thing – the legendary football manager, Bill Shankly, was born there. Shankly was to rise through the ranks of football to become one of the longest-serving and most respected of football managers ever. He made his name at Liverpool Football Club, and to this day fans of the team make a pilgrimage to the site of the old village to pay their respects. At the roadway into the old community, which has been totally obliterated by open-cast coal workings, stands a memorial stone, commemorating the fact that Shankly came from this place. The stone, erected in 1997, contains the inscription:

> Seldom in the history of sport can a village the size of Glenbuck have produced so many who reached the pinnacle of achievement in their chosen sport. This monument is dedicated to their memory and to the memory of one man in particular, Bill Shankly, the Legend, the Genius, the Man. Born – Glenbuck, Ayrshire, 2nd September 1913. Died – Liverpool, 29th September 1981. From Annfield with love. Thanks Shanks. Bill Shankly's achievements: Liverpool F. C. 1959-1974. League Champions 1963/64, 1965/6, 1972/73. Runners Up 1968/69, 1973/74. Second Division Champions 1961/62. F. A. Cup Winners 1964/65, 1973/74. Finalists 1970/71. U.E.F.A. Cup Winners 1972/73. European

Cup Winners Cup Finalists 1965/66. Semi-Finalists 1970/71. European Cup Semi-Finalists 1964/65. This plaque was laid on April 27th 1997 by Scottish Coal, Liverpool Away Supporters' Club, Network 5.

Bill Shankly was born at 2 Auchenstilloch Cottages, in Glenbuck, the son of John Shankly, who was employed in the mines. Bill was the youngest of five boys and five girls. The cottage was tiny, and as with many miners, the Shanklys were able to knock a hole through the wall to create a larger dwelling. Shankly was brought up in a footballing household, his elder brothers being accomplished players. Alec was to play for Ayr United and Clyde; James for Portsmouth, Sheffield United and Carlisle; John for Portsmouth, Blackpool and Alloa; and Robert for Alloa, Tunbridge Wells and Falkirk. Bill wished to play for Glenbuck Cherrypickers, but this team had folded before he was old enough. His first signing was with Cronberry Eglinton F. C., playing from 1931 until 1932. In December that year Shankly signed for Carlisle United, on a wage of £4 per week, before moving to Preston North End in 1933. He was to gain a Football Association Cup winner's medal with Preston in 1938. His skill on the field was recognised by the Scottish national side, and he was capped five times before the outbreak of war put his career on hold. In 1942 Bill played with Liverpool in a guest appearance against Everton. After the war, Shankly returned to Preston, where he was player and captain. In 1949 he was appointed as manager at Carlisle, moving quickly from team to team thereafter – from Carlisle to Grimsby, Workington, and Huddersfield, before being appointed as Liverpool manager on 1 December 1959.

Liverpool was languishing in the second division at that time, but their fortunes were about to change, guided by a man who lived and breathed football. Within a few years they had moved up the second division, winning it in 1962. Back in the first division they only took two years to win it, after which they became a mighty force in English football. In 1973 Shankly's Liverpool won the EUFA cup, beating favourites Borussia Monchengladbach. He announced his retirement on 12 July 1974. He died in Liverpool on 29 September 1981.

Bill Shankly never forgot Glenbuck. He was to write in his memoirs that, 'Life was not easy in the village when we were growing up. No disrespect to Glenbuck, but you could have been as far away from civilization in Outer Mongolia. The winters were cold and bitter with four months of snow.'

18.1 Glenbuck from south-east showing school to left of centre

In addition to the memorial at Glenbuck, a statue of Shankly was unveiled at Annfield on Thursday 4 December 1997. The statue was sculpted by Tom Murphy, depicting Bill with his arms outstretched, greeting his adoring fans. With his Liverpool scarf around his neck, he is cheering on the team he made his own. As the statue was being crafted, various folk who knew Bill added their comments, from his tailor, who advised on buttons, to his wife, who added a piece of clay to the work.

Bill Shankly is remembered for many amusing footballing quotes, the most famous being the time when he said that, 'Some people believe football is a matter of life and death, I am very disappointed with that attitude. I can assure you it is much, much more important than that.' He also said, 'If you are first you are first – if you are second, you are nothing.' Others were, 'The trouble with referees is that they know the rules, but they don't know the game,' and 'Football is a simple game based on the giving and taking of passes, of controlling the ball and of making yourself available to receive a pass. It's terribly simple.'

The name, Glenbuck Cherrypickers, was originally a nickname, but the team grew to like it and it eventually became its official title. How the name came about is not known now – there are stories of some of the lads marching along the street as though they were in the 11th Hussars, also nicknamed Cherrypickers; or of the team meeting outside the village shop, run by Milliken, where a basket of cherries was on display. When the team broke up and returned home, the basket was empty. Or could it be a nickname given to the team from those outwith the area, describing them as cherrypickers – folk who picked the stones from the coal in the pit.

In any case, Glenbuck Athletic Football Club was formed in 1888 and was to show their skills early on by winning the Ayrshire Junior Cup in season 1888-89. Proving that this was no fluke, the club won the trophy the following year, and again in 1890-91. In 1906 three cups fell to their skills – the Ayrshire Charity Cup, the Cumnock Cup and the Mauchline Cup.

The team was to produce fifty players who went on to have professional footballing careers. Indeed, Rev M. H. Faulds wrote that, 'It can be safely claimed that no village of similar size in all Scotland has a record to equal that of Glenbuck. Altogether, the Glenbuck story is a remarkable page in football history.' Seven sons of the glen were to be capped for Scotland – Bill Shankly (13 times), John Crosbie (twice), Alec Brown (twice), Tommy Brown (twice), Robert Shankly (once), George Halley (once) and William Muir (once). Alec Brown is claimed to have almost single-handedly won the F. A. Cup for Tottenham Hotspur in 1901, scoring four goals against Sheffield in the semi-final and the solitary goal against Southampton in the final. Another notable footballer from the village was Robert Blyth, better known as 'Reindeer', an uncle of Bill Shankly. Local tales claim that he could run 100 yards in eleven seconds wearing his football boots. Another soccer family was the Knox's. There were five sons, Hugh, Alec, Tom, William and Peter. In addition to playing in various teams, they often entered five-a-side competitions, where they excelled. In fact, in one single year they won 40 of the 41 tournaments that they had entered.

Glenbuck as a village dates back to the mid-eighteenth century. The wild countryside of Muirkirk parish was prospected for its possible minerals, and in 1795 an English-based company, led by John Rumney of Workington, took

18.2 Glenbuck Parish Church

a lease on the lands of East Glenbuck farm. In the valley of the Stottencleugh Burn an ironworks was established, located at the east end of what was to become the village. The works were in operation by late 1796 and produced iron from the ironstone mined in the hills thereabouts.

Glenbuck ironworks produce was widely distributed initially, with iron being exported as far as Ireland. The company also found some lasting fame in the fact that it manufactured the rails used in what was to be Scotland's first railway, the line from Kilmarnock to Troon. This was laid in 1810 by the Duke of Portland as a means of quickly transporting coals from his Kilmarnock area collieries to the harbour, from where it was exported to Ireland and elsewhere.

The order for iron rails was considerable. In 1810 it was noted that the contract was for 70,000 cast iron rails, an order worth around £20,000. Other sizeable orders that are known include one for cast iron water pipes for the Belfast and Dublin water committees.

Being isolated and remote from any nearby centre of population, houses were built for the workers. Perhaps the oldest was a row of six houses, built in a single terrace, overlooking the ironworks from the hillside above. This was known as Stair Row.

As with almost every ironworks in Scotland, apart from the Carron works at Stenhousemuir, the works at Glenbuck found themselves in difficulties during the Napoleonic Wars. The company was to go bankrupt in 1813. The buildings and machinery appear to have still remained fairly extant for decades thereafter, for on 23 May 1845 an advertisement appeared in the *Glasgow Herald* offering the works for sale, informing prospective purchasers that the furnace could 'be relit at little expense.' Despite the manufacture of iron in Scotland being a growing industry, the works were to remain unsold. Some old stonework associated with the works remained behind the Jubilee Row for many years.

The village went into decline once more, and it wasn't until a new, larger ironworks was established at Muirkirk that the demand for coal and ironstone grew again. Dozens of mines and pits were created across the parish, and many of these were to be found in the Glenbuck area. By 1856, when the Ordnance Survey passed through, making their maps, the village was well established. The old row of six houses still survived near the ruins of the old ironworks. Near it, but to the west, were three other houses, and in a building that may have originally been part of the ironworks was a school. It is known that the schoolmaster in the early 1800s was Thomas Clyde, as he was a creditor of the ironworks when it closed. Unfortunately, so, too, were many of the residents of Glenbuck, who had been issued with promissory tickets in lieu of wages by the company.

18.3 Glenbuck from west, with post office to right

To the west, almost a separate community, was the rest of Glenbuck, in 1856 consisting of four rows of houses, built on either side of the road that crossed the Stottencleugh Burn Bridge Number One. At the eastern side was a block of three houses, built in a bend of the stream, at angles to the road. On the west side of the bridge, on the south side of the road, was a row of three or four homes.

On the north side of the road, heading west from the bridge, was a row of seven small cottages. Immediately west of this was another row of six houses. These houses all had their own garden ground. In addition to the rows mentioned, there were a couple of solitary houses in the valley, some of which may have been shepherd's cottages or managers' homes.

The old pits at Glenbuck were comparatively small, but successfully excavated coal for many years. One of them was known as The Davy Pit (its name has been spelled variously at Davy, Davey, and Davie), its old chimney standing long after the pit had closed in 1906, until it was deemed unsafe and was demolished in 1915. The Davy Pit was operated by the Cairntable Gas Coal Company Limited. Around this time a new colliery was being sunk at Glenbuck by Burnbank Coal Company.

Death in the pits was all too common, and many miners were to lose their lives underground. Among those who died were the following selection. Thomas Haugh, an engineman, was killed on Sunday 16 June 1884 when his head was crushed by the connecting rod of the water engine wheels. Haugh had been cleaning them at the time. An unmarried man, he was only twenty years of age. On Friday 17 June 1887, at the Davy Pit, a fall of stone from the pit roof killed John Dunbar and injured three others – two of whom were his sons. A fall of stone from Galawhistle Pit on 17 October 1894 killed Thomas Davidson, a Glenbuck miner. A large lump of coal fell on William Reid in the same pit on 15 April 1899, killing him instantaneously. In Grasshill Pit, Archibald Allison was killed when he was struck by a hutch on 20 July 1922. He was only eighteen years of age and lived with his parents in Glenbuck's Grasshill Row.

By 1895 Glenbuck had grown considerably. A new large coal mine, Grasshill Number 2 pit, had been established at the west end of the village, and to house the workers a new row had been built between the pit and the western community. Grasshill Row contained 33 two-apartment houses built in a single terrace. Five coal-houses existed for the use of the families, and small allotments were located between the road and the houses. The second row of houses on the north side of the road, west of Stottencleugh Bridge, had been demolished.

When the housing inspectors visited Glenbuck in 1913 they only looked at Grasshill Row. At the time three of the houses were empty, but the remaining thirty houses had a population of 123 living in them. The rent payable to the owners, William Baird & Company, was 7s per lunar month. For this the residents shared a dry-closet per four homes. These were rather unusual in that they had sparred gates which could be locked, but which inside had seating for two persons! The houses themselves had two rooms, the kitchen having a floor space of fifteen feet by twelve feet, the room twelve feet by nine feet. The floors were made of wood and a gravitational water supply was piped to the row from Hareshaw Hill.

Although the Grasshill Row was newer than many of the houses at Glenbuck, it suffered from large cracks in the walls. These were blamed on the mossy land the insufficient foundations were laid on, plus the vibrations caused by the engines passing along the railway sidings at the coalpit, located immediately behind.

East of the bridge, on the north side of the road, were four houses in a block, plus some additional buildings. On the south side, in an angle of a field, were

GLENBUCK

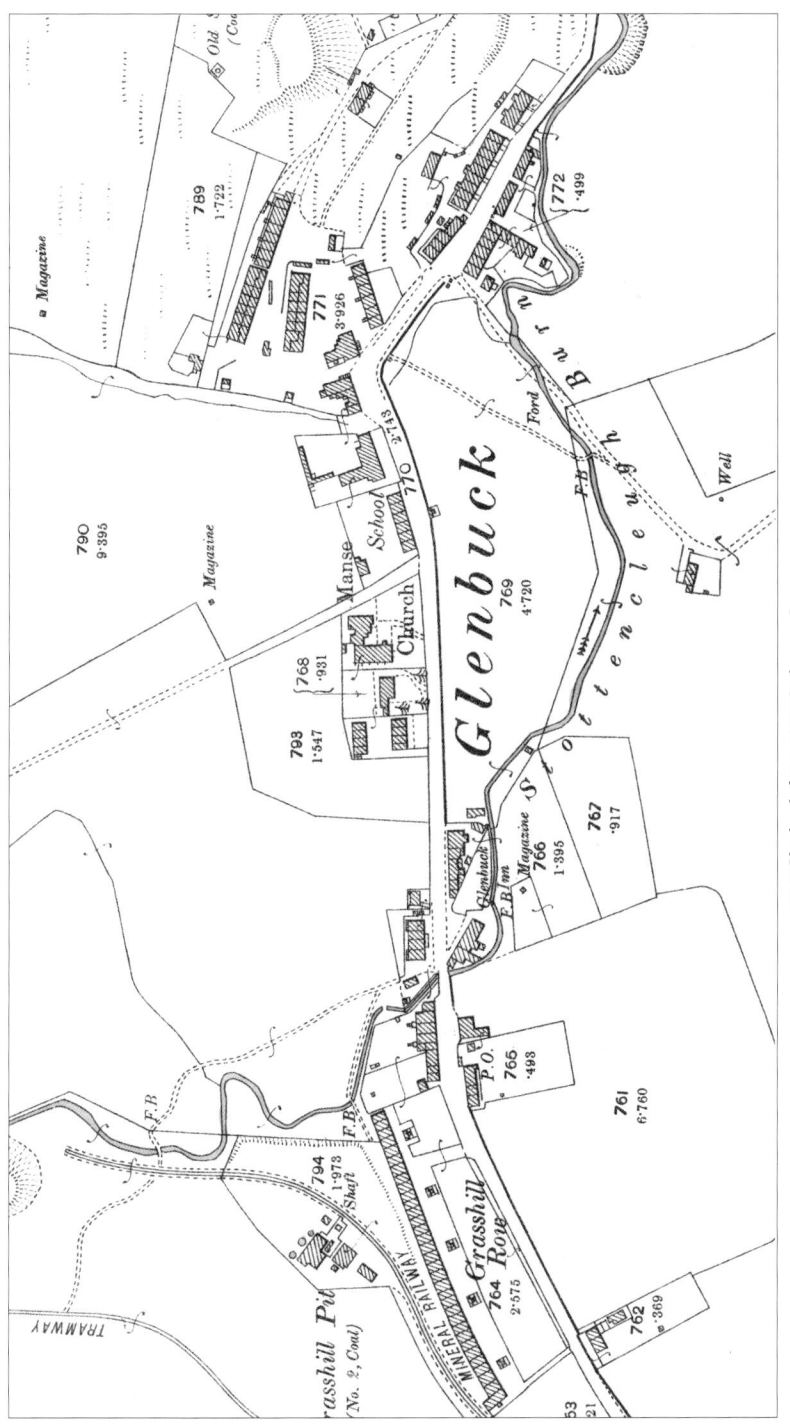

18.4 Glenbuck from 1896 Ordnance Survey map

another four or five homes. Here also was the Glenbuck Inn, or the Royal Arms Inn as it was later to be known. It was placed on the market in 1925 and was acquired by John Wilson of the Empire Bar, Muirkirk. In 1951 the license was transferred to Alexander V. Hazle of Glenbuck.

The two halves of Glenbuck had, by 1900, been joined to form one community, with houses and other facilities erected in the gap between. In the centre a stone-built church was opened on 16 July 1882, designed by the Ayrshire architect, Robert Ingram. To its side was a substantial manse, and around both were extensive grounds. The church was served by four ministers over its lifetime. On the front wall of the church building was a large stone with an inscription commemorating the local Covenanting martyrs. The church was closed in May 1954. The building stood for many years but was demolished in late 1994. The Covenanter stone was saved at the time of demolition and relocated to Muirkirk churchyard.

In addition to the parish church, there was a hall associated with the Brethren in the village. This was established in 1887 by the keen members of Lesmahagow assembly who seem to have spent much of their time in other communities, spreading the word. The assembly at Glenbuck continued to exist until 1954.

Just to the west of the church was a large house, occupied by the village schoolmaster. To the west of the schoolhouse was a small pair of rows, four homes in each. This was known as Auchinstilloch Row, but to the locals was better known as the Monkey Row. The cottages were placed on the market in 1923 but didn't sell. They were subsequently sold privately.

East of the church was a row of six houses, built facing directly onto the road. This was known as Spireslack Row and was built by William Baird & Company. The houses were small single-storey structures, and by 1914 they had been reconfigured into three pairs, to allow for greater space.

Between this row and the old row of three houses at Eastern Glenbuck was a new school, erected in 1875-6. A substantial building, two large gables faced the main road, with hipped gables to the east and west. With the increasing population in Glenbuck, the old school was deemed insufficient for the number of children in attendance. Whilst a new school was being built, the children were educated in a byre at West Glenbuck farm. During the winter of 1875-6 it was so cold that schooling had to be abandoned for a few months.

The new school was opened on Monday 13 March 1876. A total of 106 children enrolled but were immediately given a week's holiday, whilst the painters completed work inside. The only teacher employed at the time was W. S. Baikie. He had a number of struggles to contend with, for when payment was due to the school board, many pupils failed to turn up. Similarly, when a new text book was introduced in 1878, those families who couldn't afford it kept their children at home. A parent who was called to Cumnock J. P. Court that year for not paying the fees was sent to jail because he was unable to afford them.

In 1881 the school was extended, and attendance increased to 220 the following year. The closure of Lady Pit resulted in families moving away, and the school roll fell to 140. New pits being sunk brought back the population, and in 1889 the roll had increased to 220. By 1900 the roll was in the region of 300, perhaps its highest. In 1921 the pupils were delighted at the introduction of flushing toilets. Declining with Glenbuck itself, the roll fell to 42 in 1939 and to 33 in 1947. The school was closed for good in August 1951.

North of the original row of six houses were two rows of homes, built on the hillside. The front row had sixteen houses in it, built back to back with each other. This row was two storeys in height, the homes accessed from the northern side. Most of the houses were occupied by colliers, but by 1914 two of the houses were empty.

Behind this row was a second row, comprising of two terraces of houses almost joined to each other, but separated by a narrow close. The western block was a twin of the front row, with twelve houses. The row to the east had eight houses in it, all double-storey. These houses were known as New Terrace, but by 1914 all of them were empty and uninhabitable.

In the glen, where once the ironworks was located, a street of houses was formed, the buildings facing each other. Six houses were built onto the north-western end of the old school, which was converted into two houses. This became known as Old School Row. Double-storey in height, the buildings were covered with hipped roofs and the upstairs flats were accessed from external stairs to the rear.

South-east of the old school was a new row of nine houses, and next to it was a block of two larger homes. This row, which had single storey dwellings, was known as the Jubilee Row. The pair of houses was known as Rowanbank. In 1914 here lived Robert Anderson, collier, in the first house, with Constable George Forsyth in the police house next door.

On the opposite side of the street, an L-shaped block of ten homes occupied a meander of the burn, and east of this were two blocks of two houses. This was known as the Office Row. The houses were single storey in height, the houses in the close being rather small, only having a front door and window facing the lane. On the hillside above the old ironworks was a pair of houses, with small gardens to their rear. These cottages were known as Braehead.

In 1929 two new blocks of council houses were erected at Glenbuck and in November 1930 were let to the first tenants. As with many old mining communities, the name of the street was rather uninspiring – they were called 'Council Houses'! One of the families that moved into the new homes were the Shanklys, who were given the keys to number 5. The welcome addition of a bath and running hot water was to be a boon that they never experienced in their old home.

The Glenbuck Co-operative Society was established in 1887 and had a store in the village. The society had a bit of trouble in getting started, for the mine-owners weren't keen on the proposals, preferring that the residents spent their little money in the company store. At length, the farmer at West Glenbuck, James Callan, agreed that if the tenant of his cottage was to leave, the society could have it for a shop. This occurred, and on 7 May 1887 it opened for business. At first there were only fourteen members, but this quickly grew to 140 at its peak. At a meeting in 1953 it was agreed to close the society, merging the stock with that of Muirkirk Co-op. The shop at Glenbuck was then closed, and villagers had to buy their provisions from a mobile shop that came from Muirkirk.

Other commercial properties in the village included Messrs Bain & Sons, who operated a fruit shop at the building known as The Castle. Bain's premises were destroyed by fire in 1960. The post office in Glenbuck was run by the Muir family for 68 years, at the Post Office Row, opposite the Grasshill Row. Mrs Muir had taken over the job of postmistress in 1894 and served until 1912. Mrs John Muir followed until 1946, and Mrs David Muir until 1960. After this the postmistress was Mrs Anderson, whose husband owned a small mine near Ponesk.

Glenbuck had a poor supply of water for many years, despite being in an area of high rainfall and with the Stottencleugh Burn passing right through it. Up to 1909 water was drawn from local wells, one of which was located at the end of the Office Row. In that year James Young of Muirkirk was given the contract to create a new supply of water from Hareshaw Hill, piped into water valves.

The local landowner at Glenbuck for many years was Charles Howatson. He was born in 1832 at Cronberry farm, in Auchinleck parish. He always claimed that farming, sheep-breeding and Covenanting were unusually strong in his pedigree. He worked for Bairds and when that company (as the Eglinton Iron Company) acquired Muirkirk Ironworks in 1856 he was appointed as manager at the age of 23. He retired from the business in 1870. In 1859 he was married to Wilhelmina Fletcher, whose ancestors were Airds of Crossflatt. He inherited this Muirkirk farm on her death. In 1865 he acquired Dornal estate and in 1872 bought Glenbuck estate, previously owned by Col. Dickson of the Cumberland Iron Company. Howatson bought a pen of ewe hogs that were to take first place at Ayr Show in 1864. He went on to breed numerous successful rams and in 1909 was paid a record price of £250 for St Columba at Lanark market. He gained some fame from breeding top blackface sheep, resulting in them producing a heavier fleece. His sheep were to win top prizes at various agricultural shows, especially the Royal Highland Show, where he won consecutively for many years. In 1880 he erected Glenbuck House. Charles Howatson died in 1918 and is buried in Auchinleck kirkyard. He was succeeded by his only son, Captain Charles Nile Howatson, who died in 1924.

Glenbuck House was designed by the Ayr architect, John Murdoch, in the neo-baronial style that was in vogue at the time. Around the house Howatson planted woodlands, and the immediate policies were decorated with ornate gates and stonework. The house was demolished in 1948. Today, visitors can walk through the former policies towards the bird hide on Glenbuck Loch. In spring the woods are awash with snowdrops and daffodils. Old iron fences line the roads and the stone walls that survive here and there hinting at lost glories.

A new Public Hall had been erected west of the houses next to the schoolhouse. This served the community until the Second World War. The hall was closed with a declining population, but in 1948 it was taken over by Replin Company who established a textile finishing factory there. In 1953 the final meeting of a church group in Glenbuck Public Hall finished and it was expected the wooden building would be demolished soon after. However, the building went up in flames early on Monday 19 October, destroying everything.

As with most mining villages, there were plenty of organisations to entertain the residents. Amongst those in existence at Glenbuck were the

Glenbuck Yearly Friendly Society (a temperance organisation), as well as the Priesthill Tent of the Order of Rechabiltes, founded on 23 October 1897. In 1903 the John Brown Tent was opened for juvenile members – it was named in honour of the famous local Covenanting martyr, John Brown of Priesthill, who was martyred on the other side of the hill from the village. In 1913 there were 79 state members, 76 order members and 90 juvenile members.

A murder committed at Glenbuck in 1908 brought some national newspaper attention. Thomas Bone, junior (aged 28), was charged with the murder of his wife, who was nineteen years of age. He was taken to Glasgow High Court, where he was found guilty. He was sentenced to hang at Ayr prison on 29 May 1908. However, the day before he was due to be executed he received a reprieve from the Secretary of State for Scotland, his sentence being commuted to one of life imprisonment. Bone was sent to Perth jail to carry out his sentence, but on 13 November 1912, whilst the warder had a fifteen-minute break from watching him, he took a bedsheet, tied it around his neck, and hung himself from a hook on the wall. When the warder returned and found him, his body was still warm, but he couldn't be revived.

It wasn't just great football players that Glenbuck produced. The village was also noted for its famous quoiters. Tom Bone (1868-1916) was the top quoit player in the county, especially at 21 yards. He was born in Glenbuck and lived there all of his life. He started playing as a youth, and at the age of twenty became renowned beyond his village for his skill. It was said that he could throw a quoit from 21 yards and land it around a watch. In 1888 he played the noted quoiter of the period, James MacMurdo, at Cumnock, beating him by 61-42. He won the Scottish Championship in 1889 for the first time, and in 1908 won the British Championship, beating the English champion, James Hood of Liverpool. Locally, the annual competition was played for the Ballochmyle silver quoit, and Bone won the trophy fourteen times. He was to sustain an eye injury at the pit, affecting his play thereafter. He died on 15 November 1916, having never married. A new quoiting green was opened at Glenbuck on 30 April 1904. The first game played thereon was against Muirkirk, the home team winning 76-63.

The closure of Grasshill pits was the start of the decline at Glenbuck. The pits, which employed around 200 men, around 150 of which lived in Glenbuck, were first closed in May 1932, but after a period of five months were re-opened in October. The pits closed again in 1933 and were never to re-open. In 1935 most of Office Row was demolished, as was the whole of Old School Row, totalling sixteen houses.

The annual Glenbuck Old Folks' Re-Union started in 1924 and ran for many years. Speakers were invited to the village to tell of their reminiscences, the first speaker being John Rodger, headmaster of the school from 1889-1927.

In 2005 there were plans to create a new village at Glenbuck. Scottish Coal Company Ltd applied for planning permission to develop Glenbuck farm into a series of new low-impact houses and crofts. These were to be located on the site of the village, on what had been an open cast coal mine. However, these proposals never materialised.

The visitor to Glenbuck today can find little of the former community surviving. Low walls indicating Rowanbank can be seen at the roadside. Behind this the stonework of the former ironworks can be seen, built into the hillside, the arched opening the only real distinctive feature. A few walls of the manse garden remain, as do a number of mature trees that formerly grew in the church grounds. Further west, slight remains of walls can be seen to the rear of the former post office. The only substantial ruins remaining are those of Spireslack farm, located slightly to the north, the roof crumbling and the roughcast scaling from the sandstone house. From the front door one can look south over where once a thriving community existed, nowadays blighted by the remains of an open cast coal mine.

19

Haywood

*

There are still one or two cottages and buildings at the lost village of Haywood, or Crooklands and Haywood, as it was sometimes known. A minor road striking across the moor to the east of Forth in Lanarkshire makes its way to Bughtknowes, a farm. Just short of the farm is a row of modern council houses, virtually all that remains of the former community here. The public road strikes east at Bughtknowes, and shortly takes a left turn, heading to the little village of Auchengray. Just round this corner, a few hundred yards along the road, is the cottage known as the Old Manse. As its name suggests, this was the home of the minister of the local church. This stood in the same grounds as the manse, serving the local community for most of its lifetime.

Haywood Parish Church was erected in 1878 as a chapel-of-ease associated with Carnwath Parish Church. The first minister was Rev Andrew Thomson, who served there from its creation until 1884, when he gave up the charge and moved to Perth to become assistant minister at St Paul's Parish Church. He was replaced by Rev Gilbert Clark, who was ordained on 3 October 1884. The church and congregation grew in strength so much that on 28 May 1897 it was disjoined from Carnwath and erected into a parish of its own. Rev Clark was thus admitted as the first minister of the parish. He was married in 1919 to Ada Barrow. Rev Clark was quite literary in his lifetime, publishing *Home, and Other Poems and Songs*, in 1889 and a translation of the poetry of Frederick von Schiller in 1898. He died in 1930. Haywood Church served the community for around fifty years, before the congregation was to merge with that at Wilsontown, after which the church building fell into decline and was demolished. The tower had become unstable, resulting in its quick demolition.

Most Ordnance Survey maps spell the name of the village as Haywood, but it is usually pronounced as 'hey-wid' or 'hey-wood', where hey is pronounced in the Scottish way, rhyming with the 'I' in file, not lie. Some accounts, such as the *Ordnance Gazetteer*, spell the village name as Heywood. The first house in the community was Mine Cottage, erected between Tashieburn and Parkhouse in 1858 and occupied by the pit gaffer. By 1860 many other rows had been added, including the old School Row, where the original schoolroom was located, latterly converted into a house occupied by Dr Thomson.

The nearest part of Haywood village to the church was a pair of terraced back-to-back houses which lay on the north side of the road from Crooklands. The north-eastern terrace had twenty-four houses in the group, a dozen facing the main road, a second dozen facing north-west over the back yards to the mineral railway that made its way to Haywood Colliery's Pit Number 8, and other pits at Harryfoothill (where there was a lost terrace of eight houses) and beyond. The south-western group of houses was almost identical to the other, with twelve houses facing the road. However, on the back side of this row, eight of the houses were joined together to form larger dwellings. A narrow lane between the two blocks of housing led to the wash-house to the rear. This group of houses was known as Loan Street.

The bulk of Haywood village was located to the south of this, most of the community built on the south side of the Auchengray and Wilsontown Branch line of the Caledonian Railway. Two bridges crossed the railway and sidings, bringing one to the main community. On the left was the village store. Most of the buildings in Haywood were built of brick, manufactured at the nearby Auchengray Brickworks. The opening up of the coalfields in the area led to the creation of the village to provide accommodation for the miners. In the 1830s

19.1 Haywood from the north (South Lanarkshire Council)

the first mines were sunk by Thomas Nimmo. Things moved up a gear in 1862 when the Coltness Iron Company started working the gas coal below the ground, but this firm remained in the district for just a few years. The Haywood Gas Coal Company then took on the lease, and it was this company who operated in the area for the next 35 years, or so.

The Haywood branch of West Calder Co-operative Society was a single-storey building, divided into two parts. On the left was the shop, reached through a door. To the right was the main shop, the entrance door protected by a timber porch. The store had reasonably-sized windows, compared with the miners' cottages, in which were usually displayed shelves of tinned goods and other produce. The building was nothing special, being built of brick with a low-pitched roof and chimneys at the gables. The initial plans for a local branch of the co-operative resulted in much squabbling in the area. There were two sides to the argument – build it either in Haywood or else in Wilsontown. A compromise deal of building it at the little row of houses at Tashieburn was thrown out as the community was too far from either of the larger communities and would mean that a walk of one mile in each direction would be required to purchase provisions. The Rt Hon Akers Douglas MP, owner of much of the surrounding countryside, agreed to lease a site suitable for the shop in Haywood. This was signed off in September 1894 and after a quick erection, the shop was opened on Christmas Day in 1894. President of the society, James Potter, performed the opening ceremony. He was presented with a silver key by the builder of the shop, John Fairley. Once the shop started business, the first manager was James Blair.

Adjoining the shop was the group of houses known as Store Square. Six houses were built onto the store complex of buildings, and next to them were a block of four houses on the same side of Store Square. These four cottages were latterly converted into one house, Pentland View, and it survives, being restored in 2018. As with most of the buildings at Haywood, it was built of red bricks, with yellow-brick surrounds to the windows and doors. On the south side of Store Square was a long block of back-to-back homes, totalling twenty-four houses. The south side of these houses was classed as being in Lorne Street.

To the south of Store Square's houses was a hall. This was built onto the north end of a row of double-houses, eighteen in number. Following on to the south again was a second block of back-to-back homes, twenty-four in number. These two blocks had different addresses – the houses on the east side being classed as Princess Street, those on the west being Hope Street.

19.2 Haywood Store (South Lanarkshire Council)

To the west of Hope Street were five lines of housing, built nominally at right angles to Hope Street. The northernmost one had sixteen back-to-back houses. The north side of these were in Lorne Street, the southern side in Ann Street. A wide courtyard separated this terrace with a second block, containing twenty-four homes. The north side was in Ann Street, the south side in Victoria Street.

The south side of Victoria Street was part of a block of twenty-four back-to-back houses. This block had houses facing south over Pool Square to another block of twenty-four homes. The street on the south side of this block was known as Lothian Street.

The southernmost block of houses perpendicular to Hope Street had twenty-four back-to-back homes in it, the northern side overlooking Lothian Street, the south Pool Street.

Built at right angles to Pool Street was a block of two dozen houses, in the same style as most of Haywood. The terrace facing north-east was known as High Street, the other side of the back-to-back houses being known as Moor Street.

Returning to the Store, on the right of the road heading south was another series of buildings. To the right was Bank Street, with twelve houses facing north-west. At the end of this row were a number of larger adjoining buildings.

On the north side of the street, centrally placed, was a small building which was occupied by the post office around 1900. This was a sub-office under Lanark. By 1910 this post office had closed and it was relocated to a building on the south side of New Park Street.

Built at right angles to Bank Street was a block of eight larger houses. The south side of the Bank Street houses was known as Bank Square, with the same quantity of houses. The south side of the square had a block of double-sided houses, twenty-four in number. The south side of this block faced onto Park Square.

The south side of Park Square had twelve houses facing it, to their rear being another twelve, facing onto New Park Street. At the end of New Park Street was a building occupied by the village constable as a police station and policeman's house.

Between New Park Street and the end of Lothian Street was a rectangular block of land, located on which were a variety of buildings. The oldest of these was Greenbank, an older row of three cottages, shown on the Ordnance Survey map of 1860. This may originally have been a small farm. Ruinous walls from the buildings survive. One window sill has the following lines carved into it:

> Oh Annie, wert thou here tae see,
> Woefu wumin thou wad be.

On the north side of the mineral railway that made its way to Haywood Pit Number 4 was a number of industrial buildings, with a railway siding into it.

A further row of houses, known as Station Row, was located to the north of this industrial group, lying alongside the Wilsontown railway. Although they were built in the back-to-back style usual in Haywood, this row had a total of 32 houses in it. An open drain ran along the southern side of the row, and on the southern side of this was an area of open ground, here and there covered with mature trees. This was the site of Lower Haywood farm, the steading of which disappeared not long after the village was created.

Just to the west of this row was Haywood Station, the stationmaster for a time being John Paymor, assisted by his son, also John. They lived in a cottage at Station Row. The goods train which passed through at 6.00 am had an additional carriage in which miners could travel to their work.

19.3 Haywood War Memorial

On the road from Bughtknowes back to Forth were a few buildings associated with Haywood. Here was the Stone Row, five houses built at angles to the road. Just to the west of this was the School Row, six houses built back to back.

Haywood Public School followed. This has been demolished, leaving only fragmentary remains, such as part of the playground wall with gate piers. One of the schoolmasters was Matthew Biggar. Haywood also had a village institute, opened in December 1922. Although just a small building constructed of corrugated iron over timber walls, with an asbestos-tiled roof, it had the distinction of being the first ever miners' institute to be funded by the Miners' Welfare Scheme. Inside, the hall was lined with timber, and it had the additional facilities of toilets and retiring rooms. The hall was used for many meetings in the community.

In addition to the co-op, there were a few other small commercial premises in Haywood, though the co-op affected their trade and, in some cases, killed them off completely. At the Square was Hugh Dunn's licensed grocery and public house, where men could purchase beer. It survived much longer than most of the others, due to its doubling as a pub. At the top of the village was William Kechan's shop at Greenbank. It, too, sold alcohol and survived until 1920, the last proprietor being Robert Brown, a baker from Hamilton. He carried out deliveries in the district, his wife Annie operating the shop, even after his death. Other shops included John Haughan's, Dominic O'Donnell's and Mary Ann Nimmo's.

19.4 Haywood – ruins of Greenbank

A few other residents ran businesses of a different sort. Pat Muldoon was a shoemaker and there was even a clockmaker in the village for a time. James Hamilton, William Donaldson and his son ran a tailoring businesses and Susan Ross was a dressmaker, assisted by her daughter, Margaret.

In addition to the parish church, there was an assembly of Christian Brethren in Haywood, established in 1883. This continued to meet for over forty years, the brethren relocating to Wilsontown in the 1930s as the village declined. The group moved again in 1936 to the larger, and longer-lasting community of Forth.

The local football team was known as Haywood Wanderers, established sometime around 1884. Their home ground was a block of grass at the southern end of Number 8 Row. This was not the regulation size, so they moved to a new field near to Greenbank. They played in blue and white with considerable success for many years, and it is claimed that they were never beaten in any home game over a period of eleven years. Indeed, they were often claimed to be 'the dirtiest team in Scotland,' which probably explains why they were so intimidating when playing at home. The club was disbanded at the outbreak of the First World War and was never reformed. Another team which played at Haywood was Haywood Rangers, active around 1897-8. Haywood Brass Band was formed in 1869.

In the Census of 1871 Haywood had a population of 793. This increased to 1,121 ten years later, and by 1891 it had reached 1,206. It is claimed that the upper limit of the population was around 1,400.

When mining began to decline in the area, the population of Haywood followed suit. Some of the rows were cleared away, as depicted on the Ordnance Survey map of 1910. The earliest to be demolished were the five blocks which formed High Street, Moor Street, Pool Street, Lothian Street, Pool Square, and the south side of Victoria Street. The southern block of Princess and Hope streets was also removed. The block of houses on the north side of Park Square and the south side of Bank Square was removed, as was the block at the west end of Bank Square. The Station Row was cleared away by 1910.

In 1910, when a survey was made of miners' housing, the community was seriously in decline. The inspectors noted that the mine had closed about ten years earlier, after which the houses passed back to the landowners and were now in private ownership. With no work, most of the residents had moved on, and many homes were unoccupied. It was reckoned that there had been around 240 houses, but by June 1901 there were only 114, of which only fifty or so were occupied. By 1910 this number had increased once more, to about 81. Of this

19.5 Haywood – inscribed window sill at Greenbank

number 57 were tenanted by miners. Single-apartment houses were leased at a rental of £3 18s, whereas two-apartment homes were rented at £6 1s 4d.

The inspectors compiled a short summary of the state of the houses, noting that they had been erected around 1870, were built of brick with slate roofs, but that they had no damp courses – with obvious results. Many roofs did not have rhones or downpipes. The internal walls were not strapped and lathed. The

19.6 Haywood Parish Church (South Lanarkshire Council)

floors were of wood, but these were unventilated. Many internal surfaces of the walls and ceilings were broken, and some ceilings were made from wood panelling. It was reckoned that there was no overcrowding in the village. Some houses had gardens, and these were cultivated. The village had a gravitation water supply, and most residents had commandeered an empty house to use as a wash-house. Originally, water came from a local pit bottom, being pumped into a reservoir in the centre of the village, from where the water flowed by gravity to a single pump. The privies, located in the courtyard, were in a broken condition, and there were no sinks. Each home had a coal cellar. Scavenging in the community was carried out at the owners' expenses, as and when required.

19.7 Haywood Wanderers Football Club (South Lanarkshire Council)

In the 1990s mining for coal by open-cast or surface mining came into the area. The lands to the north-east of Haywood were excavated firstly, east of Burnfoot farm, but this had little impact on the site of the village. However, a second opencast, stretching from Wilsontown right to the edge of the former community came in the new millennium, obliterating the fields and moors to the west of the village.

There is little to show of the village of Haywood today. One thing that does survive, however, is the village war memorial. This was originally positioned among the rows themselves, but it was relocated to a more accessible spot in recent years, near to Crooklands farm. The old marble panels have been rebuilt in a new memorial, with a stone-built surrounding wall. The inscription reads:

In loving memory of men from the village of Haywood who sacrificed their lives in the Great War 1914-1918.

There follows a list of names – Private Alex Allan (Royal Scots), Private James Ashwood (Highland Light Infantry), Private Alex Brown (Northumberland Fusiliers), Gunner Peter Burnside (Royal Fleet Auxiliary), Private Thomas Carruthers (Royal Scots Fusiliers), Private Alex Davidson (H.L.I.), Gunner Hugh Dunn (R.F.A.), Private David Morrison (H.L.I.), Corporal David Thomson (H.L.I), Private Alex Waddell (Royal Scots) and James Whigham (Cameronian Highlanders). A second panel adds names from 1939-1945 - Private James Little (Seaforth Highlanders), Corporal James Barrie (Royal Fusiliers) and Sergeant John Walkingshaw (Royal Air Force).

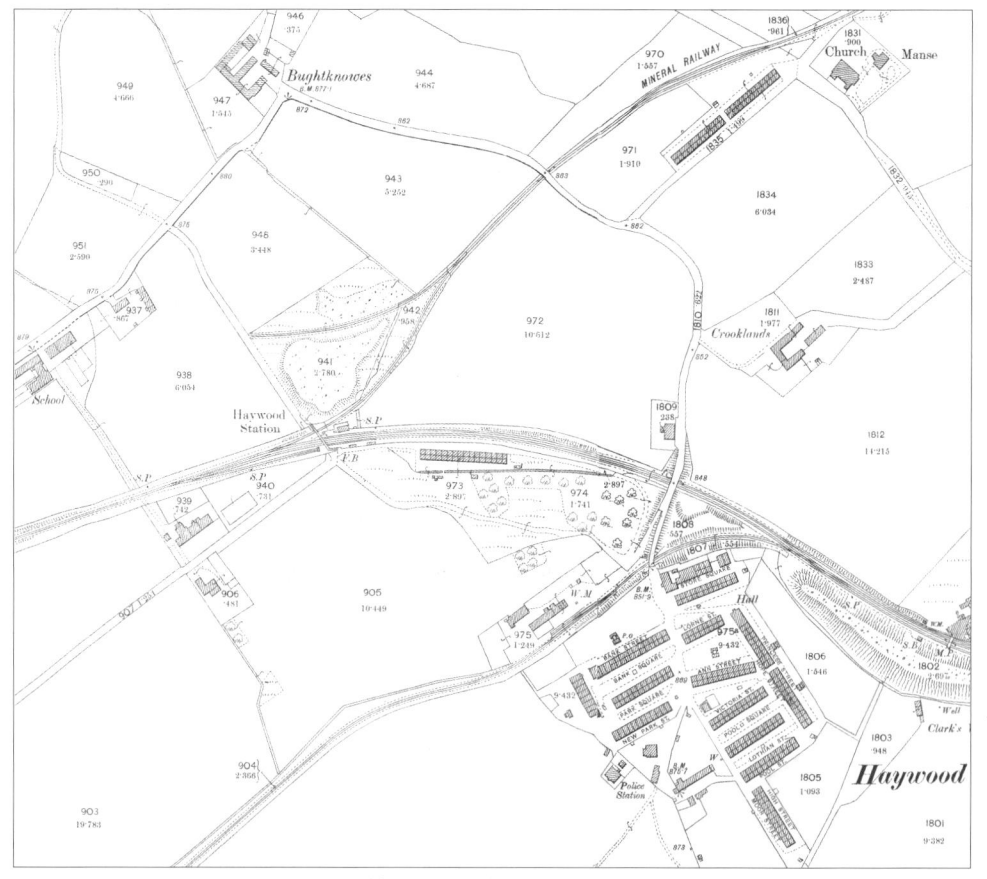

19.8 Haywood from 1897 Ordnance Survey composite map

20

Hermand

★

The Hermand Oil Works were built in the open countryside to the east of the Midlothian village of West Calder. Developed by Thomas and James W. Thornton, and then the Hermand Oil Company Ltd, the works were fairly extensive, and may have been erected around 1883. Previously, the Thorntons operated a smaller shale oil mine which was located south of Hermand Old Row, but which may only have lasted from around 1867 for eight years.

The Hermand Oil Company was formed in 1885 by James W. Thornton, and five other directors, and together they developed mineral leases they held on the estate of Hermand, Birniehill and Breich. The company prospectus noted that, 'This Company is being formed to carry on the business of Manufacturers of Mineral Oils and the products thereof, and with that view to lease the Shale, &c., in the property of Hermand, including the lands of Birniehill, and to purchase certain leases of Shale, &c., in the properties of Wester Breich, Mid and Easter Breich, with the Pits, Plant, and Houses thereon, all situated in the Parishes of West Calder and Livingstone'. James W. Thornton (d. 1885) was a coalmaster at Fauldhouse until he bought Hermand House in 1878. His brother had died the previous year, hence the decision to create a new company. In 1890 the company was dissolved and a new Hermand Oil Company was established.

With a growing workforce, the company needed to provide houses for them, there being insufficient accommodation in the parish to cope. Ground on the south side of Harburn Road was acquired, and four rows of houses were built. Each terrace was built perpendicular to the public road, and footways made their way around them.

The Hermand Rows, as they became known, were built in two different styles, although both were similar in that they had a larger building at the north end, facing onto the public road. The two western rows had larger properties, probably with two main rooms. In addition to the large house at the road end of the row, there were twelve other homes. These were built back to back, so that six cottages faced westwards, the other six facing east. This meant, of course, that windows and doors could only be built in one façade. Row number two was identical to the first row.

Adjoining these two rows were another three rows, of a similar width, again with houses built back-to-back, but the rows were slightly longer. The big difference, however, was that these three rows comprised of smaller homes, probably of a single apartment, with ten houses facing in each direction, in addition to the larger house facing the main road. The five rows, thus, had a total of 89 houses.

Half way down each row, a few yards from the front of the terrace, was a small outbuilding that served as a toilet. At the southern end of the rows were two buildings which were probably the wash-houses, and a bit of open ground around them may have been drying greens. The villagers had to get their water from one of two pumps which served the whole community. These were located at the north end of rows number one and three.

Near to Hermand were three other small rows of houses, in most cases occupied by workers at the shale-works, or else in shale mines. West of Hermand, on the road to West Calder, was the Hermand Old Row. This was located on the other side of the Murray's Pool Bridge (a name now morphed into Morrispool Bridge). As its name implies, this predated the five main rows and it is thought that the row was erected in 1867, being built to house workers in Thornton's mine and works. When originally built, this row probably comprised of twelve houses, built in a single terrace and set back from the West Calder to Harburn road. The gap between the front of the houses and the road was occupied by gardens, and a track separated the front of the houses with them. As the years passed, these houses were altered and, in some cases, extended. Half-way along the terrace, by the garden fence, was a water pump, shared by the dozen homes.

East of the five rows, on the road towards Harburn, was a small row of four houses, built on the opposite side of the road. This was known as Shuttlehall. Each house here had a garden plot either behind it or to one side. These houses were probably erected to house estate or agricultural workers and predated the Hermand Rows. In February 1844 Robert Lind, a labourer, lived here. He was fined £3 10s for two separate instances of poaching. The Linds occupied two of the cottages, according to the 1851 Census. Thomas Lind, aged 42, was a quarry labourer and a grazier, and he lived in one of the houses with seven other members of his family. Next door was James Lind, aged 68, an agricultural

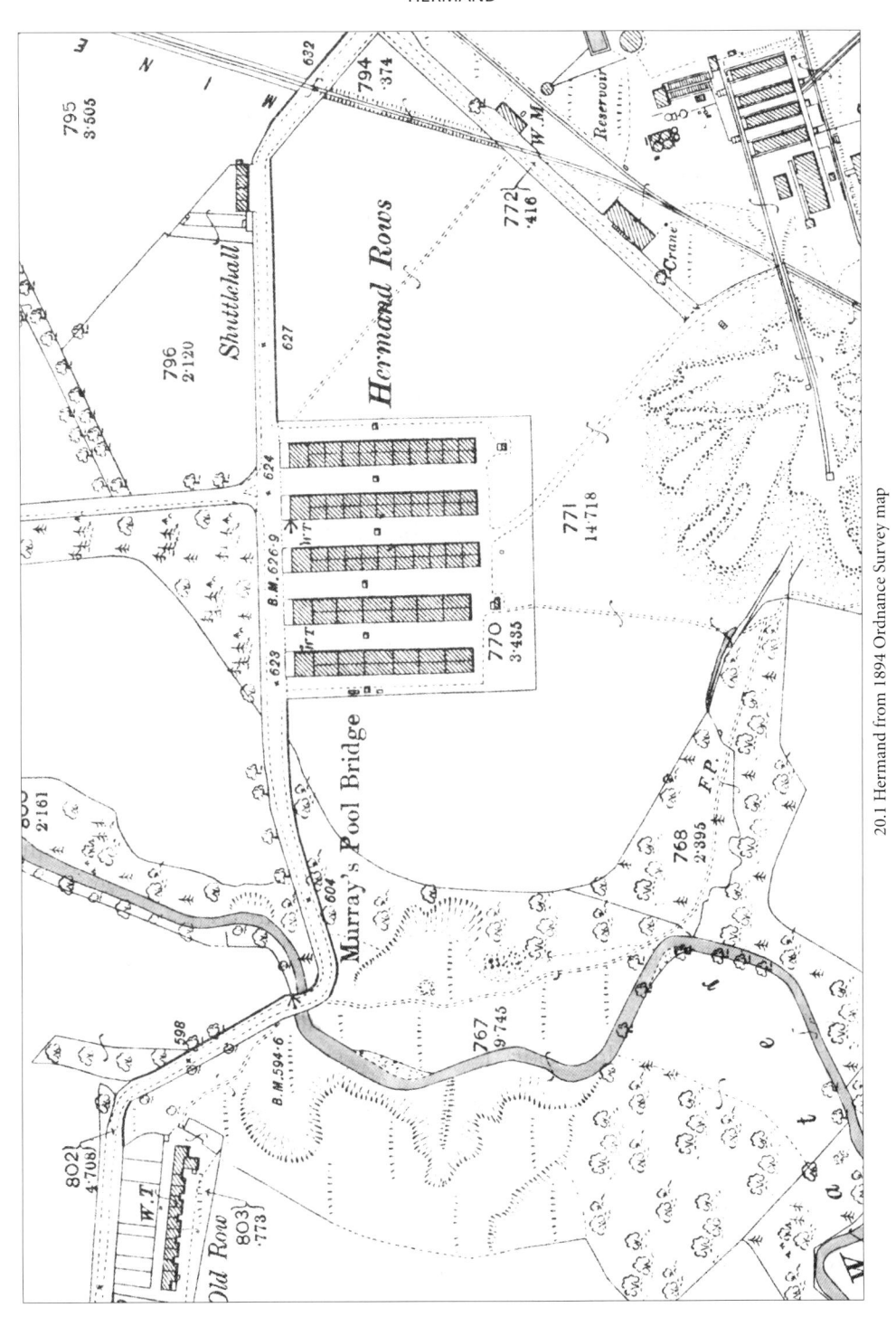

HERMAND

20.1 Hermand from 1894 Ordnance Survey map

labourer, with his wife. A third house was occupied by Robert Smith, aged 56, a stone diker, plus seven others. The fourth house was unoccupied, making the population of the three houses total eighteen.

Further on, back on the south side of the road, was another row of houses, known as Danderhall. Here were four houses, built facing onto the public highway. The back of these homes, however, faced directly into the Hermand Oil Works, the extensive industrial site covering eighteen acres and having a prominent bing at the western end, south of Hermand Rows.

Some events in the life of Hermand mirror the varied lives of Scots folk over the years. On 8 April 1911 Annie Smith, who lived at 4 Hermand Rows, spotted an eleven-year-old girl whose clothes had caught fire. She rushed to help, not thinking of her own safety, and began to douse the flames. Unfortunately, her own clothes caught fire, and she was to receive some severe burns to her own body. Luckily, she survived. In June the same year she was awarded £10 by the Carnegie Hero Fund Trustees.

Less honourable, though not involving Hermand residents, was the time in June 1891 when James Reid, a miner from Tarbrax, and William Mackay, a miner from West Calder, were walking with John Kerr past Hermand Old Row when they began to quarrel over some money matters. At the rows they stopped to fight, Mackay striking Reid twice so hard on the chin that he bit through his tongue. Although Reid and Kerr were able to get home to Tarbrax, erysipelas set in, and he died a fortnight later. Although originally charged with assault, this was changed to culpable homicide.

In 1891 a Faith Mission (P.U.) was established at Hermand with the holding of evening meetings at the rows. A tent was acquired, and sister pilgrims Barr and Hutton had been active in holding services, with the assistance of Pilgrim Donaldson.

Hermand Oil Works were closed in February 1903. The *Derby Daily Telegraph* of 19 February 1903 made a short, but telling, reference to the situation in its columns: 'The closing of the Linlithgow and Tarbrax oil works was followed on Wednesday by notices at the Hermand oil works, intimating that the works will be closed down on Saturday. The Hermand Oil Company is an extensive one, and the stoppage will mean the abandonment of a village.' The Ordnance Survey map of 1907 showed a cleared site, other than the remains of railway beds, old reservoirs and, of course, the distinctive outline of a shale bing. With the demise of the works, the need for fewer workers meant that the cottages became empty over time. At the five rows this was solved by partial demolition. The 1905 survey for the Ordnance Survey map shows that over half of the terraces' lengths were demolished – the two western rows retaining only five homes, the eastern three just seven in each, totalling 31 houses.

The houses at Hermand have all gone today. Travellers making their way along the road from West Calder to Harburn see little to indicate the former presence of a community. On leaving the village by the B 7008, Hamnavoe cottage is soon reached on the right. This occupies the site of Old Hermand. The bad bends on the road crossing Murray's Pool Bridge have been realigned, so that Morrispool Bridge is located slightly further downstream than its name predecessor. The site of the five rows is now occupied by a field, at the southern end of which are the remains of the old shale bing. Shuttlehall and Danderhall have gone, and the site of the oil works itself is virtually indistinguishable on the ground.

21
Inveraray
★

One of the most attractive places in Argyll is the village and castle of Inveraray, perched by the side of the loch at the foot of the Aray glen. The castle, seat of the Dukes of Argyll, was erected in 1745 to plans by Roger Morris, though its 'candle-snuffer' turret roofs were not added until 1877. Around it are extensive gardens and policies, covered with specimen trees, lawns and bushes. Across the bay from the castle is the village of Inveraray, the façade of houses and hotels facing the loch being a distinctive architectural feature, recognised by many. The Main Street strikes inland at right angles from the front, the church positioned in a road island.

On the grassy shore front, opposite the Great Inn, stands the town's market cross, an ancient carved floral stone cross shaft which is mounted on a stepped base within railings. It was erected here in 1839, missing the elaborate base that it once sported when it was located in the old village.

The present Inveraray Castle and village are replacements for an older castle and village and were the product of the improving 3rd Duke of Argyll. He succeeded to the title in 1743, and although the Jacobite Rebellion was still to take place, the Highlands were beginning to be tamed, and lairds wished to create modern houses and policies in the latest styles.

The old town of Inveraray stood where the present castle is now. When the new village was constructed, the residents were moved out and the buildings were pulled down. This process took around fifty years to complete.

Old Inveraray was an ancient community. When it was first established is unknown, but it no doubt owed its origins to the proximity of the castle, and the influence of the Campbells. The castle may have been erected in the early fifteenth century, to replace the Campbell's ancient stronghold of Innis Chonnell, located on an islet in Loch Awe. The tower stood around four or five storeys in height, the building being L-shaped in plan. The walls, built of rubble stonework, were plain for most of their height, only on the upper reaches being adorned with corbie-stepped gables, corner bartizans and corbel-courses. As was common at the time, a small village formed itself around the stronghold,

21.1 Inveraray Market Cross

supplying services to the laird and benefitting from his defence. The community appears to have been significant enough for King James III to establish it as a Burgh of Barony in 1472. This entitled the villagers to have a market, under the control of the baron.

Inveraray suffered considerable damage in 1644 when the soldiers under the Marquis of Montrose entered the village, burning many of the buildings. They also stormed the castle, causing much destruction.

In 1648 King Charles I raised the status of Inveraray to Royal Burgh, one of his last acts whilst held prisoner in Carisbrooke Castle. The village didn't really merit this status, being but a small community, but he was handing out baubles to the Campbells, seeking their support in the civil wars of the period. Nevertheless, it was the centre of a wide territory, and it became more important than its size would otherwise indicate. The charter confined all markets and fairs within the Sheriffdom of Argyll (excluding Kintyre) to the village. The burgh was entitled to elect a provost, four bailies, a dean of guild and twelve councillors.

Inveraray had a small market place, in the centre of which stood a market cross. In style, this was a fairly typical Scots form of structure – an octagonal base rising about ten feet in height, around which were pilasters at the edges and stone arches, on top of which rose a stone cross. The market place was located to the south of the church, at the junction of the Glen Shira road with the north-south main street.

The parish church stood to the south of the castle. Basically cruciform in plan, the building was adorned by a squat tower with steeple. Within, the church was divided into two halves – the Lowland and Gaelic congregations sharing the building. The former congregation had a minister who delivered his sermons in English, the latter had a minister who spoke in Gaelic. Each half of the church had a nave measuring 54 feet by 20 feet. The Lowland Church also had an adjoining aisle, known as the Duke's Aisle, which measured 16 feet by 11 feet 8 inches. This is where the Duke would have sat when he attended Sunday service. Both halves of the church also had lofts - the magistrates of the village usually occupying the Lowland loft. The lofts were accessed by ascending external stairs. In 1706 there was no manse in the village, but within a few years two had been built, one for each minister. The church suffered in the Jacobite attack in 1716 and it had to be repaired between 1728 and 1737, the church bells being recast in 1728 by Robert Maxwell of Edinburgh at a cost of £25, paid for by James Campbell of Stonefield. On the west side of the church was a graveyard, enclosed by a wall. The south side of this butted against the cottages in the Glen Shira road, the north faced onto the castle courtyard. The church was to the east.

The village had a tolbooth, which had been erected around 1650, adjoining the old church building. This was two storeys in height and formed the southern wing of the church. This building contained a court-house and prison cell, where the Earls and Dukes of Argyll (as Hereditary Justiciars) locked up malefactors. In the 1715 Jacobite Rising the tolbooth was attacked, rendering it ruinous. It was not to be repaired until 1723. It was here that the Circuit Courts met from 1748 onwards twice a year, in the spring and autumn. When these took place, the village was a centre of much activity, and accommodation for all of the judges and servants who accompanied them had to be found. Lesser courts, such as the Sheriff Court, Admiralty Court and meetings of the Commissioners of Supply, also held their meetings here, adding to the village's importance. The tolbooth's court room, however, was often too small for large hearings, such as in September 1752 when the Appin murder trial took place, relocated to Inveraray church.

At the start of the eighteenth century there were two schools in the village – a Grammar School and an English School. In 1706 there was no school, so they must have been established soon after a complaint at the time was sent to the duke.

One thing that made Inveraray quite distinctive was the quantity of inns or taverns in the little village. In 1748 a survey of the district discovered that there were 43 inns in the village, a figure that was regarded as 'surely too many!' However, most of these were little more than cot-houses, in which was a small brewery and a pot-still out the back, which produced whisky. The taverns were unsuitable places for accommodating travellers, and there were only three or more of them that could be classed as inns, capable of offering reasonable accommodation.

Old Inveraray had a fair number of small cottages in it. These were usually built of stone, in some cases held together with clay, but later walls were mortared. The roofs were usually thatched. There were a number of fair-sized buildings which were used by fishermen, who hauled their boats up on the shingle below the village. Most of the poorer buildings were located nearer the shore, where a couple of streets led off of the main street.

In addition to the smaller cottages, Inveraray had a fair number of more substantial dwelling houses. These were built with dressed stone and roofed with slate. Most of them were two storeys in height, but an example of a larger property was the home of James Fisher, merchant in the town and provost. He had erected a large house with a façade of 46 feet facing onto the street. The house was built from stone and rose three storeys in height, excluding the garret rooms. Most of these larger properties dated from around 1730 onwards and were built on feus with tacks of 57 years. In the market square, many of the older houses were either a storey and a half or two storeys in height. Gables often had corbie-steps, or crow-steps, and a significant number had a forestair, giving access to the upper floor. The storey-and-a-half buildings often had windows at eaves level.

In 1748, and for the following few years, the Window Tax returns indicate that there were 21 houses in the village that were liable to pay this cess, collectable on buildings containing ten or more windows, indicating that there were a fair number of larger properties. Some of these may have been the homes of lawyers, for the village had a number of these residing there, serving in the Court of Justiciary. Other large houses were the town houses of a number of Argyllshire lairds, houses that were smaller than their mansions and castles, and to which they resorted in the winter months when they could be heated more readily than their draughty and cold homes.

The main road through the community arrived at the east end, following the shore of Loch Shira, before making its way down a tree-lined avenue across the Gallows Green. Originally, a ford through the River Aray led into the market place, but around 1720 a new two-arched bridge was constructed, nearer to the castle, arriving at the north end of the market place. A road past the side of the castle made its way up alongside the River Aray, heading for Dalmally and thence to Oban. The route south to Lochgilphead and Campbeltown made its way along the shore, much as it does today.

In addition to the business carried on in Inveraray's tolbooth, the village had a thriving fishing fleet for a time. Herring and Loch Fyne are inextricably linked, and during the years when the fish were abundant, there were many fishermen residing in the village, their boats drawn up on the shore of the loch in front of the village. The harbour was little more than a stone pier, incapable of allowing all of the boats to moor simultaneously. The herring season lasted from June to New Year, and during that time fishermen made Inveraray their home, if they didn't belong there. Thomas Pennant, writing in 1769, wrote that, 'Every evening some hundreds of boats in a manner covered the surface of Lough-fine, an arm of the sea ... on the week-days, the cheerful noise of the bagpipe and dance echoes from on board; on the sabbath, each boat approaches the land, and psalmody and devotion divide the day ...'

21.2 Inveraray from painting by Paul Sandby (SCRAN)

Around the year 1750 General William Roy was in the vicinity, surveying for his great map of Scotland. This was to be the most detailed map of the country yet produced, and the detail it provided was unsurpassed until the arrival of the Ordnance Survey in the 1850s. Roy's map shows the village in its original position, stretching from the castle down to the shore of Loch Fyne. The castle is identifiable on the map from being a considerable square building, a long avenue of trees being aligned with it, stretching some distance to the south-west. Around the castle a number of lesser buildings are indicated on the map.

Roy's map indicates the street heading east from the market place to the bridge over the River Aray, beyond which was another tree-lined avenue leading to the road along the side of the loch, heading for Arrochar and the south. Although there were some buildings in the immediate vicinity of the castle, the main bulk of the village was located further south, beyond the market place, on the stretch of land west of the mouth of the Aray, and along the lochside. There seems to have been a number of streets, one making its way to the spit of land at the mouth of the Aray, where the fishing boats were tied up. From it, a shore road struck west, re-joining the main street at the shore. At the end of the bay, where a small stream ran into the loch, was a separate group of cottages, mostly single-storey, and beyond that were one or two cottages where the present village stands.

A few descriptions of the village were recorded by early travellers in the West Highlands. Major General John Campbell, cousin of the 2nd Duke of Argyll, Archibald Campbell, wrote in 1746 that it was 'a charming pretty place'.

Archibald Campbell, Earl of Ilay, had succeeded as 3rd Duke of Argyll in 1743 and decided that he wished to bring his property into the eighteenth century. Plans for the new village were made and work on it commenced soon thereafter. The Duke must have known of his plans for some time, perhaps only putting them into execution when his father died. On 9 November 1743, just a few weeks after he took the title and inherited the vast estates, he wrote to Lord Milton, stating that, 'I intend if possible to remove the Town of Inveraray about half a mile lower down the Loch, but it must be a great secret or else the feus there will stand in my way, or be held up at very extravagant prices.'

A series of possible layouts were drawn up before the settled plan was decided upon. The first person to take a feu and start building a house was John Richardson, a merchant, who began in 1748, and who was to become provost.

In 1746 the Duke issued a Summons of Removal to 126 tenants in the village, the list containing a number of notable residents in the town. These included Margaret Campbell, widow of the merchant Robert Murray; William Douglass, mason; James Johnston, smith; Patrick MacArthur, innkeeper; Margaret MacAulay, widow of the tailor, Hugh MacPaill; and Donald MacIlmauag, a boat carpenter from Fisherland in the village. However, folk were not keen to move, and in 1749 it was noted that, 'some said they wanted to know what your G[race] proposed to do with them. Others said they would build in the New Town if the houses they built in the Old Town were Comprised and full value was paid them …. Others again who have no houses and cannot build without wronging their Trade … propose to build if yr Grace let them have the loan of money at Three per Cent Intrest.'

Gradually, however, the Duke persuaded the residents to move. The Great Inn was opened in 1755, and the new Town House, with cells and court room, was opened in 1757.

Sir William Burrell made a tour of northern Scotland in 1758 and noted in his journal that, 'the Duke of Argyle intends by degrees to remove the town of Inveraray half a mile lower down Loch Fine, which now stands close to the castle'. Accordingly, in 1758 another notice of removal was made, and amongst those removed were the tenants of properties on the east side of Laigh Street. Among the twenty-two ordered out of their homes were Robert MacKellar, a fisherman who lived at Fisherland; Archibald MacNocaird, a blind man; Angus Sinclair, wright; and John Stewart, cooper.

When Thomas Pennant visited Inveraray in 1769, the new village was underway, the castle had been rebuilt, but the old village still existed. He wrote:

> This place will in time be very magnificent; but at present the space between the front and the water is disgraced with the old town, composed of the most wretched hovels that can be imagined. The founder of the castle designed to have built a new town on the west side of the little bay the house stands on: he finished a few houses, a custom-house, and an excellent inn: his death interrupted the completion of the plan, which, brought to perfection, will give the place a very different appearance to what it now bears.

The new 5th Duke, John Campbell, kick-started work on Inveraray again, following his succession in 1770. As the old town was cleared, the new town was beginning to grow. New tenements were erected to plans by William Mylne, and the occupants of the old thatched buildings in the Old Town were rehoused in them. The servants at the castle and other estate workers were moved first, and then the occupants of the larger properties were persuaded to move, on promise of long leases and compensation for moving. New manses for the ministers were erected in 1776 and temporary churches of 1772 were followed by new churches in 1777.

The last of the residents of old Inveraray had been evicted by 1778, and the site of the village was developed as part of the gardens of Inveraray Castle. David Loch saw the site in 1778, finding it, 'so totally annihilated, as not to have the smallest vestige remaining.' The present gardens occupy the location.

22
Kincardine

*

Most of Scotland's historical counties are named after towns – Ayr, Lanark, Peebles, Stirling, etc., but a few are named after other things, usually areas, such as Argyll, Sutherland, Moray and Caithness. Kincardineshire is a county that appears to be one of the latter, there being no town of that name, at least not within the shire. There is a town of Kincardine in Fife, and a few other places bearing the same name elsewhere in Scotland, but they are unconnected with the county of that name. Kincardineshire is located south of Aberdeenshire and north of Angus, and in many accounts has an alternative name of The Mearns. It was, in fact, named after a town – but the old town of Kincardine is a lost community.

To the east of the Mearns village of Fettercairn, just off a minor road linking the Cairn o' Mount road with the Auchenblae road, is the farm of Castleton of Kincardine. To the east of the farm steading, in a circular wood of ancient trees, can be found the remains of Kincardine Castle. This was a castle of enclosure, that is, it had a tall defensive wall protecting a courtyard, in which were hall buildings and an elaborate gate tower. The castle was very important in its day – for here William the Lion and Alexander II spent some time, and it is reckoned that John Balliol abdicated his claim to the throne here during the Wars of Independence. In addition to other royal visitors, Mary Queen of Scots stayed here in 1562. The castle didn't survive much longer than the queen's visit, and it was demolished in 1646.

The farm road past the castle ruins and Castleton farm continues its way through the fields, meandering slightly between hedges and the odd old tree. This was, in fact, the original main street of the burgh of Kincardine. Today, nothing of the village survives, apart from the remnants of the ancient burial ground, being little more than a clump of trees in a field, just south of the old main road. When the fields to either side of the road are ploughed, it is possible to identify small fragments of pottery among the soil, relics of the time when this was a populous village.

Detailed Ordnance Survey maps show what was believed to be the extent of the community. In front of Castleton farm was the site of the East Port, which would have been some form of gateway, originally closed at night to protect the residents from marauding thieves and cattle reivers. At one time there was a croft here, known as The Cross. The West Port protected the community at the west end, and this was positioned 500 yards to the south-west, just after a bend in the road. On 'A Map of Kincardineshire', published in 1794 by A. Arrowsmith, the main road through Kincardine is shown linking the 'Ruins of Kincardine Castle' with Fettercairn. A building named as East Port is indicated, and to the west a solitary building representing the remains of Kincardine. A rectangle indicated by a broken line is probably meant to represent the extent of the old kirkyard. From the main road a second road is shown, striking south past Inchgray to Thornton and Laurencekirk. The two roads probably joined where the original site of Kincardine Cross was.

The original houses and steadings of Kincardine were located between these two ports. Halfway along the road, midway between the two ports, stood the market cross, again marked on old detailed survey maps. It is thought that this original cross may still survive, and that it was taken from Kincardine, when the community no longer existed, and rebuilt in Fettercairn.

Some old accounts claim that Kincardine actually was larger than the street enclosed by the two ports – they say that there were houses continuing south-westwards almost as far as Fettercairn itself, and that remnants of these buildings can be identified in the fields. However, these may simply be small crofthouses which existed outwith the burgh confines.

As already referred to, the ancient burial ground associated with the parish church can still be identified on the ground. It lies about eighty yards to the south of the main road, in a field that is known as Chapelyard Park. This was St Catherine's Burying Ground, a square shaped plot where it is thought that the original church once stood – indeed, it is said that the foundations were still visible until recently. At one time it had a low wall around the square enclosure, with trees protecting it, but today it is in a tumbledown condition, the trees taking over. Even these are now hoary old specimens of beech and oak. The trees had originally been planted by Sir John S. Forbes, Baronet, as a means of protecting the site. The church here was dedicated to St Catherine of Sienna.

The last burials in the churchyard appear to have taken place in the early nineteenth century, and old accounts record funeral corteges making their way to the graveyard, the bellman walking in front, ringing the 'deid bell' as he went. The old kirkyard now has only one gravestone surviving, erected over the remains of William Taylor MA, who died in 1786. He is supposed to have been the schoolmaster at nearby Land's End. The stone, which is inscribed on both sides, is becoming difficult to read, but bears the inscription:

> WT-MA This grave contains the body of W. Taylor late in Landends of Kincardine. He died on the .. day of Octr. 1786 aged 62 years. Also the bodies of …. Also Margaret Alexander, his wife, who died the ….

22.1 Kincardine – solitary gravestone in kirkyard

The community of Kincardine was an ancient one, and it is said to have been created a burgh at some indeterminate date in the mists of antiquity. Indeed, on 11 March 1531, King James V confirmed the lands of Kincardine to William Keith, 4th Earl Marischal, re-affirming the community as not only a burgh of barony, but also the 'principal and capital burgh in the county.' Thus, Kincardine became the county town of what was known as the Mearns.

Part of the old charter reads:

> …granted for good service and for composition paid, the lands, town, tenements and crofts of Kincardine, Gallohilstoun, Palframanstoun with advowson of the Chapel of S. Catherine which formerly belonged to William and his predecessors past memory of man, and the said town was of repute a free burgh and the Sheriff Courts of Kincardine were held in the same, and the charters of the said town being lost in

the time of pest and troubles, he [King James V] de novo created the said town a free burgh and gave the inhabitants the power to pak peile and sell, with power to make baillies, burgesses, sergeants, and of having a market cross and weekly market on Friday, and a free fair twice a year, on the day of S. Catherine the Virgin in winter, and on the day of St Catherine of Senis in summer, with tolls, etc. paying annually 26s 8d of blench ferm and burgh mail whereas they paid nothing to the King aforetime.

22.2 Kincardine – view of old kirkyard from main street

Andrew Jervise, writing in the *Memorials of Angus and Mearns*, published in 1861, describes some of the land holdings in the burgh of Kincardine:

> Traces of the ancient greatness of the place are the names of adjacent fields, such as the King's and Chancellor's Parks, the Chancellor's and Deans's Crofts, the Deer or Hunting Park, the Countess' Croft, and the Earl's Inns, as also the Lorimer's, the Archer's, and the Palfreyman's Crofts. These names, it will be seen, differ from the Duray, Bakehouse, Brewhouse, Gardener's, Hen and other Crofts which, common in the vicinity of baronial establishments, are also to be found at Kincardine. As for the most part, these places are described as marching with lands belonging to some of the more ancient and powerful lords of the Mearns, the persons from whom these names were derived may have filled, in connection with the Court, the offices indicated by them.

A more precise account of the buildings in the burgh were listed in the charter issued in 1616 to Alexander Strachan of Thornton Castle when he inherited the lands from his grandfather. It reads:

> ... the croft called Hill Croft, the aiker riggs thereof, Weal [Well] Croft, Chancellor Croft, Den Croft, two crofts called Calsey Crofts, Lonie Croft, Bakhouse Croft, Lorimer's Croft, Burne Croft, Hals Croft, half of Boigs Croft and Coryismanis, Beatties Croft, Annabadies Croft, four crofts of Craigisland, of which two are called Hall Croft and Hen Croft, and two Hill Croft and Archer Croft, James Petterscheidsland, Countess Croft, Countaishauch Croft, crofts called Lochietraist, Blaikindennis, Dewresunis, Wela Croft with the shady half of Bowmanis Croft, all lying in the town and constabulary of Kincardine, lands, crofts and tenements of Gallowhillstoun, Palframanstoun, Langhauche, Suitter Croft, Temple Croft, Skinner Croft, Gois Croft, twa chaippell Crofts, Lonie Croft, aiker and Newlandis. Old extent 20s; new extent 33s.

Kincardine went into decline at the end of the sixteenth century. Indeed, it was not to be included on maps drawn by either Blaeu or General Roy. The castle no longer had any important role to play, and new communities were growing quicker elsewhere in the Mearns. Fettercairn and Auchenblae were becoming more important and, to the south-east, Laurencekirk was growing, its position on a main road helping this. The town of Stonehaven, or Stanehyve, as it was often referred to in old documents, became an important port, and eventually was to claim its place as county town in 1600. Indeed, in 1607 an act of Parliament dictated that 'the haill lieges within the schire should compeer to preserv and defend tin their courtis at Stanehyve in all time heirefter.'

The decline in official recognition as the county town and centre of jurisdiction was exacerbated by the fact that when the sheriff of the county came to hold court there was little in the way of facilities for the purpose. It was recorded:

22.3 Kincardine's old Market Cross, now in Fettercairn

...the Schiref of the Mernis alias Kincardine, and his deputtis, hes benein use this mony zeris to sit at Kincardine, quhair thair is nather ane tolbuth nor any hous to pairties to lodge into for thair intertenement, quhairby the lieges are greatulie damnifeit.

In 1665, Kincardine was part of a large estate confirmed to George, Earl of Winton. The charter includes title to, 'the hereditary office of Sheriff of Kincardine and Constable of Kincardine, Cowie and Durris, with all its privileges, and all lands, etc., round the town of Cowie, the Forrest of Cowie, called the Forrest of Month; the town and land of Kincardine, Gallowwhirstoun and Pomphray, Manstoun, with the patronage of St Catherine, and privileges of the Free Burgh of Kincardine'. However, by this time, the free burgh was in serious decline.

The old market cross of Kincardine was taken down in 1670 and rebuilt in Fettercairn. We can assume it took much the same format when it was in Kincardine, that is, an octagonal column, about ten feet tall, surmounted by a cube capital. However, it is thought that the capital may have been added in 1670 when the cross was removed, probably replacing an older capital from Kincardine that was no doubt eroded. On the present capital are carved the arms of the Middletons - a lion rampant in a double tressure, representing the arms of John, Earl of Middleton, who held the barony for a time. On the opposite side is a coronet over Middleton's initials. The other two sides bear the date 1670 and a sundial. The cross is mounted on an octagonal series of steps, six layers in total, though with constant walking over them, these have been replaced over the years.

Affixed to the market cross was a steel neck-ring, known locally as the jougs, which was used to control malefactors and deviants in days gone by. These folks would be made stand at the cross, the ring affixed around their neck, padlocked shut, and bolted securely to the cross by a chain. The remains of the hasp which was affixed to the cross can still be seen, as can the worn part of the cross where the jougs moved back and forth in the wind when it was not in use.

Marked along one side of the cross there is also an incised line, measuring 37 inches. This unusual length was referred to as an ell, a recognised measurement in Scots law, often used to measure cloth and similar materials. If there was a dispute regarding the length of the tailor's stick, it could be taken to the cross and held against the line to prove that he was not diddling the customer.

In 1828, Robert Chambers in his book, *The Picture of Scotland*, described the community as 'a small congregation of little tenements, like the out-houses of an old farm; the miserable remains of the former county-town. This hamlet, which is still called Kincardine, and boasts of having given its name to the county, contains only about sixty or seventy inhabitants.'

23

Kingscavil

*

There are still the vestiges of a village at Kingscavil, located on the old Edinburgh road, about two miles east of Linlithgow. Travellers on the B9080 (which at one time was the A9, before the arrival of the M9) will spot a church building, adjoining which are a few cottages. The church dates from 1900-02, being built on a site donated by the local laird, Captain Johnston Stewart of Champfleurie. The building isn't large, being little more than a principal nave, with a rather stunted tower for an entrance porch. Three lancet windows adorn the principal gable, and the stained glass in the building was relocated here from a church in Leith. Designed by William M. Scott of Linlithgow, the church was dedicated on Sunday 25 May 1902 and Rev Thomas Lugton served as its first minister.

Kingscavil church remains in use on two Sundays per month, the minister serving a wider parish, which includes Winchburgh and Abercorn churches. The church also has a mission hall, located in the nearby village of Bridgend, one mile to the east.

Kingscavil Church was built to replace the 'auld tin kirk', which originally lay a few hundred yards to the west of the present building. It had been erected in 1887 as a mission church for St Michael's Church in Linlithgow, to serve the growing number of residents in Kingscavil village. The tin kirk became a bit of a problem for the church, for it wasn't large enough for the congregation. Following considerable discussion, it was agreed that a new church should be built to replace it. This was to be a stone structure, and work on it was underway in December 1900 when the district experienced a considerable storm. The *Falkirk Herald* reported:

> In common with the country generally, the great gale of Thursday night and Friday morning was very severely felt, the gale being one of the most violent in recent years … the more serious damage was in the case of Kinscavil Church iron structure which was blown down and totally wrecked. The destruction of the building at this time is a

regrettable misfortune. A new church is at present being built for the congregation, and in the course of a few months the iron church would doubtless have been removed, and no inconvenience occasioned thereby. The shed used by the builders of the new church was also blown down, and the same fate befell the bell of Wester Pardovan Church.

Back in history, there was a small community at Kingscavil before the arrival of the shale mining industry, which greatly expanded it. On General Roy's map of 1747, the clachan is shown as having a few houses, named 'Kinkavel'. Certainly, in the first half of the seventeenth century, there were a few cottages which were homes to the workers at Kingscavil Quarry. In 1618 the quarry was used to rebuild part of Linlithgow Palace, King James VI ordering that the north wing should be rebuilt. This was done at a cost of £4,901 19s 2d.

By the time the Ordnance Survey arrived in 1854 to make the first proper detailed maps of the country, there were three separate rows of houses that were known as Kingscavil. To the east, within the Moor Plantation, a triangular wood of trees that survives to this day, was a row of buildings, facing directly onto the main road. There is little to indicate how many cottages this formed, but all were linked and had gardens to the rear. The Ochiltree road struck south to the west of this row, and on its western side was Kingscavil farm. Here was a collection of buildings, no doubt comprising of a farmhouse, worker's bothy, hayshed, and a circular horse-gin to power a mill.

North-west of these two parts of the village was a second row of buildings, also indicated on the map as Kingscavil. Again, the cottages were adjoining and faced directly onto the road. The frontage was slightly curved, to follow the line of the road. This part of the community was of considerable importance, for here was a smithy, at the east end of the row, and one of the middle buildings was used as a school. There were another four cottages making up the row.

The third row of houses known as Kingscavil was located to the south of the farm, on the Ochiltree road. Again, all of the houses were linked to form a single terrace. These cottages had front gardens, facing onto the road, with larger plots behind. This row probably comprised of three houses.

In the early nineteenth century, most of the residents of Kingscavil would probably be employed on local farms, or else worked on Champfleurie estate, which was located to the east of the village. By the mid nineteenth century, quarrying for sandstone was carried out, with Kingscavil Quarry being sunk to

23.1 Kingscavil (West Lothian Council)

the south of the school and smithy row. The quarry was disused by 1895.

The miners' rows at Kingscavil appear to have been erected around 1885 using brick. The Linlithgow Oil Company built them on land owned by Champfleurie estate. The houses were built alongside the Ochiltree road, with two rows on each side of the road, all parallel with each other. The bricks used in their construction were manufactured nearby, using clay quarried at Ochiltree.

The rows at Kingscavil were different to many miners' rows of the period, for each terrace only had four houses in them, there being 28 blocks of four houses. On the west side of the road, where Kingscavil farm was, there were sixteen blocks of housing. These were built facing each other, and in the roadway between were dry-closets. Each house had a very small garden to the rear. On the east side of the Ochiltree road were two similar rows of houses, but only twelve blocks of four here. Again the rows faced inward. The road south passed along the back of the middle rows of houses. The locals referred to these inner rows as 'The Front', as they faced the main road. If you lived in the houses facing the fields then you were referred to as living at 'The Back'.

A report in *The Scotsman* of 14 January 1887 gives a little glimpse of Kingscavil history:

> The little village of Kingscavil, or Champfleurie, has been enlarged by the addition to it of no fewer than 106 neat brick cottages which the company has erected for the housing of their workmen. Their presence has necessitated the erection of a school; a small mission church in connection with Linlithgow parish has also been built, a large general store has been opened, and a transformation effected in a short time, similar to what one reads of in the mining or newly-settled districts of America.

The village was fairly well served with dry closets, for there was one per four homes. The residents referred to them as 'shunkies'. At regular intervals, an old man surnamed Todd came to the village with a horse and cart to empty them. He took the bucket from each closet and emptied it into the cart. When the bucket was returned he placed a ladleful of chloride of lime in each pail.

There was no running water in the shunkies, or even in the houses, the residents needing to get their water from cast iron wellheads which were spread around the community. These were adorned with lion's heads. There were only four of these in the miners' rows, one at the north end of each row, and a further two in front of the penultimate block of houses at the southern end of the row. The water came from a supply which the oil company had created for its works, and which had sufficient volume to supply the villages of Kingscavil and Bridgend also.

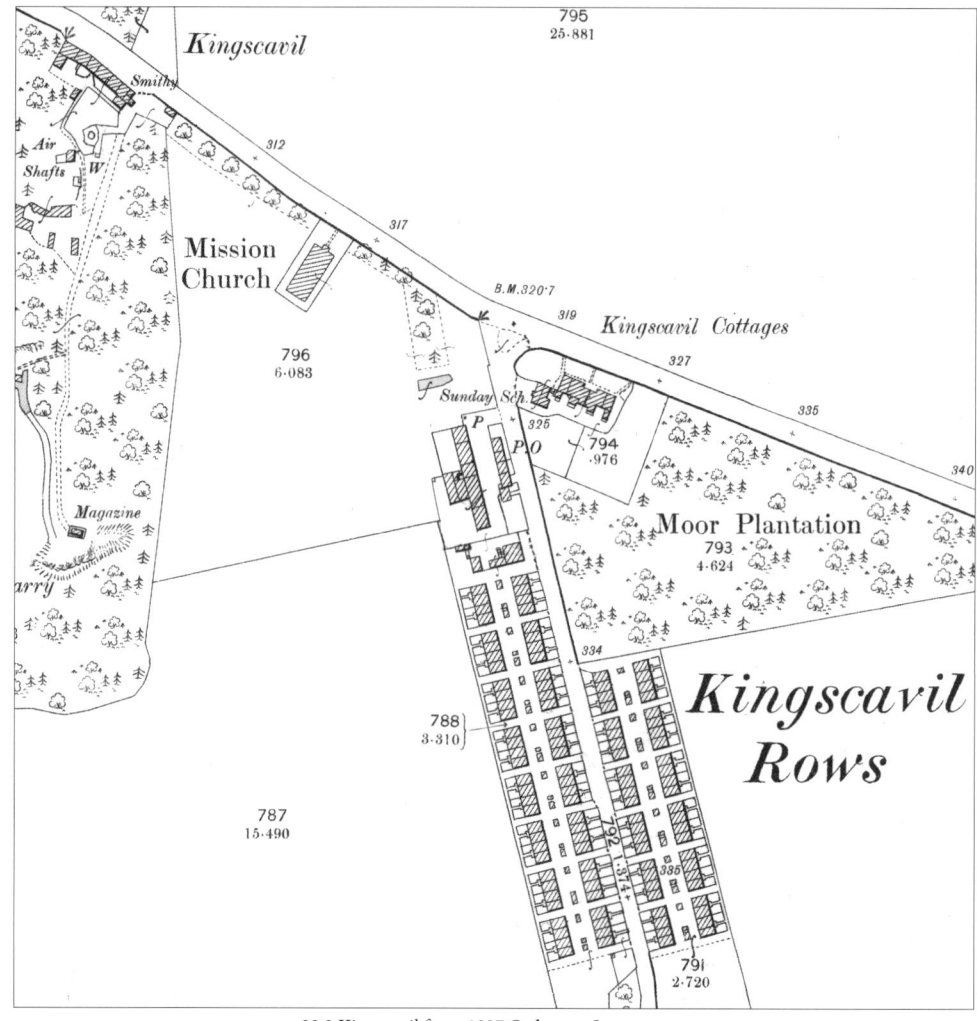

23.2 Kingscavil from 1897 Ordnance Survey map

Kingscavil was built to house workers employed by the Linlithgow Oil Company, but within a few years were jointly-owned by that firm and James Ross & Company. The large Linlithgow Oil Works was located at Bridgend, on a site now occupied by Bridgend Golf Course. The works were not too successful and went bankrupt in 1902. In later years, many of the residents worked at the Whitequarries Mine. With the sudden demand for workers when the mines were first sunk, many of the residents came from elsewhere to find employment. Surveys of the birthplaces of the early residents found that many came from Lanarkshire and Dunbartonshire. As time passed, there appears to have been an influx of Irish immigrants.

Kingscavil had most facilities that a small village had – in addition to the church there was at one time a post office, located in a building where the farm was, and a public house. The latter was positioned between the farm buildings and the rows. In 1917 the shop was run by Fraser and Carmichael, merchants. There was also a small shop run by Biddy Gallagher in the front room of her home.

Although there was an old school at the smithy row in Kingscavil, once the new rows were built this had closed. Children from the village had to walk along the main road to the public school at Bridgend. In the late nineteenth century there was a Sunday School, located in a specially-built schoolroom at Kingscavil Cottages. This building survives, now a cottage, and has ecclesiastical-shaped windows.

The houses in the rows were small, comprising only of two rooms – the front room and the kitchen. The houses did not have built-in beds like many other communities, just free-standing beds in both the kitchen and the room. In 1914 Theodore K. Irvine, who compiled a *Report on the Housing Conditions in the Scottish Shale Field*, noted that the houses were very small, had tiny gardens, and that the 'surrounding walls are in a very tumble-down condition.' At the time residents paid 1s 9d for a single-apartment house and 2s 6d for a double-apartment, which included rates. With the outbreak of war in Europe, many men were not to return from the battlefields, so much so that it was noted that between the wars, many of the houses were occupied by widows.

In 1873, a block of four houses was built to replace one of the older rows at Kingscavil. These were known as the Kingscavil Cottages and comprised four sandstone-built homes with large gardens. One of the houses was known as the schoolhouse, and the former Sunday School building was probably originally a small village school. The architect was James Campbell Walker (c.1822-1888).

Kingscavil village had its own football team for a time – Champfleurie United. They played on a football pitch which was located on the east side of the Ochiltree road, at the end of the rows. This had been granted to them by Sir Francis Tudsbery of Champfleurie and was also used for the local gala day. The team's high point in its short life was when it got to the final of the Scottish Juvenile Cup. This was played at Easter Road, home ground of Hibernian Football Club in Edinburgh, and four or five bus-loads of supporters left Kingscavil to support them.

A number of organisations existed in Kingscavil over the years. The International Order of Good Templars had a lodge there, including the Patrick Hamilton Lodge of Juvenile Templars.

The population of Kingscavil is difficult to enumerate, but in 1891 the census noted that Bridgend and Kingscavil had a population of 802. At that time, Bridgend had 86 houses in the Bridgend Rows, and Kingscavil around 114, so we can assume the population of the latter was around 460.

In 1931 the first rumblings of discontent with the conditions in the rows at Kingscavil were made. A. M. Smith, sanitary inspector for Linlithgow district, reckoned that the houses were unfit for habitation and ought to be demolished. At the time, Linlithgowshire, or West Lothian, had the highest percentage of two-apartment houses in Scotland, and not only that, it had the highest number of persons in a room in the country.

The possibility of upgrading the houses in Kingscavil or rebuilding the village on the same site was to be a non-starter, for the sewerage system could not cope. Instead a new community was established at Bridgend, where the council built 184 new houses, designed by Matt Steele, all with indoor toilets and baths, running water and electricity. The new houses had either three, four or five apartments and were built to the recently-introduced regulations issued by the Department of Health. The folk from Kingscavil were rehoused, and the old rows removed. This took place in 1937.

Where the houses of Kingscavil stood was returned to agriculture, so much so that today there is virtually no evidence to be found of their existence. Only the few houses which were associated with the agricultural trade or estate workers survive.

24
Lassodie

★

Travellers on the road between the Fife villages of Kingseat and Kelty will notice a war memorial located at Lochend, where a small burn flows under the road and into Loch Fitty. Constructed of stone, and painted a white colour, it has three bronze plaques with inscriptions on them. If one takes a few moments to stop and look at the monument, it will be noted that the memorial is to the villagers of Lassodie who lost their lives fighting in the Great War of 1914-18 and in the Second World War of 1939-45. There were 21 fatalities in the first World War, and a further four from the Second World War. Today, however, the village from where these men left to fight on the fields of Europe has gone, cleared away and the whole site obliterated by open-cast coal mining. The war memorial was originally located outside the Lassodie Public Hall but was moved when the site was cleared.

The village of Lassodie dates from after 1859. At that time the site of the community was open countryside – Lassodie House was a small country house located where the later Lassodie Mains farm was to be, an older steading known as Lassodie Mains being where Lassodie Public Hall was later to be built. Where the Old Rows were to be erected was open fields, and Lassodie House was still to be constructed. In 1851 an advertisement appeared in the *Scotsman* offering part of the estate of Cocklaw and Lassodie for sale. With it came the mining rights and it noted that, 'There are 6 or 7 seams of coal on the lands of Lassodie, which Mr D. Landale, mining engineer, Edinburgh, reports to be of considerable value, and there is also a small field of blackband ironstone which being associated with a thin wild coal, could be wrought at moderate expense'.

The establishment of a mining industry here goes back before the creation of a village. In 1825 the farms on Lassodie estate were offered to let for nineteen years, and at the same time offers were being sought for the rights to mine the coal which was known to exist below the fields. Limestone had already been worked here and was being burned to create lime for agricultural improvement. According to an advertisement in the *Scotsman* of 2 March 1825, 'The COAL on the lands of Lassodie will be let on liberal terms, and at a fixed rent, or lordship, or both, as may be agreed upon'. By September 1859 it was noted that, 'the Lassodie Limeworks are now in full operation. The lime is well known to be of excellent quality, both for agricultural and building purposes, and can be supplied at the following prices at the kilns: limeshells, 2s 5d per boll; slacked or small lime, 1s 1d per boll.'

The railway arrived in the summer of 1859, allowing the coal from the mines to be exported more readily. At the same time the lands were developed, the reporter for the *Dunfermline Saturday Press* of 23 June 1859 noting that, 'all the preparations for brickmaking, lime-burning, house-building, and coal-raising are in active operation, while some forty navvies are levelling hills and filling vales to prepare the way for the fire-steeds which are to convey its wealth to distant marts'. In March 1865 advertisements were placed in the local press aimed at builders and joiners, looking for estimates for the erection of a 'provision store, with dwelling-house, workshops, and a number of miners' cottages' at Lassodie.

The new Lassodie House was a rather grand country mansion with a sweeping drive, being built on an elevated site at what had been Braehead farm. It was the property of John Dewar. Dewar had erected a new cottage in 1877,

24.1 Lassodie – St Ninian's Church (Mary Searles)

designed by James Harley. In 1880 a new house, lodge and entrance gateway were designed by James Campbell Walker for Dewar. The original house was a double storey Victorian gothic building, the entrance porch on the west front, facing the main drive. On the south front were bay windows and a high gable, overlooking the valley towards Loch Fitty and the Hill of Beath beyond. In 1897 extensions to the house were added to the plans of John Houston. This probably included a new northern extension to the main façade, a three-storey square tower in the centre topped by a flagstaff, and a double-storey wing.

Down in the glen below the house, however, was the collier village of Lassodie, far enough away for the laird to avoid, but close enough for him to keep an eye on. One of the first buildings reached when entering Lassodie from the east end was the village school. At an earlier date an old coal-company school existed, but when education was taken over by parish school boards it was deemed as being unsuitable for education purposes. The new school building was proposed in 1873 by Beath School Board to educate the children of the miners, but was soon postponed. It wasn't built until 1877. The schoolmaster's house stood alongside, and in March 1877 an advertisement appeared in the *Scotsman* for a new headmaster to take over. He must be certificated, and would be paid £140 per annum, according to the terms. The school building was designed by the Dunfermline architect Andrew Scobie (died 1924). Built of stone, the building was symmetrical in style, with a boys' and girls' end. The two projecting wings had prominent ornate gables built into the hipped ends. Although only single-storey, the slate roof was adorned with fleches and skylight windows. In the bay between the wings were two doors, for boys and girls, over which were semi-circular pediments. The school was able to accommodate 250 pupils, was built at a cost of £2,000 and eight teachers worked in it at one time. Andrew Scobie was to design additions to the school in 1898-9 and again in 1903, when the 'manual training' classroom was added. Headmasters at the school include William Drysdale. The school was closed before 1943.

Moving into the village, shortly after the school was the village hall. This was erected around 1900. The building was constructed of timber and covered with corrugated iron sheeting. When the war memorial was first erected, it stood in the grounds of the hall.

The next group of buildings on the right was Lassodie Mains, or Lassodie Home Farm as it was at one time known. In the late nineteenth century it was occupied by John Collier. The large farmhouse, a double storey building with a porch, was located at the side of the road, replacing an older farmhouse in the steading. The new farmhouse was almost covered with ivy.

The Lassodie Arms, or Lassodie Tavern as it was latterly known, followed, located on the north side of the street just before the New Rows. The building stood over two floors, the walls painted white.

The first real part of the village followed – the New Rows. On some maps this part of the village was named as Parley. On the right-hand side was a short terrace of four houses. These had gardens to the rear. On the south side of the road, perpendicular to it, was another row of five or six houses. This was known as New Row.

The principal street followed, the south side of which had two terraces, each with ten houses in them. These were small houses, and each had a garden plot to their rear, squeezed between the house and the mineral railway that passed by.

On the north side of the road were two terraces of houses, again each one having ten homes in it. These houses were larger, and there were projecting parts to the rear. At the west end of the street was a water pump. Another was located at the east end of the street.

Striking north from the main street was a second roadway, with houses built on each side, their front doors facing directly onto the rough roadway. The right-hand, or east side, of the street had seven houses in a terrace, that to the west having eight homes in one line. Another water pump was located at the southern end of the east terrace.

A few other buildings existed at the west end of the main street, though by 1896 one of these was partially ruinous. In addition to the rows in this part of the village, there was a branch of the co-operative society. The post office also moved to this part of the village sometime around 1895. Located in a single-storey cottage, with little more than a front door and window, it had small signs announcing 'Post Office', 'Public Telephone' and 'Telegraph Office'. It was to survive here for almost fifty years, before being officially closed on 26 August 1933.

The water pumps in Lassodie dated from 1887, for on 12 September that year a new water supply was inaugurated in the village by Mrs Brownlie, wife of the colliery manager. The water came from bores on the estate, the supply collected in a large tank, the works designed by John Buchanan, civil engineer.

At the inauguration of the water supply, Lassodie Brass Band played, Rev James Clark of the Free Church having opened the event in prayer. Following a series of speeches, in which the residents were invited to use the water freely, but not to waste it, the band led the villagers through the community to each well-head, which was opened on the way.

The arrival of a water supply in Lassodie was a few decades later than the presentation of a public fountain to the residents of Dunfermline. In March 1860 Dr Henry Dewar of Aberdeen, brother of Mr Dewar of Lassodie, presented an Aberdeen granite fountain to the residents, inscribed with the words, 'Lassodie Fountain, presented to the City of Dunfermline by Henry A. Dewar MD, Aberdeen, 1860.' It was unveiled in front of Queen Anne Street Church in May 1860.

24.2 Lassodie Post Office (Mary Searles)

The road through Lassodie took a turn to the right, crossed the Lassodie Burn by a small bridge, and turned left again. At the second corner a drive led uphill to Lassodie Free Church and its manse alongside. This church stood in its own wooded grounds, the gable facing south. On this front was the entrance porch, and two lancet windows were positioned to either side. Higher up on the gable was a round window, and the gable was surmounted by an open belfry.

24.3 Lassodie School (Mary Searles)

The Free Church was keen to make its mark in the village, and early on made evangelical visits to the community. A report from 1865 noted that meetings held by the missionary were 'always crowded'. Soon a congregation had been built up and the new church building was erected. According to a Free Church report of 1875, the church was, 'free of debt and a very handsome structure'. The report, however, stressed that a manse was desirable. It said, 'They are taking steps for the erection of a manse, which is much needed as the only place the minister can get to live is in an earth-floored room in one of the cottages - a most wretched place to study and live in.' This was achieved, for a new manse was erected in 1876-7 to plans by Andrew Scobie. In May 1880 a three-day bazaar was held in St Margaret's Hall, Dunfermline, to raise funds to pay off the manse debt. Ministers serving the church included Rev James Clerk (in the late nineteenth century). Latterly, the church continued without a serving minister, and the congregation was united with Kingseat Parish Church.

When the village was cleared of residents the building was closed as an operating church around the summer of 1931. It was taken over in 1933 as a retreat, being renamed St Ninian's, West Fife Retreat and Conference Centre. This was mainly run by Rev David Patrick Thomson (1896-1974), better known as 'D. P.' He had previously been the minister of the Gillespie Memorial Church in Dunfermline. Although ministers came and went from St Ninian's, D. P. was able to be productive in writing hundreds of Christian books and articles for magazines. He published a number under the imprint, Lassodie Press. One of the visitors who spent some time at the retreat was Eric Liddell, the famous Olympic running champion who was later immortalised in the film, 'Chariots of Fire'. The retreat closed at the start of the Second World War and the buildings were used for a time as a hostel for refugees from war-torn Europe. Soon after peace resumed the building was demolished.

West of the church the road continued, again taking some sharp turns, before arriving at the west end of the village, where the Old Rows were. Just before the road passed under the mineral railway a short drive led to the right, reaching the old post office.

The Old Rows of Lassodie were strung across the hillside. There were two main rows on the north side of the road, an open track passing along the front of each. Between the main road into the community and this track were the gardens for each house. The eastern terrace of cottages had fifteen houses in it, though it may have had different numbers over the years as some cottages were joined to form larger homes.

The western row was longer, with twenty houses in it, again, probably having more at one time. This row had a right-angle bend in it at the western end, the last two cottages built onto the line at an angle. Halfway along the track in front of the western row was a water pump.

A third row existed at this part of the village, located south of the western row. This row had seven houses in it. In the nineteenth century there was a 'Colliery Store', run by James Bruce. He was also a dealer in spirits.

The folk of Lassodie supported their local junior football team, Lassodie Juniors F. C. This team was founded in 1885 and played on a field at Lochend, or Lochview, Park and it was said that they were virtually unbeaten on their home ground. This may have been due to the fact that only they could suffer the poor conditions of the park, which reputedly didn't have much grass on it. In 1887 the team reached the semi-final of the Fife Cup. The game was so boisterous that the players and team officials ended up fighting on the pitch and the referee abandoned the tie. When the game was replayed, Dunfermline won by five goals to one, going on to win the title. The club folded in 1912. Lassodie F. C. was a senior team which existed from 1884-94, playing in a black strip at Greenbank Park. Lassodie F. C. was merged with Kingseat F. C. in 1894 to create Loch Rangers.

The village had many groups and societies to entertain the residents. A Burns club existed, as well as a brass band, the upkeep of which was paid for by a penny a week taken from the miners' wages. Quoits was played on a rink, and racing pigeons were kept in numerous lofts. The horticultural society promoted the growing of flowers and vegetables and ran an annual show and the local Women's Rural Institute encouraged baking and sewing. Lassodie Literary Association held lectures and concerts in the schoolroom in the late nineteenth century. Similarly, the Ancient Order of Foresters, Court Norval No. 6308, existed in the village.

24.4 Lassodie Tavern (Mary Searles)

Health services were supplied by the locals, and Lassodie was fortunate in that it had an ambulance class, which won many competitions. Many residents were to enjoy the care of Margaret Reid, a nurse in the village, who was also able to act as a midwife, district nurse, and also as a dentist on occasion.

Lassodie existed because of coal. In 1859 the Lassodie Coal Company was established, managed by James Brownlie. He was noted as being 'cordial and satisfactory' in his management of the mines and in his relationships with the workers. The company obtained the mining rights to the west end of Lassodie grounds, and there it sunk its first pit. Around it the Old Rows were to be erected to house the miners who came in search of work. There were various pit heads constructed and abandoned over the years, and most of them were linked with railway sidings, allowing the coal to be taken to markets readily. As the years passed, the new pitheads seem to have moved eastwards, searching for new seams of coal.

Pit Number 4 was sunk near to Lassodie Mains, across a field from the school. The bing for waste from the pit was located on the south side of the mineral line, the pithead buildings on the north. In 1887 mining contractors were wanted to drive a dook mine in this pit. Pit Number 6 stood at the east end of the Old Rows, between them and the post office. The spoil heap for Pit Number 9 was positioned at the immediate end of the main street at New Rows, the pithead buildings on the opposite side of the railway from it and the village.

The last pits sunk in Lassodie Colliery were at the east end of the village, between the school and Lochfitty Burn. Pits Number 10 and 11 were sunk in 1893 and worked together. Number 10 had a shaft 360 feet deep. Pit Number 11 had a shaft that was almost 750 feet deep.

Coal from the pits was sold locally, but some of it was sent by train to Edinburgh to supply a growing city. According to an advertisement in the *Scotsman* of 24 October 1863, 'The Lassodie coals are, from the celebrated Dunfermline or Fifeshire Splint Seam, unequalled in point of quality for household purposes: and can be had fresh from the pits daily per rail, at moderate prices from: James Sword, sole agent for the Company, Scotland Street Station, Edinburgh; Junction Wharf and Old Bridge End, Leith'. Another advertisement quoted the price, 'Best splint, great and household coal, all of the finest quality for household purposes, public offices, bakers, &c., from 11s. 6d. to 15s. 6d. per ton including cartage. James Sword, Agent by direct appointment for Edinburgh & Leith.' Production from the pits grew over the years, peaking just before the outbreak of the Great War in 1914 at around 1,300 tons of coal per day.

Although it was noted that the miners at Lassodie Colliery were in general happy with their employers, they did have some disputes over the years. In February 1884, 130 miners employed at the colliery went on strike due to the employers having introduced a new way of weighing coals, known as 'Billy fair play', without having given the men fourteen days' notice. Deaths in the mines were fairly commonplace, amongst those who suffered being Thomas Reid, killed by an explosion in Number 4 Pit on 30 November 1887.

24.5 Lassodie – the New Rows (Mary Searles)

One of the employees at the colliery was John MacQueen. He was the timekeeper and storeman in the pit and died in the village on 17 March 1887, aged 74. His local claim to fame, however, was that he had been one of the crew of the *Forfarshire*, which struck the rocks of the Farne Islands in Northumberland on 7 September 1838 and was rescued by Grace Darling. He was employed as a coal trimmer, or fireman, on the vessel. When Grace Darling and her father arrived at the wreck, he was the first person she spoke to. She asked, 'Oh, honey, honey. How many more are there of you?' MacQueen was almost overcome at seeing that it was a young girl who had come to their rescue. He replied, 'God bless you, woman; God will reward you.' He may not have told his story for much of his life, for it was noted that, 'only a few months ago he gave, in interview, a thrilling narrative of his experience'. Accounts of the rescue often refer to a man in tears, which MacQueen admits was he, and that for years he did not care to speak about the rescue, as it always affected him in the same way. After his shipwreck experience, MacQueen never went back to sea, he 'had had enough of it'. Prior to becoming a sailor, he had served with Dundee Police Force for two or three years prior to 1843, followed by twenty years in the Fifeshire Constabulary, before finding work at Lassodie.

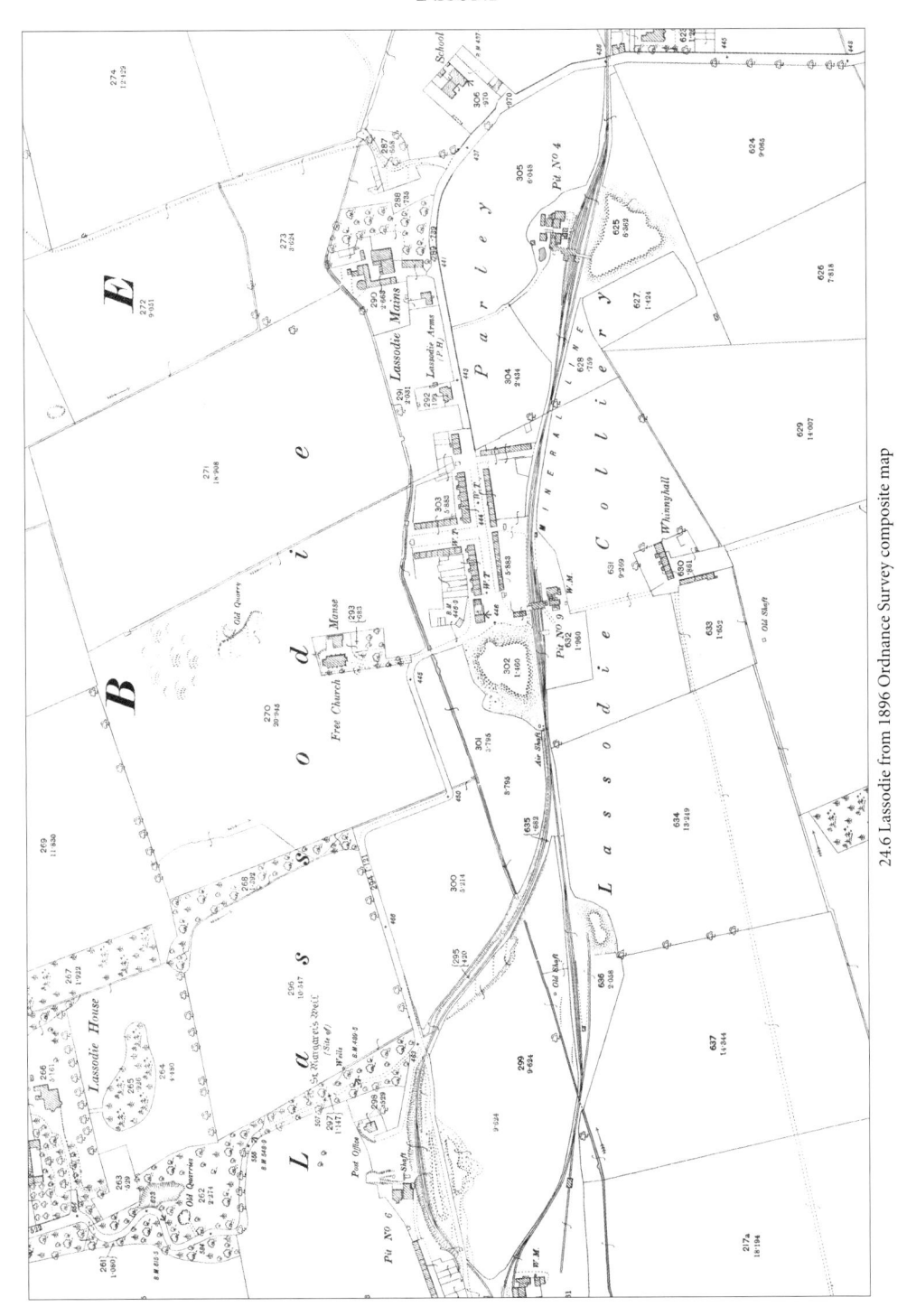

LASSODIE

24.6 Lassodie from 1896 Ordnance Survey composite map

24.7 Lassodie War Memorial

Over the years the population of Lassodie village rose and fell. In 1881 it stood at 808. By 1891 it had risen to 853. In the early 1900s the village was at its largest, with around 200 houses and a population in excess of 1,400, though this included the nearby village of Fairfield.

The Miners' Strike of 1921 is said to have been the start of decline setting in at Lassodie. At that time two of the coal mines were closed permanently, and the miners who had been employed there moved elsewhere in search of new work. By the 1926 strike, things had degenerated even more, and yet more families decided to move elsewhere.

It is said that the coal in the mines ran out in 1931, causing the industry to collapse locally. At the time there were 300 residents in the village, and they were all given a fortnight to quit their homes by the company which now owned the pits – Thomas Spowart & Co, Ltd. The mines had suffered from water ingress, and the pumps were unable to cope with the volume that built up. Spowarts had to clear the site and return it to the agricultural fields that had existed prior to the lease of the coal fields, and as such were to demolish the whole village. A number of residents refused to leave, and five men were taken to Dunfermline Sheriff Court in February 1932. Although they had rent arrears, they were ordered to leave within three weeks. As late as August 1933 there were still thirteen families living in the New Rows, but they were evacuated soon after and the last of the houses were cleared away.

By the 1940s there was virtually nothing left of the village, other than a few buildings that survived and the war memorial. The Ordnance Survey map of 1943 indicated that the Old Rows had been cleared away, other than a few random walls.

The residents from the village used to meet up every year for a reunion, where they enjoyed a meal and a blether, with a guest speaker recalling the years gone by. As the residents themselves dwindled with the passage of time, even the reunions came to an end in the 1970s.

In the 1990s a huge open cast coal mine was created over the lands that once had been Lassodie and Fairfield. The site was named St Ninians. The surface mine covered hundreds, if not thousands, of acres, eating into the hillside and removing all vestige of Lassodie, the nearby village of Fairfield, as well as the estate policies of Lassodie House. In 2013, once the coal had been worked out, restoration work commenced, but the plan had been to create a landform sculpture over much of the eastern end, where the shapes would be visible from the M90 motorway. The internationally acclaimed landscape artist, Charles Jencks, produced a scheme which had numerous mounds in the form of spirals and other shapes, and some of these were almost competed when the Scottish Coal company went into administration in 2014.

Returning back to Lassodie war memorial. Of the four names listed as having perished in the Second World War, two of them were brothers – Private John and AB Neil Mathieson MacLean. John served with the Northamptonshire Regiment and was killed in Italy on 16 December 1944, aged 39. Neil served with the Royal Navy and was killed on 25 February 1944 on H.M.S. *Inglefield*. Their sister, Effie MacLean, was to marry Joseph Connery. Joseph and Effie's son, Sean, was to become one of Scotland's greatest film stars, noted for his part playing James Bond in a number of films. He is known to have visited the village a number of times, his gran and grandpa living at a little cottage known as Bentymires, just south-west of the Old Rows.

25
Lethanhill

★

The first houses to be built at Lethanhill, high on the moor above the Doon valley in Ayrshire, was to become known as the Peewit Row. Ten houses were constructed on a fairly level stretch of the hillside, around 1849, when the Burnfoot pits were sunk. A couple of years later the 1851 Census enumerators arrived and made the first real record of who lived in the community. The surnames of the first ten families to occupy the houses were Dally, Davidson, Frew, Gibb, Higarty, Hope, Hunter, MacBurnie, MacMillan and Wilson. There were a few other families in the houses who lived with the main tenants, plus a number of lodgers. In total there were 72 residents living in the ten houses.

Some work has been done to find out where these residents came from, and it was discovered that only one family was local, being born in Dalmellington parish. The others came from Ireland, Fife, Lanarkshire, Midlothian, Renfrewshire, Wigtownshire, and from elsewhere in Ayrshire.

The Peewit Row was built on a north-west-south-east axis. On the south-west side of the row were the gardens, each looked after by the occupier of the house, the thin moorland soil coaxed into producing some sort of return, even if it was only potatoes.

The second row of houses to be erected at Lethanhill was the Whaup Row. Although built in a parallel fashion to the Peewit Row, the Whaup Row was located 500 yards further up the hill. It was around this row that the bulk of the village of Lethanhill was to be built. By 1861, when the second set of census enumerators visited Lethanhill, the population had risen to 203, living in the two rows.

The Whaup Row had 22 houses in it, again all of one apartment. The walls were built of stone, quarried at Dunaskin. The kitchens measured 18 feet by 10½ feet, the scullery 9 feet by 6 feet. As time passed, many of the houses were joined to form larger units. The conditions were poor, and in 1913 the inspectors who visited found one woman standing outside in the rain doing her washing. There were no closets, wash-houses or ash pits. A few had wooden closets. Each house in this row had a brick coalhouse, which made it appear to be a much superior place compared with the other rows. In 1914 the rent for a single-apartment house was 1s 9d, whereas a double-apartment was 3s 6d.

In the mid-1860s a new track was laid from Burnfoot, near Patna in the valley below, straight up the hillside towards Lethanhill. This allowed easier access to the village, but its steepness was to remain a problem. A secondary problem was the fact that at the foot of the hill were gates which were kept locked by the iron company. Thus, only those with permission could take carts or other wheeled vehicles up to the village. A house near to the gate acted as a gatehouse, the occupant paid to keep the key and only allow authorised vehicles through, in addition to ambulances or hearses. If any family was moving house from Lethanhill to another community, they had to ask permission from the ironworks company to allow their goods to be transported this way. Permission was usually granted, but only if any outstanding debts to the company were settled.

The new road had been vital in transporting materials for building more rows of houses. These were erected near to the Whaup Row, making a sizeable community there. By 1871 there were 190 houses, with a total population of 1,421 residents. Each house appeared to have a family in residence, plus a goodly number of lodgers.

The next phase of building saw the construction of the Step Row, the Low Row, the Diamond Row, School Row, Stone Row, Store Row, White Brick Row

25.1 Lethanhill from south-west

and Briggate Row. The Stone, Store and Whaup Row were positioned round an open area of ground that became known as the Square, the unofficial village centre.

The Step Row had 24 houses in it. It was built alongside the line of the boundary between Burnfoot and Drumgrange farms, though the line of the dike had gone. The row gained its name from the fact that, unlike most of the other rows at Lethanhill, it was built up the line of the hillside, and there were five 'steps' in the line of the roof.

The houses in the Low Row were arranged in three terraces. The first, that nearest the roadway into the village, had 21 two-apartment houses in it. The front doors were facing south-west, towards the lonely Peewit Row. In front of the houses was a narrow pathway, and alongside it ran the mineral siding that headed east to the coal mines of Corbie Craigs and Drumgrange. The Low Row was built of bricks. In each house the kitchen measured 17 feet by 11½ feet. The main room was 9 feet square, and the scullery measured around 8 feet by 7 feet. For this amount of room space, the tenants paid a rent of 2s 3d per week. Water was obtained from a gravitational supply, which often froze in winter. In the scullery was a boiler which could produce hot water. Other facilities were sparse. There was no ash pit for the whole row, and neither was there a coal house. If the call of nature came, the residents had to either use a pan in the house, or else head out into the moor. Only one wooden outbuilding served as a toilet, shared by the whole row.

The second terrace in the Low Row was located immediately to the east of the first row. This row had houses the same shape as the first row, but there were 24 of them. The houses were very damp, the main source of water ingress apparently being through the bottom of the front doors, which bore the brunt of the storms making their way across the moors in front of the houses. To the rear were gardens, stretching backward from the homes. The residents, as with most of the occupants of miners' rows, had to keep their supply of coal in their sculleries. The ashes gathered from the foot of the grates were scattered about the houses to the front and rear, building up over the years. These were seen as helping to reduce the muddy pathways on either side of the row, but in fact did little to help. The third terrace in the Low Row had a further twenty houses, again brick-built and facing the mineral line.

Just beyond the third Low Row terrace was the Briggate Row. It faced a branch line from the railway that passed in front of the Low Row. This branch was little more than a siding, constructed to allow deliveries to be made to the village store. The Briggate Row had twenty houses in it, all single apartment, apart from where two houses were joined to form one larger dwelling. A water pump was located at the west end of the row, at the side of the gardens, which had a gravitational water supply fed to it. The residents complained that the supply was poor, and that they had to share the pump with the residents of the White Brick Row. The tenants in the Briggate Row paid 1s 9d in rent per week in 1914.

The White Brick Row was built lengthways to the north-west of the Briggate Row. Originally there were 26 single-apartment houses in this row, but as with many houses in the community, a number had been joined to form one larger house. Most houses had a front door facing the rough pathway in front of the terrace, and to its side a single window. The roof was a single length of tiles, at every second house pierced with a chimney stack on the apex. The rent was the same as the houses in the Briggate Row, unless it was a double house, for which the rent was 3s 6d.

On the opposite side of the store's railway siding was the Old School Row, its back to the White Brick Row. The front faced to the south-west, generally in a downhill direction, over the allotments each house was supplied with. This row had 24 houses in it, divided into two terraces of eighteen and six houses. In style, the houses were the same as the Low Row. As expected from the name of the row, this was where the original school for the children of Lethanhill had been.

At the north-west end of the Old School Row was the Diamond Row. There were only four houses in this row, generally of the same style as the Old School Row.

Across the Square from the Whaup Row was the Stone Row. This was named from the buildings having been erected with stone quarried at Dunaskin. There were sixteen two apartment houses in this row, the houses having kitchens measuring 17 feet by 11 feet. The rooms were 9 feet square, and the sculleries were 9½ feet by 8 feet. Rent payable for houses of this size was 2s 3d per week in 1914. As with the rest of the village, there was basically no ash-pit, coal house, wash-house or closet for any house. Only in a few cases did the residents have their own self-built timber closet.

The new village attracted the attentions of a reporter from the *Glasgow Herald*, who published his article on 28 January 1875. He noted that, 'whatever may have been the condition of miners' houses in Ayrshire a few years ago', those in Lethanhill, 'were well constructed, commodious and cheap.' He complained about the condition of sanitation in the village, and the lack of means of disposal for waste. Water was obtainable from either springs on the hillside, or else from a pump which raised water from the old Number 9 pit. It was noted that this water, when added to broth or porridge, turned it black!

At the first Lethanhill and Burnfoothill re-union, which took place in Patna in 1965, the speaker, William Murphie, recalled what the village was like:

> I must say without reservation or qualification or equivocation that the 'Hill as a village was unattractive, forbidding, yes, and ugly. The drab, barrack-like uniformity of the miners' rows, planned with no eye to beauty but seemingly to conform to the alignment of the railway tracks that intersected them, presented a picture of unrelieved depression and deadness. The immediate prospect back or front was horrible, open middens and sewers, with the odd pit bing here and there. Situated as it was 900 feet above sea level and refreshed by winds austere and pure, our village should have had a clean bill of health. Yet, enteric fever was not unknown, and enteric is engendered by foul water. It should never have been, and yet the 'Hill reared hardy, tough youngsters – we're not called the 'Hill Arabs for nothing! Nonetheless, the spirit of the 'Hill folks transcended their harsh, cruel, frustrating, physical environment and in time there evolved some attempt at self-expression, cultural and even aesthetic, social recreation and fun and games.

The ironworks company established a store in the village which sold provisions to the villagers. The store received its goods at around four o'clock in the afternoon, and from then until seven at night locals could be seen queuing to buy bread and other necessities. Around 1878 the store was extended with the addition of a beer shop, where beer and ale could be bought. A number of other small shops were run by various villagers, often widows, from their houses over the years. One of the longest-lasting was Mrs Nugent's, located in the Low Row. She sold sweets, cigarettes and tubs of hot peas. She also had the novelty of a fruit machine in her premises, operated by tokens which had to be bought from her, and then spent again in the shop.

The first school at Lethanhill was located in a house at the end of what became known as the Old School Row. Run by the ironworks company, scholars' parents were charged twopence per week for their education. The growing population, and the introduction of compulsory education for children aged 5 to 13 in 1872, meant that the school couldn't cope with the numbers of children in the village, so a new school was opened opposite the eastern end of the Step Row. A single-storey structure, it had slate roofs and various chimneys from fireplaces in each classroom. In 1872 the roll was around 290, but only about 210 attended. In 1879 the roll was 212, taught by a school mistress and four pupil teachers, three of which were female. Headmasters included David Vallance, David B. MacLean, Frank Ferguson, James Parker MacAulay and George J. Donohoe.

25.2 Lethanhill School (left) and Parish Church

In 1901 the national school leaving age was raised to 14, resulting in the building becoming too small once more. In 1912 a new extension was added to the side of the school, containing three classrooms, plus teaching facilities for woodwork, domestic science, science and art. This was still to be too small, so in January 1928 a new school was opened. This was built about 150 yards to the north-west of the old school, behind the church. The school had accommodation for 300 pupils, the roll in 1950 being 195. By 1951 the roll had dropped to 140. The school outlasted the village, however, for Patna Junior Secondary couldn't cope with the numbers, and many children were bused daily up and down the hill. It was eventually closed in 1959, the pupils transferring to the new Patna Junior Secondary School, which had just opened.

When the 1928 school was opened, the older part of the original school was leased to the locals who converted it into a village hall. A committee was formed to run this.

Although most children who passed through the doors of Lethanhill school had little to look forward to when they left, other than a life in the mines, or as miners' wives, a few did manage to achieve greater things. John Hastings Millar was born in the rows in 1921. He left Lethanhill school and attended Dalmellington Higher Grade school for a time, followed by Ayr Academy. He then studied at the University of Glasgow and Trinity College, graduating as a minister in 1948. He was to serve at Glasgow Greyfriars Church before returning to Ayrshire to be minister at Crichton West Parish Church in Cumnock for many years.

Robert Murphie and his wife had three children who were to become teachers – William, Ruby and Nancy. William (born in 1895) was able to move up through the ranks of the profession, ending up as rector, or head teacher, of Fort William Academy.

In the nineteenth and twentieth century emigration was promoted amongst the mining communities across Scotland and beyond. Canada was keen to get workers into the dominion, and Australia and New Zealand made a similar call. One who headed for New Zealand was John Kirk, who lived at 68 White Brick Row. His youngest son, George Kirk, was only six weeks old at the time. It was 1868 and life in the mines was difficult. John's grandson, Norman Kirk, was born in New Zealand in 1923. Life didn't appear to have become any better for his family, for his father was often unemployed, and Norman Kirk started work clearing gutters at the age of twelve. He worked on the railways but ill-health meant that he had to move to the ferries. In his spare time, he taught himself politics and soon was serving in the Ferry-Workers' Union. In 1948 he moved to Kaiapoi to work for the Firestone Tyre Company. In the town he rebuilt the local Labour Party and it became so respected that it won the local elections in 1953. At 30 years of age, Kirk was to be the youngest mayor in New Zealand.

Kirk's political goals did not stop there. He was to be elected as Leader of the Opposition in the New Zealand parliament. At the general election in 1972 he led the Labour party to a landslide victory and he became the country's prime minister. But Kirk's health was never great, and he died on 31 August

1974 after only 21 months in office, suffering a heart attack. He was 51 years of age. His contribution to New Zealand politics was regarded as being considerable, however the *Auckland Star* reported that 'the [Labour] party owed its win more than anything else to the personality of its leader – eloquent in speech, devastating in criticism, a humanitarian with wide horizons, a man of the people writ large.' Kirk introduced laws that established the Queen as monarch of New Zealand, removed compulsory military service and improved social care. President Gerald Ford of the United States wrote that, 'Mr Kirk was an eminent leader internationally as well as at home and a valued friend of the United States. Norman Kirk's humanity, sense of justice and zeal in pursuit of peace will inspire people everywhere long after his passing.'

Although it was a few generations back, Kirk had a longing to visit the home of his ancestors. In 1968 he made a pilgrimage to the Doon valley, carrying a copy of his grandfather's birth certificate. Arriving in Dalmellington, he was to meet up with some distant cousins.

At Lethanhill the war memorial was erected in July 1920. A twelve-foot tall obelisk, it was sculpted by Kennedy of Ayr. On it are the names of sixteen men who paid the ultimate price for defending their country in the First World War. When peace resumed after the Second World War, a further three names were added to the side. The main front of the white granite obelisk reads: *Erected by public subscription and dedicated by the inhabitants of Lethanhill and Burnfoothill to the revered memory of their glorious dead who in making the supreme sacrifice during the Great War 1914-1918 nobly sustained freedom's cause.*

Not listed on the memorial, but one who played an important part in the war, was Nurse Agnes Park. She lived in Lethanhill but served with a French company at the front. When the Allied forces left one of their positions she decided to stay, treating the wounded. When relief medical staff arrived she still refused to leave, remaining to treat every last wounded soldier. She was to be presented with the Croix de Guerre for her devotion to duty and bravery in the field. When she returned to Lethanhill she was treated as a hero by the residents, and they presented her with a gold watch.

In 1921 a new road giving access to Lethanhill and Burnfoothill was built from Downieston, near Patna, across the hillside. Campaigns for a new road commenced in 1919, when local councillor, William Park, added his support to a 3,000-name petition. Ayr County Council agreed to build the road so long as the locals subscribed £150 towards the cost. This was quickly forthcoming, and the road was constructed by Peter Campbell of Cumnock at a cost of £4,065 12s 8d.

25.3 Lethanhill War Memorial

Another improvement in living conditions occurred in 1926 when electricity was supplied to the village for the first time. Electric bulbs, wirelesses and other domestic appliances could be used, and another novelty was the introduction of street lights amongst the rows. Originally, the ironworks company installed just one socket in each house, with the rule that only a wireless may be allowed to be plugged into it. As expected, this rule was flouted, for the convenience of electric kettles and other appliances was too great an attraction.

The minister from Waterside visited Lethanhill and held services in the school up until the 1880s, when the lease of a house became vacant. This building, at 165 Step Row, was converted into a Mission Hall, James Baillie being listed as the lessee. He was Irish by birth and served as superintendent of the Sunday School. The first communion service held at Lethanhill took place in 1896. The church at Lethanhill was erected in 1903 and was opened in October 1904 by the Very Rev Thomas Martin DD, Convenor of the Home Mission

Committee. A simple structure, it was erected from timber and sheeted with corrugated iron. The building fund had aimed for £299, the cost of building the church, but it raised £464, allowing an iron railing to be erected around it. Major donations of £50 came from the Dalmellington Iron Company; the Home Mission donated £51 10s and £6 7s came from overseas supporters. A management committee was formed to run the church, comprising the parish minister (Rev George Hendrie at the time), his assistant (Rev James Dalgetty), and eight villagers. These were James Baillie, James Gibson, John Gillespie, James Hampson, William Moore, Gilbert Park, John Robertson and David Wightman.

In 1936 Lethanhill and Waterside churches were erected into a quoad sacra parish of its own, separated from Dalmellington. The church marked its independence by erecting a new belfry. In April 1938 the new brick-built belfry with its bell was dedicated at a service conducted by Rev Hendrie, who had been minister of the church for over forty years. Others who took part in the service included Rev Thomas Calvert, the minister at the time, and Revs Ninian Wright and Alex Philp, ministers at Dalmellington. The new belfry was designed by Messrs J. B. Wilson, Son, and Honeyman, architects, Glasgow. The bell had previously been located in the belfry of St Valley Parish Church, Dalrymple, which had closed. The building had been purchased by Lieutenant Commander Bethell, and he presented the bell to Lethanhill. A church hall was opened in November 1936. With the population moving out, the last service at Lethanhill was held on Sunday 22 February 1953.

The church was closed in 1947 and the building was put up for sale. It was purchased by the Benquhat Silver Band. Being a timber and corrugated iron structure, it was easily dismantled and transported in sections to Dalmellington where it was rebuilt by the side of the Muck Water as a rehearsal room.

As with all mining communities, death was never too far away. Not everyone was to suffer in the pits. On 29 December 1907 a boy aged thirteen years, the son of Henry Graham, was playing on the ice on a pool in a former open-cast pit. When he fell through the ice he was drowned in the freezing water. At least two other deaths occurred on the mineral lines which passed very close to the houses. These were youths, and both were knocked down by passing coal or ironstone wagons.

Similarly, mining accidents were a frequent event in the calendar of the community. One could never tell when they were likely to take place, and the womenfolk often worried all of the time that their husbands were working in the bowels of the earth. When a fall of rock buried a miner in Pennyvenie pit on 18 November 1932, Thomas Ballantyne, a fellow miner, who lived at 175 Lethanhill, tried to attempt a rescue but he, too, was injured. He was to receive an honorary certificate and £10 from the Carnegie Hero Fund in February 1933.

Lethanhill Thistle was the local football team, playing at juvenile level. The football field was located in front of the first block of houses in the Low Row. Never the best playing surface, the field was tended as best they could by the players and supporters. Archie Ballantyne and Tom Ravie were regarded as the team's two best players. Jimmy Weir also played for Thistle, but signed for Ayr Football Club, and then Celtic, playing left-back from 1904 until 1910, winning two Scottish Cup medals and the league championship six times.

The population of Lethanhill began to decline in the late 1800s. In 1890 there were 93 houses that were unoccupied, the population at the Census of 1891 being 736. However, in 1899 the Dalmellington Iron Company sank a new coalmine to the north of the village, known as the Houldsworth Pit. Miners flocked back to Lethanhill, resulting in all of the houses being occupied and the population rising once more.

The first houses to be demolished at Lethanhill were the first that had been erected – the Peewit Row. In the early 1900s, as folk moved out of the houses, they were shut up until only one remained in occupation. However, around the same time the slag bing at Waterside was becoming so large that there was no room for more tipping. It was decided to dig a new channel and redirect the River Doon, allowing more room for the dump. A group of Irish navvies carried out this task, and for the time they worked on the job they lived in the old houses. Once they moved on, the houses were demolished.

Clearing Lethanhill began in 1947, the first residents moving into newly-erected council houses in Patna. A list for priority housing was compiled, so that married couples and sub-tenants were first to be given new homes. By 1951 the Diamond, Peesweep and Whaup rows were totally empty, and the remainder of the rows only had around ten to fifteen percent occupancy. The period of evacuation lasted seven years, the last to move out doing so in 1954. Accounts vary as to who this was – either James Stevenson, who moved out on 31 August 1954, or Robert Bryce, who had to be moved under protest to Patna at the age of 79.

LETHANHILL

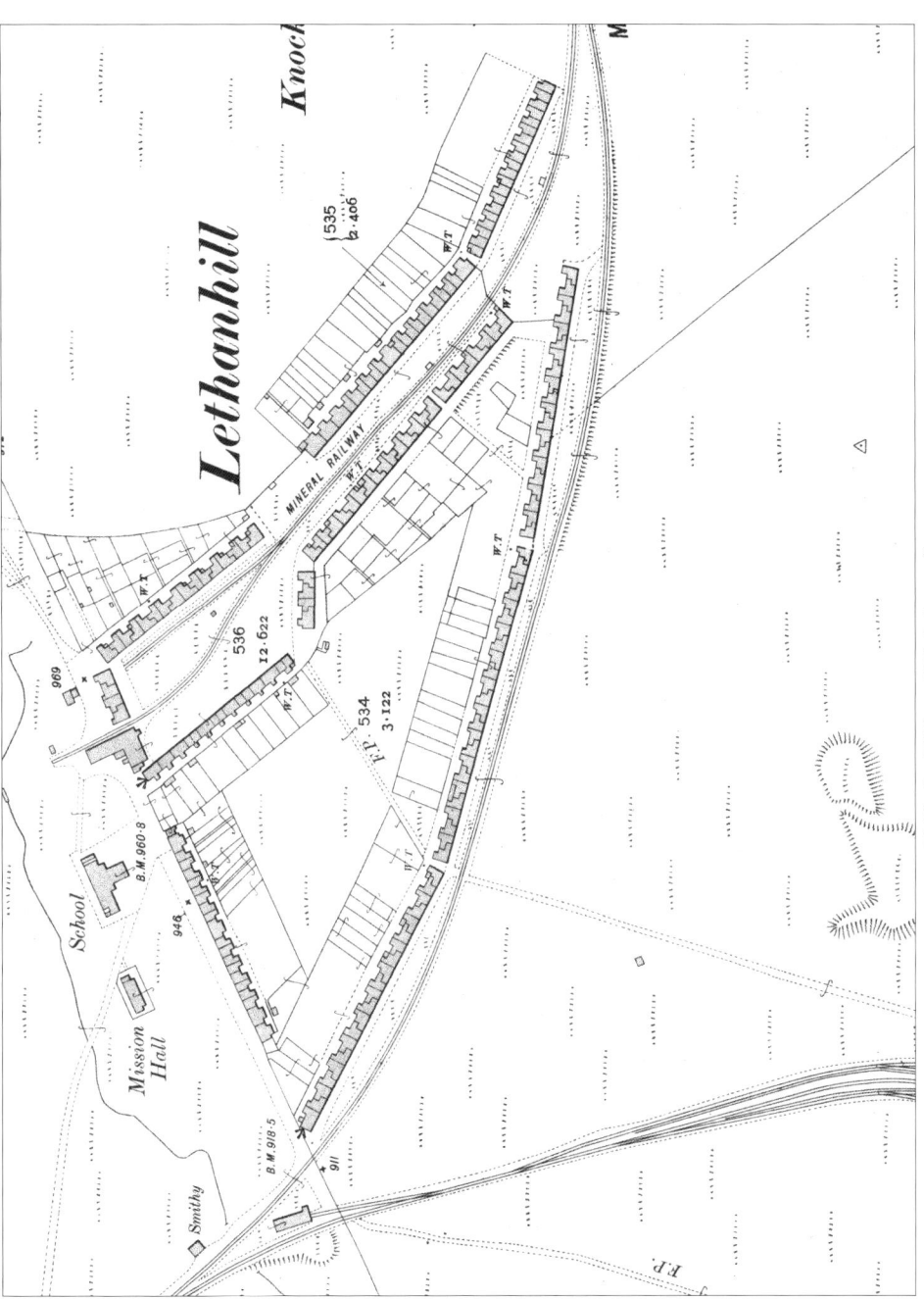

25.4 Lethanhill from 1909 Ordnance Survey map

Only the schoolhouse remained occupied, the head teacher still in residence. Appointed in 1950, George J. Donohoe was forced to remain in residence as his contract included the tenancy as part of his wages. When the school closed in 1959, with the opening of a new larger school at Patna, he was obliged to remain for years thereafter, travelling down and up the hill each school day. The house is still occupied, the last building in Lethanhill.

The school building remained until 1959, and the newer half of the building was used as a shed by the farmer up until 1983, before it, too, was flattened.

In August 1965 the first 'Hill Reunion took place at Patna Primary School, with over 400 former residents turning up to hear William Murphie reminisce about his time in the village. The re-unions continued for many years thereafter.

It is still possible to make one's way to Lethanhill. The 'new' road built in 1921 leaves the main Doon valley road just to the north of Patna, at the railway bridge. It crosses through a couple of fields before striking quickly uphill. It appears to climb in levels, soon passing the old Schoolhouse. Another level or two brings one to the war memorial, virtually the only remnant of the village of Lethanhill. The foundations of the old school and church can just be made out on the ground, but to find the footings of the rows themselves one has to venture into the plantation of pine trees which occupies the site of the old village. Soon, one will see the remains of brick walls, stone foundations and various bits and pieces that once formed parts of miners' homes.

A large block of concrete, which was formerly part of one of the buildings, lies at an angle on the side of the roadway up past the Step Row, heading towards the transmitter on the hillside. On it are painted the words, '1851-1954 Long Live The Hill'. In the immediate vicinity are the ruins of the old store, and over the fence can be seen an almost complete wall with a window, the last major relic of the Whaup Row. If one takes a wander through the pine plantation, which occupies the full site of Lethanhill, one can find more remnants. Foundations of the Stone Row protrude through the woodland floor, and the White Brick Row has more remains. There, one can see the large creamy-coloured bricks that gave the row its name, as well as the stone rear walls, and stone slabs that formed the sides of many fireplaces. The easternmost gable of the row survives to over 8 feet in height.

Of the Briggate and Old School rows, there is little to be seen. Similarly, the Low Row has more or less completely gone, but here and there can be found some brick foundations and remnants of fireplaces. At one location the iron bars that supported the sink in the scullery still stand proud from the ground. The remains of the Step Row survive in the stone foundations. Here and there, through the whole forest plantation, one can come across brick-built closets, eerily standing amongst the trees. One of the last facilities to be added to the houses, they appear to be one of the last structures to succumb to the ravages of time.

To the south-west, one can see the brick base of the old drumhead at the top of the incline down to Waterside. The site of the Peewit Row is gone, the surface here having been dug away and refilled when the Burnfoothill area was worked as a surface coal mine.

26
Longrigg
✶

Longriggend is a small community of disparate houses on the moors to the north of Caldercruix in Lanarkshire. At one time it was much larger, having a population of 1,552 in 1901, but today it is really a small community in decline, its population in the region of two hundred. The road heading east from Longriggend, making towards Slamannan, wends its way along what was described as a 'long rigg', or elongated hill, passing through forest plantations and some open fields. Just over half a mile from Longriggend itself is Longrigg farm, the steading at the roadside, its U-shaped layout typical of thousands of Scottish farmsteads of its type. Of the village of Longrigg, virtually nothing survives.

Longrigg was divided into three parts – East Longrigg, Longrigg itself, and West Longrigg. East Longrigg was, as its name suggests, the easternmost part of the community, and was more or less positioned between the county boundary (separating Lanarkshire from Stirlingshire) and a mineral railway which made its way to the Longrigg Colliery pits. There were a few houses across the border in Stirlingshire, and a short row of houses on the opposite side of the railway from the main rows. The houses on the Stirling side of the boundary comprised four small dwellings in a single terrace. These faced directly on to the road, and the houses had garden areas to the rear.

The road makes a slight bend on the line of the boundary, and here the main terraces of East Longrigg started. On the north side of the road were three long lines of houses. The east-most contained twelve homes, the four furthest east being double-apartments, the other eight containing just one apartment. The front doors opened directly onto the public road, and at the rear were areas allocated as gardens.

The middle terrace on the north side of the road contained ten single-apartment homes, again very similar to those in the east terrace.

The western terrace on the north side of the road had thirteen houses in it, seven small single-apartment houses at the western end, and six double apartment ones at the east. On the side away from the road were small drying greens and a couple of outbuildings, no doubt wash-houses and perhaps privies.

There were three terraces on the south side of the road, almost mirroring those on the north. At the eastern end was a line of ten single-apartment houses, and next to it a second row of ten single-apartments. A narrow lane between the two led from the street through to the back yard, where there was a wash-house.

The western terrace on the south side comprised nine single-apartment homes and four double-apartments, again with wash-houses to the rear. Between the western and central row on the south side was a larger building.

In 1910 the houses were inspected to find out what condition they were in. It was noted that East Longrigg had fifty double-apartment houses, the rent payable to Messrs Nimmo being £6 14s 6d. There were also 22 single-apartment houses, the rent being £4 19s 8d. The houses were built of brick and were of one storey, having been erected in the 1870s. The walls were solid, without damp-proof courses, but the floors inside were timber. The walls were rough and damp. The kitchens were of a fair size, but the back rooms in the double-apartment houses were small. There were no wash-houses or coal-cellars for the tenants, and though garden ground was available, few miners took this up. Following the inspection, the company had provided a tile drain around the houses, to try to remove some of the water that caused the dampness, put two coats of cement plaster on the exterior facades and made repairs to floors and walls. They also converted those windows which previously did not open so that ventilation was possible. Two new water stand-pipes were installed, and additional privies were erected, in the proportion of one for every two houses.

The mineral line that passed through East Longrigg made its way under the street by means of a bridge, and on the west side of the bridge were three houses, all located on the north side of the road and joined together. These were superior houses, compared with the rest of the community, for they were much larger, had gardens to the front and rear, and two of them even had front porches. On the opposite side of the road, slightly to the west, was a single cottage, again of more substantial construction, with its own garden.

Longrigg itself was built along the north side of the road along the ridge, all to the east of Longriggend. Starting at the end nearest East Longrigg, there was a short terrace of six cottages with gardens to the rear and an outside toilet at the foot of the garden, shared by the occupants.

Next in the line of buildings was Longrigg School, built onto the west end of what was the schoolmaster's house. By the 1870s this was occupied by David Scott Masterton (1852-1916), schoolmaster, who remained until his death. He had been born in Dundee and came here to teach. He and his wife, Mary Graham, had nine children, all born here, the eldest, John Masterton OBE (1878-1933), becoming a divisional inspector of mines. The school was originally funded by the local coalmasters, but it was later to come under the control of Clarkston School Board when the Education (Scotland) Act was passed in 1872. The school was extended in 1883-4, a new classroom with accommodation for 72 children being designed by Coatbridge architect, A. MacGrigor-Mitchell. In 1886 the school roll was 366. At the time, however, a fair number of pupils attended the school who lived in Slamannan parish and thus their parents did not contribute to the cost of running the school. Attempts at getting Slamannan School Board to pay for their children had been unsuccessful, and Clarkston School Board threatened to turn them away.

A little row of four houses followed, and beyond this, close to the farmstead, were two L-shaped blocks of housing. That to the east had six houses of various sizes in it. The western L-shaped terrace had eleven houses in it.

West Longrigg was the most village-like of the three communities bearing the name Longrigg. In addition to the rows of cottages facing the main road, there were further houses located to the rear, forming streets and squares of dwellings. On crossing the railway bridge (another mineral siding struck across the road at the east end of the community) there was a long row of houses on the south side of the road. This row had fourteen houses in it. Behind the homes, to the south, were areas of garden and drying greens.

A narrow lane between two rows of houses was the means of accessing the greens behind the row, and beyond it was a block of housing, formed in an L-shape. Three houses in this block faced on to the main road. At the corner was a larger building. On the road striking south-eastwards were four houses built onto the corner building. In a plot beyond this was a single house, larger in size than the usual miner's home. Across the road from this short street were the remains of an old mine, the bing still there, but which had been abandoned prior to the late nineteenth century.

On the north side of the main road at West Longrigg was a line of houses that backed onto the minor line. Although L-shaped in plan, only one cottage faced the main road. The other nine houses faced westwards, onto a street that struck north. Although originally all single-apartment houses, one of these buildings appears to have latterly contained a smithy and others were converted into a joiner's workshop. Others became a stable for the horse that was used to cart coal in the vicinity.

Facing the main road was a row of double-backed houses. There were nine houses facing the main road, the two east-most houses being larger than the rest. Built back to back to these were another nine houses, again the two at the eastern end being larger.

A wide, open square separated this row of houses from a similar-styled double-row. This had ten houses on each side, all of the same size. There were wash-houses at the end of the squares formed here, shared by the residents of the rows.

North of the second double-row was a short row of homes, built at 45 degrees to the rest of the houses. There were only four or five houses in this row, but it was demolished sometime around 1900, for they are not shown on the Ordnance Survey maps of 1914. North again from the angled row was another block of housing. Latterly (according to the 1914 map) there were three double-apartment houses and three single-apartment homes in it, but the 1890s map incorporates this row of six houses in an L-shaped block of homes. At that time there were eight houses on the north-east/south-west side, with a further five houses on the side facing south-west. Adjoining the east end of this L-shaped row was an engine-shed, with a railway siding entering it near to the junction. In 1885 it was noted that there were 98 householders in West Longrigg making up a population of 548. The sub-village of West Longrigg was erected by James Gemmell, owner of the local colliery, hence the village often being referred to as 'Gemmell's'.

In 1895 a Clarkston man surnamed Russell applied to the council for a porter and ale license for a property at West Longrigg. This pub was later taken over by Tom Sommerville, hence the row in which it was located being known as 'Toam's Raw'.

In 1910, inspectors who were compiling a report on living conditions for miners and their families, visited West Longrigg and noted that there were thirty one-apartment houses in the community, for which the rent was £4. There were also 27 two-apartment houses, the rent for which was either £5 or £6, and a single three-apartment house, the rent for which was £9. The houses were all of a single storey, built of brick around 1870. There was no damp-course in the walls, and the interior walls were plastered onto the solid brick. The apartments were described as being fairly large, and as a consequence, there was no overcrowding. There was some garden ground available for tenants, but few took the allotments up. There were no coal-cellars or wash-houses, but there were three privy middens, located forty feet in front of the houses. The houses here were scavenged at the mine-owners' expense, at the time being the Darngavil Coal Company Ltd. They appear to have been demolished fairly soon after the report was compiled.

26.1 Longrigg – David Masterton and family (Graeme Johannessen)

Mr Masterton, headmaster of the school, was also the superintendent of the Longrigg Sabbath School. This was attended by almost all of the children of the village, who were delighted to get the annual picnic. As an example, at the picnic in 1891 around 170 children marched behind Longriggend Temperance

Band from the school to Glentore farm. They played at cricket, rounders, racing and other games. They were supplied with 'buns and milk' and other refreshments before marching home.

Although most of the residents of Longrigg were employed in the coalmines, there was also a sizeable engineering works on the Slamannan Section of the North British Railway. These works were located at the Longrigg Siding of the railway, where the mineral line for West Longrigg Coal Pit Number 5 and Drumbow Colliery left the main line. In the obtuse angle formed by the railway lines were three large engineering sheds, two of which had railway sidings making their way into them.

In 1868 Nimmo & MacKillop sunk the first pit at Longrigg Colliery. For some reason, MacKillop withdrew from the partnership two years later, after which the mines were owned by James Nimmo and Company. Accidents in the pits were fairly common, and many locals were to suffer death in incidents underground.

The West Longrigg Colliery had five fatalities over its sixty-plus years of life. On 22 October 1880 Archibald MacNeil fell from a mid-working to his death. On 16 October 1882 Robert Martin fell down the pit along with the hutch. On 11 November 1902 John Menzies was killed by a roof collapse. David Butler suffered in a fire-damp explosion on 25 April 1904.

It wasn't just below ground that folk lost their lives. On 26 December 1885 Robert Robertson was killed when a 'pug' engine he was shunting at the colliery left the rails. The waggon behind was being pulled by it and it knocked against him, the buffer crushing him against the engine, killing him almost instantly. Another railway fatality occurred in June 1887 when an engine making its way from the pit at West Longrigg left the rails at a bad bend. Fourteen waggons behind then piled over and around it, being pushed from the rear by another engine. The driver of the pug, George Black, was killed. His son, a lad of fourteen years, jumped from the pug in the opposite direction and survived. He and his siblings were orphaned, their mother having died two years earlier. In 1890 Samuel MacGuire was working a dross washing machine at Longrigg when loaded waggons crushed him.

With Longrigg being built on the top of a hill – about 714 feet above sea level at the school – getting a reliable water supply was a bit of a difficulty. The Culloch Burn, which flowed at the bottom of the field to the south of the community, was often called upon as a source of water at times, but eventually water pumps were positioned about the village. The Ordnance Survey map of 1896 only shows two wells in the community – one at the west end of West Longrigg, the other to be found in the re-entrant angle of the western L-shaped terrace at Longrigg. At West Longrigg, four pumps were installed around 1910, and at the school and elsewhere pumps were installed in the late nineteenth century.

The population of Longrigg grew from zero in the 1860s (it didn't exist at the time of the 1861 Census) to 203 in 1871. By the time the next Census was carried out in 1881, the enumerators counted the population as being from either West Longrigg (333) or East Longrigg (519), totalling 852. By 1891 this had increased yet again to 1,160 (522 West plus 638 East). The number of residents started to decline thereafter, being 795 in 1901 (309 West and 486 East).

The clearance of Longrigg commenced between the two World Wars. By 1940, the bulk of East Longrigg had gone, leaving only the three houses in Stirlingshire standing and the four houses built west of the railway siding bridge. In Longrigg proper the school had been demolished, but most of the other houses still stood. Virtually all of West Longrigg had been cleared away.

LONGRIGG

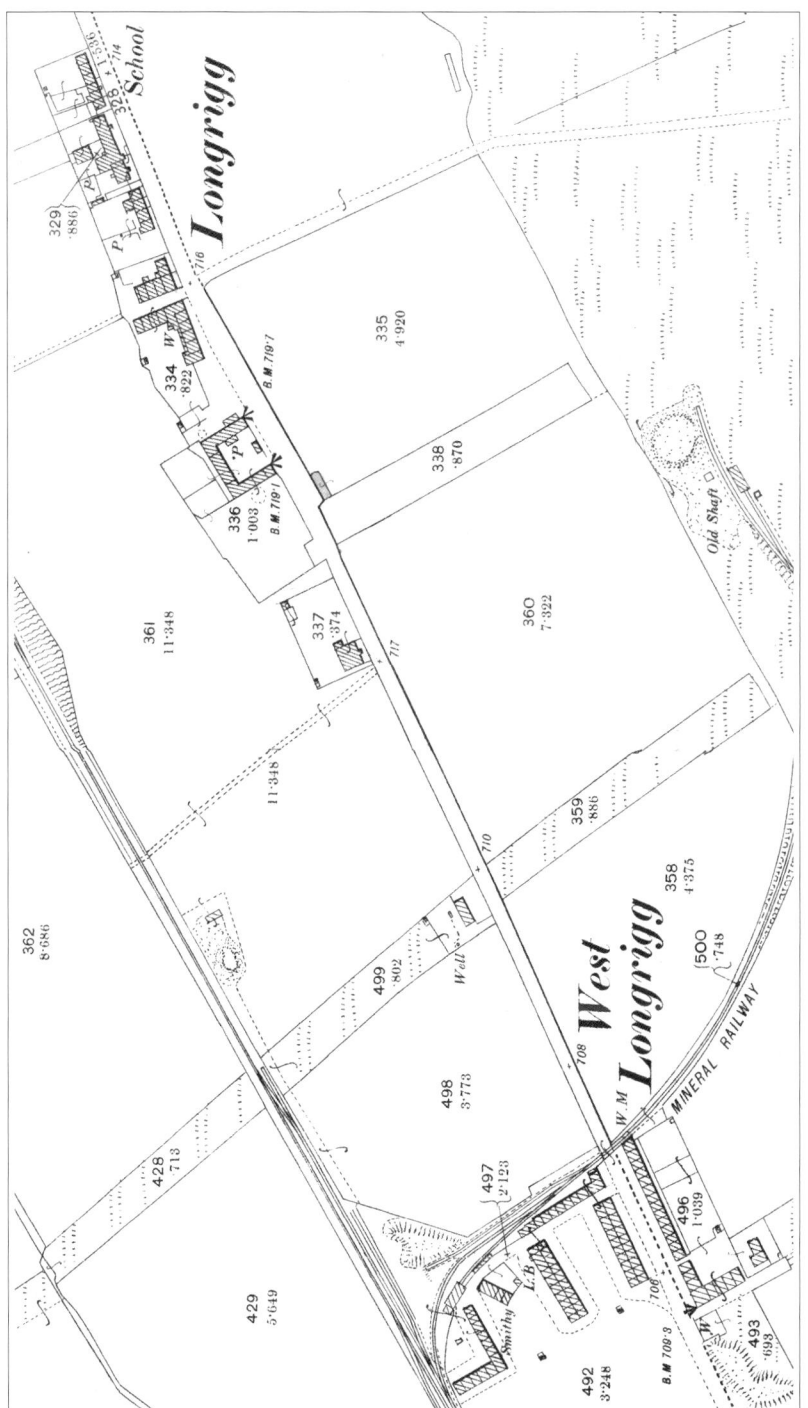

26.2 Longrigg from 1898 Ordnance Survey map

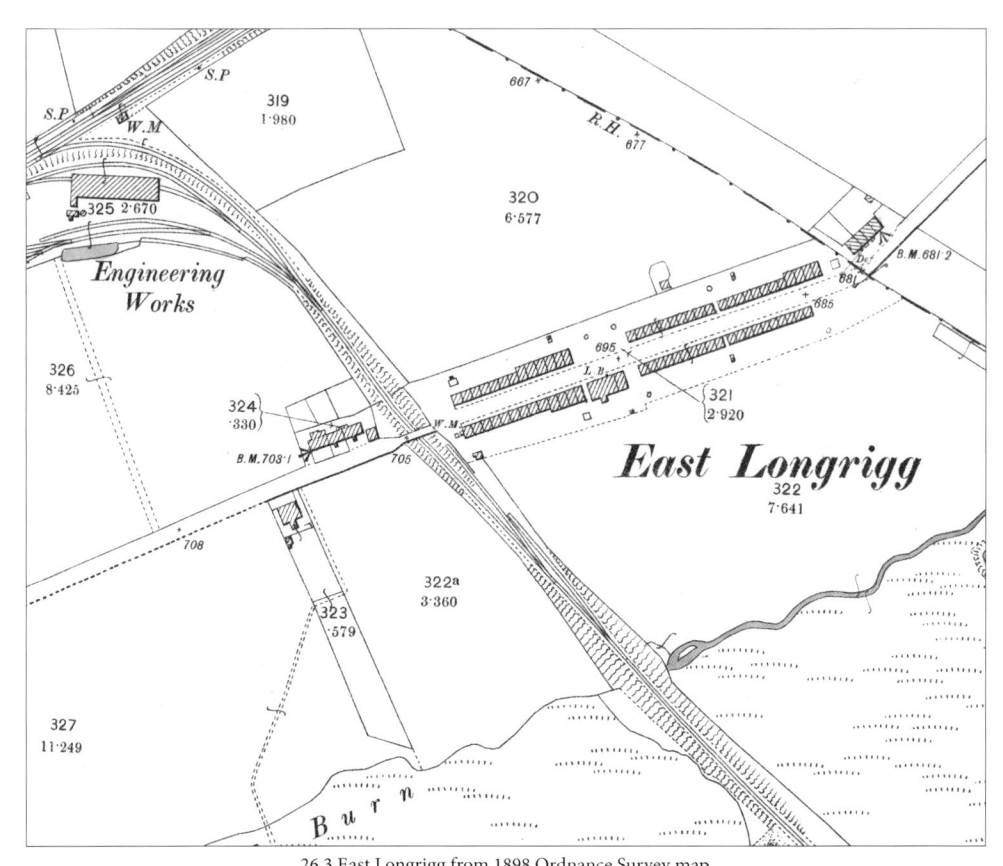

26.3 East Longrigg from 1898 Ordnance Survey map

27
Midbreich

✶

When the Ordnance Survey compiled their detailed maps of the country at the end of the nineteenth century, Mid Breich was just a farm. Around 1885 a new community was erected to the south of the farm road, between the farms of Mid Breich and Wester Breich. The houses were built by the Hermand Oil Company to house men who worked in their local mines, as well as at the Breich Oil Works. The Hermand Oil Company appear to have purchased the Mid Breich property, and also acquired the mineral leases of the adjoining Easter and Wester Breich. Although the company had started the works around 1894, it appears to have had a faltering start. A report in the *Edinburgh Evening News* of 4 September 1895 gives some details as to the position the company was in:

> The annual general meeting of the [Hermand Oil Company] was held yesterday afternoon in Lyon & Turnbull's rooms, Edinburgh. The annual report expressed the regret of the directors that they had not been able to see an opening for recommencing operations with any prospect of advantage during the year, and the company's works at Breich still remain closed. Should, however, the present improvement in the oil trade continue, they hope ere long to be in a position to recommend resuming work. The only leases held by the company are those covering the properties of Easter and Wester Breich, both of which adjoin the company's own estate of Mid-Breich, contain the same description of shale, and can be advantageously worked along with it. There has been a loss on the brickwork at Walkinshaw of £638 19s 5d, but this includes the ground-rent for Walkinshaw Refinery. This is entirely accounted for by the work being suspended for several months, first by the coal strike of last year and by the severe and long-continued frost in the early parts of this year. A rearrangement of the method of working has been made, and a fair profit is now being realised.

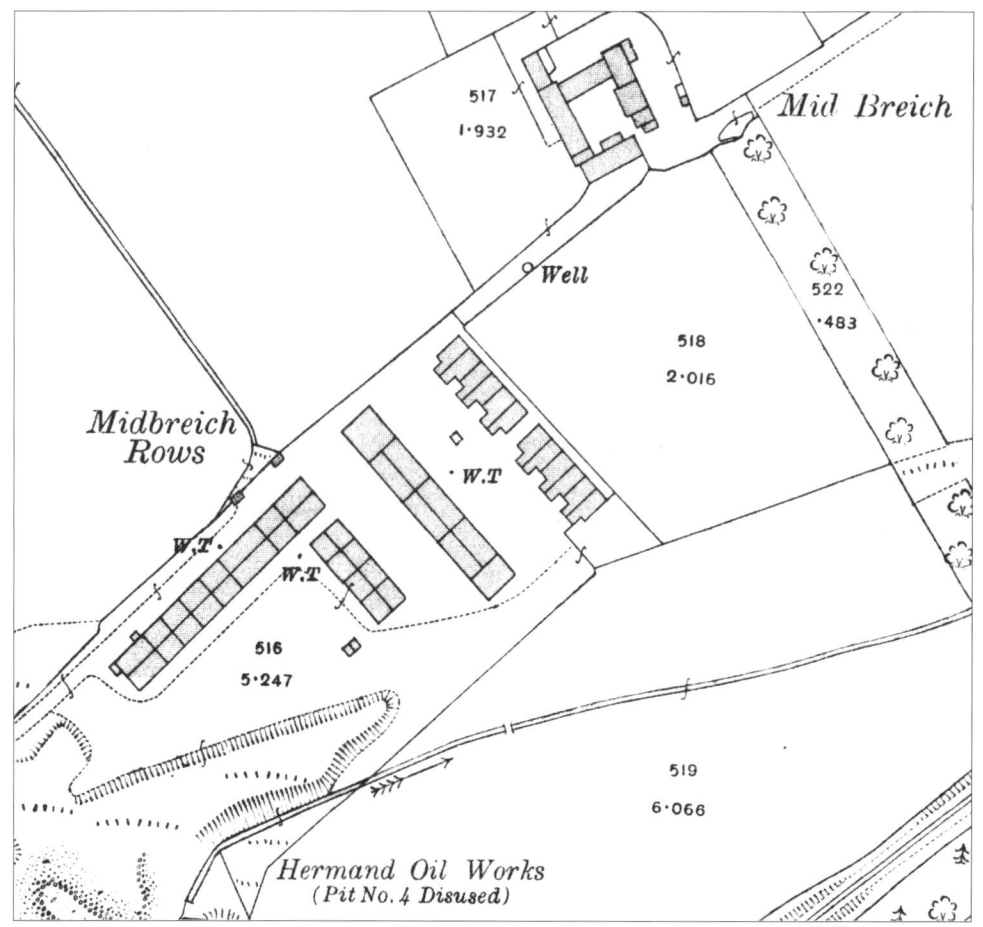

27.1 Midbreich from 1917 Ordnance Survey map

The village of Midbreich was reached from a minor road that linked Blackburn with West Calder. The old Mid Breich farm road was used as the sole road into the community. The first row reached when arriving at Midbreich comprised of back-to-back houses. There were originally twenty-two houses in total in this row, eleven facing each way. Eight of the houses were single-apartment, four located at either end of the row, whereas fourteen of the houses had two rooms.

Built perpendicularly to this row was another, containing eight houses. These were also built back to back and comprised double-apartment homes.

Parallel with the second row was another longer row, perpendicular to the farm road. This row had sixteen houses in it, again built back to back. Most of the houses in this row had two rooms, though the house at the south-eastern end of the row appears to have been larger.

The three original rows were built at the same time. Early in the twentieth century a new row of houses was added to Midbreich, built parallel with the third row. This row comprised of two terraces of six houses each. These houses, being newer, were built to a higher standard, and had better living conditions for the residents. They had two rooms in each house, in addition to a scullery.

Immediately adjoining Midbreich was the Hermand Oil Works Pit Number 4, its bing rising to the south-west of the houses. From it a tramway led eastwards, taking the shale coal to the Breich Oil Works, just a few hundred yards away. The pit-head buildings were located by the side of the road. Due to a downturn in the demand for shale coal, and a drop in quality produced in the pit, in February 1902 the New Hermand Oil Company announced that it was to cut the price paid per ton of shale to the miners from 2s 3d to 2s, and that the poorer shale coal should not be worked. The chairman of the company, Mr Chalmers, stated that the night shift in the mine would stop, and that one bench of retorts would be removed. Negotiations with the miners continued for some days but were unsuccessful.

Breich Oil Works were closed in 1903 when the New Hermand Oil Company Limited went into liquidation. A small advertisement in *The Scotsman* of 3 June that year offered for sale, 'the mineral estate of Mid-Breich, West Calder, belonging to the New Hermand Oil Company, Limited (in liquidation), and the machinery, plant, &c., of said company.' A second advertisement in the paper added some additional detail. We find that the property of Mid-Breich extended to 163 acres. On sale was, 'the whole machinery, plant, stores, &c., at the company's works. The estate of Mid-Breich is estimated to contain about 5 million tons of shale of which more than one-half is "Fells" and "Broxburn", and both seams could be easily and quickly opened up. The farm is let at an annual rent of £50, and there are 32 workmen's cottages on the estate. The machinery, plant, &c., includes the following: - one bench of 32 Pumpherston Patent Retorts, Sulphate of Ammonia plant, steam boilers, winding and haulage engines, M-L stock tanks, &c.'

The Pumpherston Oil Company (which was established in 1883) was to purchase the mineral rights to the Hermand mines hereabouts, as well as the miners' homes. It was probably after they had purchased the village that the new row of houses was added. Although the oil retorts were relocated, the mining of shale resumed, and as a result new miners and their families came to Midbreich and occupied the houses. In addition to this, some of the old houses in the rows were reconfigured, the internal walls being rebuilt to form larger houses. The oil works remained closed, and the Pumpherston company had the retorting plant dismantled and rebuilt at Seafield, so as to concentrate the company's operations.

The water supply to the village was obtained from three water pumps which were positioned amid the rows. One of these was located on the north side of the western row, between it and the farm road. Behind it was a second pump, used by the back row of houses, as well as the short perpendicular row. The third pump was positioned to the east of the long perpendicular row, and also served the new terrace of houses. In addition to these pumps was an old well, located on the farm road, just to the east of the village.

Nearer the end of the life of Midbreich, a post office was established in one of the former single-apartment houses. This was the eighth house on the first row on entering the village from the west. With the arrival of the telephone, a call box was positioned outside it.

In 1914 Theodore K. Irvine compiled a *Report on the Housing Conditions in the Scottish Shale Field*, in which he reported:

> ... twelve houses consist of room, kitchen, attic, scullery with boiler, sink and w.c. Coal cellars and dust-bins are provided. Rental 4/- per week. There are 17 houses consisting of one room and kitchen, with scullery and boiler, and eight one-apartment houses with scullery. Rent for the former, 2/9, and the latter, 2/1 per week, inclusive of rates. For the latter 25 houses, privies only are provided, and three ashpits. The kitchen floors of these 25 houses are made of cement. The size of the kitchens is 17 ft x 14 ft, and the rooms are of the same dimensions. There are no drying greens, but poles are put up for the ropes. The houses are owned by the Pumpherston Oil Company. There are forty-three houses in Breich, occupied by 224 persons.

The various shale coal mines around Midbreich operated on and off for a number of years. The Mid-Breich Shale Mine operated up until 1946, when it was closed. However, in 1948 it was reopened and worked on a smaller scale for a time.

By the Second World War many of the houses in the old rows were being vacated and the houses closed up. By September 1958 a meeting at Middleton

Hall considered the future of the houses. It was recorded that, 'Thirteen houses have been officially closed. One block completely empty and can be demolished. Houses No. 33-44 to be maintained. The remaining houses to be closed when vacated. Demolition of the closed block to be carried out by the demolition squad after demolition at Pumpherston has been completed. Tenants in Deans Village, employed at Westwood, should be considered for empty houses in this village.' The houses numbered 33-44 referred to the new terrace.

Today, most of the site of Midbreich is covered in woodland, the old road still providing access to Mid Breich farm.

28

Mossend

★

To the north of West Calder, on land beyond the West Calder Burn, is the site of a sizeable community known as Mossend. There is a modern scheme of houses bearing the same name, located just to the south of the old village, and regarded as being part of West Calder itself. One of the streets here is known as Mossend and following it will bring one to the site of the old village.

Mossend occupied a diamond-shaped piece of land on the west side of the road. The community was built by Young's Paraffin Light and Mineral Oil Company to house its workers from Polbeth Shale Pits. The first houses were erected around 1870. Travelling from West Calder, the first block of houses reached originally had six homes in it, though these were latterly of different sizes. As the years passed, the first four houses were merged to form two larger dwellings, the last two remaining the same size. Immediately after this short row were three terraces of homes, separated by narrow lanes between them. (The gap between the first row and the three terraces was larger.) The first two terraces had six houses in each row, the third terrace having eight homes. The front of the houses faced onto a pavement which separated it from the road, unimaginatively known as the Front Street. To the rear, the houses had new sculleries added to them at some time, improving the facilities of the miners who lived here. A lane passed by the rear of these houses, separating them from the allotment gardens that were arranged behind. In most cases the garden associated with each house was not directly behind it.

At the end of the three terraces was a road striking to the west. This was known as Mid Street, from its position through the centre of the community. The street had houses lining both sides, four terraces on the south side, and a mirror image of four on the north. The terraces were built close to each other, the intervening street being rather narrow, with no room for pavements. On the south side of the street, each of the four terraces had six houses in each row. The north side of the street was very similar, though over the years some of the houses were to have had small sculleries added on. The houses in Mid Street had some allotments to the rear of the houses.

MOSSEND

Front Street took a bend to the left to the north of the Mid Street junction. The west side of the street was lined with a further six terraces of homes, separated from the road by a pavement. Nominally, each of these terraces had six houses in it, but as years passed some of the houses were joined together to form larger dwellings, suitable for bigger families. As with most of the other rows at Mossend, many of the houses were to have sculleries added to the rear.

On the opposite side of the road from the northern Front Street houses, was Mossend Cottage, a sizeable building which was located immediately below the pit bing. This predated the village by many years, originally being a small farm.

28.1 Mossend – Front Street (West Lothian Council)

A third street existed at Mossend, linking the north end of Front Street with the west end of Mid Street. This was known as East Street, even although it was located at the west side of the community. There were five terraces here, each with six houses in it. It was the same story here regarding houses being joined to form larger homes. The street was narrow, and on the north-west side of it, across from the homes, were a series of small buildings, being outhouses. Behind the rows at East Street was a large triangular area, surrounded by the other rows, used as a recreation area, but in some places fenced off to create gardens.

It was in East Street that one of the residents appeared to run an illicit off-sales. Archibald Kerr was hauled before the Justice of the Peace Court in Edinburgh on 26 March 1872 under the charge of having trafficked excisable liquors in his house. A girl surnamed Reid had been sent to his house by a woman named Bryce. She was to ask for a pint of Scotch porter, which she duly received from Kerr after she paid him two-pence. At the court the girl stated that she had purchased porter from the same house on previous occasions, and that it was produced from a cupboard in the kitchen. The woman named Bryce claimed that she was concerned at the amount of shebeening that was taking place from the house, and had set up the sting. At the court, it was related that the law allowed the sale of table-beer up to the value of 1½ pence, so long as a licence was obtained. The prosecutor therefore said that the accused should be found guilty. However, the agent for the defence claimed that the charge came about as a result of one person using the law to gratify a personal spite. As a result of the doubt over the case, and the fact that there were no other witnesses, the charge was found not proven.

Shebeening seems to have been a common problem in many mining villages, where wives and widows tried to make a living. In March 1871 Agnes Renny, wife of John Renny, was convicted of trafficking in excisable liquors at Mossend without owning a licence. She was sentenced to pay either £7 or else serve six weeks in prison.

In 1914, when Theodore Irvine compiled his *Report on the Housing Conditions in the Scottish Shale Field*, he noted that, 'There are 140 double-apartment houses. The water is supplied by four stand-pipes. The rental is 2/3 per week, inclusive of rates. There are no coal cellars, wash-houses, or sculleries. Dry privies exist, but are practically public nuisances. The refuse is removed weekly by the Oil Company. The sewage is disposed of in an open channel. There is a contrast in black and white about these houses - the gables are blackened with tar, whilst the fronts and backs of the house are whitewashed.'

The report was to be instrumental in bringing about improvements to Mossend. Originally, all houses had two apartments within them. In the 1920s, many of the houses were extended to the front when new brick-built sculleries were added. These had doors to one side, leading into a small vestibule. A water-closet was located to the right, and a coal-shed was incorporated into the porch.

The residents of Mossend obtained their water from a couple of pumps. These were located by the side of the road, one in the southern part of Front

Street, the other in the northern part. There was a bleaching green in the village, where the womenfolk laid out their washing to dry in the sun. In June 1879 James Nelson, a young boy of around eleven years of age, was found guilty of having stolen items of clothing from the green. He was sentenced to be confined for five years in Leith Industrial School.

28.2 Mossend from south-east (Almond Valley Heritage Trust)

Most of Mossend's residents were employed in the local pits. Across the road from Front Street was the Mossend pit, its bing stretching from the village to the pithead, piled above the West Calder Burn. At the north end of the community was a railway siding which allowed pugs with coal trailers to access the pit. The pit was closed by 1897, however. Jacob Shore from Mossend was killed in an accident in Addiewell Number 15 shale pit on Tuesday 29 October 1872. He and John Morgan, pit sinkers, were descending into the shaft in a 'kettle' when, about seventy fathoms down, Shore mistook the instructions and the 'kettle' in which they were descending was misguided, striking some scaffolding. The 'kettle' was upset, throwing out Shore, who fell ninety feet to the bottom of pit, dying instantly. Morgan managed to save himself by grabbing hold of the chains and holding on to them until he was rescued.

Another pit fatality occurred on 25 June 1923 when Charles Kane was killed when the roof of Number 32 shale mine, owned by Scottish Oils Limited, collapsed. Kane lived at Mossend and was a leading official of West Calder Junior Football Club. In 1938 John Rossa, a shale miner who lived at 59 Front Street, was one of five killed following an explosion in Westwood Shale Pit, Blackburn. Rossa was severely burned when the explosion took place on 7 January. He was sent to Royal Infirmary in Edinburgh, where he died of his injuries on 25 January.

At the end of the nineteenth century, Mossend had its own football ground, located in the field to the north of the Addiewell and Polbeth Railway. This was home to Mossend Swifts, a senior football club which was founded in 1879. The club was noted for its various victories, one particular one being in season 1888-89 when they beat Hibernian 2-1 in the Scottish Cup. The game was played at home in front of a crowd of 2,000, which was more than double the village's population at the time. Mossend Swifts won the East of Scotland Shield twice, in 1888 and 1895. They won the King Cup three times (1888, 1889 and 1897) and the Linlithgowshire Cup in 1885. The Rosebery Charity Cup fell to them in 1889. Two Swifts players were to be capped for playing with Scotland. Robert Boyd was capped twice, once in 1889 against Ireland and again in 1891 against Wales. He also played for Leith Athletic for a period. At one time five Ellis brothers played for the Swifts, James Ellis being capped in 1892 against Ireland. He played centre forward for Hearts and Leith Athletic, in addition to Swifts. Other notable players who passed through the Swifts ranks include George Hogg, who played for Hearts for eleven years, and Thomas Nicol, who played for Burnley, Blackburn Rovers and Southampton. The field was abandoned when Mossend Swifts amalgamated with West Calder Football Club in 1903 to form West Calder Swifts. The latter's ground at Burngrange Park was used. With the outbreak of the First World War the club failed to continue and was disbanded around 1915. A second football ground was created with terraces formed to improve the view for spectators. In the 1920s and 1930s Mossend Amateurs played in the West Lothian Amateur League. Wattie Ross was their chairman and Billy Rutherford club secretary. A new Mossend Swifts existed around 1932-34, playing in the Edinburgh and District League.

In 1871 Mossend had a population of 940. This dropped slowly over the next ten years, being 669 in 1881, before gradually rising once more, in 1891 being 730.

MOSSEND

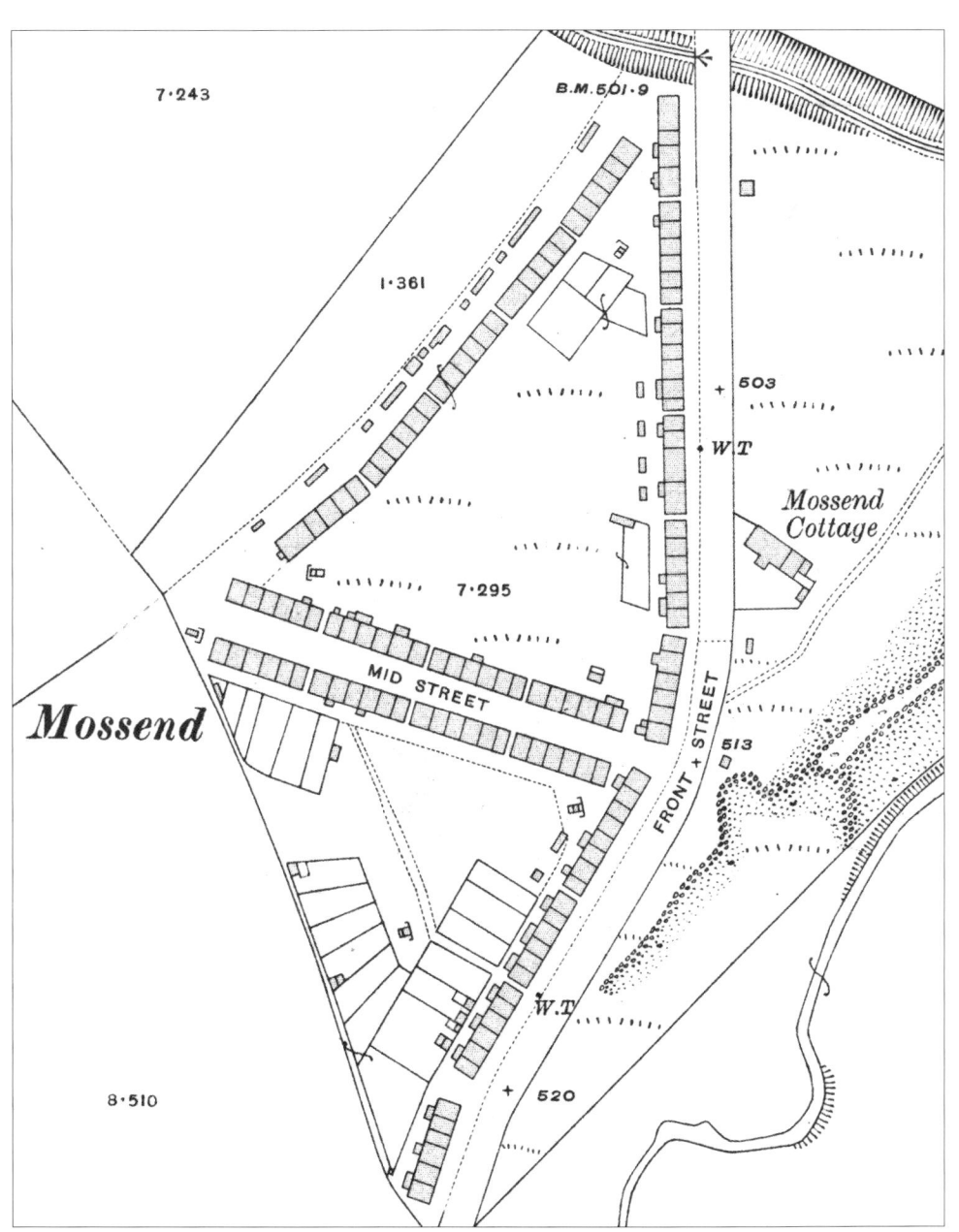

28.3 Mossend from 1917 Ordnance Survey map

The houses at Mossend were gradually cleared away as they became vacant. The mines had closed, the workers moving to new homes elsewhere, leaving properties vacant. After the Second World War the clearance of the community was sped up, although it took some time to totally clear the village away. In the late 1950s most of East Street had been removed, leaving Front Street mostly occupied. In 1958 there were twelve houses closed up, and as the residents moved out, others followed. At the time there were no totally empty terraces. Many homes were taken down in the 1950s, but it wasn't until around 1968 that the last of the houses were demolished. Mossend Cottage was also gone. Mid Street was also cleared, and by the time the Ordnance Survey compiled their 1970 map of the area, only six of the original ten terraces in Front Street were still standing. By merging smaller houses, there were only 32 homes in these six rows. Most of the residents were rehoused in Polbeth. Today the site is a field of rough grazing with scrubby trees. On the ground, traces of the houses can still be found, and what was Mid Street survives as a track into a farmer's midden. North of the site of the village, new homes have been erected on what was originally Clovenfordsykes farm, contrasting unimaginably with the simple miners' home that lay to the south.

29
Oakbank

*

The last resident of the village of Oakbank, West Lothian, moved out in 1984. Mrs Mary Shearer had lived in the village for most of her life, running the village shop and post office with her late brother. Although the village that their shop had served had gone, they managed to continue by delivering papers to East Calder and selling goods to passers-by. In fact, the Shearers had virtually been the last residents for twenty years. Mary Shearer was 81 years old when she left, moving to a more suitable house. When she moved out, the demolishers moved in and cleared away her house and the remaining buildings, one of which was Mrs Shearer's former shop.

Prior to Oakbank being demolished, there had been a bit of a dubiety regarding ownership. According to local lore, when the oil works and coalmines in the area closed down, the villagers were gifted their properties by the late Colonel Hare. Proof of this was difficult to come by, and there were no official records of the transaction having taken place.

West Lothian Council, who hoped to tidy up the remains of the mining community, carried out research in the national records and discovered that the village was still officially owned by Young's Paraffin Oil Company (a division of BP) and D. B. Marshall of Newbridge (known at the time as the proprietor of the Marshall's Chunky Chicks business). Once ownership had been confirmed, the village was cleared away, leaving only the bowling green, still used by residents of East and Mid Calder villages.

The village of Oakbank was established in 1860 by Sir James Simpson, who established the new oil works at Oakbank. This was taken over by a new company in 1864, known as Midcalder Mineral Oil Company Ltd. This firm was not very successful and in 1869 the works were acquired by the Oakbank Oil Company Ltd. This firm was more successful, at least initially, but a drop in the price of oil and a poor choice of retort in the works for refining shale coal almost brought the company to its knees in 1886. However, the business was reorganised, the works were extended at a cost of over £30,000, and it continued for some more years.

In the shale oil industry, the Oakbank Oil Works had a high reputation for its developments. In 1873 the manager of the works, N. M. Henderson, designed a new type of retort which greatly increased yield and efficiency. Henderson retorts were copied and established at many other works. However, they were quickly superseded when the chief chemist at Oakfield, (Sir) George Thomas Beilby (1850-1924), developed yet another improved retort, in collaboration with William Young (1840-1907) of the Clippens Oil Company at Straiton. Patented in 1882 and known as the Young and Beilby Retort, this became one of the more popular retorts thereafter, with half of all 5,000 retorts in Scotland being of this type by 1889, allowing the Scottish shale oil business to compete with foreign oil producers. Beilby had started work at Oakbank in 1869, and in 1914 was knighted for his contribution to chemistry and fuel economy.

The houses at Oakbank were built alongside the railway that made its way to the Oakbank Oil Works of the Midcalder Oil Company. Located east of the Linhouse Water, the road into the village headed south from the village of East Calder, a dead-end route that terminated on the western Pentland Hills outliers. On entering the village, to the left, was the first terrace of houses. This comprised four blocks of six houses. Each of these had at one time a tiny garden

29.1 Oakbank from north-east (West Lothian Council)

to the front, but these appear to have disappeared as the years passed – certainly more recent photographs don't show them. To the rear of the houses were washhouses and some outside toilets. On the opposite side of the street was the bowling green.

Houses in these four blocks were single-storey, built of brick and with slate roofs. Each house was narrow, and to the front were small porches, with two doors giving access to a pair of houses. These porches were timber lined and built on brick foundations. To the side of the porch was a single window, lighting the front room. The doors were reached by concrete steps.

On the same side of the street as the first terrace of houses were five blocks of housing. Each block contained twelve houses, built back to back to each other. Again, these houses at one time had small gardens on the road side, and washhouses to the rear. These houses had an upstairs, and the terrace was distinguished by the six dormer windows on the slate roof. As the houses were back to back, there was the same to the other side, and the chimneys were positioned half way up the roof, not on the ridge.

On the other side of the street, next to the bowling green, was a short row of buildings, almost perpendicular to the street, in which were five houses. Next to it was the original village school, latterly to become the institute.

South of the school, between the roadway and the mineral railway, were three more blocks of housing. That nearest the school had six houses on two floors, twelve in total. South of it was another row of twelve flats, six over six. To reach the upper flat residents had to climb an external stairway. Next to it was a row of seven houses, all single-storey and built along a slope, the roof being stepped. These three rows were the oldest in the village, being recorded in 1868.

The road through Oakbank took a sharp turn to the left beyond these rows. Facing the road was a block of sixteen houses, eight flats on each storey. Behind it, parallel with the road into the oil works, were two other blocks of housing, eight houses in each. Finally, at the southern limit of the village and almost at the oil works were two more blocks of housing, eight houses in each, built back to back.

In 1871 the population of the village was 355. When the Census of 1881 was compiled, the population had risen to 506. By 1891 there were 979 people living in the village.

The village had a number of water pumps in it. There were two serving the blocks at the southern end of the community. A further four served the northern part of the village.

The oil works at Oakbank were located to the south of the village. The works and village were built on the estate of Colonel Stewart Hare of Calderhall, hence the confusion at a later date as to the ownership of the community. In 1919 the business was bought over by the Anglo-Persian Oil Company, a subsidiary of BP. The works at Oakbank were closed in 1931.

In March 1921, there was a serious fire in one of the blocks at Oakbank. The flames engulfed twelve dwellings, totally destroying them, and leaving the residents homeless. Three people were to die as a result of the fire – John Gordon, his wife Jessie, and his stepson, John Sinclair. The conflagration was to be a major disaster in the village, however the oil company was able to rehouse those who had lost their property. The three who had suffered in the fire were buried at Kirknewton.

As with many mining communities, the residents of Oakbank were keen on making the most of their little leisure time. Oakbank Mossgiel Burns Club was established in 1923 and held annual Burns Suppers until at least 1949. The bowling club was established in the late nineteenth century and a bowling green was laid out in the village.

In addition to the Shearer's shop, there was a general store in the village, originally Oakbank Co-operative Society. This was established in 1872. In 1883, it had 188 members on its books, generating sales of £9,333. By 1891 membership had increased to 304. The co-op amalgamated with West Calder Co-operative Society at a later date.

Originally, there was a school in the village just south of the bowling green and on the same side of the road. In 1901-2 a new school building was erected by the East Calder and Kirknewton Parish School Board, located slightly north of the village at Hoghill farm. The headmaster appointed was a Mr Miller, who had previously worked as headmaster at Wilkieston School. At the time of his appointment, there were five other teachers working in the building. They taught a total of 222 children.

When the new school building was opened, the old school was converted into the village institute and reading room. This survived until 1930, when the new hall, or institute was opened. It was later to become a house and was one of the last buildings in the village to be cleared away.

For the children, the residents of the village organised an annual gala day, the first one taking place in 1925. These ran until 1960.

OAKBANK

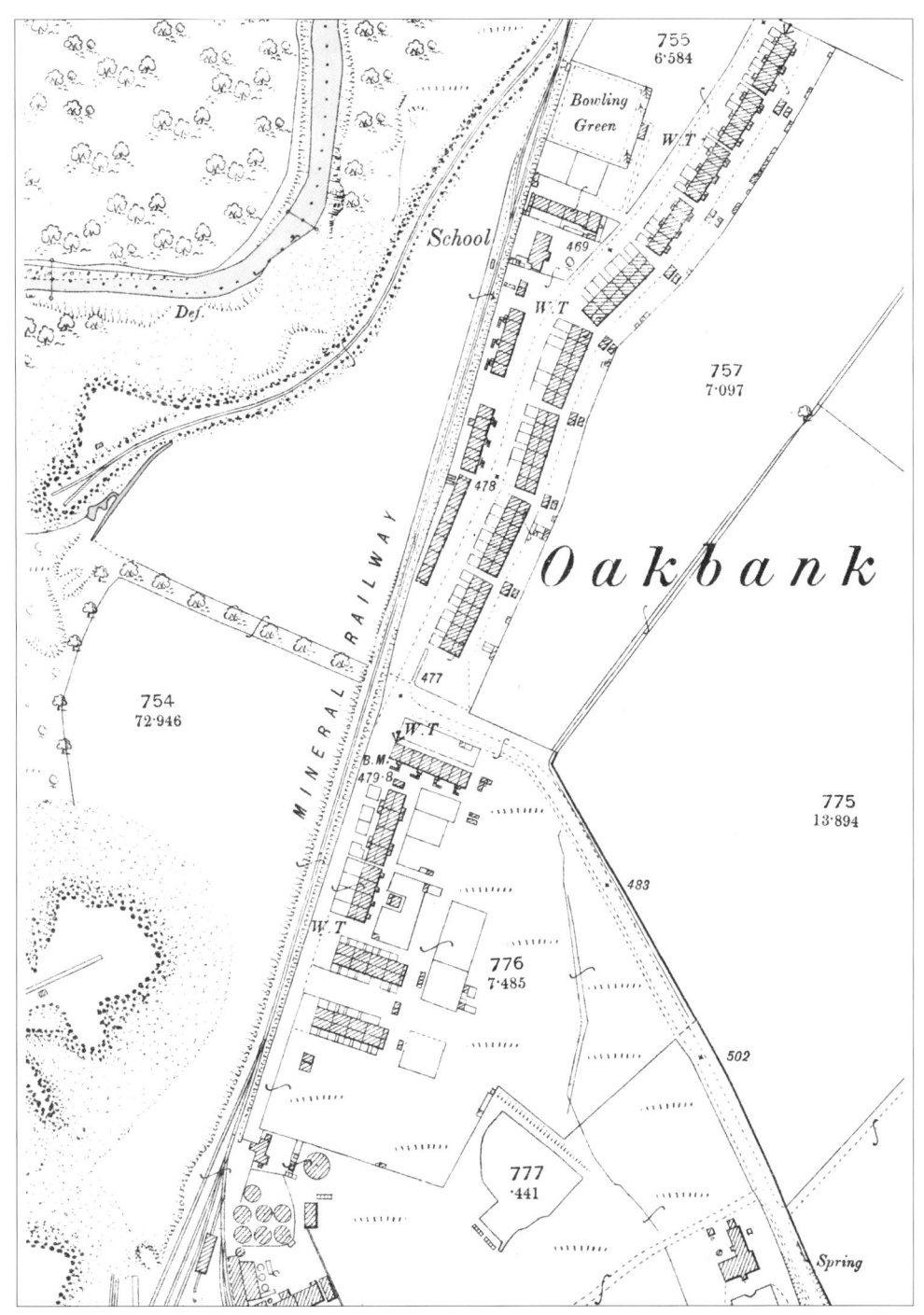

29.2 Oakbank from 1895 Ordnance Survey map

The parish church of East Calder, which was almost two miles away from the village centre by road, established a mission in the village, Rev MacKerracher being appointed as missionary in 1902. Some residents attended the United Presbyterian Church in East Calder instead.

The fitter young lads of the village formed a number of football teams. Oakbank Rangers played in senior ranks in 1880-82. In the following year Oakbank Thistle was formed, again a senior team. A third senior side, Oakbank Harp, existed for a short period. There were three different Oakbank junior teams. Oakbank United played from around 1898 until 1904. Oakbank Athletic Football Club played in season 1908-9. The longest surviving junior team, Oakbank Thistle, was formed sometime before 1912 and played in junior leagues until at least 1951, by which time support had dwindled with the falling population.

In 1914, a housing report into the condition in workmen's houses was compiled. Oakbank was one of the villages selected for inspection, and the compilers found that there were 165 houses in the village. These were very small – simply a room and kitchen. In many cases, the layout of the dwelling was such that it comprised simply of a kitchen and attic, the latter used for sleeping in, in addition to the beds in the kitchen. There were also three houses that were even smaller – these only had a single apartment. The average rent in the village was two shillings per week. At the time, there were wash-houses for ever four houses.

It was around the time of the inspection that the houses were improved with the installation of running water. The old wooden porches in some rows were replaced with brick-built sculleries and toilets. These small extensions had no pretence at any architectural niceties, being rather utilitarian blocks, built with facing brick, topped with flat roofs and having narrow windows. Nevertheless, the residents were delighted when they were added to their homes.

The outbreak of war meant that little could be done to address the conditions in the village. Demand for shale oil also tumbled after the war, and in 1931 the Oakbank Mine was closed. The oil works were closed around the same time, and were demolished soon after. The old 'Bogey Brig', which the residents knew well, was demolished in 1937.

In 1951, Oakbank village, too, was in decline. Although many residents were being rehoused elsewhere, or else had moved further afield in search of work, the village still had two shops. The village school was still open, three teachers educating 73 pupils. In 1959 two empty houses were acquired by the Rover Scouts, and they held many activities there before abandoning them in 1963.

Although the village has gone, some of the community facilities enjoyed by the residents continue. Oakbank Bowling Club still has an active membership, playing on the same green. Its members come from nearby villages. The Institute remained in use as a social club as recently as 1996.

Today the site of the village is reached by driving along Oakbank Road from East Calder. Hundreds of detached bungalows have been erected as part of an expanding Livingston, though the residents may well think of themselves as belonging to East Calder. Beyond, the minor road enters open countryside, but one can see that there has been something here before. A footpath runs alongside the road, and here and there are lamp-posts, hinting at an earlier need for night-time lights. Some stone walls confirm that this was not just rural countryside. Oakbank Garage Services is on the right, occupying what had been an open space north of the bowling green, and next to it is the bowling green. Oakbank Bing has been graded and planted with bushes and trees, now an open parkland owned by West Lothian Council. Part of the regrading resulted in the southern part of the village, beyond the dog-leg in the road, being covered over and it is planted with trees.

30

Oldtown of Roseisle

★

To the south-east of the Moray fishing village of Burghead, at the crossroads formed by the B 9013 and the B 9089, is a small community known as College of Roseisle. It was here that a very ancient Early Christian settlement once existed, for references to its ancient church survive. There can also be found the more recent 'County Houses', so called as they were erected by the county council. About half a mile to the north, on the sloping hillside of Tappoch, are a number of small farms, all bearing the name Roseisle. Here can be found East, Mid and West Bank of Roseisle, Easter Backlands of Roseisle, and Wester and Easter Oldtown of Roseisle. To the south of the latter two farms was the site of the ancient village of Oldtown of Roseisle, or simply Roseisle as it was named on some early maps and plans, a community cleared away in the mid-nineteenth century.

When Timothy Pont compiled his map of Moravia sometime around 1583-1614, he jotted down the two communities of 'Old Rofsyil' and 'New Roffyell'. To the west of the communities, and linked to the sea by a stream, was the Loch of Rofsyll. Robert and James Gordon compiled maps around 1636-52, that of Aberdeen, Banff and Moray to Inverness noting simply 'Rofyll'. The Loch of Roseisle was immediately south of the village, an elongated stretch of water. To its east, marshes linked it with the Loch of Spynie, which was at one time a major loch in the area until it was drained considerably. West of the Loch of Roseisle was a third loch, sometimes referred to as the Outlet Loch, which stretched from College of Roseisle towards Burghead Bay. These three lochs and intervening marshland almost meant that Roseisle and Duffus were located on an island. The crossing points, between the lochs, were at College and the aptly named Bridgend farm, half a mile to the east of the former.

The village of Roseisle was located on a fairly main trackway that extended from near Lossiemouth, across the central spine of this island, to Burghead in the west. The roadway through Bank of Roseisle is almost all that remains of this route, Lossiemouth Airfield having obliterated the eastern stretch, and the policies of Gordonstoun having closed off the central part. West of Roseisle itself the road has degenerated to a track alongside the Roseisle forest. A transverse route from the south came from near Nairn to College. The fourth route was more upland in nature, having to make its way across the slopes of Tappoch, passing Kean and Begrow, to Duffus. As this was the shortest route from Roseisle to the parish church at Duffus, it became known as the Kirk Road.

30.1 Oldtown of Roseisle (Gordon Castle Muniments)

An old estate plan of 1773 shows the farms and lesser properties on Duffus estate, with Oldtown of Roseisle being depicted. The village has a fair density of cottages and crofts indicated on the map. The houses and out-buildings were more-or-less gathered along a central street, but here and there other buildings were accessed down little lanes that led from the main road. The plan indicates the numerous small plots of ground associated with each house, all carefully numbered.

Within Roseisle was a large granary building, described as being five bays long and being roofed in slates. This sizeable building must have dominated the community, and reference is made to it being replaced in 1733-4. The work was completed by the mason Thomas Chrystie at a cost of £404 14s 0d Scots. It was used to store the grain paid in kind by the tenants on the estate to the local laird, in this case one of the Gordons of Gordonstoun.

In the 1780s plans were drawn of the lands of Roseisle by lands surveyor, Alexander Taylor. He was one of three brothers who may have been the sons of William Taylor, employed as a surveyor at Fort George. Alexander found work with Grant of that Ilk in 1768 as a salaried surveyor and seems to have remained in the north-east for a number of years, carrying out work for other major landowners. By 1782 work drawing estate plans had dried up in Scotland, mainly due to a few years of poor harvest, so he went to Ireland where he found employment making maps, becoming one of Ireland's greatest cartographers. He died in 1828.

Taylor's plans were to identify who owned which part of the community, so that the lands could be reallocated as part of an agricultural improvement scheme. Where small plots and runrig fields had existed around the village, the proposal was to create new larger farms, with regular field patterns. The difficulty arose over the ownership of the lands, for much of it was the property of the Duke of Gordon, but other strips and holdings were owned by the Gordons of Gordonstoun. It was in 1773 that it was decided to drain the Loch of Roseisle and reclaim the land for agriculture. One victim of this was the Mill of Roseisle, which became redundant thereafter.

It was to be another fifteen years or more before the intermingled properties on Roseisle were to be sorted out. In that year, Alexander Penrose-Cumming of Altyre succeeded to the Gordonstoun estates. He set about making arrangements for development once more, but his plans were thwarted by a rival claim to the property – one that was taken all the way to the House of

Lords in 1800. In 1810 parliament approved of an excambion, where properties were swapped and what had been a tapestry of ownership was redefined into manageable estates.

The plans drawn of Oldtown of Roseisle show a fair-sized village, arranged alongside a road making its way east-west. Unfortunately, the plan doesn't identify any particular building by name or use, but it is detailed enough to depict the individual buildings, adjoining enclosures, probably kailyards or stackyards, and surrounding runrig fields and allotments. At the west end of the village were a series of buildings, one a large L-shaped block, one leg blocking the west end of the street. On the north side of the roadway were a number of buildings, their gable-ends facing the street, narrow lanes passing between and leading back to either buildings at the head of the lane, or else through gaps to the fields beyond. On the south side of the street the buildings appear to be more random, some facing east-west, others north-south, others U-shaped, some L-shaped, and one building having a rather fanciful L-shape, with three wings sticking out at various places.

Bruce B. Bishop in *The Lands and People of Moray* reckoned that there were around seventeen houses in Roseisle in the seventeenth and eighteenth century, plus an inn. As a result, he reckons that the village had a population of around seventy to eighty. Each house had a stretch of land associated with it, operated on the runrig system. He has also identified a few early occupants of the village, such as Isabel Simpson and Jane Thayne who lived in 1632. Other names appear in the kirk session minutes, and there we find Isobell Brown created some scandal by 'marrying so soon after her husband's death, she being with child at the time.' Similarly, the church authorities were concerned to discover that William Spence's new wife, Janet Scot, gave birth only ten days after their wedding in 1787.

Walter MacFarlane makes reference to Roseisle (he doesn't use the Oldtown part) in his *Geographical Collections Relating to Scotland*, compiled prior to his death in 1767. He writes:

> The next considerable countrey village is Ross Isle, it is a mile south east from the Burgh and two long miles westward from the kirk, ther is two gentlemanis dwellings in it, the one built by Robert Sutherland and the other built be William Sutherland upon the Carseward of Ross Isle, it is a very convenient lodgeing with a good orchard, a garden

chamber, a convenient pidgeon house, a good girnel house with a great many other conveniences, offices houses and the like, all built be the said William Sutherland of Rosehaugh, proprietor of the town of Ross Isle, hath very large cornfields round about it, lies to the westert of a loch joining to Outlat where a great many water fowls resort. It is bounded on the north side with the sea, there are two of three publict inns in the same town.

In 1797-8 a Farm Horse Tax was applied across Scotland, and the list of owners helps us to identify some names of people who lived in various communities. At Roseisle, which obviously included the farms and crofts bearing the name, we find the following: Alexander McDonald, George Bannerman, Alexander Bannerman, William Forsyth, James Gregor, James Nicol, John Hendry, John Grant, Robert Hendry, John Cobban, James Collie, William Sutherland, John Scott and Charles Ross. Between them, these men had 55 horses, 24 of which were not liable to pay duty.

The 1851 Census gives us an indication of who lived at Oldtown of Roseisle, or 'Village of Roseisle' as it is listed thereon. There were three farms referred to as 'Old Roseisle', occupied by John Jeans (who farmed 110 acres), John James (farmer of 112 acres) and Alexander Gordon (farmer of 117 acres). These men had sizeable households, Jeans having 9 residents in his house on census day, James and Gordon both having 13 people in their house on census day. In addition, Old Roseisle is noted to have other houses, occupied by James Watson, cartwright, Margaret Ross and James Nicol, who farmed forty acres.

Listed under the 'Village of Roseisle' were thirteen dwellings, having a total population of 54 at the time. A number of heads of the household were listed as crofters, the implication being that they farmed a stretch of land. Two of them were known as James Bannerman, perhaps cousins, a third was James Hendry, and William Forsyth was an overseer of 35 acres. Archibald Fraser was a farm servant; Alexander Petrie was a house carpenter; and John Dunbar was a blacksmith. George Reid was a cartwright; John Innes and Archibald Forsyth were labourers; Margaret Bannerman listed herself as a 'washerwoman'; Alexander Rhind was employed as a mason in addition to being a crofter. Archibald Forsyth had eight people in his house, four other households having seven apiece.

With the settlement of the land-ownership difficulties associated with Oldtown of Roseisle, the village was removed in the mid-1800s. By the time the Ordnance Survey arrived to make their detailed maps of Duffus parish, the village had gone, leaving just Wester and Easter Oldtown farms, with a variety of other steadings bearing the Roseisle name – Backlands, Bank and College, much as is indicated on modern maps. In 1861, when the Census was compiled, only the two farms bearing the name Old Town existed where once the village stood.

An ancient flint arrow-head was discovered in the ground at Oldtown. This was just one of many ancient artefacts discovered in the vicinity, indicating that man has occupied this fertile stretch of countryside for thousands of years. On the summit of Tappoch, the hill that rises above the site of the old village, is an ancient burial cairn, and on the slopes around it are many relics from the Bronze Age, including cup and ring marked rocks, a souterrain, stone cists (in which human bones were found) and bead ornaments.

The dispersed residents of Oldtown may have moved, in many cases, to the planned village of Cummingstown, which is located one mile to the north, basically a single main street built along the shore. This village was established around 1808 by Sir William Cumming Gordon, principally with the intention of attracting fishermen, but it lacked one important ingredient – a suitable harbour! By the time of the first Census in 1841 the new community still only had ten households whose livelihood came from the sea – six employed as fishermen, working from nearby Burghead or Hopeman, and four coopers. The rest of the residents were either agricultural labourers or else worked in the quarries that existed along the shore.

31

Rattray

*

On the main road linking the small Aberdeenshire villages of St Fergus and Crimond, two minor roads strike north-east onto the flat farmlands. They actually meet up, and another byway leads north-east, towards the low promontory known as Rattray Head. This isn't some great headland, rather, it is a low stretch of dunes and skerries, but one which forms a major change of direction on the east coast of Scotland.

On the way towards the coastguard lookout and the former Shore Station associated with Rattray Head Lighthouse, the road passes an old ruined church in its kirkyard on the right, and shortly afterwards arrives at Old Rattray farm, where the public road ends. Between the kirk and farm the ancient Royal Burgh of Rattray once stood, a community of some importance in its day.

The church is referred to as St Mary's Church, and is currently located in the parish of Crimond. It is claimed that it was established here as a memorial by the family of one of the sons of an Earl of Buchan who was drowned accidentally in a well at the community. According to the *View of the Diocese of Aberdeen*, ''Tis said that a son of --- Cumine, Earl of Buchan, was drowned accidentally in a well here – whereupon this chapell was founded for his soul.' Some say this was in AD 911 and that it was a son of William Comyn. In the nineteenth century a stone inscribed 911 was inserted into the kirk walls. Another early reference to the church is made in the *Registrum Episcop. Aberdon*, where it is noted that, 'Between the years 1214 and 1233, William Cumine, Earl of Buchan, granted the lands and mill of Stratheyn and Kindrochet to Cospatric MacMadethyn, for the payment of two stones of wax, at Whitsunday, yearly. This rent was afterwards given by the Earl of Buchan, in the town of Rettre in Buchan.' The payment of goods was changed into one of cash at a later date. Another payment is recorded in 1451, when Master Richard of Forbes, Chamberlain of the Crown Lands in Mar and Buchan, arranged for six shillings to be paid to the chaplain of Rattray from the lands of Strichen. In 1460 James III confirmed a charter for the payment of £5 Scots and two stones of wax to the chapel.

31.1 Rattray Kirk

The church ruins measure around 45 feet internally longways, by about eighteen feet across. The walls, which were built with small stones held together with lime, are three feet thick. At the east end of the ruins are three arched windows, the central one taller than its neighbours, and to the west there appears to have been one solitary window, with the entrance doorway on the south wall. The kirkyard walls were for many years in a rather ruinous condition, but a former parishioner paid for their repair in 1848.

From the church eastwards to the farm of Old Rattray was the ancient village of Rattray. The street was fairly straight, but no doubt there would have been a variety of lanes and closes off it, striking north and south. An old account tells of its foundation as a Royal Burgh: 'There being a hot contention, under Queen Mary, between the Earl of Errol and Marischal, about the superiority of this little town of Rattray, the Queen, to prevent further dispute, erected it into a royal borough; whence, at this day, there is no custom paid at its markets, nor do its inhabitants hold by the tenure of common tenants, but as feuars; the town having lost its honours and magistracy, and yet none but the king being properly superior of it.' The date of erection of the village into a Royal Burgh by Mary Queen of Scots was 6 March 1564.

Even earlier, perhaps as far back as the thirteenth century, the village had been created a Burgh of Barony by Robert III. In 1324 there is reference to the harbour at Rattray, the earliest known.

The village appears to have been quite small for much of its lifetime. In 1561 there were only eight residents in the community. By 1696, when the Poll Tax was compiled, the village still only had eight tenants plus their associated families. Of these eight, four of them were employed as fishermen. Archaeological digs discovered that the village extended from Rattray Castle to the kirk, and nothing existed beyond either of them. The few buildings that were identified were located on both sides of the road, the more industrial or commercial tending to be on the north side of the highway, adjoining the loch, or harbour, the residential and agricultural ones being on the south side.

In 1888 the Laird of Rattray wrote a paper for the Buchan Field Club in which he gave some of the known history of the burgh. He made reference to an eighteenth-century estate plan, but unfortunately this is now lost, and has been for some time. However, from the talk, we find that there were 37 plots identified in the community, perhaps indicating that there were 37 houses and associated families. Each plot is thought to have had around 75 Scotch acres allocated to it, allowing the tenant to keep a few cattle and sheep. Other old charters make reference to some of the properties, including Greathead's Croft, Schivas Bank and Spring's Land. One charter of 1507 refers to a market cross existing in the community, something that is otherwise unknown. If one did exist, the implication is that there was a weekly market in the burgh at one time.

When an account of Rattray was written for the *View of the Diocese of Aberdeen*, in 1732, the village still had nine or ten houses, at the time belonging to the lairds of Haddo and Broadland. In the *New Statistical Account*, written in 1840, Rev Alexander Boyd gives a short history of the final years of the village:

> The Burgage lands were of considerable extent. There is now only one feu remaining. It measures about three acres imperial, and is possessed by Robert Sellar, who is thus an heritor in the parish. The oldest charter upon the feu, extant, was granted in 1627. In that year a burgh court, holden at Rattray by the Hon. John Hay of Crimonmogate, William Dalgardno of Blackwater, and David Rires of Strathstedlie, bailies of the burgh of Rattray, a jury of thirteen honest men, citizens of the said burgh, find that Magnus Smith, father of William Smith, died possessed

of four roods of land in the said burgh. Upon this, David Rires, one of the said bailies, superior of the lands of Rattray, granted a charter on the said four roods, in favour of William Smith. The next charter is granted in 1675, by William Watson of Haddo, bailie of the burgh of Rattray, superior of the said lands, in favour of Isobel Watson, spouse of Alexander Bisset, in Bilbo. The latest charter is granted in 1711, by Charles, Earl of Erroll, superior of the lands of Rattray, in favour of the daughters of the said Alexander Bisset and Isobel Watson.

Rattray owed its early prosperity to the sea, for it once boasted of a harbour. Access to this was by way of a channel that was protected by the castle. Once through the channel, what is now the Loch of Strathbeg was a safe haven of the ocean, where boats could be harboured in admittedly shallow water. This, however, suffered constantly from the blowing sands that form the dunes along the shore. Eventually, when the sands had engulfed the harbour entrance too much it was abandoned, and the site of it is now unknown. The lack of trade and an income forced the residents to move elsewhere, resulting in the community going into terminal decline.

An old account, published in *Fraser's Magazine*, August 1859, gives the story behind the demise of the harbour:

> One account ascribes the divorce [of the Loch of Strathbeg with the sea] to the effects of a furious gale from the east, about 1700, which in one night closed up the channel, and raised an impenetrable barrier of sand. So complete and sudden was the calamity, that a vessel which was then lying at anchor in the estuary is said to have been permanently imprisoned. The river, which had previously been known as the Water of Rattray—from the little village at its mouth—when thus dammed up and enlarged became the Loch of Strathbeg. That the accident, however, had occurred at an earlier period, or that the river-mouth at least had been previously much contracted, appears from the account supplied by Robert Gordon of Straloch, who wrote in 1656, 'Jam littora incipiunt in meridiem deflectere, ubi exiguous sinus est Strabeg, olim porta nobilis, nunc arenis penis obrutus; manent hie oppidi Ratray vestigia, quae nunc portus fortunam sequuntur.' When 'Strabeg' had been 'porta nobilis' is not known; but it would be curious should

further research prove that the storm which 'over blew' the parish of Forvie was the same which destroyed the port of Rattray.

Other accounts, such as the *Statistical Account of Scotland*, claim the great storm that blocked the harbour entrance took place in 1720.

To the north of Old Rattray farm is a low eminence known as Castle Hill. It doesn't rise very high above the surrounding countryside, but here stood the ancient Rattray Castle, seat at one time of the Cumine (or Comyn) Earls of Buchan. It is said to have fallen into ruins shortly after the Earl of Buchan was defeated in a battle at Inverurie by King Robert Bruce in 1308. The blowing winds covered what was left with a layer of sand, but this, through time, became converted into loam, resulting in the site of the castle becoming covered with a deep soil, producing crops of grain and grass, according to the *New Statistical Account* of the parish. On the south-eastern edge of the Castle Hill is the site of an ancient well, perhaps that in which the Earl's son was drowned.

It is said that within the courtyard area of the castle were at one time some industrial kilns, but these were probably destroyed in the 1730s, when the last of the foundations of the building were removed.

To the north-west of Rattray, by the side of the Loch of Strathbeg, is a rough field known as the Battle Fauld. Here, at some unknown time in history, Sir James the Rose was slain by Sir John the Graham. The fight was over the hand in marriage of the daughter of the Earl of Buchan. Sir James' grave is in the field, and the story was long commemorated in ballad form. The English folk rock band, Steeleye Span, recorded the song 'Sir James the Rose' in 1976, including it in their album *Rocket Cottage*.

The site of the Royal Burgh of Rattray is now pleasant green fields. As early as 1858 Rev John Pratt, in his *Buchan*, noted that, 'Ancient coins are occasionally turned up by the plough or spade, near the site of the old Burgh of Rattray.' These appear to have been 'generally gifted away to the curious', and no record of their dates or place of unearthing recorded. Detailed Ordnance Survey maps indicate the various sites where items have been unearthed over the years, including coins southwest of the Castle Hill and urns near to Old Rattray farm.

In August 1888 the Buchan Field Club visited Rattray and were guided around by Rev James Forrest of Lonmay. In the record of their visit, it was noted that they were:

…conducted to the Castlehill of Rattray and the Banks of Loch Strathbeg. Here Mr Cumine of Rattray and Mr and Mrs Henderson of the farm of Old Rattray joined the excursion. After lunch on the grass-clothed slopes overlooking the Loch, a business meeting was held at the Castlehill. The members proposed at the previous excursion were unanimously admitted members of the Club, and Mr Cumine was proposed and seconded as a member of the Club. Dr Gregor, Pitsligo, was also unanimously admitted an honorary member. In the absence of Mr Boyd, Mr Gray, solicitor, Peterhead, reported that enquiries had been made as to the alleged font dug up at Forvie, with the result that it appeared the stone was not a font but of the nature of a piscina.

Mr Forrest said the Castlehill was believed to have been the site of a Castle which once stood on a rock in the sea and belonged originally to the Comyns. There was a tradition that it was blown over with sand one Sunday evening while the inmates were engaged in playing cards. Others said it was buried because of the plague. In confirmation of this it was said that when some workmen dug into it about 1740, a man who drove his spade through the panel of a door was immediately suffocated. If it belonged to the Comyns it must have been erected sometime during the 13th century, when the configuration of the sea coast there was certainly very different from what it is now. In making some drains for the farmhouse of Rattray not long since, a well-made causeway was discovered at the foot of the mound under which the Castle is said to be buried.

Up to the end of the 17th century there was no loch there but only a widening of the mouth of the river Rattray or Strathbeg water. Between 1700 and 1720 it would appear that the outlet began to be choked with sand, and somewhere about the latter year a great sand storm occurred which completely choked up the channel, enclosing in the harbour of the burgh of Rattray a small vessel laden with slates. This was the last vessel that ever sailed into the harbour of Starny Keppie, as the place where the harbour was is named. The slates that were taken out of it were used in roofing the house at Haddo, in Crimond, and some said the Manse of Lonmay.

31.2 Rattray Castle

More recently, a fairly comprehensive archaeological dig has taken place over a considerable part of the site of the ancient burgh and castle site. Much of the lands were under threat from intensive farming and erosion, so between 1985 and 1990 various spells of field walking and digging took place. The archaeologists discovered that the castle stood on the site of a former motte hill, which dated from the late twelfth to thirteenth century, after which it was abandoned. The site was later adopted for the erection of a timber hall, succeeded in turn by a stone manor or castle, dating from the early fourteenth century to the late fifteenth century. Around 1500 the castle appears to have been abandoned and the stone robbed for other buildings.

In addition to supposed fishing sheds and associated structures on the lochside, the archaeologists discovered that most of the buildings excavated on the north side of the road were industrial in nature. Among a number of kilns that were unearthed were fragments of pottery, indicating that the manufacture of jugs, jars and other containers, was carried out here. Some of the pottery ware was decorated with patterns scored into the clay prior to firing. Another building excavated appeared to be a metal-workshop, where different pieces of ironwork were manufactured, perhaps for shipping, or just as local blacksmiths.

The castle mound was excavated, and here a number of kilns were found, as well as three later-stage buildings. This confirmed an earlier excavation, made in the 1730s by a Mr Arbuthnott, who 'caused dig up an eminence at the S.E. side of the castle hill, where he found a great number of stones, supposed to belong to the kitchen of the castle, as the workmen found very large hearth stones covered with ashes.' Today, a World War II pillbox can be seen on the mound, used to overlook the nearby naval base.

32

Riccarton Junction

★

The reopening of the railway line from Edinburgh south through Gorebridge and Stow to Galashiels heralded the return of trains through part of the Borders. In the main a commuter line, the success of the railway resulted in calls for it to be extended further, following the old route through Hawick and Newcastleton south to Carlisle. Whether or not this will ever come to fruition is yet to be seen. Should the line be resuscitated, it is unlikely that the lost railway village of Riccarton Junction will be rejuvenated.

When it opened the first time, the Waverley Route was a new railway line which made its way from Edinburgh south through the Scottish borders to join the main London to Glasgow line at Carlisle. It was opened to traffic on 1 July 1862 by the North British Railway Company, but it was officially known as the Border Union Railway. Much of the route was through pleasant glens and rolling countryside, populated by small towns and villages, many of which were to have stations created to serve them and their surroundings. However, south of Hawick, the line took a more remote route, crossing the Roxburghshire hills before dropping to Newcastleton. In the middle of this area a railway junction existed, the other line heading for Hexham and Newcastle. This was known as the Border Counties Railway. It was at this junction, remote from anywhere, that the railway company established a village for many of its employees. Like many mining communities created by coalmasters, Riccarton Junction did not have the services of an access road, the residents requiring to either walk down the glen to Riccarton, or else across the hillside to the Hawick road.

The railway junction was a fairly important one on the Edinburgh line and it was selected by the railway company to be the site of a station and service depot. Numerous sidings were laid to the west of the junction, within the arc made by the curving lines, and here a large three-road engine shed was positioned, capable of holding six engines. Next to it was a two-road carriage shed. A number of cranes next to it were used for lifting engines and carriages. To the south of this was another large building, part of which contained a smithy.

RICCARTON JUNCTION

At the junction of the main lines was a station platform, used by passengers to change trains, in addition to the residents of Riccarton Junction itself. It had no other purpose, there being stations nearby which served the residents of the district more readily – Saughtree Station was on the Newcastle line, near to a public road, Steele Road Station to the south, and Shankend Station to the north.

Within a field to the north-east of the station and junction was built a number of houses which formed a small community. The first houses were erected in 1862, an advertisement in the *Carlisle Journal* of 22 July that year asking for tenders:

> North British Railway. To be let, the building of six workmen's houses at Riccarton Junction. Plans and specifications may be seen, and further particulars obtained by applying to the resident engineer, Mr John Ridley, at Thorlieshope, Liddesdale, who will receive tenders until the 29th day of July inst. Thorlieshope, July 19th 1862.

In September 1862 tenders were invited for the erection of a further two cottages. The drawings were held by the resident engineer, by this time Sheriton Holmes.

32.1 Riccarton Junction from south-east

Built alongside a steeply climbing roadway was a line of semi-detached double-storey homes, no doubt the first eight houses erected in the village. There were four blocks of these, each with small gardens to the front. Larger garden plots were located to the rear (on the north-west side of the houses), and here were outhouse privies, one per house.

The longest terrace of houses was built almost perpendicularly to the first row. This had a series of houses along it, each of different sizes, but all double-storey. The first terrace had sixteen houses in it. Those to the western end were in general smaller in size, with outside toilets. A narrow pend passed through the middle of this row, and to the east of it were the larger houses, each having a toilet built onto the house.

Continuing the line of the long row, but built on the opposite side of the covered burn, was a row of eight houses. Again, these had outside toilets to the rear.

There were one or two other houses at Riccarton Junction. Situated in front of the main row was a solitary house, two storeys in height. This was the station-master's house, known officially as No. 1 Riccarton Junction. Built of stone, it was a substantial structure, three bays wide, with a projecting porch. Stationmasters who lived here included William MacAdam (died 1924), George Cameron Gray (1908-1910), W. M. Forrester (1910), Isaac Bell (1912), Walter Irving (1920-1931), Robert Blyth (from 1935), Robert Duncan (from 1939) and R. Gall (from 1951).

Leysburnfoot was a shepherd's cottage located just to the west of the village, but within striking distance of it. Within the gusset of the railway junction was a house and garden. In total, there were 37 houses in the village. At its height, Riccarton Junction had 118 residents.

Riccarton Junction, as the community was officially known, had its own post office, a sub-office under Hawick, the principal town being around thirteen miles to the north. This post office was located within one of the platform buildings.

The platform buildings were originally erected of timber, which was to cause some difficulty. In August 1863 the waiting room went on fire, the blaze extending into the whole range of buildings, which included the booking office and refreshment room. As the telegraph office was also burned to the ground, no message could be sent for assistance, and it wasn't until the following morning that a man walked along the line to Hawick to notify the authorities.

The refreshment room at the time of the fire was run by the Misses Steele. In 1896 Miss Steele served refreshments to the Chinese ex-Viceroy, Li Hung Chang, who was on a sight-seeing tour of Scotland. In 1924 the refreshment room was run by Mrs Sarah J. Wyllie, who it was who probably acquired a liquor licence for it. It was later run for many years by Mrs Graham (died 1945) then her daughter Lillah Graham until 1947. It was then taken over by Mrs Mary Ann Milligan. By 1951 the refreshment rooms were run by British Railways themselves.

Also in the platform buildings was a shop, which sold provisions and other goods. This was operated by the Riccarton Junction Co-operative Society Ltd. Sales in 1909 amounted to £605 15s 10d, earning a dividend of 3s 4d in the pound per member. On 13 September 1943 the society was taken over by the Hawick Co-operative Society Ltd.

There was a school at Riccarton Junction, located at the eastern extremity of the field in which the village was built, and the highest building in the community. Known as Riccarton Public School, the school building was situated in a playground. The school originally had outside toilets and an enclosed playground for infants. Sometime between 1900 and 1916 a schoolhouse was erected to the immediate west of the school itself, home of the schoolmaster. This was a storey and a half building, occupied, as part of their office, by Ronald MacDonald, and other schoolmasters. The school was closed in 1963, pupils from the area having to travel by train thereafter to either Newcastleton or Hawick.

32.2 Riccarton Junction from south-west

Another building that was added to the community between 1900 and 1916 was the village hall. This was built onto the end of the long row. Social events were regular occurrences, meetings that were keenly supported in such a remote community. A regular whist drive took place, the funds used to ensure the upkeep of the building. Among the various organisations that existed over the lifetime of the village were a carpet bowling club, Women's Rural Institute (founded 1944), and the Sports Committee. The latter committee organised the annual picnic and sports, with events such as the married women's race, single men's race, high jump, etc. There was also an evening dance after the picnic, held in the recreation hall. Quoiting was played. At Christmas the Children's Entertainment Committee organised a dance, and distribution of parcels from the Christmas tree – 75 being distributed in 1935. There was never a church building in Riccarton Junction, but in the 1870s the railway company issued 'church tickets' to allow residents to travel to the nearest church, ten miles distant. At a later date, services were held in the engine shed, followed by the waiting room at the station. The minister had to travel to the village to take the services.

Snow often caused difficulties for the residents of Riccarton Junction, being located high in the hills. A mapmaker's benchmark on the signal box at the north end of the station was 867.9 feet above sea level. Long winters with deep snow meant that the residents were often snowed in, though the railway was usually cleared by snow-engines. However, on a number of occasions trains had to stop at the station and wait until the drifting snow had been cleared. An example of this took place in November 1904 when the Pullman train from London to Edinburgh got stuck in drifts, caused by a fall of twelve inches of snow. Similarly, in January 1867, the line was closed as the train could not make it through the drifts.

In 1935 the London and North Eastern Railway Company erected a generating station to provide electricity for the station, previously having to be lit by Tilley lamps, which required regular cleaning and re-fuelling. The two diesel electric generators produced 250 volts, used to light the station. This electricity supply was later extended to two other houses in the community, probably the stationmaster and schoolmaster's homes. There had been an older electricity power house which exploded in September 1922, seriously injuring signalman, Frank Porter. The explosion destroyed the power house, engines, batteries, a store and the blacksmith's shop. Electricity for the rest of the village did not arrive until 1955.

Other events in the life of Riccarton Junction noted over the years include the fatal railway accident in December 1865 when the engine-driver, John Wright, who lived in Riccarton Junction, was killed and the stoker was injured when the express train from Carlisle halted, waiting on the train from Newcastle to join it. Unfortunately, the second train ran into it, and the engine was derailed. Another fatality occurred in September 1882 when a pilot engine ran into some detached goods carriages. A Mr Davidson was killed. On 27 December 1887 a pilot engine struck John Armstrong, pointsman, cutting his head in two. He was only 25 years of age.

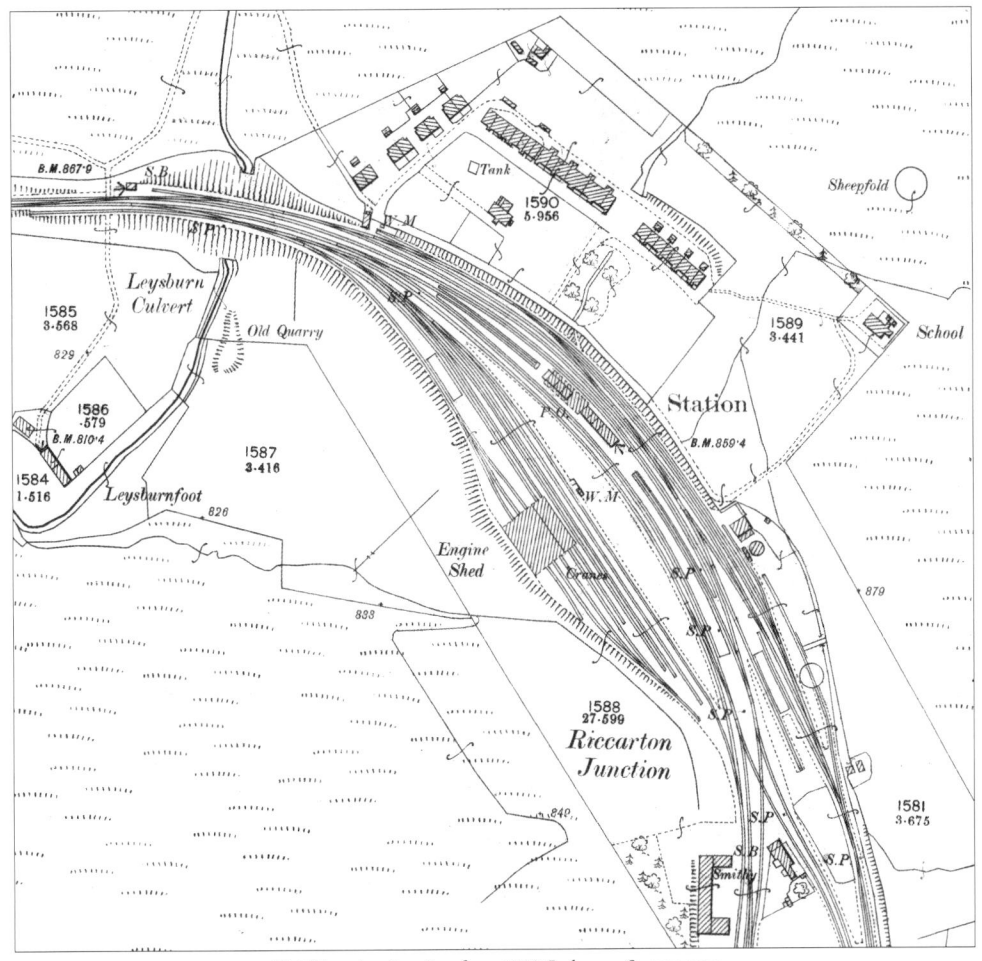

32.3 Riccarton Junction from 1898 Ordnance Survey map

On a more positive note, on 1 December 1892 a wedding took place within the waiting room on the station platform. The couple, who were Scots, lived in England, but the laws of the time prevented them from being married south of the border due to the short period of time they had spent there. Accordingly, they journeyed back to Scotland and were married in a snowbound station waiting room by Rev Smith of Newcastleton Free Church.

The lack of a road into the village was something that caused the residents much trouble over the years. In 1946 the villagers sent yet another letter to Roxburghshire County Council, asking for one to be made, but the council simply requested that the London and North Eastern Railway Company made its 5.56 train from Edinburgh stop at the station, making travel a bit easier. In 1946 a feature in the *Daily Express* described Riccarton (as it was sometimes simply known) as 'the lost village'. In August 1951 A. J. F. Macdonald MP visited Riccarton Junction to inspect the village, and see the difficulties experienced by the residents for himself. In 1963 the village was to be connected to the outside world by a road for the first time, when a track was laid from Whitterhope summit, about three miles distant.

Riccarton Junction Station was never to be a money-spinner for the railway companies. In the Border Union Railway returns for 1920 (perhaps its best year) the station only brought in £529 in passenger ticket money, and £1,177 in goods charges.

The railway through Riccarton Junction was never greatly popular or profitable, and on 15 October 1956 the Border Counties line from the village through Kielder and Hexham was closed. The main north-south line remained in operation until 6 January 1969, when Dr Beeching axed the line in an attempt at making British Railways profitable. With no purpose for the village remaining, it quickly went into decline and the houses were abandoned. All that remains is the former schoolmaster's house and school building. The station-master's house remains as a roofless shell.

In the 1980s the BBC made a film entitled 'The Slow Train to Riccarton'. Depicting the old station, the programme also contained interviews with some former residents.

In 1997 a group calling themselves the Friends of Riccarton Junction was formed with the intention of restoring the station and establishing a heritage centre. A long lease of the property was obtained from the Forestry Commission and following successful fund-raising, the former generator building was restored as an interpretive centre. In 2004, further grants enabled the platform to be restored, some rails to be laid alongside the south-bound platform, and a telephone box replaced where one had formerly stood.

Things took a turn for the worse at the Friends' annual general meeting in 2005 when members were disappointed to discover that there had been very little progress with the restoration works. As a result, an extraordinary general meeting was held on 11 April 2008, at which the organisation was wound up. The site remains as it was, and any restoration work is again starting to deteriorate.

33
Roughrigg

★

Sitting almost exactly on the boundary between Stirlingshire and Lanarkshire was the village of Low Roughrigg. The community was wholly within Lanarkshire, however, the border indicating a difference in land ownership, and the coal company which built the village only held the mineral rights for the Lanarkshire side of the border. The village was located between the old railway and the coal sidings that branched from it.

Roughrigg Colliery was established in 1857 by J. & J. Cross, but the coal company had difficulties in accessing the Slamannan Railway and thus getting its coal to the markets. In 1861 a new branch line was laid into the pits, but this required to pass through the neighbouring property to the east. The rent payable to cross the land, and the cost of major cuttings and embankments, resulted in the company failing in 1864. In 1865 the Roughrigg pits were sold to Forrester & Robson. Robson left the partnership in 1872, after which the mines were operated by Robert Forrester. The mines produced what was described as 'first class' steam coal, but this was obtained from thin seams. In addition to producing coal, coke kilns existed at Number 8 pit and were operational at the end of the nineteenth century. In December 1901 Forrester's lease on the minerals expired, and the pits were abandoned. A number of the pits were subsequently operated by a variety of other companies for a short period of time.

The oldest structure in Low Roughrigg was a short row, probably at one time three houses, but one of which was converted into a school building. This row existed prior to 1859, when it is represented on the Ordnance Survey map, and thus was probably erected in 1857 when Cross first established the pit here. The school, which was 616 feet above sea level, served a wide and disparate community, including an old row of miners' houses at Westfield, or Westfield Row, to the south-west, comprising of a terrace of seven homes.

By the time the map-makers had returned to survey the area in 1896, there were a number of new terraces erected in the village. Facing the school was a long row of houses, formed in two terraces. The row immediately across the road from the school had eight houses in it, with gardens to the south. Adjoining this row was a second terrace, in this case with ten houses in it. Again, there were allotments to the south. Between the two terraces a narrow lane led to the back gardens, and here was a wash-house.

When the new railway branch was laid linking Low Roughrigg with the Monkland and Slamannan railway it passed immediately to the north of the old row. The line of the road to the east of the school had to be remade, so the road was constructed to the south of the row, before swinging round to the north and down through a cutting under a railway bridge.

To the west of the cutting, parallel with the two terraces, was another block of housing. These were a different style to the terraces, for they were built back-to-back. There were ten houses on each side of the row, and a wash-house was located to the north of them, adjoining the railway.

The road from Low Roughrigg south, towards Roughrigg farm and Roughrigg village, left the community at the east end of the long row. It passed through a gap between the end of the row and two buildings. A few hundred yards down the hill was a row of houses, six in number, with gardens in front.

Westfield Row was to be the nucleus of the later village of Roughrigg, which with the community at Lower Roughrigg, formed a mining community on the moors. This row, which existed in 1859, was considerably extended to the west, with the addition of more houses. This formed a long terrace, with gardens to the south side. The old Westfield Row was reconfigured, a couple of the smaller houses being joined together to form larger homes.

On the opposite side of the road from Westfield Row was another row of buildings, some of which were houses. In addition to four homes was a public house and the village store, the latter two at the eastern end of the terrace.

Roughrigg had a number of railway sidings passing through it, and the villagers often had to cross them as they made their way around the community. On the east side of the main line adjoining the road to Roughrigg farm, was a long line of housing. This seemed to have an indeterminate number of homes in it, the houses being joined or subdivided over the years. In general, there were around sixteen homes in it.

Running parallel with this row, to the south of it, was a long row of houses, its style quite unusual for mining communities. At the south-western end was a block of eight houses, four facing one way, and four facing to the rear. Each house was L-shaped in plan. Adjoining these houses were five other houses,

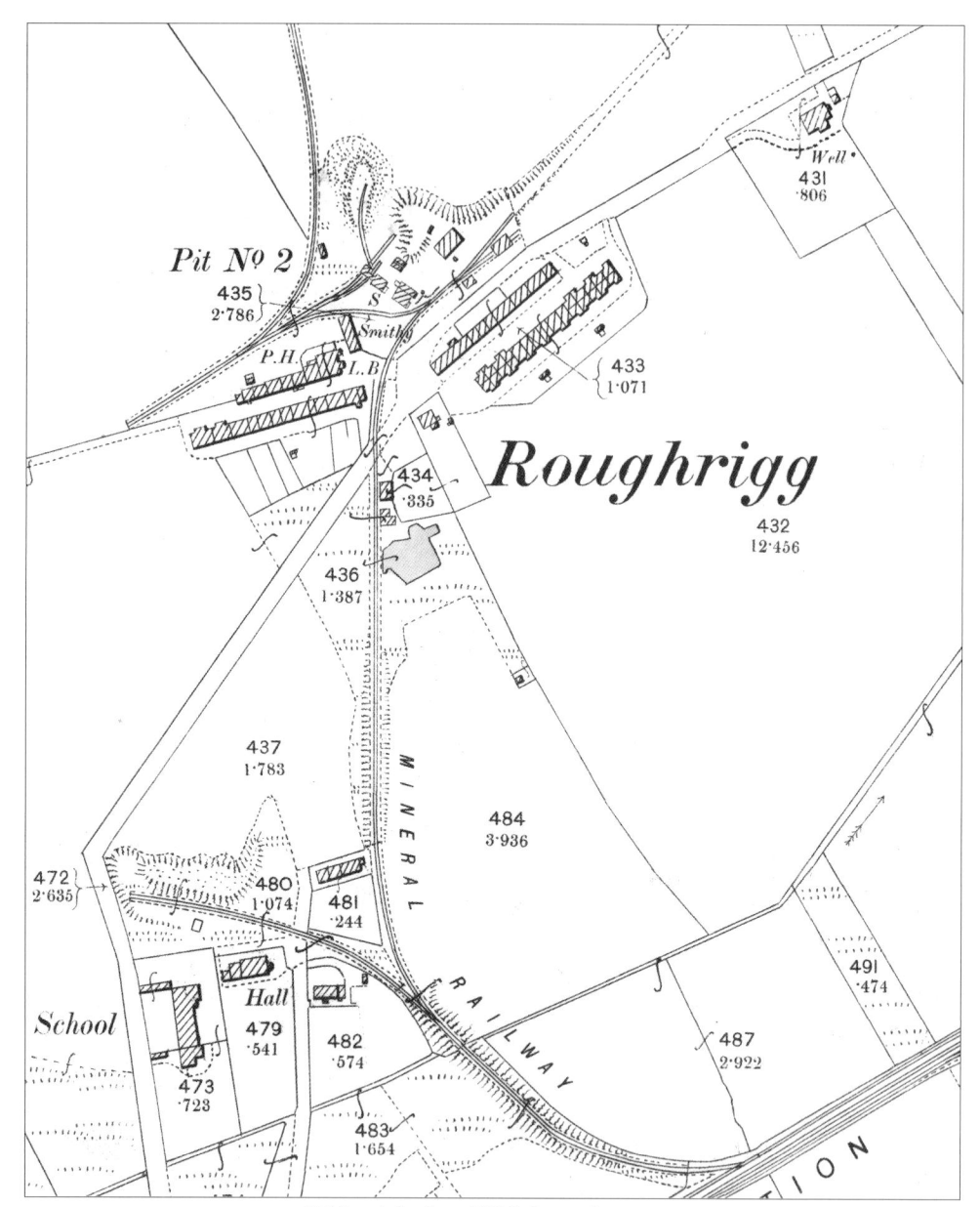

33.1 Roughrigg from 1898 Ordnance Survey map

and abutting the end of these were another twelve L-shaped houses, again built back-to-back. To the south-east of this row were allotments and two wash-houses.

Roughrigg village was dominated by Roughrigg Pit Number 2, which was positioned just to the side of the rows. A series of mineral lines led to various pithead buildings and coal bings. There were numerous other pits in the immediate vicinity, Pit Number 5 being located across the field to the north-west; Pit Number 3 immediately to the north; Pit Number 10 next to Low Roughrigg; Pit Number 11 along the North Monklands railway to the west; and Pit Number 12 was to the south of Low Roughrigg.

South of Roughrigg, on the road towards the larger community of Longriggend, was a school building and hall. The school replaced the old place of education at Low Roughrigg and was a much larger building, erected to cope with the increased number of pupils as a result of the new houses. Adjoining the school was the schoolmaster's house, the headmaster in 1887 being John MacArthur. In 1886 the roll was 324, with an average attendance of 244. In 1891 barrels were ordered for the school to collect rainwater to 'supply the children with drinking water'.

Near to the hall was a single cottage, and close to it was a little row of three houses.

The road from Longriggend to Roughrigg School was created by the joint efforts of Messrs Forrester of Roughrigg Colliery and the school board. In 1885 Robert Forrester complained to the school board that the condition of the road was deplorable and that this had been abused by a new bridge over the road for a railway siding created by Messrs James Nimmo & Company. Apparently, water was gathering under the bridge, and the children walking to the school had to wade over their ankles. When built, the road had not been meant for carts, only for pedestrian traffic, such as workers making their way from Longriggend to Roughrigg pits, or children going to the school. In 1891 the school board was remonstrating with Lanarkshire County Council, requesting that it make a new road from Longriggend to Roughrigg.

For worship, villagers at Roughrigg travelled to Longriggend. However, for a period from around 1873 to 1888 there was a gospel hall in the village, used by the Christian Brethren. John Burleigh was the leading light in the brethren. There was also a mission station of the Free Church, which had a large Sunday school. Among ministers who served there was Rev Craig.

In 1871 the population of Roughrigg, which included Westfield and Peesweep Row, numbered 365. By 1881 it had grown to 689 but it started to decline once more, in 1891 being 470 and 436 by 1901. It was noted in 1884 that there were a large number of vacant houses about Roughrigg. In the following year the Longriggend Registration District return noted that there were 96 householders in the community, with a population of 514.

In 1910 the houses were inspected to see their condition. There were nineteen single-apartment houses, the rent payable being £2 12s 0d, and four double-apartment houses, the rent for which was £4 7s 0d. The houses had been erected around 1870 of brick without damp-proof courses. The internal walls

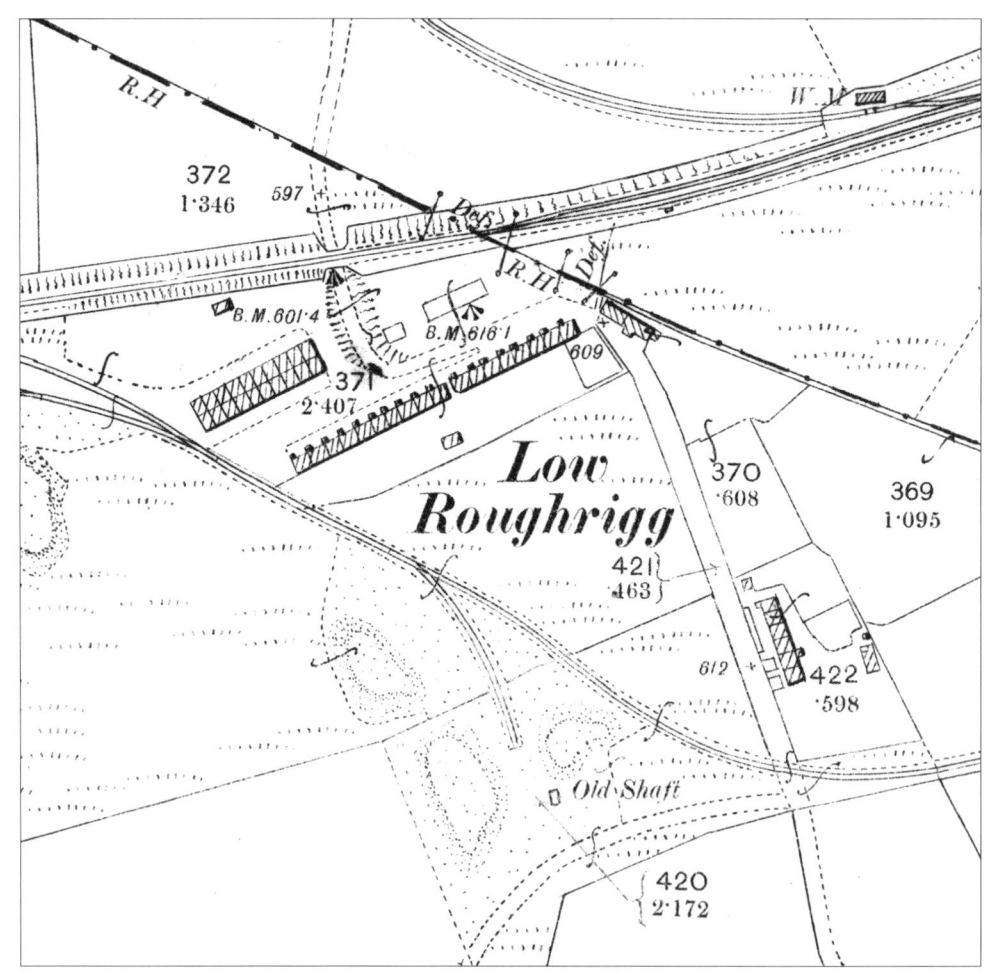

33.2 Low Roughrigg from 1898 Ordnance Survey map

had plaster applied directly to the bricks, but the dampness simply seeped through. The floors were of wood, some of which were ventilated. There were no wash-houses or coal cellars. Two privy middens served the houses but there were no sinks. There was a supply of gravitation water, obtained from standpipes. The owners occasionally carried out scavenging work.

Roughrigg began to be abandoned at the start of the twentieth century. At Low Roughrigg the back to back houses were cleared away before 1913. The western row of the long terrace had similarly been cleared away by that date, leaving just the eight houses of the eastern terrace. The two buildings built at the east end still existed also. Of the southern row, only two homes remained, one of which was formed from two cottages.

At Roughrigg, the mine had been closed by 1913, and the surface buildings and mineral railways removed. The row along Roughrigg farm road was partially demolished, leaving a rather random selection of houses, of various sizes, bastardised out of the old terrace. The row of houses behind still existed.

By 1913 a number of houses in the Westfield Row had been demolished, leaving a gap in the terrace. Surprisingly, the original seven houses of Westfield Row survived, as did the far western end. The row of houses with the public house and store also survived. There were a couple of other cottages with gardens still in existence.

On 24 June 1913, the inspectors for the Royal Commission into miners' houses visited Roughrigg and were very scathing in their report: 'These are not houses at all, and are really held together by the work of the tenants. There are no sculleries, no coal-cellars, no washhouses; two dry-closets or privies (of a kind) for twelve tenants; scavenging done, sometimes and somehow; one stand on the street for water; rent, 1s. weekly, plus rates, for a one-roomed house, and 1s. 8d. weekly, plus rates, for a two-roomed house. The whole place is most discreditable.' At the time, the houses were owned by Messrs Sinclair.

Roughrigg Football Club played in the senior football ranks for a short period, but little is known about the club.

Miners from Roughrigg sometimes suffered injury or death in the local pits. Probably the earliest major incident was when William Roberston, described in the *Hamilton Advertiser* as a collier, residing in Roughrigg, was crushed and severely bruised when the roof of Number 2 Pit partially collapsed. He appears to have survived. Similarly injured was Robert MacKibbin, who also lived in Roughrigg, who was injured by a fall of stone from the roof of

Roughrigg Number 8 Pit whilst he was putting up a prop. He was attended to by Dr Boyd of Slamannan and sent to the Royal Infirmary. Less lucky was Thomas Welsh, aged 57, who was killed in Lochend Colliery, near Caldercruix, on 24 July 1917. Welsh lived at Roughrigg, but travelled to Lochend to work, the pit there owned by James Nimmo & Company. Welsh was in the pit brushing with a man surnamed Campbell. A shot was fired, and the pair began to clear up the rubble. At some point, a stone weighing around six hundredweight fell from the roof, crushing Welsh on the head and body. Campbell ran for help, and the stone was removed, but Welsh was dead. His body was brought to the surface and was transported back to Roughrigg on a cart.

Compared with many of the other villages in New Monkland, Roughrigg lasted longer. The *Third Statistical Account* of the county of Lanark, written in 1960, noted that the village was in the 'process of dissolution', the residents being rehoused in either Plains or Caldercruix.

34

South Cobbinshaw

★

The Cobbinshaw Loch reservoir is a man-made loch located in the moors to the south of West Calder, on the edge of West Lothian territory. It was created in 1818 to supply water to the Union Canal. It was later operated by Edinburgh Water Works but was subsequently taken over by the North British Railway Company. Most folk have not seen it, for it is partially surrounded by forestry, but along its western side runs the former Caledonian Railway, from where one can gaze across the open waters to the open countryside on the far side. From a minor road near Woolfords an even minor road strikes east, through the trees, crosses the railway and arrives at North Cobbinshaw farm. In the immediate vicinity are a few other buildings, and the site of Cobbinshaw Railway Station.

The station was opened on 15 February 1848, and rather than just serve the immediate farm, it actually served two local villages – North Cobbinshaw and South Cobbinshaw. North Cobbinshaw was the smallest. Here, however, was the local post office and a few cottages by the side of the railway, mainly occupied by railway workers. The station was closed on 15 February 1966.

In 1891 an illustrated weekly newspaper, *The Graphic*, depicted a scene from the district on the cover of the Saturday 24 January edition. An engraving by J. Nash shows a group of men enjoying ice-yachting on a frozen loch surface. The caption reads, 'Ice-yachting on Loch Cobbinshaw – "Ready About" – result, "Man overboard",' with one of the ice-sailors having tumbled from the yacht onto the surface of the ice.

To reach South Cobbinshaw, one continued along the road past North Cobbinshaw farm and then over a causeway that still makes its way across the reservoir towards South Cobbinshaw farm. The farm sits on a low hill, and the road continues beyond it, down the other side, across a small stream. Just beyond this, where a few trees still grow tall, was the village of South Cobbinshaw. The name has sometimes been spelled as Cobinshaw or Cobbingshaw.

The village was established around 1870 when the South Cobbinshaw Oil Company obtained the mineral rights to this part of the estate. The company was owned by three shareholders – Hugh Rose (one of the Craig and Rose paint manufacturing family), Sir James Falshaw, Baronet (1810-1889), who was to serve as the Lord Provost of Edinburgh from 1874-75, and Jonathan Hyslop, who had moved from Wishaw and who was noted as the author of *Colliery Management*, published in 1880. Under the peaty moors the rocks contained shale coal, part of a large field that was worked to the south at Tarbrax in Lanarkshire, and to the north-west, well into West Lothian. The South Cobbinshaw Oil Company erected a new oil works at this site around 1870. In addition, they built brick kilns, to use the clay and blaze produced as a by-product of refining the oil.

Being located in a very remote part of the parish of West Calder, at the western extremity of the Pentland Hills, there were few men living locally that could provide a workforce. Accordingly, the oil company needed to build homes for workers who were to come to the new industry. Around sixty houses were built, and to these flocked men with their families.

The South Cobbinshaw Oil Company overstretched itself somewhat and was dissolved on 31 August 1876. The mines hereabouts were abandoned, and the workers moved on to find employment in other areas. Most of the houses were left behind, their doors open to the wind, and they started to fall into disrepair. According to the 1882 Valuation Rolls, five of the houses were let out to monthly tenants, and a sixth was occupied by Rev William Johnston. Fifty-six other houses were unlet.

The shale below the ground remained, however, and it was still an important commodity. The rights to it were acquired by Young's Paraffin and Mineral Oil Company, Ltd., and soon that firm was opening up the shale field once more. Once again, miners returned to the village, and soon all of the houses were occupied by families. The village bloomed for some years, and soon additional facilities were being added.

The former brickworks at Cobbinshaw, which lay on the southern side of the South Cobbinshaw Railway Siding, was acquired by the South Cobbinshaw Fireclay and Brick Company Ltd in 1884. The company was run by Thomas Scott of Edinburgh, Robert Munro of Bathgate, Andrew A. Rose of Edinburgh and Hall Grigor of Inverkeithing. The company operated the brickwork for less than five years, the business being wound up voluntarily on 8 January 1889. Bricks produced at the works were stamped with the name 'COBINSHAW'.

SOUTH COBBINSHAW

The Ordnance Survey map of 1893 depicts the village at its zenith – in 1891 the Census reckoned that there were 309 residents. At the north end of the community were two rows of houses, built parallel to each other, with doors facing west to the upper stretches of Cobbinshaw Loch. The front row had twelve houses in it, all of a similar size. At the north-western end was a small extension, no doubt containing a wash-house or some other communal facility. The row behind also had twelve houses in it, and again a small extension existed at the northern gable.

Built parallel with these two rows were three other terraces of housing. At the west end was a block of six houses. These had doors facing south, and on the north side of the row were three projections, perhaps containing wash houses or dry closets. At the eastern end of this row was a carved stone benchmark, used by the map-makers to set levels. This one indicated that the village at this point was 888 feet above sea level.

East of this row was another line of houses, but these ones were what were termed 'double-end' houses, being built back to back. Each side of the row had six houses, so that each house only had windows on one façade. The row was built of brick – mainly red in colour, but with lighter bricks around the door and window openings, plus forming quoins at the corner of the row. The roofs were covered with slates, and chimneys lined the ridge.

East again was a third row in the central line of houses at Cobbinshaw. This had six houses in it also, with a wash-house attached to the eastern end.

Parallel with this last row, and lying to the south of it, was a sixth row of houses, this one containing six homes. In total, there were 54 houses for mineworkers and their families.

During the early years of Cobbinshaw's lifespan, water had to be drawn from a pump located below the village, near to the Birk Burn. In 1901 the Caledonian Mineral Oil Company piped in a new supply to the rows, but this was to prove troublesome, and the flow of water was never great.

There was a small store in the community, in the 1870s operated by William Lind. He was the son of the tenant farmer at South Cobbinshaw farm.

The first school at Cobbinshaw was located at the western end of the community, and probably dated from shortly after 1870, when the village was created. In July 1880, the West Calder School Board advertised in the *Glasgow Herald* for a certificated female teacher to work at Cobbinshaw Public School. She was to be given a salary of £55 plus 10 per cent of a government grant to teach the thirty children on the roll at that time.

In 1894 a new school building was erected, the older school being totally insufficient to cope with the children in the community. The new building was located to the west of the northern rows, where the road took a turn to the right. This one had a fenced off playground, unlike the old school, and was to be extended at some point before 1905. Shortly after the new school opened, the old one was demolished and the site cleared away.

The teacher at the school at the turn of the century was John Anderson, who lived in Tarbrax. On 16 January 1903, once he had completed his day's work at the school, he was walking back to his home in Tarbrax. To make walking easier, he was wont to follow the mineral line that ran from Viewfield Coal Pit to the Tarbrax Oil Works. Unfortunately, he was unaware of an approaching mineral train that was making its way to the Tarbrax Works and it ran into him, killing him instantaneously. He was noted in newspaper reports of the time as being, 'a promising young man'.

34.1 Cobbinshaw Parish Church (Almond Valley Heritage Trust)

Being just over five miles from the parish church in West Calder, the mining families didn't attend very often. Missionaries from different denominations were to visit the community on various Sundays, and over time it was agreed to have a new place of worship erected there. This was to be a timber building, clad with corrugated iron, and was built to the west of the new school. A small porch at the southern end gave access to the chancel, lit by plain-glass windows on each side. At the north-western end was a fireplace to heat the building, and the gable on the southern end was topped by an open belfry with bell. Across the road from the church was a well. The church became a member of the United Free Church at the union in 1929. Although the village was in decline, the church appears to have continued for longer than the community it was built to serve. Worshippers from Woolfords, North Cobbinshaw and even Tarbrax, came to worship there, but eventually the dwindling congregation resulted in its closure in 1938. The last minister, Rev Dr Hugh Young, had just died at an age in excess of ninety years, and the village of Tarbrax was also in decline – at the time only forty or so of the former 300 houses there being occupied.

In the late 1880s and into the 1890s a Faith Mission under the Protestant Union was established at South Cobbinshaw with some success. Prior to the First World War, an assembly of Christian Brethren was established in the village. This appears to have flourished for only a few years but is known to have still existed in 1922.

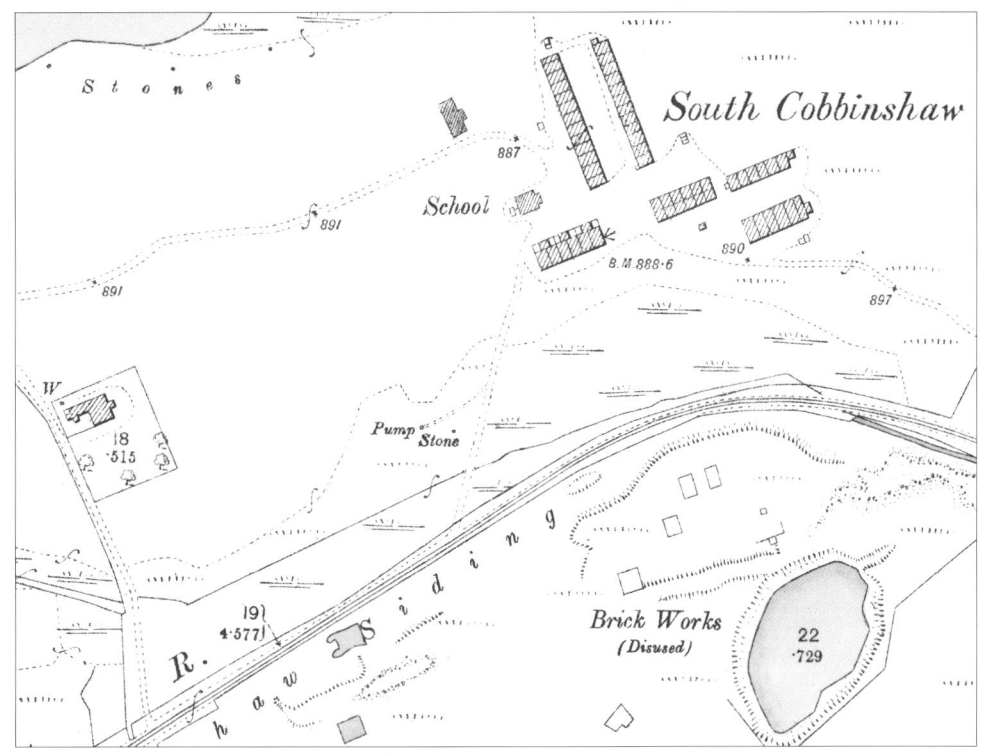

34.2 South Cobbinshaw from 1895 Ordnance Survey map

At the west end of the low ridge on which the village was built stood the manager's house. It faced to the north-east, looking slightly uphill to the village. It was located in its own walled grounds, with service wing to the rear and a gravel drive to the front porch. In the grounds was a pump, used for drawing fresh water.

The main mines and works at Cobbinshaw lay to the east and south of the community. A track from the village led alongside the Birk Burn to the Cobbinshaw Pits, numbered One and Two. These were still in operation in 1905. From them a tramway was used to draw shale coal to the Tarbrax Oil Works, which lay to the south, just over the boundary in Lanarkshire.

An older tramway continued north-east to the mine on Cobbinshaw Hill. Located almost on the summit of the 965-feet high hill, it was known as Cobbinshaw Mine and was in production in 1893. It was disused by the time the map-makers arrived to survey the area in 1905.

A tramway from Cobbinshaw Mine led north-west to an older mine, certainly closed by 1893, which was also reached by a minor railway known as the South Cobbinshaw Siding.

The mines at Cobbinshaw were to become the property of the Caledonian Mineral Oil Company Ltd., which owned the nearby Tarbrax Oil Works and various other pits. This business was reconstituted into the 'New' version in 1893. In 1896 Cobbinshaw Mine was managed by John Allan. At that time 100 men worked underground with a further 21 working on the surface.

By the turn of the twentieth century the works at Cobbinshaw were in decline, and the workers moved elsewhere in search of employment. The poorer quality houses were abandoned and left to become derelict. The Caledonian Mineral Oil Company collapsed into administration in early February 1903, and what remained of the houses were purchased by a private business. They had been offered for sale at £70 for twelve. Other buildings were demolished, and the slates on the roofs and salvageable timber and bricks were placed on the market.

The First World War kept the village alive for a bit longer, but by the early 1920s it was more or less abandoned. The houses were cleared away by 1925.

Visitors to South Cobbinshaw today will find little to indicate the fact that a fair-sized community once existed on this remote moor. The former manager's house still has some of the trees growing in what was the garden. Only the slightest of foundations can be discovered associated with the old rows.

Similarly, the old brickwork is difficult to make out on the ground, but the round pool of water where clay was excavated still survives. To the east, on Cobbinshaw Hill and by the Birk Burn, are rounded spoil heaps associated with the mines there. Nature is slowly reclaiming them, too.

The only tangible remnant of South Cobbinshaw is to be found elsewhere. When the church was closed it was partially dismantled and the corrugated iron and timbers were taken to Woolfords farm, where it was rebuilt, to form a small meeting hall for the local community.

35
Southfield

✶

There is a small community known as Southfield in existence today, located one mile to the south-west of the village of Slamannan in Stirlingshire. It comprises of a few cottages, Southfield farm itself and Loanhead, strung along the southern side of a minor road. Immediately to the east of it, almost half a mile distant, is a stretch of woodland, located alongside the Culloch Burn, a tributary of the River Avon. The wood occupies the ground on which the original Southfield village was located, as well as some industrial buildings where the villagers worked.

The coke works were located to the south-west of Southfield. A mineral railway from the main line made its way to the works, and from it various sidings made their way to different parts of the site. A separate siding made its way back into Southfield Colliery Number 2 Pit, which was positioned at the east end of the village, holding the workers' housing together like bookends.

The eastern half of the village of Southfield comprised of three parallel rows, each of the same length and format of houses. The southernmost row, which lay alongside the mineral railway that led into Southfield Colliery's Number 2 Pit, had fifteen houses in a single terrace.

Behind this row, and slightly higher up the hill, was the middle row, again comprising of fifteen houses. A third row, again with fifteen houses in it, was positioned to the back of the second row.

At the western end of the three long rows, were two other rows, erected at right angles to them. The eastern one, which faced onto the road leading up to the Southfield Road, had ten houses in it.

Immediately behind the row, on its western side, was a second row, this one having twelve houses. This row was superior in some respects to the first, in that the houses had gardens to the west. At the back of the gardens, reached by a path from the rows, was a well, the principle source of water for the community.

The rails of the mineral line passed to the south of this part of the village. On the south side of the line, and facing directly onto it, was another row of houses, nine in number. These appeared to have been much smaller in size. This was the original Southfield Row, erected at the same time as the two pits, and in existence sometime before 1860, for they appear on the Ordnance Survey map of the time, the only houses in Southfield.

At the west end of the railway row was a large building, used as an engine shed. On the north side of the siding, west of the two north-south rows, was another building, subdivided into two.

Many of the men from Southfield worked at the Southfield Number 1 Pit, which was located just a few hundred yards from their homes. This pit was sunk prior to 1860, at which time it had little more than a mineral siding into it, with some small pithead buildings. By the late nineteenth century, this pit was abandoned and the site cleared away. To the south-west of the old pithead a new colliery was constructed, far larger in size. The railway was extended, and there were numerous sidings and gantries to load coal. The pit was considerably extended, with the erection of a series of coke ovens, between the old pithead (which continued to work the coal seams below the ground) and Southfield village.

Other men from the village were employed in the Southfield Colliery, Pit Number 2, which stood at the east end of the rows. This pit dated from much the same time as the original Pit Number 1, but was not to be developed like its elder sister. The shaft was partially open, and a pool of water lay in front of the pit. The coal spoil was dumped in a small bing to the south of the pit head. The proximity of the pit to the village sometimes caused problems, such as in July 1874 when four boys from the village, Charles Bell, Peter Easton, John Radcliffe and John Thomson, were charged with malicious mischief at the pit. Radcliffe was fined five shillings, or five days' imprisonment, whereas the others were admonished.

Not all of the workers at the pits were men. In 1880 Jane Winning was working at the pithead, pushing hutches to the pit mouth. She fell down the shaft, tumbling 300 feet to her death. She was only seventeen years of age. Other deaths in the local pits include that of James Kidd, a blacksmith from Loanhead. On 31 October 1896 he was working on a siding at the pithead of Number 1 Pit, repairing a waggon with his son. As he lay underneath it, other waggons which were being shunted, bumped into it, causing it to roll over his arm and leg. He died eighteen days later in Glasgow Royal Infirmary. On 19 February 1890 James Whyte, husband of Ann Grossett, was accidentally killed at Southfield Colliery.

35.1 Southfield from 1897 Ordnance Survey map

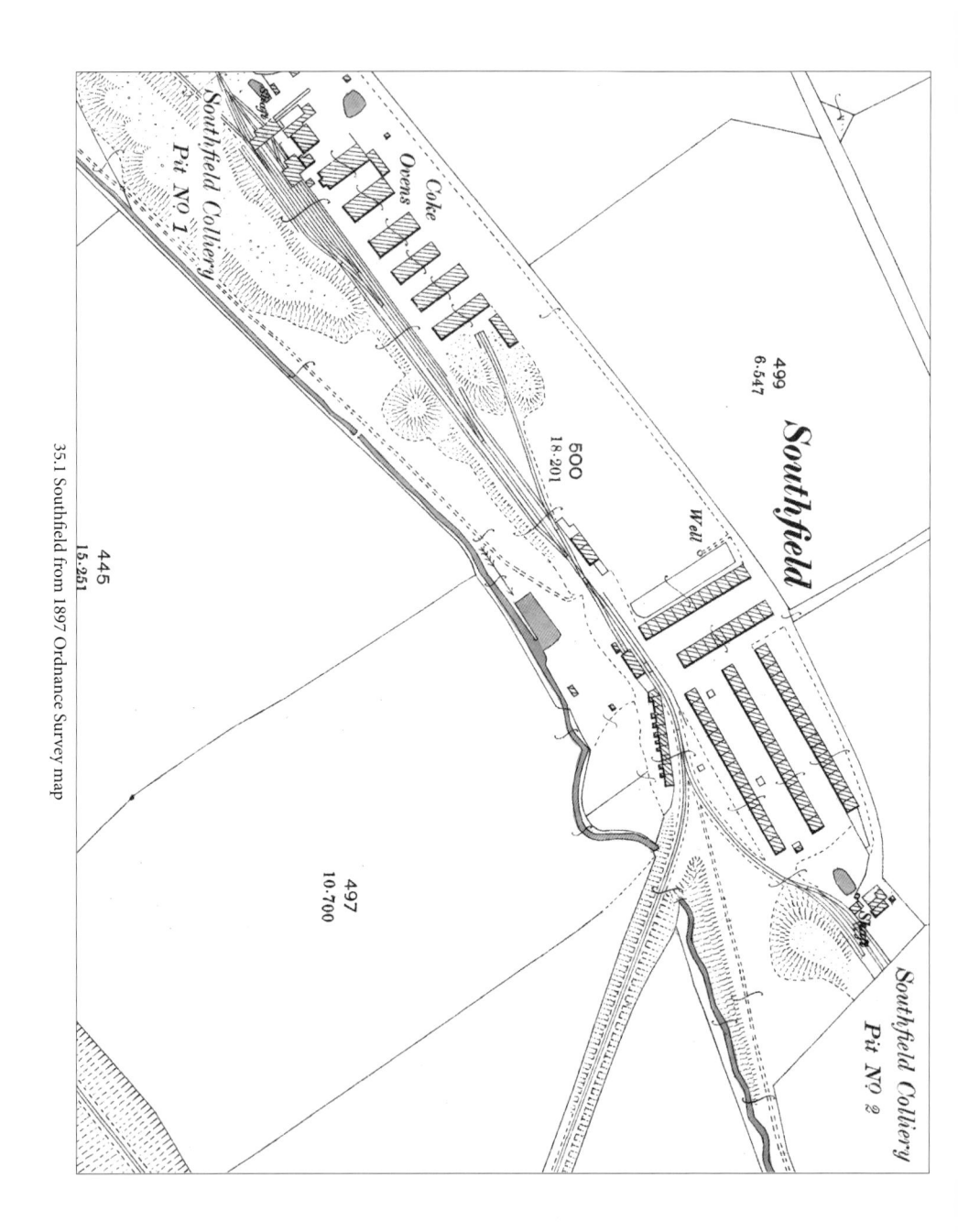

There was an 'adventure school' at Southfield, established by the mine-owners, Messrs W. Black & Sons, in 1878. Slamannan School Board was unhappy with the provision of this school and repeatedly tried to have it closed. In June 1879 the board sent J. Biggan, of Airdrie, to inspect the school, after which they sent a letter to Messrs Black, advising them to close it. In 1880 there were 70 pupils on the roll, under teacher David Hunter. The school was still operational in 1894 but was eventually taken over the by school board.

The residents of Southfield appear to have enjoyed their football, and a number of teams existed in the community. Southfield Football Club was a senior team which was founded in 1880 and played for three seasons or so. At a later date Southfield Rangers played at senior level (around 1887-1891). Other teams may have existed, though they may have been one and the same. These were Southfield Athletic (noted in 1888-89), Southfield Swifts (1890), Southfield Corinthians (active 1890-91), and Southfield Football Club (1894). Southfield seems just to have played on a field loaned by the neighbouring farmer, and the conditions were sometimes deplorable. In November 1888 they lost by six goals to nil against Gairdoch in the Stirlingshire Cup, but lodged a complaint due to the late arrival of their opponents! Within a few weeks they won by the same amount, beating Airdrie Fruitfield at home. In February 1889 the club played against Redding Athletic but an accident occurred involving two players, Robert Whyte of Redding and a man surnamed Stirling of Southfield. The former died a few days later.

Other clubs for sports and pastimes existed too, such as the draughts club, which was active in 1895, beating Falkirk in the first round of the Stirlingshire Association Trophy. There was also a group of Christian Brethren in existence in the 1880s, their annual excursion for the children being a highlight in the community's social calendar. This often went by special train from Slamannan to places like Linlithgow, where they visited the palace and played cricket, football and other games, plus went boating on the loch. By 1888 there was a non-denominational Sunday school in the village.

Not everyone in the village was God-fearing and upstanding. In December 1895 a miner named Andrew Archibald, aged 44, who lived there was charged with having murdered his second wife, Isabella Rutherford. Archibald and his wife had been drinking heavily on a Monday evening and then began to quarrel. He chased her from the house, running after her with a poker, striking her repeatedly. Eventually, both returned to the house, and the wife went to bed.

She remained in it all day Tuesday, and it was not until the Wednesday that Archibald sent for the doctor, who pronounced her to be dead. Archibald was later arrested by Sergeant Fyfe. Other random incidents from the village's history include the time when the prostate body of Alexander MacLauchlan was found on a public thoroughfare within the village. It was early on a Monday morning in April 1886, and the 58-year-old labourer was suffering from exposure, having lain there most of the night. He died before a doctor could be found. In 1871 William Hamilton, who was in the habit of walking along the railway line to Slamannan for a daily newspaper for his employer at the pit, was killed. As he made his way, he heard the North British passenger train from Airdrie approaching, so he stepped off the line onto a siding. However, a train was shunting there, and he unfortunately got his foot stuck in the points. Unable to remove it in time, the engine and five waggons knocked him over, seriously injuring him. He died as he was being transferred to Edinburgh Royal Infirmary.

The whole community and pits at Southfield were all cleared away soon after the turn of the twentieth century. An advertisement in *The Scotsman* of 26 August 1908 gives a very clear indication of what happened to the remnants of the community:

> Sale of building material of workmen's houses at Southfield, Slamannan, on Friday first, 28th August 1908 at eleven o'clock. Shirlaw, Allan & Co. have received instructions from Messrs. Inkster, Dunn & Co. to expose for sale by auction as follows: 123,000 Ballachulish slates, 7,600 Welsh slates, 139 sheets corrugated iron, 1,100 square yards sarking, 10 in. by ⅝ in.; 425 square yards flooring, 6 in. by 1⅛ in; 18,500 feet of battens, 5 in by 2 in; 675 feet of battens, 4 in by 2 in; 600 feet of battens, 6½ in by 2½ in; timber, various, 220 doors, windows and shutters; firewood, etc. Also stones and bricks of 3 rows of houses.

By the time of the First World War there was little to indicate that the community had existed, other than the line of the old railway and an odd bing and mound here and there. The whole site had been planted in trees, which quickly obliterated the community, hiding any fragments from view.

36
Westerton

★

Westerton was a small community of three rows of houses, located in the parish of Kirkliston, West Lothian. The rows lay on the northern side of a minor road that linked Newbridge with Pumpherston, near to a large bend on the River Almond.

The village basically stayed the same size for all of its lifetime, and there were very few community facilities – the residents being expected to make their way to the nearby villages of Broxburn (a mile and a half away), Newbridge (a similar distance), or Kirkliston (2½ miles). Westerton, or the Westerton Cottages, or Westerton Rows, as they were variously known, was built in a single phase, around 1885.

All of the rows at Westerton were the same size and format as each other – with fourteen houses in each terrace, making a total of forty-two homes. Each house had a small scullery and two rooms. The walls were built of brick and the roofs were covered in slate. The ridge had clay tiles on it, every other ridge tile having a projection not unlike a capital B on its side, making the skyline quite distinctive and decorative. Each front door had a small slated canopy, supported by timber struts, perched on stone corbels. In general, the style of the houses was slightly more decorative than most other miners' rows.

The houses in the Front Row, which was built parallel with the road, had their backs to the road, and between the houses and the road were small enclosed gardens.

The front of the Front Row faced onto a narrow roadway, on the other side of which was the Middle Row. Again, this had fourteen houses in a single terrace. To the rear were small gardens, smaller than those in the Front Row.

A narrow lane, only passable on foot, or perhaps with a wheelbarrow, lay beyond the garden fence, and backing on to this were the gardens of the Back Row. This row had an open roadway on the northern side of it, running alongside the fields.

Each house at Westerton had a small porch, projecting in front of the main façade, and adjoining that of the neighbour's. The area occupied by the community extended to around 2½ acres. The village had a drying green, located at the north-eastern end of the rows.

In 1891 the Medical Officer of Health for Linlithgowshire was scathing about the supply of water to the village. He noted that the community had around 500 residents at that time (giving an average occupancy rate for each house of almost twelve people), but that there was no proper water supply. It was recorded that Westerton was 'greatly in need of water. To [Westerton] the owners of the houses - Young's Paraffin Oil Company - contemplated laying a pipe from the Kirkliston and Dalmeny works. This might have been accomplished, but that consideration was given to the fact that other districts would in the near future be in want'. However, water was later supplied to the community by pipe to a water pump, located at the south-western end of the Middle Row.

36.1 Westerton – No. 4 Westerton Cottages in the 1930s (Almond Valley Heritage Trust)

In 1914 Theodore K. Irvine visited Westerton and reported on what he saw:

The village consists of 41 houses, built in three rows of equal size. The homes are built of brick and consist of a room (12 ft x 12 ft), kitchen (12 ft by 12 ft with two bed recesses), and a scullery with sink (7½ ft x 6 ft). Outside dry closets, coal cellars, and small gardens are provided for each tenant. There is a common drying green but no wash-houses. All refuse is removed twice weekly by the company. The rent, inclusive of local and county rates, is 3/- weekly. Population, 257. One of the houses, with a wing added, has been converted into a billiard and games room. Daily papers are supplied, and there is a small library. The workers pay 1.5d per week for use of the reading room.

The men who lived at Westerton were employed in local shale coal mines, owned by Young's Paraffin Light and Mineral Oil Company. Near to the village was the Newliston Shale Mine, where a number of them worked, and many others were employed at the slightly more distant Ingliston mine.

An explosion in Ingliston Mine (Pit Number 36) on 24 January 1921 resulted in the injury of five men, two of whom lived in Westerton. The shale mine had always suffered from gas and, on this occasion, this was to ignite, severely burning the men, mainly around the face and other exposed parts. The injured were transferred to Edinburgh Royal Infirmary for treatment. The Westerton men were James Greenan (aged 35) and Robert Sneddon (aged 28). Luckily, all five survived.

As with many mining communities, the residents of Westerton established an institute, or community hall, where they could hold various meetings and spend some of their precious leisure time. This institute was formed within one of the empty cottages - number 15 - the north-eastern end cottage in the Middle Row. This was established around 1900. Within the room was a billiard table, where the Westerton Billiard Club met.

The parish church at Kirkliston ran a Sunday school at Westerton for the children living there. This operated for many years and was still teaching the children Bible stories in 1950. The United Presbyterian minister of Winchburgh also assisted in running the Sunday school for a time.

At the north-east end of the rows, in a field extending to 1.8 acres, was a football pitch, much used by the men and lads of the community. In the 1940s,

Westerton Amateurs played in the Lothian Amateur League. Their local derby opponents were Kirkliston Amateurs and matches between the two clubs often attracted largish crowds.

Snippets of life in the rows can be found in the local newspapers. In March 1866 James Oliver, a miner who lived at Westerton, was sent to prison for twenty-four hours for assaulting his wife on 20 February. Breaches of the peace often took place in miners' rows, and Westerton was no exception. In March 1899 the *Linlithgowshire Gazette* reported on 'A Hot Time in Westerton Rows'. Apparently, Richard Jones Williams, his wife and his daughter Ellen, had been in the house of William Pollock (a pit bottomer) and his wife, where she ran a small shop. The Williams' son, John, had apparently claimed that he could beat all of the Pollocks, and Mrs Pollock had asked the Williams' to chastise their son. A fight ensued, whereupon Mary Pollock, William's daughter, was dragged by her hair, and William Pollock was punched on the nose. The sheriff at

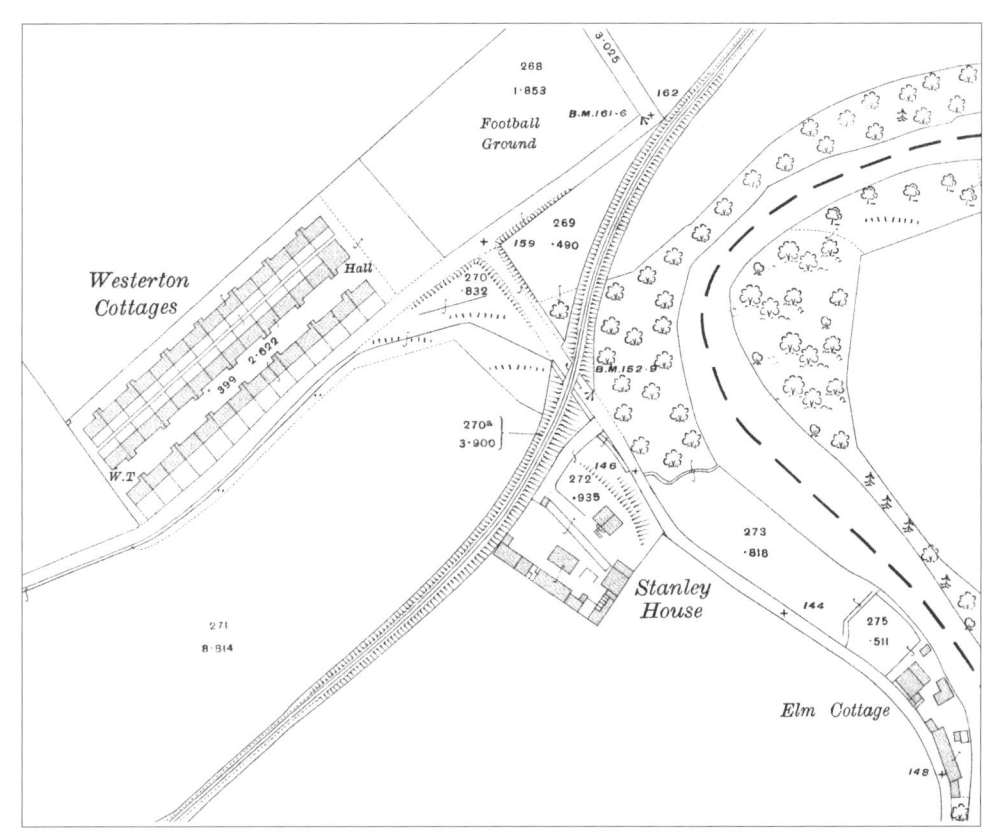

36.2 Westerton from 1915 Ordnance Survey map

Linlithgow found the charge not proven and said that both the Pollocks and the Williams had acted in a very improper way. The quarrel didn't finish there, however, for on 2 March Mary Pollock threw a pail of water at Ellen Williams on the drying green at Westerton. She was taken to court again and claimed that she threw the water at Ellen as she thought she was about to strike her. The sheriff asked, 'Are you now prepared to let bygones be bygones?', to which she replied, 'Well, it is very hard. Every time that we appear outside the door, they put their fingers to their nose and wave handkerchiefs as we go along the street.'

In Kirkliston village, centre of the parish of the same name, the war memorial stands at the junction of Main Street with Queensferry Road. The obelisk, which was erected soon after the end of the first World War, states that it was 'Erected by public subscription by the inhabitants of Kirkliston, Newbridge and Westerton districts'. Some of the names on the memorial are of residents who lived at Westerton, including Private Peter MacLeary, Cameronians, who was killed at the Battle of the Selle on 23 October 1918. He was only nineteen years of age.

The houses at Westerton survived until the 1960s, after which they were demolished and the occupants rehoused. In April 1954, the *West Lothian Courier* reported that 'Westerton is on the way out, as the houses are to be closed as they become vacant. This little hamlet, which was originally built to house shale miners, was, from the time it was built, a happy go-ahead community, and there are many in the district who will hear with regret of the "passing" of this village.' By September 1958 thirty of the houses had been abandoned and closed down, including the miners' institute. Only twelve houses were still occupied, and the residents were being offered new homes elsewhere. Some of the houses had been demolished and the site of them cleared away as much as possible. The whole site had to be cleared away and restored to ground level by Martinmas 1961.

The site of the rows has returned to agriculture, the field often being used to grow barley and other crops. In 2009, when a new natural gas main was being laid through the site, an archaeological watching brief was carried out. Although the field looked as though nothing had ever been in it, below the soil the workers found the shattered remains of the foundations of the houses.

37
Whiterigg

*

The village of Whiterigg started with a single row of houses, located by the side of a minor road to the north-east of Airdrie, in New Monkland parish. The community was established in the late eighteenth century, but grew around 1840, when the coal was worked on a larger scale. An advertisement in the *Glasgow Herald* of 17 June 1803 read: 'Alexander Shanks, coalmaster at White Rigg, near Airdrie, has for sale a quantity of coal for the use of smiths at 2/6 per cart, allowed by all who have used them to be the best in that part of the country.' The houses were built by William Black and Sons, coalmasters. The business was later to be taken over by United Collieries Ltd. When the Ordnance Survey arrived in 1859 and made the first detailed maps of the district there were already dozens of abandoned coal mines.

By 1859, Whiterigg comprised of three rows of housing – the original row, which was made up of a random selection of houses in a single terrace, a company-built row of twenty houses to the east of it, latterly known as Whiterigg Row, and to the east of this second row, a further row named South Standrigg Row. On the maps of the time, the village was spelled Whiterig, but by the 1890s it had gained a second 'g' to become Whiterigg. The old row was actually split into two by the Slamannan branch of the railway, the straight line adopted by the railway builders passing directly through what had been a continuous row. At least one house had to be demolished to allow the track to be laid, and the house immediately north of the line was retained, but it had to have a new gable erected, built at almost forty-five degrees to the front wall.

The Old Row, as it was known, lay to the east of the old community. It had twenty single-apartment houses. In 1910 the Lanarkshire Medical Officer visited the village and made remarks on the houses. He noted that the houses were very damp, small and built of rubble. The occupants paid a rent of £3 18s per annum.

South Standrigg Row was located adjoining the Ballochney railway branch line. The houses were some of the oldest at Whiterigg, having been erected around 1835 by William Black and Sons to house miners employed in the local

37.1 Whiterigg – Meadowhead Cottage (North Lanarkshire Council)

pits. There were actually two blocks of housing here – one containing four single-apartment houses, the other much longer, with 28 single-apartment homes. The buildings were single storey, the walls constructed of stone. As there were no damp-proof courses, the stone allowed the moisture to rise from the moor and into the homes. Internally, many of the houses had brick floors, whereas others had timber floors. Although the houses only had one room in them, this was regarded as being of a reasonable size, allowing it to be used to accommodate a fair-sized family. Each tenant had the right to use part of the allotments to the south of the row, but it was noted that many of the miners didn't bother with them, perhaps the soil being unsuitable for growing crops. The occupants did not have any sanitation within their homes, instead using open privies across the roadway from the house. In 1910, the last of the occupants were being rehoused, the owners of the property having had notice served on them to have the buildings closed down.

On the south side of the railway bridge was the village school, in existence in 1838. This was provided by the local coalmasters, and the children had to pay one penny per week to attend. Two teachers were employed to educate the miners' children.

In the immediate vicinity were various places of employment for the occupants of the rows. To the east were extensive oil works. South of the village, across the North Burn, was a chemical works, located in the gusset of the railway lines. Whiterigg Chemical Works were established in 1856 and survived for thirty years. It was here that John Patison (1828-1905) experimented in low-temperature carbonisation, which was to assist in prolonging the period of shale-oil production in Scotland. At Airdriehill, a little further south, was a coal pit, in operation in 1860. The miners at Whiterigg had a powder magazine in the field to the west of the old row.

In 1867 the area around Whiterigg was to undergo major development when the new Stanrigg Oil Works was established. It was constructed on the site of the old oil works, and numerous railway lines and sidings were laid into the factory, which comprised of many industrial buildings. East of the workmen's cottages was a high bing where waste material from the works was dumped. The works were established by Messrs Black of Whiterigg and Thomas Jeffrey. They leased 1,000 acres of mineral rights, and by 1869 were producing 50,000 gallons of crude oil per month from 15,600 tons of shale coal.

37.2 Whiterigg – Airdriehill Square (North Lanarkshire Council)

In December 1869 a reporter from the *Airdrie, Coatbridge, Bathgate and Wishaw Advertiser* visited the new oil works and reported on what he found:

The works as seen from a short distance along the line presents no inviting appearance to the traveller. Everything is black and gloomy which is heightened as dusk approaches by the gleaming lights which blaze constantly from the waste gas which escapes from the retorts through large vertical pipes. We were shown over the works by Mr Jeffrey, while the manager of the establishment, Mr Thomas Abernethy, explained the whole process of distilling the pure white liquid from the black coal. The coal being broken into small pieces, the retorts were charged, these being simply cast iron pipes about twelve feet in length and about sixteen or eighteen inches in diameter. Following distillation, the volatile matter distilled from the coal is conducted by pipe to the condensers where they are condensed into thick dark oil, along with a little water. Eventually, from all of this process oil is distilled. From the last distillation, the pure oil is obtained being light and nearly colourless, and it is hard to imagine that the almost crystal-like liquid before you has been produced from that grimy heap of coal which we saw thrown into the retorts at the other end of the works.

The arrival of the oil works meant that more housing was required for the workers employed there. By 1897 a number of new houses had been added to the old row, and a few buildings were by now erected on the west side of the road. A public house was one of the buildings on the west side of the street, and a railway station was now established on the railway line. Next to the old school a public hall had been erected in the gap in the row, a facility much used by the miners, oil workers and their families. The oil works was closed in 1903, resulting in a population drift from the local communities.

The biggest addition to Whiterigg was the erection of a large block of housing known as Airdriehill Square. This was located across the railway line from the old chemical works, which by this time had closed, no doubt superseded by the oil works. The houses were erected in 1874. Airdriehill Square was built in what had been an open field, surrounded by a loop of a mineral railway which served a number of mines.

Facing the main road was a row of houses, sixteen in total, usually referred to as the Front Row. These houses had narrow frontages but were deep in plan, and the central houses had small extensions to the rear, within the Square. Each house had a door and a window facing the road, the terrace of homes rising gradually up the brae.

The northern end of the Square backed onto the railway line. This row comprised of nine houses, the north-east one being larger than the rest, being linked to the eastern row. Again, the houses were single-storey, had slate roofs and chimneys. It was known as the Bottom Row.

The southern, or Top Row, had ten houses in it, again small in size, each with a front door and window. To the south of this row, in a rectangular field, was a washhouse. As with all of the rows at Airdriehill Square, the houses were built of brick, but there was no damp-proof course included. The floors were of timber, but the walls were poorly finished and suffered from dampness.

The eastern, or Back Row had a total of fourteen houses in it. In the centre of the Square were two washhouses. At a later date, outdoor privies were added to many of the houses, often just a timber structure, in most cases adjoining the front door. Another improvement was the introduction of electricity. This was only used to light the houses, with wires supplying a bulb in each room. Tenants were unable to use the supply for anything else, though many connected wireless sets and other equipment into the bulb socket.

The enlarged community meant that the old school in Whiterigg was no longer big enough to cope with the number of children who attended. In 1869 a new schoolroom was provided by Mrs Black, wife of the coal-owner.

In 1875, yet another new school building was constructed in a field to the south of Airdriehill Square, near to the Eastern Gatehouse, which guarded the drive to Airdriehill House. The owner of the house, James Waddell, who sat on the school board, was paid a feu duty at the rate of £12 per acre for the site. Airdriehill School was erected by Clarkston School Board, the local coalmaster, William Black, being one of the board members. Basically 'H' shaped in plan, the school was divided into boys' and girls' ends and could accommodate over 300 pupils. Next to the road, adjacent to the school, was the schoolmaster's house.

The first schoolmaster was in fact the teacher at the old Whiterigg School, Mr L. H. Horne. The school was formally opened on 31 January 1876 but had been open to pupils before this. Mr Horne was paid the full cost of running the school, having to pay the teachers and other running costs from his income. A few problems occurred at the school, in particular the difficulty in getting children, especially boys, over the age of twelve to attend. The schoolmaster sent a note to the Board of Education explaining this:

> This being principally a mining district, the School Board has found difficulty in securing regularity of attendance, especially in the case of children above twelve years of age, whose parents require their assistance in the mines or mills, and also those who are required to attend to the house or youngest children when the parents are working. In the majority of cases the excuse has been that they were unable to pay fees or to provide boots and clothing for their children.

In 1879 the school had accommodation for 365 children, with an average attendance of 103 day and 27 evening scholars. It received grants of £90 9s 0d and £15 15s 6d. In 1886 the roll was 208.

The next headmaster at the school was James MacLuckie, who proved to be a popular man in the community. Indeed, the school was usually referred to as MacLuckie's School. He served as headmaster at the end of the nineteenth century. The school was closed in 1922, the approaching Airdriehill Quarry causing damage to the building by blasting.

The rising number of Roman Catholics living at Whiterigg meant that the local parish decided to erect a new church to serve the parishioners. St David's R. C. Church was built on Ballochney Road, to the east of the Easter Gatehouse, opening in October 1900. It stood in extensive grounds, with the presbytery building standing alongside. The building was erected from stone, and the steep slated roofs were prominent in the area. Within the chapel was St David's School, the chancel of the building being separated by folding partitions to create classrooms, and a curtain covered the altar. The headmasters here included a Mr Johnston. This school was soon to be too small and a new school was erected to the north of Whiterigg. The old school closed in June 1931.

The site of St David's new school was the old Whiterigg farm. It was positioned here to replace the old catholic school at Whiterigg and also that at Meikle Drumgray, further north. It drew its roll from a wide area. The school was officially opened by Bishop MacIntosh from Glasgow. Among the headmasters who served there were Paddy Lally and Hugh Hendrie. The roll in

1940 was 374, but with the number to be added to with the arrival of 35 evacuees from Glasgow, another teacher joined the staff. Following the demolition of most of the mining communities hereabouts, the school was closed on 23 December 1959. Pupils were transferred to the new St David's Junior Secondary School in Plains, which was officially opened on 21 March 1960.

The water supply to the village did not arrive until around 1900. Prior to this, the villagers had to get water from wells and springs, or sometimes from the North Burn, though this also served as something of a sewer. One of the better-known springs was located adjacent to the Ashy Bing at Whiterigg. The ice-cold water rose from the ground, and it gained a reputation for having some form of healing qualities. It is said that folk came from far and near to draw this water, such was its fame.

The sanitary conditions at Whiterigg were often of a seriously poor standard. In 1849 there was an outbreak of cholera in the community, claiming the lives of many of the residents. The mine-owners, not fully understanding the cause of the disease, had the houses white-washed in an attempt at improving the sanitary conditions. The houses were again whitewashed in 1866, according to a report in the local newspaper: 'William Black, the proprietor of the village of Whiterigg, is paying great attention to its sanitary condition. The houses are being whitewashed both outside and in. Whiterigg in its new dress looks mightily improved and the sight should tempt some more of our coalmasters to go and do likewise.'

Eventually it came to be known that cholera was a symptom of dirty water, so new supplies were laid into the community. When water was piped into the village, it was only available from pumps, positioned around the village. In the old part of Whiterigg village, the pump was located next to the post office. At South Standrigg Row there were two pumps in front of the rows. At Airdriehill Square, both pumps were rather inconveniently located at the southern end. Another pump was located in the street at St David's presbytery.

Sometime prior to 1898 a new public hall was erected at Whiterigg, on the south side of the railway bridge. A public house was positioned on the street on the north side of the railway, opposite the post office. The latter was a sub-post office, under Airdrie. In 1887 the public house was occupied by Morrison Bisset.

Stanrigg Oil Works were closed in 1903 and the site was demolished and most of the remnants cleared away. Only old track beds of railway lines, bings

WHITERIGG

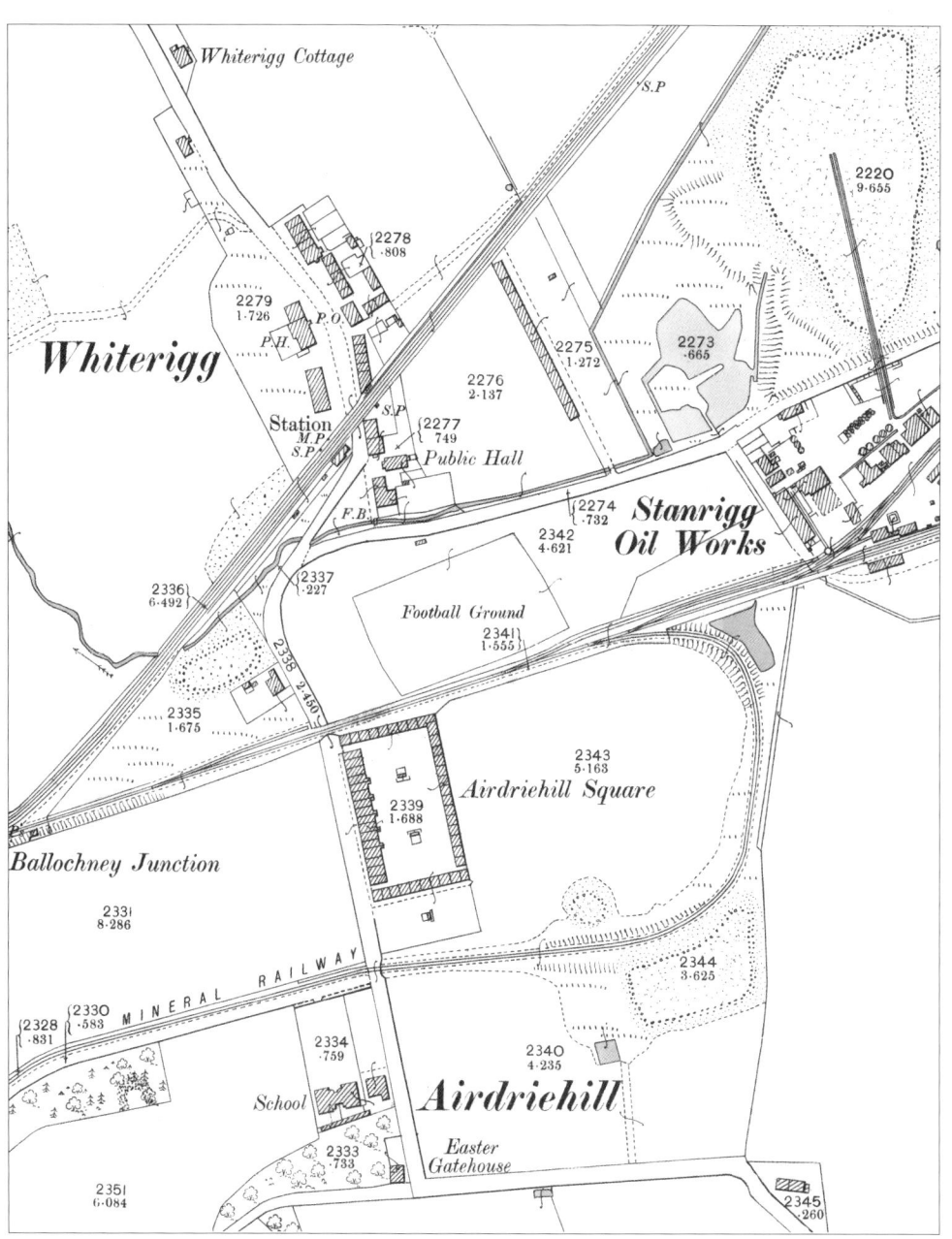

37.3 Whiterigg from 1898 Ordnance Survey map

and pools associated with cooling ponds remained. Residents at Whiterigg had to look elsewhere for work. Some found employment in Airdriehill Quarry, which had expanded considerably, almost reaching the new school. The quarry was owned by Shanks and MacEwan.

In 1930 a small coal mine was established just to the east of Airdriehill Square. Owned by Willie Makin, the pit operated for a few years under different owners before closing.

As with most mining communities, Airdriehill had its own junior football team. Airdriehill Shamrock played in the local leagues at the end of the nineteenth century. Its football ground was located between Whiterigg's older community and Airdriehill Square, between the road and railway line. It was granted to the team by Mr Waddell of Airdriehill House on a lease of 99 years at a rental of one penny per annum. As the new century dawned, the team struggled to continue, and it was agreed to merge with three other minor teams from the locality – Darngavil Star, Greengairs and Plains Bluebell – to form a new team. This was called Darngavil United and played at the village of that name.

A number of players from the mining community ranks made it as professional players. One of these was Jimmy 'Whitey' McGowan, who was to play with Partick Thistle for eighteen years. He was capped for Scotland on two occasions. Another was John Devlin, who played for Hibernian, Kilmarnock and Walsall. For the latter team, he was long remembered for having scored five goals against Torquay United in 1948. Matthew Costello played with Chesterfield, Thomas McGuigan played with Ayr United then Hartlepool United before retiring. Ally McGowan played for Wrexham. Thomas Brannen played for Wrexham and Airdrieonians. Archibald Banned played for Albion Rovers. Jim Kane played for Third Lanark and St Johnstone.

As in all places, random deaths occurred throughout the years. One melancholy example was the time when James MacGowan, a miner who was passing through Airdriehill Square on his way home from work, spotted the legs of a young boy dangling out of a tub. Apparently, the two-year-old, named James Conners, had fallen head first into the tub and was unable to extricate himself. Although there was only four inches of water in the bottom of the tub, he drowned.

According to the Census of 1881, Whiterigg had a population of 553. This increased to 640 in 1891, but by 1901 Whiterigg was in decline and most of the residents were moving elsewhere. The old Whiterigg Row of ten houses was demolished before 1935. Lanark County Council planned to clear the remaining residents, and as new council houses were erected at Caldercruix the villagers of Whiterigg were rehoused there. For a number of years an annual re-union was held, when former sons and occupants of Whiterigg came together to reminisce about life in their former village. The last of these is thought to have taken place around 1947 in St David's Hall. Although most of the villagers were re-housed, the lack of accommodation in the area meant that others were keen to take on the houses. Thus, some of them remained in occupation until 1952, when it was decided to demolish the houses as soon as they became vacant.

38

Woodend

✶

On a low promontory, between a little burn flowing from Woodend farm into the Barbauchlaw Burn, stood Ogilface Castle, *caput* of the Barony of Ogilface. It was never a large edifice, being perhaps little more than a defensive tower with a stair wing to one side, the steep embankments down to the streams adding to its defence. It is thought that the castle may have dated from the sixteenth century, and that it passed through the hands of the Wood, Murray and Livingstone families. By the seventeenth century it was in ruins, and local tradition claims that it was used as a hideout by the Covenanters.

Ogilface Castle was very much in ruins by the time the village of Woodend was erected to its north, just across Woodend Burn. The village comprised of one street, with houses on both sides of the road from Armadale to Avonbridge, in West Lothian. Leaving Armadale behind, the minor road drops to the bridge over the Barbauchlaw Burn, a series of old quarries on the left. On the other side of the burn the road climbs again, and makes a turn to the south-west. It was from here along the road towards Woodend farm that the village was located.

Woodend village was built on what had been an old coach route from Airdrie to Bathgate. The line of this can still be made out on the ground, but around 1790 a new roadway was constructed further south, passing through Armadale Cross, and leaving the old road to fall into disuse. The village was probably constructed sometime in the late 1850s, for the Ordnance Survey map of 1854 doesn't show any buildings here. To the south-west of Woodend farm, however, it indicates the original Woodend Pit, which worked coal and ironstone, there being two coal and ironstone pits in the vicinity. The community also had a smithy and store. The village was erected by the Coltness Iron Company, which was active in the district working the minerals. By 1868 the village contained 39 houses, located in three terraces – the Office, Stable and School rows. All of these were built of stone, which was quite unusual for mining communities in Lothian at this time.

The Coltness Iron Company acquired the mineral rights on Barbauchlaw in 1856. Woodend Pit was opened in 1870 and over the years numerous pitheads were created to work various seams. Pit Number 2 was just to the west of Woodend farm, whereas Pit Number 5 was to the north. Extensive colliery bings survive in the vicinity. A mineral railway siding from the Bathgate – Airdrie railway left the main line at Woodend Junction and meandered alongside Barbauchlaw Glen to the pits.

38.1 Woodend from the west

Deaths in the pits were all too common. Some died on the surface, such as John Thomson, jammed between two railway carriages belonging to the Monkland Railway Company at Woodend Colliery on 4 February 1862. Others were to suffer underground, often from rocks falling from the roof of the pits.

There were five main terraces of houses in Woodend, four of which were located on the north side of the road. On climbing up from the Barnbauchlaw Bridge the first row on the right was known as the East Row. This originally had twelve houses in it, but by merging some of the small homes, it latterly had fewer. Unlike the other rows at Woodend, this one sat back from the road, a series of gardens being located between. Around the houses were narrow paths, front and rear. House number one was occupied by James Calder, clerk.

Staying on the north side of the road, the second terrace was known as Office Row. This faced directly onto the road. As with the other rows, the number of houses changed over the years but, when built, this row had thirteen houses in it. Half-way along the terrace was a narrow close, allowing pedestrian access to the back of the houses, where gardens were to be found across the back lane. In 1917 there were only nine houses in the row.

The third row on the north side of the road was called the School Row. This originally had twelve houses in it, and a similar close passed through the houses to the rear gardens. By 1917 there were only ten houses, some of the houses having been merged together.

The last, or fourth row, on the north side of the main road was located round a bend from the main road. Again, there were initially twelve houses in this row, but the last house was about twice the size of the rest, and by 1917 there were ten homes. This terrace was known as West Row.

On the south side of the road through Woodend, the first row reached from the bridge had fifteen houses in it. These houses had no back lane, the gardens leading directly off the homes, but a close or pend half-way along the row gave easier access. This row was known as the Stable Row.

Beyond the Stable Row were a few random buildings. Further along the street, still on the south side of the road, was Woodend Public School, a comparatively bigger building in a large playground. This play area was divided into two, with areas for boys and girls to play separately, and in the corners were sheds. The school had initially been funded by the mining company, but in 1879 the seminary was transferred to Torphichen School Board. The school had accommodation for 120. In 1884 it was noted that the average attendance was 115. In 1900 there were 205 scholars on the roll, but by 1933 it had fallen to 80.

Sometime around 1900 a schoolhouse was erected on the piece of ground between the school playground and the glen of the Woodend Burn. This is the only house of the original Woodend to survive today. Teachers who lived there included Mr J. F. Slingsby (appointed 1894), Mr Christie, William Black and James Brodie (died 1950).

Just west of the school was the village institute, or miners' welfare club. Among the various events held in the building were dances. In the Victorian period Woodend Friendly Society was formed. The Woodend and Armadale Floral and Horticultural Association held regular shows in Woodend Public School from at least the 1870s up to 1914. The association was reformed in 1931.

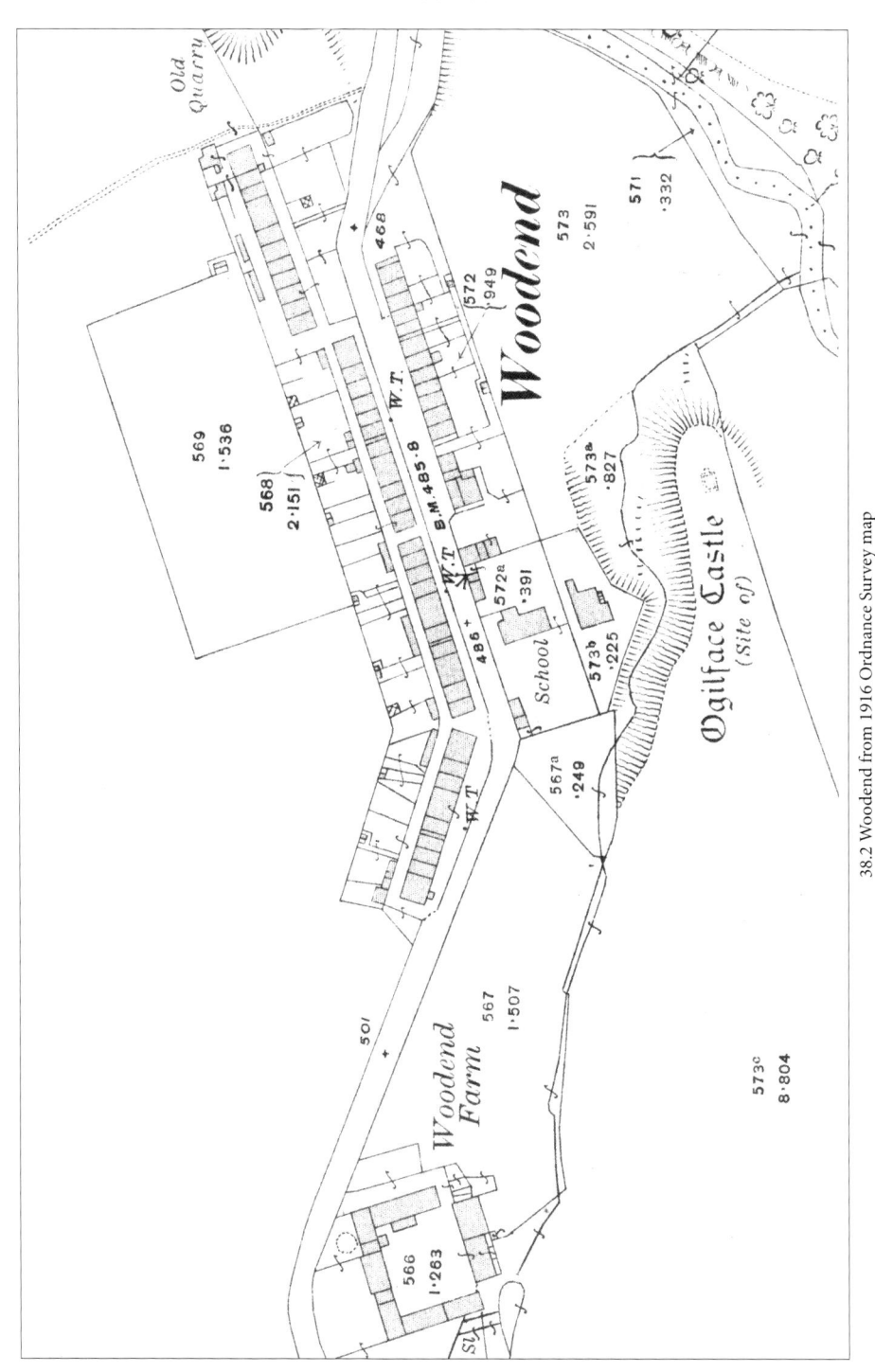

WOODEND

38.2 Woodend from 1916 Ordnance Survey map

Woodend Sabbath School was popular with children, the superintendent for many years being Alex Ballantyne (1848-1925).

On 30 November 1899 a major storm, during which thunder and lightning roared and hail struck the ground with considerable force, took place across much of West Lothian. At Woodend eight houses were damaged by the lightning. It appears to have struck the end house of one of the rows, occupied by Mr MacEwan, destroying the chimney. Many slates were ripped off, and the electrical charge ran along the ridge to the next seven houses, ripping off slates for about two feet to either side of the ridge. Many rhones were thrown from the walls. Internally, Mr MacEwan's ceiling collapsed, his kettle on the hob was knocked through a window and his sister and child were blackened with the soot. Three men who were standing outside were knocked to the ground.

Water was brought into the village in the early years of the twentieth century. Three pumps along the main road allowed residents to draw water. One was located in front of the West Row, the second in front of the School Row and the third in front of the Office Row.

Woodend had its own football team, which played on a pitch located to the immediate north of the Office Row. The oldest recorded team from the village was Woodend Jubileans who existed in 1887. They were later renamed Woodend Athletic. By the turn of the twentieth century, the local team was known as Woodend Excelsior. Other teams which played at Junior level in the village included Woodend Thistle. Woodend United played in the 1920s and Woodend Celtic played in juvenile leagues around 1910. Some other teams used the pitch also, such as Armadale Volunteers.

By the time of the 1891 Census, the population of Woodend had risen to 346, most of the menfolk employed in the local mines. The census also confirmed that they lived in 62 houses, making an average of five and a half persons per property. For the next ten years the population was fairly static, the census of 1901 calculating the population as 341.

Woodend was still occupied when the Second World War broke out. At the time, the residents had been promised new homes in Armadale, but the war put a hold to that. Ownership passed from the Coltness Iron Company to the National Coal Board on 'vesting day' on 1 January 1947. In 1944 there had been an agreement that the residents would be rehoused in Armadale, but in 1948 many tenants complained that they were being by-passed when new homes became available. West Lothian Council considered various options for

Woodend's future. By this time the houses were not of a standard that was acceptable, so the choice was between rebuilding the houses or pulling them down. The latter was chosen, and in the 1950s the rows were cleared. The last of the residents had been offered new council houses in Armadale, located just one mile away on the other side of the burn.

39

Woodhead

*

Due west of the Kirkcudbrightshire village of Carsphairn, in the valley of the Garryhorn Burn, can be seen remains of a sizeable mining community. The Woodhead Lead Mines today form a most interesting industrial archaeology site, one that is spread across the slopes of Garryhorn Rig. Remains of buildings and chimneys are positioned randomly across the hillside, gradually crumbling into the ground once more. In recent years they have become more recognised for their historical and archaeological importance, and as such have become protected.

In 1838 prospectors were in the area and discovered considerable pockets of lead, plus copper, zinc and silver to a smaller degree. The lead had first been noticed by the farmer at Woodhead, who reported it to his landlord, Colonel MacAdam Cathcart (d. 1865). The discovery was acted upon quickly, and the following year new lead mines and associated buildings were established. These veins of ore, or galena, dip towards the north-north-east at around sixty degrees. The veins also contain zinc-blende and chalcopyrite.

Colonel MacAdam Cathcart was a very forward-looking landlord, and he wanted the best conditions that he could for the workers at his new mines. He was very 'hands-on' and took a deep interest in the on-going work. In his journal he wrote:

> Visited the Mine this day, found the water course going on well ... entered into agreements respecting the intending buildings at the Mine after examining the different offers and conferring with the intending contractors on the spot.

Writing in March 1844, Rev David Welsh, minister of Carsphairn and contributor of the parish entry in the *New Statistical Account of Scotland*, was enthusiastic about the new mines and of the possibilities they brought. It is worth quoting him at length:

Nothing has yet been done in the way of purifying the lead. The ore which has been extracted, lies in the state in which it was dug out; but preparations are beginning to be made for washing and purifying it, and it is presumed that no expense will be spared in carrying on the operations on the most approved plans. There is abundance of coal and lime upon the estates of the proprietor on the Ayrshire side, and it is hoped that an exchange favourable to Carsphairn may be made.

Since the preceding pages were written in 1839, Carsphairn has undergone a wonderful change, chiefly on account of the mining operations carried on within the parish. Since the operations commenced, the population has been nearly doubled. In that part of the parish in which lead was discovered, and in the bosom of a remote mountain, where the silence of nature was seldom broken, unless by the barking of the shepherd's dog, or the call of the shepherd, there is now a scene of industry and activity, which requires to be witnessed in order to be understood; and which cannot be contemplated without astonishment.

The proprietor of the mine, the Honourable Colonel MacAdam Cathcart, has spared no expense in obtaining all the necessary apparatus for crushing, washing, and smelting, on the most approved principles. The wheel used for moving the crushing apparatus is about 30 feet in diameter, driven by water obtained from the neighbouring mountains. The smelting furnaces are constructed on the most approved plan; and large houses have been built, and preparations are making in them for separating the silver from the lead. The proprietor has been acting hitherto as if it were his object to exhibit the whole operations in the most perfect manner, rather than to enrich himself. It is to be hoped, however, that the liberal manner in which hitherto he has conducted the whole business, may meet with an ample reward. The Honourable Colonel M. Cathcart retains the mine entirely in his own hands. He has appointed skilful and steady men as overseers; and he takes pleasure in personally superintending the whole.

Everything is done by the proprietor to promote the comfort of the workmen. A large village has already been built upon the side of the hill, additions to which are still making; and from the situation which it occupies, and the cleanliness of its appearance, it presents a picturesque object to the traveller in passing among the wild mountains. The proprietor has likewise evidenced his liberality in his attention to the mental cultivation and moral improvement of the workmen.

Though there are workmen from different quarters, yet greater part are from Leadhills and Wanlockhead, —men who had enjoyed the privilege of excellent libraries, and who regretted their separation from these means of entertainment and improvement. So soon as the Colonel and the Honourable Mrs Macadam Cathcart were made acquainted with their desire of forming a library, they sent a number of books, which laid an excellent foundation for a library, and which, by various means, is rapidly increasing. In addition to this, they have built an excellent school and school-master's house; the school-house is more ample and commodious than any in the district, and they give a liberal salary both to the schoolmaster and female teacher.

The mining operations have changed Carsphairn from being one of the most rural and pastoral parishes in this country, into one of comparative bustle and activity. More money now circulates in one week than was circulated, a few years ago, in the course of the year.

The writer of the *New Statistical Account* makes reference to the number of miners travelling from Wanlockhead and Leadhills in search of work, and this is noted in an account of Leadhills made in 1841. When Joseph Fletcher paid a visit in order to compile evidence for a Royal Commission on Children's employment he noted that:

> At the time of my visit [to Leadhills] there were a number of families remaining in the village, the heads of which, to the number of perhaps 80 had gone to work at the newly opened mine at Carsphairn in Galloway about 60 miles distant, where there is as yet no permanent home for those dependent on them.

However, it was not too long before rows of miners' houses were built. These were strung across the hillside in terraces. At the western end of the community were the Higher Row and Lower Row, but above them were more rows of houses, including the Office Row. North east of the two named rows were

WOODHEAD

39.1 Woodhead from east

39.2 Woodhead from east

further houses, seemingly randomly spread about the complex, as though the miners were given free rein to find suitable ground for building. Some of the rows were named Bone's Row and Weir's Row, probably after some long-term occupants. Mill Row was where the smelters lived. It had five houses within it.

In the 1841 census there were 22 houses occupied, with a population of 200. Ten years later the number of houses had increased to fifty, with the maximum population achieved at Woodhead, 301 persons. All of the houses were single storey and roofed with slates.

As well as miners from Leadhills and Wanlockhead, Colonel MacAdam Cathcart also brought in the experience of miners from Cornwall, many of whom were appointed as overseers.

The manager at the mines for much of the time was Peter Wilson, and he kept a diary from which it is possible to glean some interesting facts. Up to the end of 1852, 5,700 tons of lead was produced, providing an income, minus the cost of smelting, of £88,065. Averaging this out over the twelve years previously provides an annual income of around £7,300. There was probably further income, for every ton of lead also produced eighteen ounces of silver, which was sold at a much higher rate. Lead was sold at an average rate of £16 per ton, though the price was sometimes as high as £24 per ton. The cost of smelting was worked out at eleven shillings per ton, including fuel costs.

There were two veins of lead ore worked at Woodhead, named the Woodhead Vein and Garryhorn String. Mine shafts, adits, levels and ventilation shafts were created across the hillside, creating a complex series of tunnels and linking shafts. The upper three levels were named the Top Adit, Middle Adit and Deep Adit levels. Below this were two other levels, the Eleven Fathoms Level and the 25 Fathoms Level.

The miners required dynamite in order to blast into the rocks, and a powder magazine was located near to the Upper Row. This was a small square building, topped by a hipped roof.

There were at least nine shafts at Woodhead, dropping vertically to seven different levels where the lead was worked. The deepest, which was 312 feet deep, was sunk in 1843. From the shafts the levels spread out into the hillside, where miners worked in cramped conditions, between masses of whinstone. Light was provided by candles, and there are records of two banksmen being given three candles each for twelve hours. The overseer was allocated 5,961 pounds of candles at a cost of £173 17s 3d.

On the surface a crushing plant was established, shown on detailed maps as a 'crushing machine', to break the rocks that were brought to the surface. To drive this plant a large waterwheel was constructed, thirty feet in diameter.

To get sufficient water to drive the crushing wheel and for other purposes three extensive lades were dug out of the hillside. One contoured at around 950 feet above sea level, feeding a rectangular reservoir known as the Weaver's Dam. A second lade was positioned about 750-800 feet above sea level and contoured from the Garryhorn Burn right into the centre of the community – it was probably this lade that drove the crushing machine's waterwheel. A third lade was located higher up, contouring at approximately 1000 feet above sea level, diverting water from the Garryhorn Burn and adding to it water from lesser streams. Water was also obtained from the north; the headwaters of the Green Burn being diverted over the shoulder of Garryhorn Rig and into two sizeable reservoirs located in the pass. The lower, and slightly smaller of the two reservoirs, had a sluice which controlled the flow of water from it, and this was directed down a lade towards the smithy and crushing machine.

A washing plant was constructed, where the ore was cleaned. Boys were employed to carry out this task, being paid around one shilling per day. At one point there were twelve lead washers under the age of fourteen years, including six aged ten years. Linking the different plants were small mineral lines, the stone transported along them in bogies. A smithy existed to work metal, and near to it was a wright's workshop.

A smelting plant was built where the lead ore could be placed into furnaces and melted. This was a short distance downhill from the crushing plant, linked with it by a short pathway. Arranged around a courtyard, and only one storey in height, the smelting houses were the largest buildings in the whole works, and two major furnaces had the smoke directed through underground flues and up the hillside to two chimneys built above the complex. The lower chimney still stands to a height of around fifty feet. The higher chimney has collapsed and only stands around fifteen feet in height. The slag and impurities were taken off, leaving the natural lead to be poured into ingots. Smelters were paid eighteen shillings per week and were given a free house and fuel.

Lead from Woodhead was taken by track over the hill towards Lamloch and from there north to Dalmellington, where it was stored in what the locals called the 'Leid Yard'. Continuing on, the lead was taken to the port of Ayr, from where it was shipped south through the North Channel and Irish Sea to

Liverpool and even exported to the Netherlands, where the lead was converted into sheets used for roofing and other plumbing purposes. The same road was also used for hauling coal and limestone from the Ayrshire coalfield to the smelter.

The amount of lead produced at Woodhead varied over the years, but the works produced the greatest quantity within its first five years, after which production diminished. The total quantity of lead mined at Woodhead was 6,712 tons.

Wages at the mines were paid depending on the output. In January 1839 the Colonel expected to pay the miners around £3 per month, but as the pits deepened the men found it more difficult to keep up with production. Later, miners were paid about eighteen shillings per week, though their labourers only received around twelve to fourteen shillings.

As with all mining operations, there were a number of fatalities. One of these was reported in the *Dumfries Standard* of December 1849:

> On Monday last, a miner named John Bone lost his life through an accident at Woodhead Lead Mine. Deceased had fired a blast, and was proceeding to remove the rubbish, when a large mass of rock, which, unknown to the workman, the gunpowder had detached from its bed, fell upon him. The stone was immediately removed, but so severely had he been crushed that, although little external injury was visible, he survived barely half an hour. With the above exception only one death has occurred at Woodhead Lead Mine for upwards of twelve months. Considering that the present year has been so rife with disease, it is doubtful if any other village in Britain, with a population of from three to four hundred individuals has the same cause of thankfulness to the Giver of health and life.

A second fatality is recorded in 16 January 1852. On that day David Wilson was killed in Harris' Jerry Shaft.

In his circuit tours, Lord Cockburn paid a visit to Woodhead. He noted that, 'it looks like a colony of solitary strangers who were trying to discover subterranean treasures in a remote land.'

In 1843 a new school was erected at Woodhead, located below the Lower Row. This replaced an earlier school, for it is noted in 1841 that John Kidd was

WOODHEAD

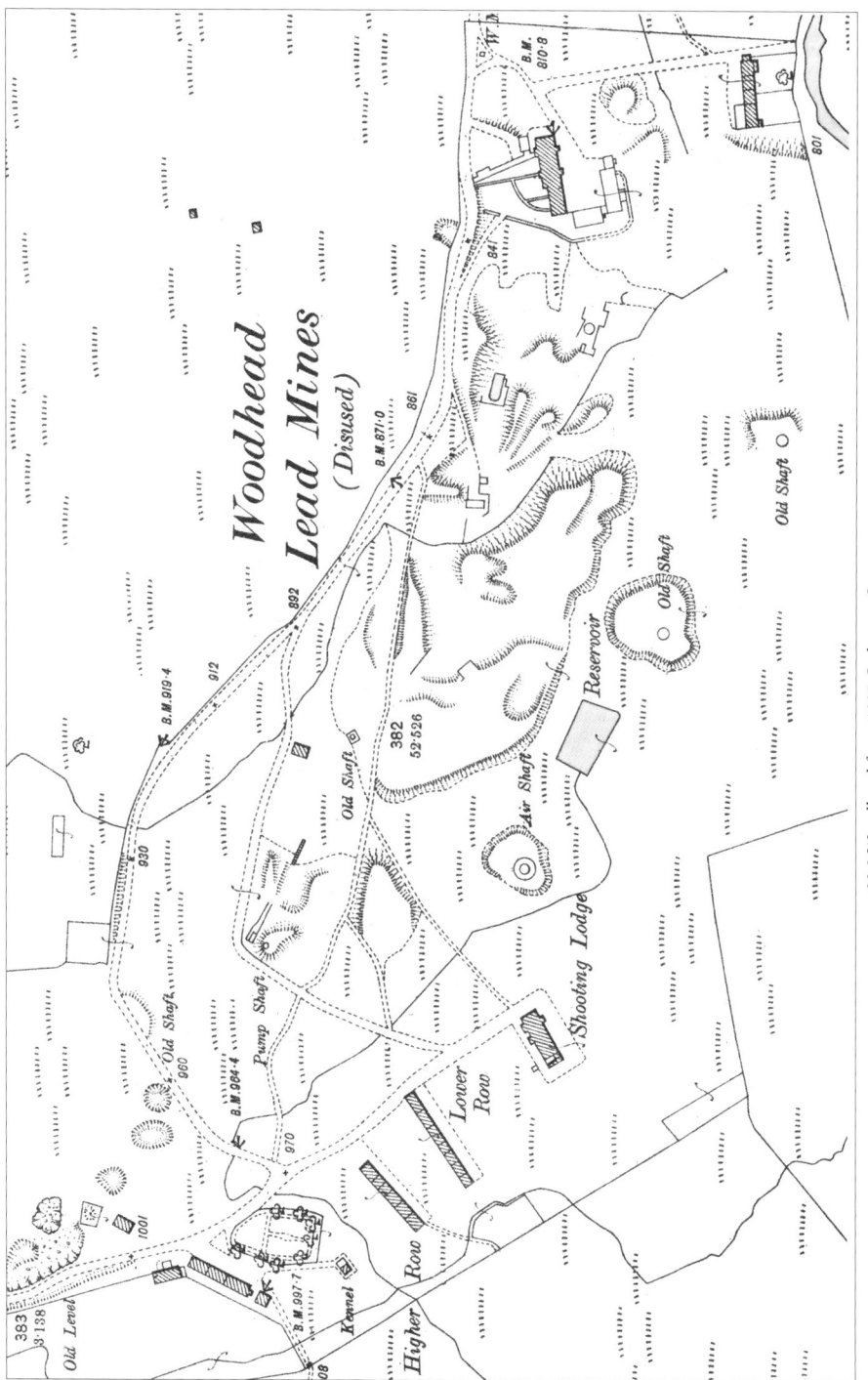

39.3 Woodhead from 1895 Ordnance Survey map

employed as a teacher at the village, which had 46 children under the age of 13. The next teacher was Charles Stuart MacLean, who was assisted by his wife, Eliza Finnis. According to the *Dumfries Standard*, 'in the seminary recently opened at the lead-mines, Carsphairn, the Hon Colonel MacAdam Cathcart has there built a most commodious schoolhouse and we congratulate him in the fortunate election which has been made of a teacher who seems in every way fitted from the success which has accompanied his labours during the short period since his appointment to be an unspeakable benefit to the numerous and increasing population of the mines'.

There were 49 pupils at Woodhead school in 1851, aged from five to fourteen. Within the next few years it is thought that the school was closed, for around that time many miners left the works in search of new jobs, the production of lead dropping considerably. The building was later converted into a shooting lodge for the Cathcarts and remained in use as such for a century thereafter.

The miners at Woodhead wished to establish a church of their own, but Colonel MacAdam Cathcart would not allow them to build one on his property. Most of the miners were English, and they adhered to the Wesleyan Methodist Church. James MacMillan of Lamloch was more sympathetic and allowed a place of worship to be built there. Until it was erected he allowed the miners to worship in his kitchen. In January 1844 it was decided to build a church, and the miners, along with assistance from the Free Church congregation in Dalmellington, set about constructing it. Lamloch Church was built to the south west of Lamloch House, by the side of the Lamloch Burn, at the nearest point on MacMillan's property to Woodhead village. The miners walked over the hill track, a distance of one and half miles, meaning that worshippers had a round trip of three miles to worship. This was a favourable distance compared with the six-mile round trip to the parish church in Carsphairn. However, in 1841 there were eighteen Free Church members at the church who travelled there from Carsphairn. The church was closed in 1876 and the building reverted back to MacMillan.

In addition to the school and church the Library Society was founded in 1840. In 1849 the library had over eight hundred books on its shelves, including a 'splendidly bound copy of the Encyclopaedia Britannica', which Colonel MacAdam Cathcart had presented. 'The library was probably part of the school, and everybody within a ten-mile radius of the mines was allowed to borrow from it so that the fruits of this judicious liberalism are apparent not only in the well-thumbed volumes which may be found in almost every cottage, but in the superior intelligence and orderly habits by which the inhabitants of this district are so honourably distinguished.'

A number of causes, including a slump in demand for lead, resulted in the mines at Woodhead being closed. In February 1852 a number of miners and other workers were given notice to quit, and in 1853 a fair number of residents of the mines emigrated to the United States, in particular to Pennsylvania. Nevertheless, some folk still remained at the houses, and writing in the first edition of *Rambles in Galloway* (1876), Malcolm Harper noted that he saw nearly one hundred workers, 'all busily engaged at work on the surface.' By the time the second edition of the book appeared in 1896, he noted that the mines had been abandoned for several years. In 1861, according to the Census, there were only 88 people living at the mines; by the 1891 Census this had dropped to fourteen people, living in three houses. The houses at the village were gradually abandoned, and the last house to be occupied was in 1954. Sometime between 1917 and 1920 the Ore Supply Ltd company of Newton Stewart did some prospecting at Woodhead, but it is not thought that they carried out any mining.

In the kirk at New Abbey, south west of Dumfries, is a stained-glass window in memory of Rev James Stewart Wilson. He was educated at the little school at Woodhead, from where he went to Edinburgh University and studied for the ministry. He was to become the minister at New Abbey.

40
Woodlands

✶

The M8 motorway makes its way between Glasgow and Edinburgh, thousands, if not millions, of vehicles passing along it every day. The last stretch of the route to be created was the section between Bargeddie and Newhouse, this part of the route being dual carriageway for many years. When the new motorway was created it took a route slightly to the south of the old A8, and at Kirkwood, west of Coatbridge, it was to obliterate much of the remnants of the lost village of Woodlands. This was its proper name, as recorded on Ordnance Survey maps and other official documents, but in many cases it was also known as Kirkwood, that being the name of the colliery to which it was attached, and the main road through Woodlands had houses known as Kirkwood Row.

Most of Woodlands had gone before the motorway, however, so it was not to blame for its demise. It was gradually cleared away and the houses demolished from the beginning of the twentieth century onwards, the residents being rehoused in council houses erected at Drumpark, Kirkwood, Kirkshaws or Old Monkland, large council estates forming the west end of Coatbridge.

Woodlands village was strung along the side of the road that once linked Old Monkland with Langmuir and Bargeddie. It was located on the north bank of the North Calder Water, near to the spot where the lesser watercourse of the Luggie Burn had its confluence with the greater river. The Luggie had been crossed for years by an ancient bridge, known as the Luggie Bridge, to be replaced sometime between 1858 and 1896 by a second, wider bridge, just upstream from the old bridge, which remained. A few yards downstream from the old bridge a third crossing made its way over the Luggie, as well as the North Calder – the Woodlands Viaduct. This was built to carry a mineral railway serving Bredisholm and Braehead collieries, but by 1896 it was closed, leaving the viaduct to stand for a few years before it was cleared away prior to 1910.

Before the creation of Woodlands village this was a rural area. Near to the old Luggie Bridge was the Luggie Mill, which had a waterwheel powered by water taken from a lade filled from the Luggie itself. The mill was in ruins before 1858. In the same corner of the Luggie was Rosebank, a sizeable villa.

WOODLANDS

The discovery of workable coal resulted in a major change in the area. At the confluence of the Luggie and the North Calder, but on the opposite side of the Luggie from what would become Woodlands, was Braehead Colliery Pit Number 5. Here coal was worked deep below the ground. On the surface were a series of pithead buildings and numerous railway sidings branching from the main line here. Braehead Number 2 was to be closed before 1896. Kirkwood Pit had been opened by a Mr Hendry in 1862. In 1881 its manager was Robert Gray. By 1910 it was owned by United Collieries Ltd, which oprated a variety of other mines in the district. There were four different Kirkwood Colliery pits, all located within a short distance from each other.

Where Woodlands was to be built was originally a field nestling between the road and the North Calder. Other fields lay on the north side of the road, rising up Kirkwood Hill. A small cottage, known as Meadowlands, stood by the side of the road, with small gardens to either side.

The creation of the Kirkwood Colliery was to result in the building of houses at Woodlands to house the many miners who were employed there. The colliery was located on the north side of the road, immediately east of the Luggie Burn, and numerous railway sidings and colliery bings were to be formed over an extensive area. Pit Number 2 was located by the side of Woodlands road itself. A total of 79 houses were built for colliery workers. These were all brick-built, but the quality of construction was such that they were erected as cheaply as possible. All of them were single storey in height. The walls did not have any damp-proof courses included, meaning that moisture seeped up the walls from the ground. Internally, the walls had been plastered directly onto the brick, resulting in a cold, damp surface which did not take paint very well. In most cases in the rows the floors were of timber, in many cases ventilated, but there were some homes with brick-lined floors.

The houses at Woodlands were mainly located on the south side of the road, though there were some on the north. Most of the houses on the south side of the road dated from around 1872. Starting at the old Luggie Bridge at the west, the first row of houses contained eight dwellings, built along a shallow dog-leg. The front doors faced directly onto the road, and on the other side of the dwellings were gardens, stretching back to the North Calder. At the west end were three two-apartment homes, the rent for which was £5 2s in 1910. Adjoining these were five two-apartment houses, but these were slightly smaller, reflected in a rent of £4 4s. In many cases the second apartment was used as a scullery. Most of the community was regarded as not being overcrowded in 1910, though occupation of them was still quite high. The biggest percentage of houses in Kirkwood Row did not have the luxury of a wash-house, but they did have a coal cellar to store fuel.

Following on were two rows of houses built in a similar style. The western one had six two-apartment cottages in it. The rental payable in 1910 was £4 18s. Again, the front doors led directly onto the road and gardens were located to the rear, across a lane. On the south side of this lane was a wash-house. The third row also had six two-apartment houses in it, again with gardens over on the other side of the lane. The rental paid in 1910 was £6 2s.

A close between rows of houses here led south to a hall, a sizeable building which was erected prior to 1896. This was the property of Kirkwood Christian Brethren, a popular evangelical movement common at the time in many mining communities. Better known as the Gospel Hall, weekly services were held here, in addition to midweek prayer meetings and a popular Sunday School for children. The Kirkwood Brethren appear to have continued their existence until around 1933.

The fourth row at Woodlands had sixteen one-apartment houses in it. Half of these faced the road, and a lane to the rear gave access to the ones behind. This lane also separated them from the North Calder, which here made a sweep towards the houses, meaning that there was no room for gardens. The rent payable was £4 4s in 1910.

The fifth row of houses was built in a narrow stretch of land between the river and road. There were fifteen houses in this terrace, but not all were of the same size. The six east-most houses were smaller than the rest, being single-apartment homes built back to back. The houses at the back were reached by a stair, and they overlooked the river. These six houses were rented at £4 4s in 1910. The west-most houses were double-apartment homes, the rent for which was £5 14s.

Row number six was built back to back like the fourth row. The ground here sloped steeply from the roadside, meaning that a second layer of houses could be included at the back of the terrace, facing the river. It had eighteen homes in it, six on the lower level, and twelve single-apartment houses at street level. On the south side of the row were external stairways, leading to the upper floors. The rent for these houses was £4 4s in 1910.

The final row on the south side of Woodlands road was more or less the

WOODLANDS

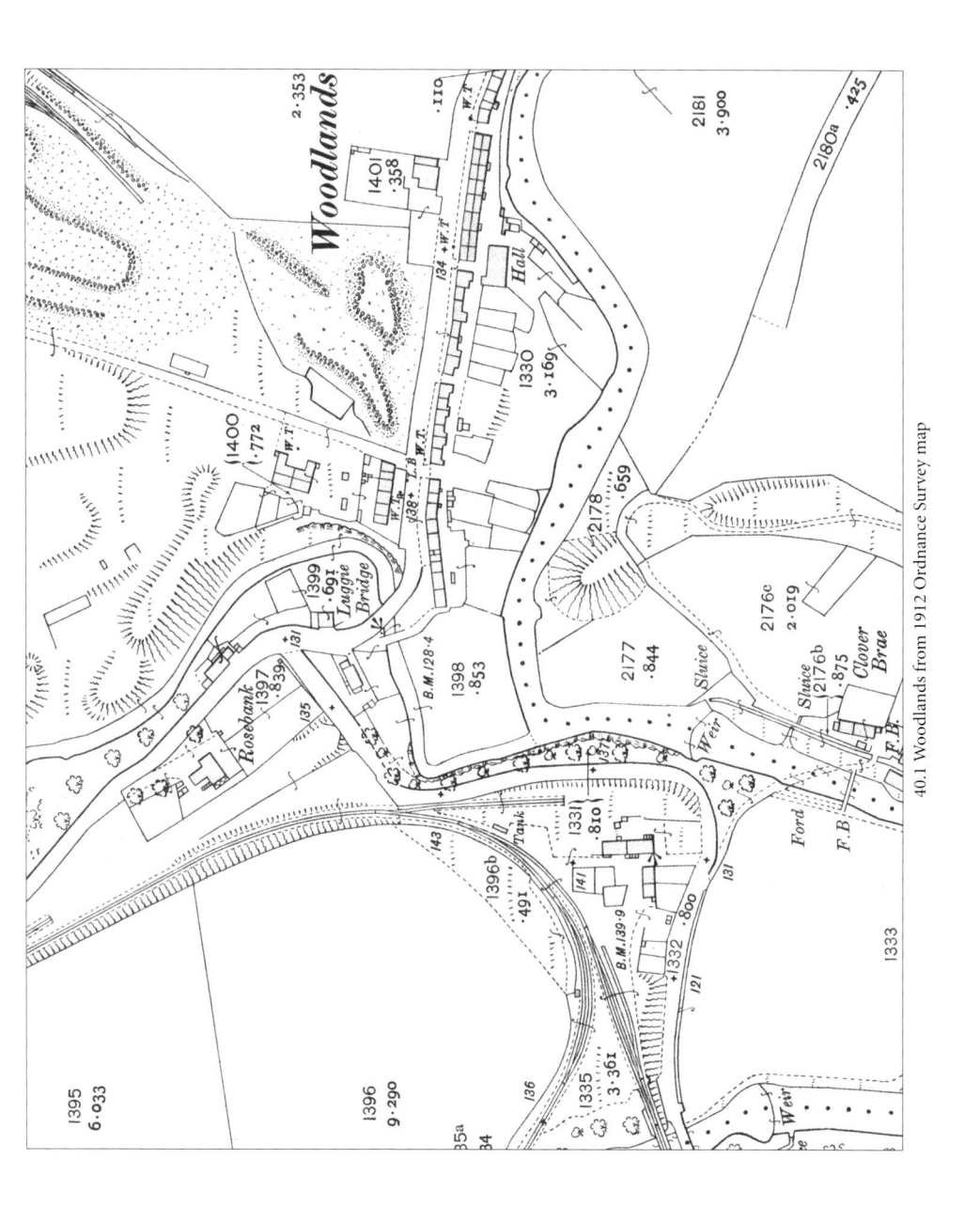

40.1 Woodlands from 1912 Ordnance Survey map

same format as the sixth row. It had seventeen one-apartment houses in it plus one two-apartment house. Six of these were at street level, the houses built back to them being reached by a flight of stairs from the back lane. Under these back houses were a line of six single-apartment houses at lane level, their back wall built into the embankment. The rent payable in 1910 for a single apartment house was £4 4s, and a double-apartment house was £5 14s.

As said, there were few houses on the north side of the road. Between the Luggie Burn and the pit road was a short terrace of six two-apartment houses, complete with gardens, though these were often uncultivated. This row of houses was known as Beech Row and rental in 1910 cost £5 15s 6d. The houses were all single storey, built of brick like the rest of the village, the roofs arched and covered over with felt. No damp courses were included in the walls, resulting in dampness throughout the terrace. Internally, the wall surfaces were simply plastered onto the inside of the brick wall. The floors were laid on the ground, in some cases made of brick, in others having timber. It was reported that the internal condition of the walls and ceilings were poor. The houses were built around 1873 with sizeable kitchens and small bedrooms attached. At the time it was reckoned that these houses were not overcrowded. The houses did not have the benefit of wash-houses or coal cellars, the residents of the row having to share one outside sink located at the front of the row. To the rear was one open privy midden

Behind Beech Row was a further block of houses. At the east side of Kirkwood pit bing was the old Meadowlands cottage, followed by a sizeable house. At the far end of the village, facing the last row of houses, was a pair of cottages in large gardens.

Water was to be supplied to Woodlands village and water pumps were installed at various locations through it. Two pumps were located on the north side of the village, one at the row of houses and another at the block behind it. A third pump was positioned at the lane between the first and second rows. A pump was located just east of the close leading to the gospel hall, and another at the next close. There were a couple of others elsewhere in the village. The water came from a gravitational supply, but the drainage was by surface water channels which often were blocked and stinking. Outside sinks were provided for washing purposes, but these were filled from water from the standpipes. Waste water was just emptied into open drainage channels which took it to the river. The village was regularly scavenged at the expense of the mine-owners.

Children who lived at Woodlands attended the school at Old Monkland and were expected to walk the lane which became Woodside Street each day. It is recorded that a number of these children had to walk to school and back in bare feet. Others had poor quality footwear, and on arrival at school the teacher allowed them to dry their socks and 'gutties', or plimsolls, on the radiators, ready for the return walk.

At one time the owner of Woodlands was John James Bannen, who practised as a solicitor in Coatbridge, living in Airdrie House and latterly at Alderford House, Langloan, Coatbridge. He had a son, Ian Bannen (1928-1999), who became a well-known actor in a variety of films and television shows.

Woodlands had its own football ground, located among the spoil heaps and bings of Kirkwood Colliery, north of the village. This was the home ground of Woodlands Football Club, which played at junior level in the late nineteenth century. This club may have folded and the ground was taken over by Kirkwood Thistle and then Kirkwood United. These two clubs played in the junior leagues, the former having a light blue strip. Among players from this team who made it in greater things was John (Jock) Cameron (1877-1956). He was born in the rows and played for Kirkwood Thistle in his youth before signing for St Mirren. In 1904 he moved to Blackburn Rovers and after three years was signed by Chelsea. In 1913 he moved to Port Vale, remaining for a year and latterly managing them for a short period. He was capped twice for Scotland: in 1904 against Northern Ireland and 1909 against England.

The first houses to disappear at Woodlands were also the oldest – Meadowlands, cleared by 1910. Kirkwood Colliery had closed by this time, and the village was in decline. The remainder was emptied and the residents moved into new homes in Coatbridge.

Appendix

✶

Village	Parish	County (Historical)	Grid Reference
Adamsrow	Newton	Midlothian	NT 324701
Arden	New Monkland	Lanarkshire	NS 801683
Avonhead	New Monkland	Lanarkshire	NS 808698
Balclevie	Elie	Fife	NO 492012
Benquhat	Dalmellington	Ayrshire	NS 464096
Binnend	Burntisland	Fife	NT 240872
Bothwellhaugh	Bothwell	Lanarkshire	NS 720581
Burn Row	Slamannan	Stirlingshire	NS 857715
Cullen	Cullen	Moray	NJ 507664
Darnconner	Auchinleck	Ayrshire	NS 576240
Darngavil	New Monkland	Lanarkshire	NS 783688
East Benhar	Whitburn	West Lothian	NS 917620
Eastfield	New Monkland	Lanarkshire	NS 832685
Fairfield	Beath	Fife	NT 128918
Fochabers	Bellie	Moray	NJ 348593
Forvie	Slains	Aberdeenshire	NK 020266
Gavieside	West Calder	Midlothian	NT 021642
Glenbuck	Muirkirk	Ayrshire	NS 749296
Haywood	Carnwath	Lanarkshire	NS 974546
Hermand	West Calder	Midlothian	NT 028628
Inveraray	Inveraray	Argyll	NN 096091

APPENDIX

Kincardine	Fordoun	Kincardine	NO 667748
Kingscavil	Linlithgow	West Lothian	NT 030763
Lassodie	Beath	Fife	NT 123924
Lethanhill	Dalmellington	Ayrshire	NS 436103
Longrigg	New Monkland	Lanarkshire	NS 835707
Midbreich	Livingston	Midlothian	NT 005644
Mossend	West Calder	Midlothian	NT 016636
Oakbank	Kirknewton	Midlothian	NT 078665
Oldtown of Roseisle	Duffus	Moray	NJ 138674
Rattray	Crimond	Aberdeenshire	NK 085575
Riccarton Junction	Castleton	Roxburghshire	NY 539978
Roughrigg	New Monkland	Lanarkshire	NS 830715
South Cobbinshaw	West Calder	Midlothian	NT 020572
Southfield	Slamannan	Stirlingshire	NS 848721
Whiterigg	New Monkland	Lanarkshire	NS 780674
Westerton	Kirkliston	West Lothian	NS 105719
Woodend	Torphichen	West Lothian	NS 907691
Woodhead	Carsphairn	Kirkcudbrightshire	NX 529937
Woodlands	Old Monkland	Lanarkshire	NS 709633

Bibliography

*

Bishop, Bruce B., *The Lands and People of Moray – Part 19 – Roseisle, Burghead, Cummingston, and Hopeman prior to 1850*, J. & B. Bishop, Elgin, 2004.
Cramond, William, *Reminiscences of the Old Town of Cullen, 1812-18*, John Adam, Aberdeen, 1882.
Donaldson, George, *Reminiscences of Haywood*, Hamilton Advertiser, Hamilton, 1935.
Dunbar, John G., *Sir William Burrell's Northern Tour 1758*, Tuckwell Press, East Linton, 1997.
Duncan, Robert, *Bothwellhaugh: A Lanarkshire Mining Community 1884-1965*, Workers Educational Association, Glasgow, 1986.
Findlay, Alistair, *Shale Voices: A Creative Memoir of Scotland's Shale Oil Communities*, Luath Press, Edinburgh, 2010.
Gibson, Rev Ivor, *The Spirit of Lassodie*, Trojan Press, Leslie, 2003.
Irvine, Theodore K., *Housing Conditions in the Scottish Shale Field – Evidence and Suggestions to the Royal Commission of Housing (Scotland)*, Scottish Shale Miners' Association, 1914.
Lindsay, Ian G., and Cosh, Mary, *Inveraray and the Dukes of Argyll*, Edinburgh University Press, Edinburgh, 1973.
Love, Dane, *Ayrshire's Lost Villages*, Carn Publishing, Auchinleck, 2016.
Lucas, Hugh; Devlin, Eddie; & Reilly, John, *The Lost Villages*, Lanarkshire Family History Society, 2015.
Pennant, Thomas, *A Tour in Scotland in 1769*, W. Eyres, Warrington, 1774.
Rice, Catherine, *'All Their Good Friends and Neighbours', The Story of a Vanished Hamlet in Angus*, Abertay Historical Society, Dundee, 2014.
Watt, Archibald, *Highways and Byways Round Kincardine*, Gourdas House Publishers, Aberdeen, 1985.

MAPS

Plan of Cullen, Peter May, 1764
Plan of Inveraray, Inveraray Castle Archives.
Oldtown of Roseisle, 1773-4, Gordon Muniments, National Records of Scotland.

WEBSITES
Abandoned Communities, www.abandonedcommunities.co.uk
Scottish Mining, www.scottishmining.co.uk
Shale Oil – a History of Scotland's Shale Oil Industry, www.scottishshale.co.uk

OTHER SOURCES
Forbes, E. J., *Dissertation on Local Mining Industry* [New Monkland], c.1955, copy at Airdrie Library.

Index

*

Accidents (industrial), 18, 23-4, 30-1, 47, 70, 100, 107, 115, 141-2, 150, 205, 219-20, 229, 241-2, 271, 279-80, 289, 295, 309, 320
Accidents (other), 119, 120-2, 141-2, 219, 284, 291-2, 306
Adair, John, 35
Adam, Andrew, 16
Adam, Robert, 75
Adamnan, St, 134
Adamson, Rev John, 17
Adamsrow, 11, 15-21, 330
Airdriehill, 100, 114, 300-4, 306
Alexanders of Ballochmyle, 85, 91
Allan, James, 131
Allotments and Gardens, 22, 62, 77, 79, 114, 118, 150, 167, 170, 191, 193, 210, 213, 225, 228, 238, 255, 268, 275, 277, 288, 293, 299
Anderson, John, 31
Anstruther, Lady Janet, 34
Anstruther, Sir John, 34-5
Archaeological excavations, see Excavations
Arden, 22-6, 30, 330
Ardross, 35
Argyll, Dukes of, 174-6, 179-81
Armstrong, Rev R. S., 36
Avonhead, 27-32, 330
Avonhead Coal Company, 27
Avonhead Colliery, 30, 32

Ayrshire's Lost Villages, 11, 13

Baird & Company, William, 86, 91, 150, 152, 155
Balclevie, 33-6, 330
Ballochmyle Colliery, 91
Ballochmyle Rows, 90-2
Ballochney, 72
Balquhatstone Colliery, 69-70
Balquhatstone House, 71-2
Bands, 29, 41, 63, 106, 110, 165, 201, 204, 219, 229
Bank (savings), 106
Bannen, Ian, 329
Bannen, John, 329
Barblues, 22-3
Baxter, John, 16
Beilby, Sir George Thomas, 246
Benhar Coal Company, 103, 107-8
Benhar, see East Benhar
Benquhat, 37-44, 219, 330
Bent Coal Company, 55, 61
Binnend, 45-54, 330
Binnend Oil Works, 45
Black & Sons, Messrs William, 291, 298, 304
Bone, Thomas, 156
Boswell, James, 80, 126
Bothwellhaugh, 55-66, 330
Bowling Greens, 62, 245, 247-8, 251
Boyd, Robert, 242

Braehead Colliery, 325
Breich Oil Works, 235
Brethren Assemblies, 89, 118, 152, 164, 277, 285, 291, 326
Brickworks, 39, 101, 159, 233, 282, 287
Bronze Age, 257
Brown of Priesthill, John, 156
Buchan, Earls of, 258, 262
Bucklyvie – see Balclevie
Burghs, 12, 77, 79, 175, 184-5, 188, 258-62, 264
Burn Row, 67-73, 330
Burn Row Riot, 70
Burnfoothill, 214, 217, 223
Burns Clubs, 44, 89, 106, 109, 204, 248
Burnside Row, 88
Burntisland Oil Company, 45, 47
Burrell, Sir William, 129, 180
Busby, Lady Jean, 62

Caledonian Mineral Oil Company, 283, 286
Cameron, John, 329
Carsphairn, 37
Cathcart, Col. MacAdam, 314, 318, 322
Chambers, Robert, 13
Chemical works, 300
Cholera, 304
Church 284-5
Churches, 17, 30, 36, 40, 47-8, 60, 72, 77-8, 82, 87-9, 91, 94, 100, 105, 124, 126, 128, 133-7, 139, 147, 152, 158, 164, 174, 176, 181, 183, 190-1, 193, 198, 201-3, 215, 218-9, 250, 252, 258-9, 270, 277, 284, 285, 287, 295, 303, 322
Clarkson, David, 25
Clifton Ironworks, 27
Coal mining, 16-23, 27-8, 30, 32, 42, 55, 6, 85-69, 94-5, 100-1, 107, 123, 143, 149-50, 157, 197, 208-9, 212, 223, 236, 295, 298, 306, 325
Cobbinshaw, 281-7
Cockburn, Lord, 320
Cocklerow, 17
Coke ovens, 289
College of Roseisle, 252
Colliery squares, 11, 16
Coltness Iron Company, 95, 160, 308, 312
Common Colliery, 90, 92
Commondyke, 87
Commonloch Row, 12
Connery, Sean, 209
Cook, Robin, MP, 62
Co-operative Societies, 57, 85, 89, 91, 99, 104, 120, 141, 154, 160, 200, 248, 269
Corbie Craigs, 42, 44
Courthouse, 126
Covenanters, 37, 84-5, 105, 152, 155-6, 308
Craighall Mines, 17
Cricket, 72, 229, 291
Crooklands, 158, 167
Cuffabout, 15
Cullen, 13, 74-83, 330
Cummingstown, 257
Dalmellington Iron Company, 38-40, 42, 219-20
Danderhall, 172-3
Darling, Grace, 206
Darnconner, 12, 84-94, 330

Darngavil, 95-102, 306, 330
Darngavil Coal Company, 228
Darngavil Colliery, 95, 100-1
Davy Pit, 149-50
Derncleugh, 33
Dewar, Dr Henry, 201
Dewar, John, 198-9
Douglas & Boag, 27
Drowning, 119, 219, 258, 306
Drumbreck, 112
Drumgray Colliery, 95
Dryburgh, Jane, 120-2
Duffus, 13
Dun, Roger, 37

East Benhar, 12, 103-111, 330
East Longrigg, *see* Longrigg
Eastfield, 112-18, 330
Edmonstone Colliery, 17-18
Eglinton Iron Company, 86, 155
Electricity supply, 12, 39, 60, 196, 218, 270, 302
Elie, 33-6
Ellangowan, 33
Ellis, James, 242
Emigration, 64, 143, 216, 323
Ennis, Lawrence, 143
Errol, Earls of, 134
Excavations (archaeological), 135-6, 257, 260, 264-5, 297
Ex-Residents' Committees, *see* Reunions

Fairfield, 119-123, 209, 330
Fallahill Colliery, 107
Farm Horse Tax, 256
Fell's Row, 141

Ferm-touns, 13
Fettercairn, 182-3, 187-8
Findlater, Earls of, 13, 74, 79, 83
Fires, 89, 100, 154, 172, 248, 268
First World War, 41, 65, 122, 142-3, 167-8, 197, 217, 297
Fletcher, Joseph, 316
Flockhart, Alexander, 18
Fochabers, 12-13, 124-31, 330
Football, 42, 49, 62, 94, 100, 110, 116, 141, 144-7, 164-5, 195, 203, 220, 242, 250, 279, 291, 295-6, 306, 312, 329
Forvie, 132-136, 263, 330
Friends of Riccarton Junction, 272-3

Gardens, see Allotments
Gavieside, 137-143, 330
Gemmell, James, 227
Gibson, Hugh, 84-5
Glasgow Herald, 28, 68, 148, 213, 283, 298
Glasgow Steam Coal Company, 27
Glenbuck, 144-157, 330
Glenbuck House, 144, 155
Gordon Castle, 13, 128, 130
Gordon, Dukes of, 124, 126-7, 129-30, 254
Gordon, Robert and James, 252
Gordonstoun, 252, 254
Gorehill Colliery, 23
Gospel Halls, 60-1, 118, 139, 277, 326, 328
Graham, Sir John the, 262
Granary, 254
Grantown, 23
Grasshill Pit, 150, 156

Green, Richard, 47-8
Greenbank, 162-3
Greengairs Colliery, 95
Grocery – see shops

Hainchin', 101
Halls (public, etc.), 48, 50, 60-1, 63, 77, 104, 124, 128, 155, 160, 163, 197, 199, 216, 248, 270, 277, 287, 295, 301, 304, 326
Hamilton of Bothwellhaugh, James, 55
Hamilton Palace Colliery, 55, 59, 62, 64-5
Hamilton, Duke of, 103
Harbours, 12-13, 74-5, 178, 260-1, 263
Harper, Malcolm, 323
Harryfoothill, 159
Haywood, 158-168, 330
Haywood Colliery, 159, 162
Hendry, John, 29
Hermand, 169-173, 330
Hermand Oil Company, 169, 172, 233, 235
Hermand Oil Works, 172
Heywood, *see* Haywood
High Binn, 50, 52
Highland Clearances, 13
Hotels (*see also* Inns *or* Public Houses), 65, 77, 83, 124, 174
Howatson, Charles, 155

Ingliston Mine, 295
Inns (*see also* Hotels *or* Public Houses), 78, 80, 125, 128, 152, 174, 177, 180, 186, 200, 227, 255-6, 275
Institutes, 41, 61, 104, 163, 247-8, 251, 295, 297, 310

Inveraray, 12, 174-181, 330
Irish immigrants, 25, 107, 194, 220
Ironstone mining, 23, 39, 71, 112, 148, 197, 308
Ironworks, 23, 27, 148-9, 153, 155, 211
Irvine, Theodore K., 141, 195, 236, 240, 295

Jack, William, 27
Jervise, Andrew, 186
Johnson, Dr Samuel, 80, 126
Johnstone, William, 25
Jougs, 129-30, 188

Kelt, M. & J., 27
Kilconquhar, 34-6
Kincardine, 12, 182-9, 331
Kincardine Castle, 182, 187
Kingscavil, 190-196, 331
Kirk, John, 23
Kirk, Norman, 216-17
Kirkwood, 324
Kirkwood Pit, 325, 328-9

Lady Pit, 153
Lady's Tower, 34
Langloan Iron Company, 96
Lassodie, 119-20, 122, 197-209, 331
Lassodie Coal Company, 204-5
Lassodie House, 198-9, 209
Lead mining, 314-5, 318-20, 323
Leases, 11, 17, 23, 27, 91, 95-6, 103, 107, 130, 148, 160, 169, 181, 208, 216, 233, 272, 274, 300, 306
Leisure, 42, 44, 49, 61-3, 72, 89, 101, 106, 156, 196, 204, 248, 270, 291, 295, 310

Lethanhill, 210-223, 331
Library, 41, 106, 295, 316, 322
Liddell, Eric, 203
Limerigg, 67
Limeworks, 198
Linlithgow Oil Company, 192, 194
Little, James, 32
Loch, David, 181
Longrigg, 112, 224-232, 331
Longrigg Colliery, 224, 229
Longriggend, 23, 30, 32, 113, 115, 224, 228, 277-8
Longriggend Colliery, 112
Lorimer, Professor James, 50
Low Binn, 50-1
Low Roughrigg, 274-9

MacFarlane, Walter, 255
McPhee, John, 62
MacQueen, John, 206
Market Cross, 13, 76, 83, 129, 174-5, 183, 185, 188, 260
Markets, 125, 128-9, 175, 185, 259-60
Marshall, William, 130
Masterton, Scott, 226, 228
May, Diana, 37
May, Peter, 77
Medical officers, 12, 25, 294, 298
Melanosis, 17-18
Merrilies, Meg, 33
Midbreich, 169, 233-37, 331
Midcalder Mineral Oil Company, 245-6
Middleton, Earls of, 188
Midtown Colliery, 23
Millar, Rev John Hastings, 216
Millerhill, 17, 19, 21

Mills, 80, 85, 254, 258, 303, 324
Monktonhall Colliery, 20-21
Moray, Earls of, 55
Mossend, 139, 238-244, 331
Mossend Pit, 241
Muirkirk Ironworks, 155
Murder, 92, 156, 172, 176, 291-2
Murdoch, James, 30
Murphie, William, 214, 216, 222
Mylne, William, 181

National Coal Board, 20, 42, 107, 312
National Union of Mineworkers, 12
New Statistical Account, 17-18, 75, 85, 135, 260, 262, 314, 316
Newton, 15-17
Newton Parish Church, 17
Niddrie & Benhar Coal Company, 107
Niddrie Coal Company, 19
Nimmo & Company, James, 112-14, 118, 225, 277, 280
Nimmo, Thomas, 160
North Cobbinshaw, 281, 285, 331
Nurses, 204, 217

Oakbank, 245-251, 331
Oakbank Oil Works, 245-6, 248, 250
Occupancy, 18-19, 91, 103, 294-5, 326
Ogilface Castle, 308
Oil-refinery or Oilworks, 23, 45, 47, 50, 137, 139, 141, 169, 172-3, 194, 233, 235-6, 245-8, 250, 282, 284, 286, 300-1, 304
Old Cullen House, 82
Oldtown of Roseisle, 252-7, 331

Park, Agnes, 217

Parley, 200
Patison, John, 300
Peden's Stone, 105, 107
Pennant, Thomas, 74, 129, 134, 178, 180
Playfair, James, 75
Police stations, 57, 89, 153, 162
Pont, Timothy, 252
Populations, 19, 26, 32, 39, 42, 47, 50, 53, 62, 90-1, 103, 111-2, 125, 128, 150, 165, 196, 208, 210-11, 220, 224, 227, 230, 242, 247, 255, 256, 260, 268, 278, 283, 294-5, 306, 308, 312, 318, 320, 323
Post Offices, 38, 40-1, 77, 79, 82, 89, 137, 154, 162, 195, 200, 236, 245, 268, 281, 304
Pratt, Rev John, 132, 135, 262
Public Houses (*see also* Inns *or* Hotels), 28-9, 32, 80, 98-9, 112, 115, 164, 195, 275, 279, 301, 304
Pumpherston Oil Company, 235-6

Quarrying, 38, 170, 191, 257, 303, 306, 308
Queen, Michael, 30
Quoits, 49, 101, 106, 139, 156, 204, 270

Raeburn Row, 137, 139
Railways, 19, 21, 46, 85-6, 95, 148, 162, 198, 229, 266-74, 281, 324
Rattray, 12, 133, 258-265, 331
Rattray castle, 260, 262-3, 265
Reading Rooms, 41, 49, 61, 106, 139, 141, 248, 295
Rechabites, 41, 63, 89, 156

Redrow, 17-18
Rehousing, 64, 92, 101, 111, 118, 143, 181, 196, 220, 244, 250, 280, 297, 307, 312-3, 324, 329
Rent, 19, 25, 38, 68-9, 73, 97-9, 108, 116, 141, 195, 211-12, 225, 227, 236, 240, 250, 258, 278-9, 295, 325-6, 328
Re-unions, 40, 44, 65, 139, 157, 209, 214, 222, 307
Riccarton Junction, 266-273, 331
Robertson, Tommy, 110
Roseisle, 252-7
Ross, Katherine, 126
Roughrigg, 274-280, 331
Roughrigg Colliery, 274, 276-7, 279-80
Roy, General William, 179, 186, 191
Royal Commission of Housing, 12, 116, 279
Runrig, 254-5

Salterhill, 69
Sand (blown), 132-4, 261, 263
Sandford, Dr Daniel, 50
Schools, 18, 22-3, 29-30, 32, 38-9, 48-9, 61-2, 80, 82, 85-8, 103, 105-6, 111-13, 124-5, 128, 139, 148-9, 152-3, 159, 162, 176, 195, 191, 199, 214-6, 222, 226, 247-8, 250, 269, 277, 283-4, 291, 299, 302-4, 310, 316, 320, 322, 329
Scone, 13
Scott, James Rankine, 119
Scott, Sir Walter, 33, 35
Seafield, Earls of, 75, 77
Second World War, 197, 209, 217, 265

Shale coal, 23, 27, 45-6, 137, 141, 143, 169, 191, 233, 235-6, 238, 241-2, 245, 282, 286, 295, 300
Shale oil (*see also* Oilworks), 23, 27, 46-7, 169-70, 246, 250, 300
Shankly, Bill, 144-6
Shearer, Mary, 245
Shebeens, 29, 122, 240
Sheriffhall Colliery, 17
Sherry, Peter, 23
Shields, John, 100
Shops (*see also* Co-operative Societies), 25, 28, 40, 47, 53, 56-7, 72, 89, 99, 104, 120, 141, 147, 154, 159-60, 164, 195, 203, 214, 245, 248, 251, 269, 275, 283, 296
Shotts Iron Company, 23
Shuttlehall, 170, 173
Simpson, Sir James, 245
Slains Castle, 132
Slammanan Station, 67
Slum Clearance Acts, 12, 44, 92, 111
South Cobbinshaw, 281-7, 331
South Standrigg, 298
Southfield Colliery, 288-9
Southfield, 288-92, 331
Sports – *see* Leisure, *or name of sport*
Spowart & Co., Messrs Thomas, 122, 208
Square Town, 11, 15-16, 18-19
Squatters, 92
St Ninian's, 202-3
Standrigg, South, 298
Stanrigg, 22
Stanrigg Colliery Disaster, 100
Stanrigg Oil Works, 300
Stanrigg oil works, 304

Starryshaw, Coal Pit, 107
Station Row, 67
Statistical Account (Old), 74, 82, 95, 262
Stevenson Forvie Centre, 135
Stewart of Champfleurie, John, 190
Stewart, James, 1st Earl of Moray, 55
Stonehaven, 187
Store – *see* shops
Strachan of Thornton, Andrew, 186
Strathclyde Park, 65
Strikes, 70, 92, 205, 208, 233
Sunday (Sabbath) Schools, 30, 41, 60, 80, 100, 139, 195, 218, 228, 277, 291, 295, 312, 326
Swinlees, 90

Taylor, Alexander, 254
Taylor, William, 184
Third Statistical Account of Scotland, 101, 118, 280
Thomson, Rev David Patrick, 202
Thomson, T., 111
Thorn Row, 69
Toilets, 58, 113, 139, 153, 163, 170, 196, 212, 225, 240, 247, 250, 268-9, 302
Tolbooth, 78-9, 126, 130, 176, 178
Tyninghame, 13

United Collieries Ltd., 298, 325

Walker, William, 90
Walker's Row, 90, 92
War memorials, 37, 41, 65, 122. 167-8, 197, 199, 209, 217, 222, 297
Wardrope, James, 69

INDEX

Wash-houses, 22, 60, 118, 120, 159, 167, 170, 225, 227, 247, 250, 275, 283, 302, 326

Water Supply, 19-20, 25, 39, 47, 53, 69, 82, 97, 99, 105, 120, 123, 154-5, 167, 170, 193, 200-1, 212-4, 225, 227, 229-30, 236, 240, 247-8, 250, 283, 288, 294, 304, 312, 328

Weaving, 74-5, 80

West Longrigg, *see* Longrigg

Westerton, 293-7, 331

Whinnyhall, 47, 50-1

Whiterigg, 101, 114, 298-307, 331

Wilson, Agnes, 37

Wilson, Dr John T., 25

Wilson, James, 18

Wilson, Rev James Stewart, 323

Wilson, John (Dundyvan Ironworks), 23

Wilson, Peter, 318

Woodend, 308-11, 331

Woodend Pit, 308-9

Woodhead, 314-323, 331

Woodlands, 324-9, 331

Young's Paraffin Light Company, 137, 142, 238, 245, 282, 294-5